The
Balloonist

The Balloonist

The Story of T. S. C. Lowe—
Inventor, Scientist, Magician,
and Father of the U.S. Air Force

Stephen Poleskie

FREDERIC C. BEIL
SAVANNAH

Published by
Frederic C. Beil, Publisher, Inc.
609 Whitaker Street
Savannah, Georgia 31401
beil.com

LIBRARY OF CONGRESS CATALOGING-IN-PUBLICATION DATA

Poleskie, Steve, 1938–
The balloonist: the story of T. S. C. Low—inventor, scientist, magician,
and father of the U.S. Air Force / Stephen Poleskie.—1st ed.
    p.   cm.
Includes bibliographical references.
ISBN 978-1-929490-27-1
1. Lowe, T. S. C. (Thaddeus Sobieski Coulincourt), 1832–1913.
2. Balloonists—United States—Biography.
3. Engineers—United States—Biography.
4. Aeronautical engineers—United States—Biography.
5. Military engineers—United States—Biography.
6. United States—History—Civil War, 1861–1865—Technology.
7. Aeronautics, Military—United States—History—19th century.
8. United States. Army—Biography. I. Title.

TL620.L6P65   2006
973.7'3—dc22
[B]
                                                    200622469

Manufactured in the United States of America
First edition

To
Jeanne Mackin

Contents

Prologue

A Brief History of Ballooning, or How War Was Taken to the Air

It could be argued that the balloon was the most significant of mankind's achievements. For the first time ever, a human being was able to leave the surface of the earth and travel in the skies.

The French brothers Étienne and Joseph Montgolfier had long been considered the originators of the hot-air balloon. However, recent research has revealed that on August 8, 1709, almost three-quarters of a century before the Montgolfiers, a Brazilian priest, Bartolomeu de Gusmão, demonstrated a model hot-air balloon at the court of John V of Portugal. An artist of the time, Bernardino de Sousa Pereira, recorded the event in a painting now in the museum of the city of São Paulo, Brazil. According to one Salvadoro Ferreira, who witnessed the feat, the small balloon was constructed of thick paper and inflated by hot air, the fire being contained in a clay bowl suspended below the neck of the envelope. Other reliable witnesses included Queen Maria Anna, the Papal Nuncio, and Cardinal Conti, who later became Pope Innocent III. It was reported that the balloon reached a height of twelve feet before two panicked valets, fearing it would set the royal drapes on fire, used their staffs to batter the strange flying thing to the ground.

On April 25, 1783, the Montgolfier brothers, papermakers by trade, successfully flew their first balloon at Annonay, near Lyons in France. Propelled by hot air from a wood-and-straw fire, the balloon was reported to have risen to a height of about a thousand feet and traveled horizontally three thousand feet before the hot air cooled and it fell to earth. They had begun their experiments years earlier with tiny paper bags and the smoke from their fireplace.

Two months later the brothers gave another public demonstration at Annonay with an improved balloon that rose to a height of six thousand feet. This ascension was witnessed by a visiting American diplomat greatly interested in scientific discovery, Benjamin Franklin, who described the event in his journal. The success of this balloon resulted in a summons from the king himself, Louis XVI, who wished to see the new invention.

For their command performance the Montgolfiers constructed an even larger balloon, and hung a basket underneath it. In the basket would be the world's first aerial voyagers: a cock, a duck, and a sheep.

This balloon was launched at Versailles on September 19, 1783, before the astonished gaze of King Louis, Marie Antoinette, and their court. The brightly decorated craft climbed to approximately 1,800 feet, and, carried by the winds, flew two miles before coming down. When the balloon was found, the cock was discovered to be somewhat the worse for his adventure. Learned minds of the time speculated that the cock, while admittedly a bird, but not used to flights higher than three feet, had been weakened by the great altitude to which the balloon had ascended. Further investigation suggested, however, that it was more likely that the poor fowl had been trampled on by the overly excited sheep. The avid Ben Franklin was also present at this demonstration.

King Louis was so impressed with the flight that he awarded the brothers the Order of Saint Michel. From that time on, all hot-air balloons would bear the title *montgolfieres*.

Having demonstrated that it was safe for animals to venture into the skies, the Montgolfier brothers concluded that human beings should be next. The brothers constructed another, larger balloon specifically for this purpose. This magnificent new balloon was over forty-nine feet in diameter, and superbly decorated in a blue-and-gold color scheme, emblazoned with the royal cipher, signs of the zodiac, eagles, and smiling suns. Below its neck was a wicker gondola capable of holding two men and the fire necessary to keep the envelope inflated.

Louis XVI, worrying over the experiment's success, proffered that a couple of prisoners, who had been sentenced to death, might volunteer to fly in the *montgolfier* if they were offered a chance of freedom. However, Jean-François Pilâtre de Rozier, a man who had been a very active supporter of this project from the start, protested that the honor of being the first person to fly should not be given to a criminal.

Pilâtre de Rozier won his argument and on October 15, 1783, made a tethered flight to a height of eighty-five feet. By carefully tending the straw fire in the gondola, the prototype aeronaut was able to remain airborne for a full four and one-half minutes.

Such was the progress of technology in those days that a mere seven months after their first successful attempt at launching a balloon, the Montgolfiers were preparing to put two men into the skies for an untethered flight.

Having proven himself as an aviator, Monsieur de Rozier was now ready to take up a passenger. On November 21, 1783, de Rozier and the Marquis d'Arlandes became the first men to be carried in free flight by a balloon. They made their ascent, before cheering crowds, from the garden of the Château a Muette in the Bois de Boulogne, Paris. A southerly wind carried them five miles in twenty-five minutes, before the first aerial voyage in history ended in a farmer's field. A dream of five thousand years had been realized; man had safely flown through the skies.

Unfortunately, two years later, on July 15, 1785, de Rozier, the first man to fly, would also become the first man killed in a flying accident when a balloon he was using in an attempt to cross the English Channel inflated with hot air and hydrogen, caught on fire and crashed in flames.

Despite their achievements the Montgolfier brothers, with their hot-air balloons, were beginning to feel competition from the phlogiston-filled balloons of Professor Jacques A. C. Charles. The lighter-than-air gas phlogiston would later be renamed hydrogen by the French chemist Lavoisier.

On August 27, 1783, Charles successfully launched a small, unmanned phlogiston-filled balloon from the Champs de Mars in Paris. This balloon was airborne for about forty-five minutes before coming to earth at Gonesse some fifteen miles away, where it was attacked by panic-stricken villagers wielding pitchforks who, believing it to be some strange device of the devil, were not satisfied until the balloon's rubberized silk skin had been reduced to shreds.

Benjamin Franklin, by then a rabid follower of the balloon experiments being conducted in France, had viewed Charles's launch. Franklin was dismayed to hear many of those in the crowd around him dismiss the balloon as being of no practical value. Even members of the French military present at the ascent, with whom Franklin discussed the balloon's flight, failed to recognize the potential of lighter-than-air craft as an instrument of war. One officer remarked on the balloon's qualities as an entertaining toy and laughingly asked, "Of what use is it?" Franklin, always quick to grasp the significance of any new invention, made his now-famous reply: "Sir, of what use is a newborn baby?"

Following his great success with his model, Charles designed and built a man-carrying balloon. On December 1, 1783, the professor and one of the two brothers who had assisted him in constructing the skin, Marie-Noel Robert, became the first men to fly in a hydrogen-filled balloon, ascending from the Tuileries Gardens in Paris before a crowd estimated to number four hundred thousand.

On September 15, 1784, Vincent Lunardi, secretary to the Neo-politan ambassador, rose from the grounds of the Honorable Artillery Company to become the first aerial voyager in England. He described his balloon in letters to his guardian, Chevalier Gherado Campagni, rejecting the Montgolfiers' method of inflating the balloon with hot air as being too dangerous in that it required a constant fire being carried aloft to be applied to the contents of the envelope. Lunardi chose instead to use inflammable air produced by the action of vitriolic acid on metals or semimetals.

The greatest of the early balloon journeys was the first aerial crossing of the English Channel by the Frenchman Jean Pierre François Blanchard and the American Dr. John Jefferies in a hydrogen balloon. On January 7, 1785, they took off from Dover, Kent, in a balloon which had only a small margin of lift considering the weight of the two men and their equipment. At one stage of the flight the balloon began losing height so rapidly that the aeronauts, to avoid going into the water, threw overboard everything they could to lighten it. They conspicuously arrived in France wearing only their undergarments.

Newspaper accounts of the accomplishments of the Montgolfier brothers, Professor Charles, and other balloonists of the time generated tremendous interest in the balloon as a sporting vehicle and as a money-maker for showmen and daredevils. Ballooning became such a fad that "even women" trusted going aloft in the fascinating new conveyance, the first woman to fly being a Madame Thible, who ascended from Lyons in a *montgolfiere* with the French painter Fleurant.

Artists and craftsmen also got in on the act, decorating every conceivable object, from cabinets and bureaus to vases and snuff boxes, with images of balloons. Some wealthy people even arranged "balloon rooms," where everything including the chandeliers was decorated with or took the shape of a balloon.

Several days after de Rozier's first flight with a passenger in the Montgolfier hot-air balloon, Professor Charles had also taken up a passenger, one André Giraud de Vilette. Afterwards, in a letter to the *Journal de Paris,* de Vilette commented on the ease with which he had been able to view Paris and its surroundings. He wrote, "From this moment I was convinced that this apparatus, costing but little, could be made very useful to an army for discovering the positions of its enemy, his movements, his advances, and his dispositions."

In the not too distant future Napoleon Bonaparte, consummate dreamer as well as master military strategist, would become the first commander to recognize the possibilities of the airship as an instrument of war, and form an air corps using balloons.

After Napoleon's experiments little further thought would be given to using balloons as part of a military strategy, even though the idea went back, at least on paper, to 1670. In that year the Jesuit priest, Father Francesco de Lana-Terzi, designed a balloon-ship, which was the precursor of lighter-than-air craft. He doubted that God would ever allow it to be built as he perceived its immense capacity for destruction. With uncanny foresight, de Lana-Terzi described the ease with which his balloon-ship could bomb fortresses, fleets, and cities.

No nation would successfully establish a corps of war balloons until the American Civil War. This would be accomplished, although not without considerable opposition and difficulty, by the balloonist Thaddeus Sobieski Constantine Lowe.

The
Balloonist

1

The Great Western *Takes to the Air*

The morning of June 28, 1860, dawned crisp and clear. A colorless mist rose off the river as three men, driven in a smart cabriolet, departed central Philadelphia in the early light and headed across the empty fields in the direction of the gas works at Point Breeze. As the road was one not usually traveled by such a fine carriage, the driver kept his horses at a walk, mindful of the ruts and potholes filled with the previous night's rain. The cabriolet belonged to Garrick Mallery, editor of the *Philadelphia Inquirer,* who was to be the passenger of honor on the inaugural flight of the balloon *Great Western.* Excited by the possibility of the airship's flight, no one in the carriage gave much thought to the fact that the nation they lived in was on the verge of dividing itself.

The tall and handsome young man with the full black moustache seated in the center, whose dark eyes were clearly focused on the future, but who could not stop talking about the weather, was the balloonist Thaddeus Sobieski Constantine Lowe, designer and builder of the mammoth airship now being inflated at Point Breeze. Despite the morning chill, the carriage's top was folded down so Lowe could see the sky. The winds aloft had brought a clearing trend from the west.

The two other men listened patiently as the day brightened, and the balloonist commented on every departing cloud, every wisp of wind. Discreet looks passed between them indicating that Lowe's fascination with the weather was becoming insufferable. Yet while they wished the balloonist would allow the carriage closed, and stop talking about the conditions, they were well aware that in a few hours, although they would be along merely for the ride, it would be he who would have the ultimate responsibility for the success or failure of the first attempt of the *Great Western* at leaving the earth.

The other man in the coach was John B. Dickinson, a former sea captain who had volunteered for the crew of what Lowe eventually hoped would be the world's first transatlantic flight. While taking a tour of the airship in progress, Captain Dickinson, upon seeing the lifeboat that

Lowe had designed to hang under the gondola of the *Great Western*, had expressed a strong interest in becoming part of the venture. The captain had pointed out that if the airship was unfortunate enough to go down in the Atlantic Ocean, it would be useful to have someone on board with the knowledge and skill to sail the small vessel.

The rising sun was in the process of restoring the color and nuance to the landscape when T. S. C. Lowe and his party arrived at Point Breeze. They found Professor John C. Cresson, president of the Franklin Institute, and chairman of the board of the gas works, already at the mooring. He had been there for some time supervising the inflation of the massive gas bag of the *Great Western*. It was on Cresson's orders that the Point Breeze Gas Works had built and installed special twenty-inch mains for this purpose. The airship's envelope was beginning to take its shape, and the meters showed that with the present flow the balloon should have four hundred thousand cubic feet of gas in the bag in four hours.

Lowe was pleased with the progress. Satisfaction showed on his face. Looking at the sky, the balloonist remarked, as it had become a clear and still morning, the crew should have no trouble with the inflation. He noted, however, that Point Breeze, as its name implied, was in a location rather vulnerable to the forces of the wind. Lowe stressed to Cresson the need to have a high fence installed to protect the balloon on subsequent occasions if the wind should pick up while the bag was in the early stages of inflation. The balloonist was concerned that a sudden stiff wind could drive the underinflated bag across the ground, possibly tearing it to shreds. Cresson agreed on the advisability of a wind fence, and said that he would take the matter under consideration and have something installed as soon as it was feasible.

Although the hour was still quite early, a festive atmosphere prevailed at the launch site. People, in their Sunday best attire, strolled about marveling at the balloon's massive size or sat on the ground eating breakfast from picnic baskets. Attracted by a series of articles in Mallery's paper on the airship's progress, throngs of curious had made their way out from the city by all manner of conveyances. Moreover, the crowd was growing almost as fast as the balloon was taking shape. The editor mingled with the onlookers, wandering contentedly around the area observing the goings on and hastily scribbling in his notepad. From time to time Mallery stopped to talk to people in the crowd. Some of the bystanders publicly ridiculed the whole operation, and predicted dire circumstances for Lowe and his crew. A few of those who recognized Garrick Mallery even took the trouble to advise him that he was unwise to risk his life in such a foolish experiment.

Mallery scorned the warnings and wrote in his paper that the comments were a response of "the large and respectable class who never believe aught but their senses. We, on the contrary, were so unscientific as to feel much more secure in the magnitude of our conveyance, particularly after a careful inspection of its great strength and manifold skillful appliances. Besides, it was contrary to nature that the *Philadelphia Inquirer* should not be well up in everything."

As the morning progressed, dreamy and calm, the balloon continued to expand. A bit after noon the mass of varnished fabric had become an airship and was pulling at its restraining ropes. One hour later, the balloonist, the newsman, and the sea captain, waving bravely, climbed into the gondola. The ground crew began to loosen the mooring cables. Their strong arms had difficulty holding the ropes as the giant airship was tested for lift. Fortunately for Lowe there was no wind, for the balloon, even with all its sandbag ballast on board, was bobbing impatiently, displaying a tremendous desire to leave the unremarkable landscape it was squatting in and rise into a sun-streaked sky.

Lowe ordered the ropes released one by one, then began to throw out ballast. The airship was rocking back and forth, straining at the last of its restraints, when the balloonist broke the neck of the gas valve to let the envelope blow off its excess gas. The occupants of the gondola quickly ducked their heads down and covered their faces with handkerchiefs to avoid the acrid stench of the blown coal gas. When they looked up again, they were greeted by a mass of shouting, waving, and running people rapidly receding below them.

Inside the rising gondola the occupants were surprised by the strange sense of a lack of motion. When the airship had climbed a few hundred feet above the ground, Lowe stabilized the ascent, whereupon the newly birthed aeronauts each grasped a small American flag and waved it out a porthole at the throng of transfixed observers.

Having practiced it many times on the ground, Lowe had no difficulty now in climbing up into the "hoop." This was a small platform, located between the car and the gas bag, through which all the guide ropes were routed. The plan was that flyers would take turns standing watch up there during the Atlantic crossing. Unfortunately, as he was presently the only one on board qualified for this duty, Lowe would have to spend most of his time in the hoop. Luckily for him this was planned to be a short trip.

The balloonist kept his craft fairly close to the ground as it passed over the perfectly laid-out streets of Philadelphia. He was taking delight in giving the citizens of that metropolis a good view of what many had called his "unmanageable airship." The great mass was not even supposed to get off the ground; the balloon, however, had risen into the air with the grace of a sea gull.

Lowe himself still was not sure that this was all not an illusion, one of the more vivid of his many dreams of flight. The wind on his face and the clear shouts of the people below brought a smile to Lowe's countenance. He began to sing at the top of his voice to reassure himself it was all real, not just the legerdemain of his early magic shows. Despite all the obstacles put in his way, all the comments of his detractors and unbelievers, and his own moments of self-doubt, the *Great Western* was aloft. Lowe checked his lines one more time, paused a moment to enjoy his triumph, then went back below to get on with the work of the rest of the flight.

The passengers were peering out the windows excitedly, pointing here and there at things they recognized, immensely enjoying their first-ever view of the world from above. Mallery observed that only the gondola had a reality for him, as Philadelphia below appeared to be nothing but a model—tiny, cardboard buildings, with dyed green sponges for trees, standing next to painted-on streets and parks.

Over the outskirts of the city now, Lowe tossed out more ballast, careful not to hit anyone, or anything, and the mammoth airship began to climb. As he watched the ballast hurtle down, the balloonist speculated on the destruction he might have wrought to the fine houses and public edifices they had just passed over if the sandbags he had been throwing had been bombs.

At about a mile above ground the balloonist caught the west wind. Stopping the ascent, Lowe set the balloon on an easterly course toward the Delaware River. From the gondola Lowe studied the shining water through his telescope. The river at that point stretched from north to south like a giant mirror laid on the landscape, the wind so still he could barely discern a ripple on the water's surface.

With the light winds, it was not until late in the afternoon that the *Great Western* floated over Camden, New Jersey. Lowe spotted the tracks of the Camden and Atlantic Railroad, a line that, if followed, would lead them across the low hills and checkerboard farmlands to the ocean.

The airship was now at a height of fifteen thousand feet, Lowe announced proudly, demonstrating the workings of the altimeter he had designed. He also computed that they were moving over the ground in an easterly direction at approximately six miles per hour. At their present height, the curvature of the earth was becoming apparent, and the balloonist imagined he could faintly see the distant ocean through his telescope. The lack of oxygen that accompanied this altitude was causing the pioneering aeronauts to experience a carefree sense of exhilaration. They took turns climbing, somewhat unsteadily, up the ladder to the hoop. There each man stood for a while enjoying the view and, following Lowe's example, singing into the wind mightily while holding onto the ropes.

The state of science was such that the aeronauts were unaware that the false sense of well-being presently overtaking them was one of the symptoms of hypoxia, a condition that occurred when the body was denied a sufficient supply of oxygen. All three of the men had unconsciously increased their breathing rate. While the outside temperature was rather cold due to the high altitude and setting sun, the occupants of the cabin were feeling a tingling, warm sensation. They found themselves sweating. At the controls, Lowe was having difficulty seeing out the window, concerned by the apparent rapid deterioration of his vision as night was approaching.

Mallery stared at the jumping pages of his notebook. He was extremely tired. He knew that it had been a long and adventurous day, which was not yet over. As much as he wanted to write down his sensations, he could not make his pen move across the paper. Mallery flipped back through the pages he had written earlier in the day, observing the steady decline of his script. It was not the fatigue; he was sure of that. Mallery had often come home from a sixteen-hour day and written entries in his diary that were as clear as those he had penned in the morning. He shook his head several times, unable to comprehend what was happening to him. Mallery wondered if his present dizziness might be caused by something he had eaten from the basket of food they had carried with them.

After consuming most of the bottle of "Monongahela" whiskey he had brought along, Captain Dickinson was stretched out happily on one of the benches, lustily singing old sea chanteys.

Attempting to take readings, Lowe was having trouble focusing his vision on his instruments. The markings seemed to blur and disappear. He shook his head and blinked his eyes. Then the balloonist remembered the impromptu talk on the need for oxygen he had given to an audience at a lecture in New York City. How could he forget it? That was the evening Lowe had first met his wife, Leontine. He had come into the hall and felt faint, and opened the windows, much to the disapproval of the audience, which had prompted the lecture. Lowe was aware that neither he nor anyone else understood much about the effects on the body caused by depriving it of oxygen at high altitudes. He also knew that, as fragile as it was, the human body had the ability to adapt.

Lowe had read of tribes of Indians that spent their whole lives on mountains in South America at altitudes such as the balloon was at now. He and his two traveling companions, however, were flat landers, and at their present altitude the atmospheric pressure was almost half of what they were used to on the surface. As Lowe had stressed in his lecture, breathing oxygen was essential to life. He was aware that man could live for weeks without food, and days without water, but only minutes if totally deprived of oxygen, which was was not stored in the body. Once taken into the lungs, most of the gas was absorbed into the bloodstream and carried to other parts of the body to be used to oxidize food material and produce energy transformations. Because life was a breath-by-breath existence, man continued to live only so long as he was able to continually replenish the oxygen he consumed. Lowe realized that if he was going to persist in his exploration of the higher altitudes, he would need to devote some of his time to developing a supplemental oxygen source. However, for the moment, unaware of the danger that confronted them, the three men just sailed on, fearless in their ignorance.

The hour getting on toward evening, the sun down below was beginning to disappear. But for the crew in the airship, high above the clouds, the sky was still blue, although the moon had already made its appearance. The rays of the sinking sun behind them colored the tops of the clouds with a phosphorescent coating of pink and blue and gold, giving the look that the surface was on fire. Lowe peered out his window, mesmerized by the glow.

With the sun finally vanished below the horizon, the gas in the bag began to cool rapidly, contracting and causing the balloon to begin a hasty descent. Although they had not reached their destination, Lowe decided it would be wisest to land where they were, rather than try to prolong the flight by throwing out ballast, or engaging his mysterious and untested propeller wheel.

The airship had descended very low and was hovering over some fields near a town, which they later learned was Medford, New Jersey. From his lofty vantage point en route, Lowe at one point had glimpsed the sea, but now after almost nine hours of flying, during which the balloon had been blown on a rather circuitous course, the grand airship was coming down still some thirty-eight miles from the ocean, and a mere twenty-six miles from where its voyage had begun.

A gaggle of people, some holding lanterns, had gathered on the ground below the backing and filling balloon. Many in the group were waving and shouting, apparently encouraging their strange visitors to land. Lowe bellowed through his megaphone for someone to catch and hold the rope he was going to drop. Then turning to Mallery and Dickinson, the balloonist reminded them of the landing procedure he had briefed them on before they took off. Now breathing normally and beginning to regain their senses, his two passengers relaxed and took a crouching position while holding on to the gondola's hand rail. With a great hissing noise and a coughing of putrid fumes, Lowe released the remaining gas in the envelope.

The passengers clung tightly to the rail, ready for a harsh jolt, but Lowe brought the airship to the ground with a grace that denied its great bulk. His critics would have to "acknowledge the corn," the *Great Western* had successfully flown and come back down again in one piece.

Mallery would later write in a newspaper article: "The monster in ascent and descent and in that generally most difficult matter of landing, was as thoroughly under the control of its skillful builder as ever a horse in harness." He was also convinced of the possibility of the Atlantic flight, stating, "We could have been over the sea at short notice. . . . It is a curious coincidence that, on this 28th day of June, 1860, the *Great Eastern*, largest seagoing vessel, arrived, inaugurating, it is said, a new system of ocean navigation, and on the same day, the *Great Western*, still larger in proportion to rivals of its own kind, left the city of Philadelphia to commence a yet more novel era in the navigation of the air."

In spite of Mallery's and other writers' many newspaper articles about Thaddeus Sobieski Constantine Lowe and his airship, there were still things the people of Philadelphia wanted to know. Who was this "Professor" Lowe who had sailed his great airship so boldly over their town when so many had predicted his failure? Some said he wasn't even a professor at all; they had heard he just adopted the title while traveling with a magic show. They said he was some kind of a showman, married to a French actress in New York. Most knew that he had tried to fly his airship there in Central Park the year before, but had failed. Why was the Franklin Institute giving him all this money? He wasn't one of their own, not from Philadelphia, not even from Pennsylvania. The papers all said he was ambitious to excel, and to make himself known, and hard-headed, and an independent thinker, yet as far as anyone knew, he had very little education. Could all the gossip going around be true? Had the balloonist really been born in New Hampshire, the son of a poor grocer who had also worked as the town cobbler?

2

Lowe's Early Life, and Things to Come

The stillness of a prolonged summer drought hung over the village of Jefferson Mills, New Hampshire. The streets were nearly empty. The men were gone, sweating in the shimmering fields. Nor were there any children, all having tramped off to the woods to wade in the cool streams and ponds. What few people did pass were mostly women going about their errands. There was a surveyor measuring something. The millinery shop was open, as were the apothecary and the farrier, but the grocery was strangely closed. The grocer's wife was the reason.

Clovis Lowe, who had been a drummer boy in the War of 1812, and had served for a time in the state legislature, paced the floor in front of the stove in his small frame house. The heat was murderous. Clovis' job, at the moment, was to keep watch on the boiling water. The dry wind that blew off the mountains barely ruffled the kitchen curtains, yet carried in dust through the open windows with every passing horse or wagon. The screams from the bedroom upstairs had been going on for some time. Clovis knew from past experience that they would go on for much longer.

With the morning came a fainter noise, a baby's cry, then a peaceful stillness. Clovis stood at the foot of the bed holding the small bundle he had just been handed by his wife Alpha. As the man owned the local grocery store he was quite good at estimating weights. He figured what he had in his hands to be about six pounds. By candlelight that night, Clovis Lowe would carefully scribe in the back of the worn family Bible: Born August 20, 1832, a son, Thaddeus Sobieski Constantine. The grocer already had more children than he could afford, so he also was the village cobbler.

Her husband had winced at her choice of a name. But during the long months of her pregnancy Alpha had been reading *Thaddeus of Warsaw*, a popular romance novel, so she named her new son after the hero. This book, by the Scottish writer Jane Porter, chronicled the life of one of the foremost families of Polish history, which traced its legacy back to King Jan Sobieski. In 1683 Sobieski had raised the siege of Vienna by the Turks, thereby stopping their march on Europe and saving Christendom from a Mohammedan usurpation. Perhaps Alpha had been expecting similar great things from her son.

Years passed as an uneventful parade of chores and then school. August 20, 1843, Thaddeus Lowe celebrated his eleventh birthday. Given his family's limited means, no silver spoon had been bought at Thaddeus' birth; the celebration was modest. His mother baked him a molasses cake, which he shared with his siblings and a few friends. The birthday boy received a small pocket knife for his present. In that same year, 1843, Professor John Wise of Lancaster, Pennsylvania, announced his plan for a transatlantic balloon flight; and Jefferson Davis, the future Confederate leader, entered politics as a delegate to the Democratic State Convention in Jackson, Mississippi. News traveled slowly in those days, and neither of these items were major events, of interest mainly in their local area. Isolated as the Lowe family was in New Hampshire, young Thaddeus, sitting on the back porch cutting notches in a birch strip with his new knife, had no way of knowing of these two men, nor how they would someday be entwined with his own place in history .

Later that year Thaddeus moved with his family to a larger house in nearby Jefferson. To his delight young Lowe's new home was just across the street from the public school. He did not regret the move from the smaller yellow frame house, with its two-mile walk to school. While the trip had been picturesque, winding through a fertile valley surrounded by the White Mountains, it was bitterly cold in winter. And the tedious journey took him only to the Coos County School, which provided him with a lackluster education at best, being limited to the standard grammar school curriculum.

Shortly after the move, his parents, faced with a faltering financial situation, made the difficult decision to send their son away. Thaddeus was "bound out" to an outlying farmer. The boy was obedient and endured with silent resentment the stern discipline of the farmer and his wife, who treated young Lowe as if he were a servant. While Thaddeus was curious about everything, the farm he had been sent to had no books other than the Bible. When Lowe asked his foster parents for time to visit the sparsely stocked local library, he was brusquely told he would do better to busy himself with his chores. During the long winter nights Thaddeus would often crouch in a corner of his bedroom, which he shared with the farmer's children, reading by a small candle, rubbing his hands together for warmth while on the bureau next to him the water in the wash basin turned to ice.

For all his hardships Thaddeus discovered living conditions at the farm to be even more arduous than at home. Faced with rocky soil and a short growing season bracketed by severe cold in winter and drought in summer, New England farming was an uncertain business at best. Most of what was grown had to be sold, which meant the choicest bits did not end up on the farm family's table. Thaddeus found the food wretched, consisting mostly of mutton, game, pudding, and the occasional fish, accompanied by fresh or dried beans and corn, usually washed down with weak tea.

Thaddeus did not mind that his family had need of the very small amount of money he was earning. He just considered it his misfortune that he had been sent to the farm while his older brother had been allowed to go to Boston to learn a trade. Despite his hatred of farm work and the people he had to stay with, it was a contract of honor which his father had entered him into, so he made the best of it. As the weeks passed, the conduct of the farm family toward him did little to cause him to develop a fondness for farming, nor for his situation.

Each night, as Thaddeus hung his robe on a peg before slipping into bed with the other children, he would look out the window in the direction of Jefferson and think of his family, covering his face so that no one could see he was crying. Finally he could stand it no longer. One afternoon, when he was working the fields alone, Thaddeus just put down his rake, vaulted over the stone fence, and walked back home.

Full of misgivings, his father welcomed him back. Clovis apologized to his son, saying that he had sent him away for his own good, hoping he might learn farming. The events, however, had left a mark on the boy. Their bond of trust was broken. A wall had been erected between them, and many years would pass before father and son would again be able to communicate freely.

Away from the farm and back at school, Thaddeus' total misery was soon replaced by complete happiness. The boy discovered new interests in botany, chemistry, and geology. He began studying in earnest, absorbing all he found on these subjects. Thaddeus could not learn fast enough, and never had enough books to read even though his teacher often lent him volumes from his own personal library.

Time passed quickly. Thaddeus grew into a handsome, studious boy, tall for his age. He had become extremely sensitive to criticism, but equally responsive to praise, moldable more by a kind word than a thrashing. Clovis, who had an admiration for learning, knew his son wanted to go to college, probably even Harvard; he was frustrated, however, by the knowledge that despite his hard work and frugality this did not seem possible.

Although Thaddeus loved the mountains that surrounded his

home, most times he felt imprisoned in his valley. He dreamed of following his older brother, Joseph, who only last spring had left for Boston. While his brother had apprenticed to the trade of boot-and-shoe cutting like his father, Thaddeus aspired to something higher, although he did not yet know what. As he looked at the hills surrounding him, Thaddeus imagined that whatever he did do, one day he might become so famous at it that perhaps a mountain might even be named after him. Whereas his father's fortunes had improved somewhat in the larger town of Jefferson, Clovis Lowe could still by no standard be considered wealthy. While everyone in the area traded in his store, the grocer was not one to dun a person who was slow to pay his bill, nor could he let any family be deprived of necessities. Thus his own family oftentimes went without on account of Clovis' generosity.

Though only a simple storekeeper, as well as the village cobbler, Clovis was fairly well educated for his day, having attended such schools as were available to him, and had passed on to his son his habit of reading. He had also traveled as a drummer boy, which was more than most people in the town who rarely went outside of Jefferson. Thus Clovis' opinion was highly regarded throughout the county, and he had even served for a time as a selectman and delegate to the state legislature. It was not uncommon for men from the town to stop by Clovis' store to seek his advice. Clovis was the rock, the person in town people came to when they needed to make a difficult decision.

Despite his generosity, Clovis was not a spendthrift. He kept careful books, obsessively recording every purchase and expenditure. He was loathe, however, to add up the columns at the end of the week and made no attempt to balance his accounts. Thus Clovis never knew whether he was operating at a profit or a loss. The only thing he was sure of was that he never had enough money. This was another trait he would pass on to his son Thaddeus, which would not serve the boy well when he became a man.

Whenever he had free time, Thaddeus had to help his father in the store by stocking the shelves, bringing in wood, taking out the ashes, and sweeping up. He especially liked to be around the store in the evening when the men stopped by on their way home from work. It made the boy feel like a grown-up, sitting around the wood stove reading the newspapers and discussing the day's events. Young Lowe enjoyed showing off his knowledge to the older men of the village, who considered him to be a kind of prodigy. Although he alternately worried about never having anything original to say, or being too bright for his own good, Thaddeus did not hesitate to express his opinion, and to defend it boldly.

A strange, and unbelievable, article appearing in the extra edition of the April 13, 1844, *New York Sun* had completely flabbergasted the regulars gathered at Clovis' store. The immense implications of the story became the subject of considerable heated discussion. The glaring headline read: "Astonishing News! Atlantic Crossed In Three Days! Signal Triumph Of Mr. Monck Mason's Flying Machine!" The newspaper article went on to describe the passage of the "steering balloon" *Victoria* from northern Wales to Fort Moultrie near Charleston, South Carolina. The airship was supposed to have crossed the Atlantic in seventy-five hours, with a crew of eight aboard, all men well known to the English aeronautical community. The piece contained many convincing technical details of the airship, and was colored with electrifying entries taken from the logs kept by Mason and a member of the crew, Harrison Ainsworth. The story proclaimed: "The air, as well as the earth and the ocean, has been subdued by science, and will become a convenient highway for mankind. Not only had the Atlantic never been crossed by air before, but a passage of about three days was incredible when measured against the three weeks it took surface vessels."

When word got around about the ocean crossing, people could not believe their ears. Those who wanted to know rushed to the store to see the facts in black and white for themselves. A large group gathered around the cracker barrel expressing loud and varied opinions.

Someone remarked that Captain Monck Mason had been with Charles Green when he ballooned from London to Germany in 1836, so he would have the necessary experience to make such a trip.

Another man reminded the speaker that the Atlantic was a lot wider than the English Channel.

Others maintained that the story must be erroneous. And so the conversations went wandering back and forth throughout the evening and well into the night.

Even young Lowe expressed his opinion, having read several books on the Montgolfier brothers and the other pioneers of ballooning. He had often lain in front of the dying fire late into the night reading about balloons, imagining himself a balloonist, flying across the ocean in an airship of his own creation. Thaddeus Lowe's comment to the gathering that day revealed his dreams and his frustrations. If men had flown across the Atlantic in the air, then the skies were indeed conquered, he pointed out, wondering secretly what was left for him to do.

Young T. S. C. Lowe, however, need not have worried. Two days later another article in the *Sun* reported that the newspaper had contacted its correspondent in Charleston and been unable to confirm the arrival of an airship from England. The paper concluded that the story was a gigantic put-on. It was subsequently discovered that the piece was the work of a down-on-his luck writer named Edgar Allan Poe. Newly arrived in New York from Philadelphia with his sick wife, the author had concocted the fantastic tale and then sold it to the *Sun* as a straight news item in a desperate attempt to earn some money. Poe's balloon hoax would become a legend in journalistic circles.

The deception had been believed by so many, not just because it was so skillfully written, but because it was what the public was expecting. At the time, ballooning was being widely covered in the newspapers and in the new illustrated magazines such as *Harper's* and *Leslie's.* A legion of itinerant balloonists were traveling back and forth across the country making ascensions in cities large and small. Everyone had a good laugh at Poe's deception and what the newspapers were calling "balloonitics." As for young Thaddeus Lowe, he was pleased to learn that there was still something left for him to do with his life.

In the spring of 1845 the first bits of news about the war with Mexico began to reach Jefferson. Like most schoolboys, Thaddeus followed the war news closely. One story that especially held his interest was the scheme suggested by John Wise, the leading balloonist of the day, to break the deadlock at the siege of Vera Cruz by bombing the Castle of San Juan de Ulua from the air. Wise proposed to construct a balloon a hundred feet in diameter. He maintained his balloon could carry a load of up to eighteen thousand pounds of bombs and torpedoes. He planned to have the balloon maneuvered into position by guy ropes, keeping it high above the range of the Mexican gunners, while the aeronauts dropped their deadly missiles onto the helpless troops below.

Unfortunately, or perhaps fortunately for those in the fortress, the army never showed any interest in Wise's proposal. His idea, which had attracted wide comment after it was first published in his hometown Lancaster, Pennsylvania, newspaper, was ridiculed in all the journals but one. The Philadelphia *Public Ledger* halfheartedly suggested that Wise's strategy be given a try. And in another article the governor of Kentucky was quoted as saying while the idea was doubtlessly the product of a man of genius, he was sure it would be very difficult to enlist volunteers for a balloon service.

Thaddeus Lowe was one of the few people who had taken the matter seriously. He discussed the idea with his teacher, who was of the opinion that the balloon and the crew would probably be blown up along with the target. Despite his scorn of Wise's plan, the teacher did provide his student with the information that balloons had been used

successfully as instruments of war more than a half-century earlier.
As proof of this he lent the boy a book on Napoleon's campaigns.

Thaddeus was astonished to learn that as far back as 1794 Napoleon had ordered four military balloons constructed. He named them
the *Entreprenant, Celeste, Hercule,* and *Intrepide.* To operate these
balloons Napoleon had created what he called a "Company of Aerostiers" as a branch of the Artillery Service, under the command of one
Captain J. M. J. Coutelle.

On June 26, 1794, during the battle of Fleurus in Belgium, Captain
Coutelle had made an ascension in the tethered hydrogen balloon *Entreprenant.* The startled Austrians did not know what to make of this
strange craft hovering tauntingly overhead, just out of reach of their
guns. From his lofty vantage point Coutelle had complete knowledge
of the Austrian force's deployment. Information of their movements,
signaled to the ground by the captain, played a crucial part in the Austrian's defeat. Coutelle's flight at Fleurus was significant in that it was
the first operational use of an aircraft in war. The borrowed book also
revealed to young Lowe that the French had used a military observation balloon with success yet one other time in that same year, at the
siege of Mayence.

A boy of vivid imagination, Thaddeus saw himself in a balloon
floating over enemy lines with Captain Coutelle, spying on the enemy's movements and warning his troops below. From high up above
he could also spot for the artillery, allowing them to hit targets they
could not even see. Even at the young age of thirteen, T. S. C. Lowe
was giving the military uses of balloons serious thought. He could
not understand why the newspapers had made such a folly of Wise's
proposition when balloons had been used successfully in combat in
Europe more than fifty years earlier.

The thought, however, of using balloons for military purposes
also perplexed the young man. Lowe could not help wondering how
a thing that had so much to offer science and human progress had
been so quickly made into an aid to human destruction. As he lay on
the grass watching the clouds pass in the melancholy New Hampshire
sky, Thaddeus wondered about this paradox for some time. There
must be a reason for everything, the boy concluded, even if he could
not immediately perceive it. Then he quickly turned his active mind
to other things. Thaddeus Sobieski Constantine Lowe was young and
had much to accomplish before the matter of war balloons would become his main concern.

Although he had been dreaming of the skies most of his early life,
Thaddeus Lowe would not begin experimenting with flight until age

fifteen. While his initial attempt to take a creature aloft was made only with a large kite, the affair was as flamboyant as any he would have later on his with full-size airships. But he didn't accomplish this in his hometown of Jefferson; he had to run away to Boston first.

In the summer of 1847 Lowe's father decided, as his family was growing again, and his finances were still not doing well, they should move to Randolph. This town had been Clovis' birthplace, and he had dreams of returning to a farm there and opening up a guest house.

Thaddeus listened patiently to his father's schemes, but he was secretly making plans of his own, knowing it was time for him to set off. He realized it would not be easy to leave as he loved his family. But he wanted to go to Boston, like his brother Joseph. After considerable discussion the matter was settled. Although he was sorry to see his son go off, Thaddeus' father wasted no time in talk, but agreed to write a letter to Joseph. Hopefully Joseph would find an apprenticeship for his younger brother as a boot-and-shoe cutter. The father reminded his son if things didn't work out, he could always return to the steady habits of home.

With the passing of each summer's day, Thaddeus was more impatient when Joseph's answer had not returned. Moreover, T. S. C. Lowe was not sure that he even wanted to follow in the cobbler's vocation. Although he thought not unkindly of his father and brother, Thaddeus considered himself much more intelligent then they were. It was a difficult decision to make, but he felt he had more to do with his life. He had been brought up to believe that duty to one's family came before duty to oneself. Nevertheless, one moonless night Thaddeus packed his kit and slid down a rope, secretly leaving without saying good-bye.

In August 1847, toting his carpetbag on his shoulder and with two half-eagles tied in a sack hidden under his shirt, young Thaddeus Lowe began his journey from his home in Jefferson to Portland, Maine, more than a hundred miles away. Lowe walked the dugways and hitched rides on Owensboros with farmers, who often gave him food and a place to sleep in exchange for doing chores. At that time, ten dollars was an "almighty sum" for a boy of fifteen. Thaddeus had been saving this money since he was twelve. Despite his unusual height and ungainly appearance, Lowe moved with a fluid grace, a skill he had learned from playing with Indian children when he was young and hunting with them when he got older. Considered a clever lad and a hard worker, Lowe had never had any difficulty finding jobs and was good about saving his money.

When he finally arrived in Portland a month later, T. S. C. Lowe was overwhelmed. He had never seen so many buildings. Red-brick structures as tall as three stories lined the streets leading down to the wharves. The waterfront bustled with activity. Numerous drays and wagons rattled to and fro over the cobbled thoroughfares, the drivers shouting and fanning their horses with enthusiasm. There was commerce everywhere, with hawkers and peddlers doing business right out on the sidewalks as well as in the shops. The fishmongers shouted from their carts and blew loud on their horns, selling porgies at five cents a pound. The salt air smelled of drying fish, wood, leather, tea, tar, tanning acid, and the dozens of other odors of cargoes coming and going to various ports around the world. After some searching, the awed mountain boy finally found a place to stay in exchange for doing odd jobs while he waited for a ship that would take him to Boston. A few days later he learned of a lumber boat going that way and arranged to have a berth on it as a cabin boy.

Threatening clouds hung over the harbor as Lowe's ship set sail the very next day. Never having been on the water before, the up-and-down movement, as the old hull creaked and groaned across the swells, did its best to upset the boy's digestion. He spent the better part of his first morning with his head hanging over the rail. But Lowe soon became used to the boat's motion. He loved the surge of power as the sails caught the wind, plowing the bow through the white waves, and the sudden change of direction as the boom came around causing the hull to tip, and the boat tacked off on a new heading. He decided that if he wasn't to become a balloonist he would be a sailor. By the end of the trip, however, Lowe had set his choice firmly in favor of ballooning. The vast number of rats scurrying back and forth between the ship's deck and hold, which one of his duties was to contain, and which he was told were an integral part of any sea voyage, had turned his mind to the clear skies.

After a sea voyage that lasted the better part of three days, young Lowe finally arrived in Boston. If he had been impressed by the city of Portland, Boston must have seemed to the boy to be the center of the world. The harbor was choked with boats of all sizes and descriptions. Masts towered above water as sloops, frigates, and whalers lay at anchor. Many ships in the vast armada were flying flags from nations which Thaddeus, even with his vast knowledge of geography, could not identify. The lumber boat had to wait in the harbor for a full day for a slip to be vacated.

When his ship finally docked, Thaddeus Lowe ran down the ramp, relieved to be on land. He had no intention of ever going back to sea. Stories he heard from members of the crew of young lads being shanghaied and forced to go on voyages of sometimes two or three years, during which they were flogged for disobedience, had left him terrified.

Looking around him, the new arrival realized that he had been ridiculous to even consider remaining in Coos County. How could anyone with an interest in life remain there for long when there was such a stage as Boston? Lowe's eyes danced about the many people engaged in diverse activities, from lawyers to chimney sweeps. The narrow, crooked streets hummed with the gabble of merchants, market men, ladies, priests, strumpets, street urchins, soldiers, and sailors; and rumbled with the clatter of horses, oxen, carts, coaches, broughams, and cabriolets. He could not stop long enough in any one place to catch his thoughts before his senses were assailed by some new experience or idea. Here, Thaddeus told himself, was where he would make his reputation.

The directions Lowe had received from a passerby to his brother's cobbler shop led through a labyrinth of dark and winding streets, lined with dank cavernous warehouses, where it appeared that even at midday the sun never greeted the ground. He wondered if he had been purposely led astray. The newcomer did not need to use his imagination to suspect that this neighborhood, the turf of rival street gangs, was not a place a person ventured into at night, especially if one was alone. To Thaddeus everyone appeared suspicious of everyone else, and he himself became the subject of numerous inquiring glances.

After a long, but for Thaddeus fascinating, trek through the tangle of narrow, foul-smelling streets, Lowe found his brother's place of work. Joseph asked his employer for the rest of the afternoon off. The two left the shop and set off walking, with Joseph catching up on the news from home. Thaddeus told of his falling out with his father over not wanting to move back to Randolph, and of their reconciliation, and how he had left without telling anyone. Out of indifference, or perhaps respect for their father, Joseph listened while saying little. What his thoughts were he did not divulge. The two boys had always tended to side with their mother in disagreements anyway. To them Alpha Lowe was an honored and beloved woman, possessed of exceptional energy, a strong will, and high moral principals, whom they loved deeply. While Thaddeus had yet to take a serious interest in the opposite sex, these were traits he would discover in the woman whom, after the briefest of courtships, he would eventually marry.

In a short while the brothers came to a pleasant area with a green meadow and many trees. Overwhelmed by his rapid passage through what must have been the heart of the city, Thaddeus allowed that he

felt more comfortable now that they had arrived in the country. Joseph laughed, explaining they had not reached the outskirts, but were
still in Boston, only in an enormous park called the Common, which
sat right in the middle of town. Displaying his newly acquired urban-
ity, Joseph led his brother to the other side of the Common, where he
showed the newcomer the wonder of Beacon Hill, lined with its elegant red brick houses that led in orderly rows up to the massive yellow
dome of the State House. Setting his bag down to admire the setting,
Thaddeus asked his brother how much farther to their house.

The would-be shoemaker was disappointed when Joseph revealed
they were merely "sight-seeing" in Boston. Thaddeus was being apprenticed to a William Otis Nash, who had taught his brother shoemaking. The boy who had come so far to get his start in the big city
would be living further down the south shore in the small town of
Hingham. Sensing his brother's disappointment, Joseph reminded
Thaddeus that he couldn't expect to start at the top and should be
grateful, as Nash, French, and Company was one of the best boot-
and-shoe manufacturers in New England. He assured his younger
brother that he would not come out on the "little end of the horn" in
this situation. For Thaddeus, who had banked so much, against his
better judgment, on working with his brother, it was a painful revelation. He went silent, torn between elation and despair over what
might become of him.

Thaddeus Lowe soon learned that, according to the custom of
the times, as an apprentice he was now legally bound to William
Otis Nash, the master craftsman, and that he must obey Nash as he
would his own father. Even his leisure time was subject to Mr. Nash's
control. If Mr. Nash wanted Thaddeus to go to church services with
him on the Sabbath, he would go. In exchange for his labor, and his
obedience, Thaddeus Lowe would be housed, fed, clothed, and taught
the skill of boot and shoe making. If he showed promise, in time he
might progress to the rank of journeyman and then finally to master
craftsman. As a master, Lowe would have the opportunity to leave Mr.
Nash's employment and open his own shop.

All in all, Thaddeus Lowe was content with this arrangement, even
though he was anxious and eager to get ahead, as he was only too
aware it was a miserable time for workers, especially the young and
unskilled. Thaddeus knew that, despite child labor laws, thousands
of children his age or younger, who should have been in school, daily
worked in shops and factories throughout the Boston area, usually
for as many as ten to twelve hours per day, for minimal pay. More often than not these young people operated dangerous machinery, and

worked with caustic substances, for employers who had little regard for their health or welfare, let alone their future.

Thaddeus found that for black persons the situation in Boston was even worse. They suffered kinds of abuse different from their counterparts in the South. Most could find no work at all outside of hard labor and servants' jobs because, even if they were skilled at something else, no employer would hire them. In addition Northern cities harbored many escaped slaves who could find work only at the risk of being discovered and returned to their former owners under the terms of the Fugitive Slave Law, to be dragged back to the South in chains.

Coming from the country, young Lowe had been astonished by these revelations. His shock was amplified by the discovery that at any time of the day the streets of Boston swarmed with people, many of whom look to be engaged in debauchery and lewdness, yet nobody appeared to be doing any work. There was also a vast number of people who apparently had naught to do but occupy their time solely with the task of cheating other people. And while his upbringing had been far from puritanical, Thaddeus was also bewildered by the forwardness of the women who accosted him in the streets.

While he was fascinated by his new situation, and was determined to succeed in spite of all that went on around him, privately Lowe was extremely lonely and somewhat distraught. He had been away for less than two months, most of that on the road, but he was already beginning to miss his family and the comforts of home. He wished he would receive a letter from his father. Thaddeus realized, however, that although Joseph had probably written home and told of his arrival in Boston, his father would not write until he wrote first. Thaddeus had written several letters, but had torn them up without posting them.

During the weeks that followed, as the youngest apprentice, Thaddeus Lowe mainly did chores and ran errands for the journeyman. But he soon progressed from building and keeping the fires to cutting pieces of leather. Eager to learn, Lowe applied himself to his tasks and worked hard at his new trade. Mr. Nash could not help notice his new apprentice's skill with his hands. After working in the shop only two months, Lowe was given an assignment usually reserved for the most experienced shoe cutters, that of making a congress boot.

The congress boot was designed to have a u-shaped opening on each side. Even expert boot makers had great difficulty in making neat, matching, cutouts in the tough leather. Lowe stuck his knife into the leather and, proceeding as if he had thrown caution to the wind, skillfully made the cuts. His congress boot was perfect on his very first try—as was each one he cut out after that. Curious to see how the pawky young man accomplished this, Mr. Nash and his foreman secretly watched Lowe as he worked. They were surprised to see him lick the knife blade before each cut, a trick he had learned as a child from the Indians he had watched cutting hides. Mr. Nash was so impressed with the usefulness of this innovation that he ordered a bowl of water to be put on the workbench next to each of of his congress boot cutters. Unknown to Mr. Nash, some of his more duplicitous cutters soon replaced the water in their bowls with rum.

As weeks turned into months, Lowe and his master developed a cordial relationship. Passing time by the fire in the evenings, the two often had conversations on a wide range of subjects. Nash became impressed with the scope of his precocious apprentice's mind. To encourage the young man, he arranged Lowe's work schedule so he could continue his studies and explore his scientific experiments. Self-absorbed and ambitious, Thaddeus took advantage of Nash's generosity and bent his whole soul to his books. He did, however, fear that his interests were too broad, and he was too easily distracted. Lowe struggled to keep his table clear of its clutter of notes and drawings, and to concentrate on just one book, one subject, at a time. Yet his imagination kept intruding. All too often he found his thoughts wandering off into the sky.

With the coming of spring, the interest of the young men of Hingham turned to kite-flying, a favorite sport due to the proximity of the windy shores of Hingham Bay. Lowe saw kites not only as a recreation but, like Benjamin Franklin, as a means for scientific exploration. He tried his hand at building and flying kites, and soon surpassed most of the local boys at this activity. Not content to just watch his creations fly, Lowe decided to construct a kite large enough to carry a small animal aloft. He remembered what he had read about the Montgolfier brothers' early experiment in which they sent up a cock, a duck, and a sheep, and he wanted to test the reaction of animals to altitude himself. To this end, Lowe built an enormous, multitiered kite, and then persuaded a friend of his to lend him his dog for a flight. However, on the night of the scheduled experiment, the lad declined to have his dog go for a kite ride, fearing for the safety of his pet, much to the disappointment of the group of boys who had gathered to witness the historic event.

Not one to say nay, Lowe scoured the neighborhood for wild, "fice" dogs, which were normally everywhere. Finding none, he hurried to Mr. Nash's shop. Thaddeus had his own set of keys, as he opened up in the morning and closed again at night. A big black tomcat lived in the shop. This huge and wild feline was kept to manage the rat population attracted to the choice bits of leather. Did he dare take this tom for his experiment? Lowe wondered. His audience was still waiting anxiously. He could not disappoint them, knowing they would be huffed if he didn't send something up. Lowe promised himself he would bring the cat right back to the shop. The novice scientist was very confident of his kite and sure no harm would come to the animal.

After some coaxing, Lowe managed to lure the cat into the wire cage he had constructed for the purpose of taking the dog aloft. It was more than large enough for the cat, who cowered in the corner, its eyes open wide. As an afterthought, on the way out, Lowe picked up a small peg lamp standing on a table near the door. He would use the lamp as a marker to show the kite's position while it hung in the night sky.

The site chosen by Lowe for the cat's flight was an athletic field east of Hingham Centre, where there were no buildings or trees to impede the kite's progress. The town clock was striking ten as Lowe and his self-appointed assistants approached the field with his monstrous kite and all his other paraphernalia. Word had gotten out about what Lowe was planning. Attempting to pass through town unnoticed, he had picked up, nevertheless, quite a boodle of curious followers. Although it was admittedly a very minor production, for the first time in his life Thaddeus Sobieski Constantine Lowe found himself alone at the center of the stage.

Red tissue paper was wrapped over one half of the lamp, and it was tied on midway up the kite's tail. The cage containing the now howling cat was secured to the end. After another check to be sure things were firmly fastened, Lowe ordered the kite go.

Struggling against the brisk wind, the boys held the massive creation in check. As they paid out the line an extremely strong breeze from the bay caught the kite and took it aloft with great speed, blowing it in the direction of the town. Although six lads held the stout line, they had all they could do to keep their footing as the giant kite, powered by the small gale, slowly dragged them across the ground.

The rope tethering his kite had been marked by Lowe with a supply of buttons, empty thread reels, and scraps of leather at every ten feet, so that he could tell how far aloft the kite was. By the time it reached a thousand feet, the boys were having difficulty restraining the twisting demon. They were relieved when Thaddeus had them tie the line to a stout post at the edge of the field. His kite in a fixed position now, Lowe decided to take a tour of the town to observe it from various angles. The glowing lantern, showing first red and then white as it swayed with the wind, made a highly visible marker.

By the time the town clock chimed midnight the wind had died significantly, so Lowe had the kite pulled down. Although the lantern was still brightly lit, the huge cat was almost invisible—a ball of black fur crouching in the corner of the cage. Only the glowing green reflection of the lamp light on its eyes gave a clue that the animal was still there. A low moaning sound was coming from the corner of the cage—a growl that sounded at the same time threatening and as if its originator were on the verge of death.

Thinking he would stroke the cat to reassure him everything was all right, Thaddeus began to cautiously unlatch the cage. The tom stood up and arched its back, letting out an earth-shattering howl. Lowe jumped back, just as a black streak, its claws bared, flew out the door, and disappeared into the darkness with the gaggle of boys in hot pursuit.

Lowe was left to disassemble the kite and drag his gear home. He hoped the boys did not catch the cat as he knew if they did it would not be well for the poor frightened creature. Feeling guilty about the whole incident, on the way home Thaddeus swore to himself that he would never again involve an innocent animal in his experiments. He would not send a living thing aloft until it could be himself. As soon as Lowe had his first free moment, he began plans for a larger, man-carrying kite.

An article appeared the next day in the local paper about the strange light that had hung in the sky over Hingham on the previous night. That evening at supper Mr. Nash referred to the article and asked Thaddeus if he could venture some scientific explanation for this seemingly unexplainable phenomenon. Expecting his apprentice's usually witty riposte, Nash was confounded when Lowe merely responded he had no opinion and could not imagine what might have caused a light to appear in the sky. The lad quickly finished his meal and asked to be allowed to leave the table before Nash was able to pursue the matter further.

The next morning the black tom was discovered missing from the shop. It became a mystery as to what had happened to it since everyone was sure the animal had no way of getting out. Lowe felt very bad. He knew the cat had trusted him and he had let it down. He was sure the poor frightened puss had come to harm at the hands of the pursuing mob of boys. His haste at abandoning the creature embarrassed him. Nevertheless, several days later, much to Lowe's relief, the old tom cat reappeared, a bit shabby and dirty, but seemingly none the worse for having been away. The next day, as Lowe worked at his bench, he felt something rub up against his leg. He looked down to see the black tom looking up at him with its large dark eyes, on its toes, its back arched magnificently, and he knew he had been forgiven.

From then on Lowe managed the details of his existence with a sober and dignified optimism, eventually completing his apprenticeship and leaving Hingham for Boston to join his brother. While he learned many new things in Hingham, Lowe never discovered that the very streets he was walking had been trod by an ancestor of a man who was to play an important part in his later life, and the life of the nation. No one in the community cared that in 1637, only seventeen years after the landing of the Pilgrims at Plymouth Rock, young Samuel Lincoln, a weaver from Hingham, England, had emigrated to Hingham, Massachusetts, marking the beginning of the Lincoln clan in America. At the time Lowe lived in Hingham, Abraham Lincoln was nothing more than a little-known congressman from Illinois.

3
A Magic Show, a Bride, and a Balloon

In the spring of 1850 Lowe reluctantly returned to his parents' home in New Hampshire. After spending two fairly content years as an apprentice with William Nash, Lowe had gone into the shoemaking business in Boston with his brother Joseph. During his time away from home, Lowe had saved a good deal of money. He hoped to have enough to go to college. A serious illness, however, forced him to return to Randolph before he was ready. Confined in a dark room during the long summer months, Lowe despaired of ever getting well. But by September he was feeling fit enough to go about. Lowe's appetite for entertainment revived; he agreed to take his brother, Charles, to a magic show. The gaily colored poster had caught his attention: Professor Reginald B. Dincklehoff, World Renowned Chemist, Appearing for Three Nights Only at the Randolph Town Hall.

Professor Dincklehoff's show was no mere feat of legerdemain, as he boastfully proclaimed at the beginning of his act, but "the wonders of science revealed right before your very eyes." This mention of the word "science" piqued Lowe's interest. He had thought he was accompanying Charles to a simple magic show, but this was different. When the professor asked for a volunteer from the audience to assist him, Lowe did not have to be coaxed up onto the stage.

To someone like Lowe, who had an avid knowledge of science, the show proved to be quite elementary. But the unsophisticated audience, made up mainly of merchants and farmers from in and around Coos County, had been quite entertained and impressed, rewarding the professor with many rounds of enthusiastic applause after his closing demonstration.

Dincklehoff had also been impressed by his volunteer assistant. He recognized that the young man of eighteen had an alert and questioning mind. He was pleased to learn of Lowe's interest in science, and that the youth had not only studied in school, but had continued to make experiments on his own. As he was never sure who would turn up in his audiences on any given night, Dincklehoff asked Lowe if he would like to work as his assistant for the rest of his engagement. He could offer only a very small salary; however, the professor assured the young man that he would learn a great deal. Tired of languishing at his parents' home, Thaddeus readily accepted the opportunity. The relationship proved so cordial that by the time Dincklehoff had to depart it had all been arranged, and Lowe left town with the professor and his magic show.

Lowe toured with Dincklehoff for two more years, until the aging chemist decided to retire. By then Lowe had become so attached to the life of the traveling showman that he used his savings to buy Dincklehoff's equipment and his act. Lowe donned Dincklehoff's frock coat and top hat, officially adopting the title of "Professor of Chemistry." Except for substituting "Coulincourt" for what he considered the rather drab "Constantine," Lowe kept his own name. He had enough money remaining to purchase a portable laboratory. Now Lowe could experiment with gasses, something he would need to be familiar with if he was to pursue his not-forgotten dream of becoming a balloonist.

"Professor" Lowe's lectures were an immediate success, drawing huge crowds wherever he went. His new act all but eliminated the simple magic tricks of his predecessor. Instead, Lowe concentrated on demonstrating the basic facts of chemistry with the flair of a showman. A nation that was facing a growing division, as it moved from the agricultural to the industrial, needed to be entertained. Lowe's combination of fascination and education provided the perfect diversion from the conflicts between the North and South now appearing more regularly in the newspapers.

Lowe enjoyed his traveling life. During two years on tour, he had continued to grow in popularity, attracting large audiences throughout the country, and earning an enormous amount of money. Remembering his earlier goal, he decided to add several small balloons to his repertoire. He contrived to use these in a special experiment.

In his youth Thaddeus Lowe had often lain for hours on a hill near his home studying the movement of clouds. He observed that clouds traveled in different directions. The higher clouds generally moved from west to east, while the lower ones often proceeded from east to west.

After a considerable number of tries, Lowe determined he could regulate the height at which a balloon stopped rising by adjusting the amount of hydrogen it contained and ballast it carried. By varying the thickness of the coat of varnish he covered the balloon's skin with, the professor found he could also control the rate at which the gas was lost and, therefore, the time a balloon would stay aloft.

As a new feature of his show, able to be done only at outdoor performances, Lowe would release a number of brightly colored balloons. Then he would announce confidently that the red ones would go high and fly east, while the yellow ones would stay low and head west. To the delight and amazement of his audiences, most of the time the balloons performed exactly as he predicted. Lowe would then send a boodle of lads to retrieve the balloons, for a copper penny apiece, calling out almost the exact spot where each balloon would be found.

This often-repeated experiment not only added to Lowe's fortune, but convinced him that the sky's winds were as constant as the earth's rivers. He believed that although sometimes the wind's currents varied in width, if one knew them they could be followed as predictably as the streams. Lowe felt that if he could invent a device that could change a balloon's altitude, without the need to vent precious gas or toss out ballast, he would be able to find the proper flow and travel the skies with speed, and complete reliability.

On February 14, 1855, Lowe arrived in New York City to deliver a lecture to the largest and most sophisticated audience he had yet performed in front of. He had rooms at the grand and luxurious Astor Hotel, the gilded ballroom of which was to be the site of his performance.

There was a rustle in the audience as Professor Lowe took the stage. No longer the rough bumpkin from Jefferson, New Hampshire, he had grown handsome and acquired a poised and cultured manner equal to his good looks.

Accustomed to more boisterous settings, often outdoors at fairs and carnivals, Lowe immediately became aware of the silence in the room. Heavy brocade drapes had been drawn over the windows to keep out the cold and the noise of traffic in the street. The only sound, save the occasional cough, was the tinkling of the cut glass droplets on the huge chandeliers swaying unperceptively overhead; yet there was no air.

Lowe's face became flush. He could not breathe. His nostrils were clogged by the scent of wet leather, and tobacco, and of a hundred different perfumes and powders. The whole densely packed panorama of faces seemed to him to be drawing the oxygen from the room. Almost in a panic, Lowe leapt from the platform. Saying he must have air, Lowe ran to the nearest window and threw aside the drapes. Unbolting the latch, the professor pushed open the sash to the cold winter night and leaned out, taking several deep breaths. Leaving the window open, Lowe walked back to the stage. The night air, saturated with sounds and odors, lazily wafted into the smoky grayness of the hall. His lecture would have to compete with the noise of the clomping horses, rattling carriages, the shouts of the drivers, and the smell of tomorrow's bread being baked in the hotel kitchen, but at least now he could breathe.

As Lowe returned to the lectern, he noticed many of the faces in the affluent Gotham audience were registering curiosity, amazement, and even shock. Some gave him a well-mannered look of hostility. There were many whispered comments. People of the upper class just did not open their windows; they might risk an attack of something or other. A number of the women clutched their partners' arms and made a display of drawing their fur wraps around their shoulders and shivering.

Feeling his actions had been challenged, an idea raced into Lowe's head. He immediately launched into an impromptu lecture on the beneficial effects of oxygen. Oxygen is the most abundant of all elements, he began, staring down the unsuspecting audience, present in the atmosphere to the extent of 21 percent by volume, in the oceans to the extent of 85.5 percent; and as a constituent of rocks and minerals, constituted 46.7 percent of the solid crust of the earth. These and many other facts flowed from the professor's finger tips, as the now heroic stuff flowed in through the open window. Lowe concluded by pointing out that oxygen comprised 60 percent of the human body, and, being a constituent of all living tissues, humans, as well as other animals and most plants, oxygen was required in a free or combined state to maintain life. The audience was immediately charmed. Most thought that his opening of the windows was an integral part of his lecture. Gone was their hostility toward him and their fear of the fresh night air. More than a few present would sleep tonight with their window sash bravely open a crack.

A skilled lecturer, when Lowe spoke his eyes swept the room, embracing the entire audience, allowing no one to feel left out. But tonight he found his gaze being drawn repeatedly to a petite, attractive woman, wearing an outrageous feather hat, in front of him in the very first row. This mysterious woman was so tiny and had such fair skin that she appeared almost to be a gaily attired porcelain doll.

Confounded by her presence, Lowe tried to avoid the woman's stare. However, whenever their gaze met, the professor saw that her quick, dark, eyes were following his every motion, her spirited face registering total absorption in his every word. She was looking at him with a cordialness that inspired his confidence. Lowe was befuddled and irritated with himself for his lapse of concentration. Apparently his audience did not notice Lowe's dilemma, for at the end of the lecture he was surrounded by an unusually large group of scientific enthusiasts. Nevertheless, he could not restrain his eyes from wandering over the heads of his admirers; he was searching for the exotic beauty with the feather hat.

At last the crowd dispersed. As Lowe was putting away his equipment for the next day's performance, he chanced to ask a reporter he had met earlier if he happened to be acquainted with the petite woman with the feather hat who sat in the middle of the front row.

The reporter allowed as how he did know the woman, and revealed her name was Leontine Augustine Gachon. Although she was only nineteen, she had already established herself as somewhat of an actress. When he asked Lowe if he wished to meet her, the professor did not hesitate to give his consent.

As they made their way downstairs the reporter told Lowe the woman's story. Leontine Gachon was not just another French refugee. Her father had been a palace guard for Louis Philippe, the "Citizen King." Welcomed back in 1814 from his exile in Philadelphia by Louis XVIII, and restored to his Orleans estates, Louis Philippe soon became a favorite of the French middle class and by 1830 had been proclaimed king himself. But the Citizen King's reign was marred by extreme corruption on the home front and a disinterest in foreign affairs. So, in 1848 the populace revolted against him. The Gachon family had fled out the back door of the Tuileries with the royal entourage just as the Republican mob was coming in the front. Her father had left the Citizen King in London and brought his family to New York.

Leontine was, the reporter related, an independent girl who had a fine education, but now, through her own initiative, had gone out and made her mark in acting, a field for which she had not been trained.

Lowe and the reporter found the Gachons seated in the lobby, almost as if they had been expecting the professor's arrival. After introductions and a short, polite conversation, Professor Lowe graciously invited the party to take a late supper with him.

At the table in the hotel's dining room Leontine's mother and father, knowing little English, spoke infrequently. But Leontine made up for their silence. Her questions about Lowe's work, asked with her charming French accent, totally enchanted the professor and made him realize her intelligent comprehension of science. Overwhelmed by Leontine's attractiveness, Lowe had difficulty keeping his mind on the conversation. He knew from that moment, for the first time in his life, he was in love. The day, by coincidence, was Saint Valentine's Day.

The courtship was short. Lowe knew he had only one week in New York before he had to begin a tour of the South. Lowe romanced the young actress with a sense of breathless urgency, displaying the same resolve he showed when pursuing scientific knowledge. He was determined not to leave New York without Leontine as his bride.

And so it was, a mere seven days after they had met, that the New York papers announced: "The famous professor of science Thaddeus Sobieski Constantine Lowe and the actress Leontine Gachon have been wed by a justice of the peace in the ornate salon of the Astor Hotel, where the professor is staying."

As the sun rose the next morning, the newlyweds departed Gotham on Lowe's tour of the South. They would happily combine his lecture tour with a wandering, extended honeymoon. After a long train ride, their first stop was in Zanesville, Ohio, where Lowe performed before a packed house, his new wife sitting off to the side of the stage beaming mightily. From there the couple went by boat down the Muskingum and Ohio rivers to the Mississippi, where they joined up with a troupe of a hundred performers on a showboat that was touring up and down the river bringing entertainment to the various towns.

Once on board the showboat Leontine did not sit idle. When she learned the troupe had no need for serious actresses, she laughingly agreed to become part of a dance routine. A Mr. Ralph Keller, who worked in the dance act with Leontine, later wrote his recollections of the trip and described Lowe as "an ingenious odd sort of Yankee with his long hair braided and hanging in two tails down his back." Lowe was also in charge of a museum on board that displayed a garish collection of wax reproductions of human freaks and celebrities. This job pleased the scientist no end, and he took great joy making new creations by adding to or subtracting from the models as he saw fit.

He was tired of the sameness of meals they were getting on the boat, Lowe complained one day at supper. The food was good, but he wanted a change of diet. As there was no performance on the next day and the steamer would be anchored in the river near a wood, Lowe proposed he would provide the troupe with something different to eat.

Although he had not hunted in years, Lowe had been a skilled stalker of game during his boyhood days in New Hampshire. As he had anticipated, dawn found the showboat anchored in the stream near a large island. He borrowed a rifle from one of the security men and rowed ashore to hunt wild turkeys. Several shots were heard in the woods along the bank, and a smiling professor returned shortly with two big birds slung proudly over his shoulder. Lowe presented them to the cooks to prepare for dinner, only to be informed that these were not some breed of Southern wild turkey he was not familiar with, but rather turkey vultures. The cook proclaimed the fowl not fit for human consumption and refused to cook them.

Not to be deterred, Lowe replied he would cook them himself. Thaddeus and Leontine went to work preparing the birds, concocting elaborate sauces using her French recipes. They held a special dinner after the regular meal and served up the vultures to their friends. Eager for a change, their guests dived in. Everyone chewed on the tough meat bravely, but the looks they gave each other soon revealed that the meat-eating scavengers made for a rather unappetizing meal, no matter how well it was seasoned. The growling spasms in his stomach that evening made Lowe realize he should have heeded the cooks' advice.

When the cold winds of winter came to the Midwest, the Lowes left the showboat and took an apartment in New Orleans. This was a natural place for Leontine as many of the citizens were from France, and the French language was widely spoken. Settled in after their adventures on the Mississippi, Leontine encouraged her husband's study of aeronautics and his plan to construct his own balloon. To support themselves and earn funds for the balloon, Lowe gave lectures while Leontine assisted on stage with the chemical experiments. Together they made a group of marionettes, and Leontine used them to give puppet shows for children. She had learned puppetry in Paris and was both imaginative and skillful with her troupe, one of whom, with its eagle beak and full moustache, bore a striking resemblance to her husband. Despite the charming streets and cafés, and the many activities the couple were engaged in, Thaddeus and Leontine were overcome by a homesickness for the Northeast. The Lowes did not remain long in New Orleans, but returned to New York early in 1856.

While in New Orleans Lowe had hoped to see an ascension by the famous French balloonist, Ernest Petin, who now resided in the city. On Christmas Day 1852 Petin and several of his companions had gone into the water when his balloon had developed a catastrophic leak while attempting to fly across Lake Pontchartrain. Alas, Lowe was never able to see the Frenchman fly. Petin had an unparalleled record of cancellations due to improper inflation, bad weather, a vandalized balloon, and a general lack of finances.

One playful evening, when the Lowes were established back in New York, Leontine revealed to her husband that she had been attracted to him the minute he first strode onto the lecture platform in front of her. Reconstructing the history of that escapade, Leontine confessed she had given her card to a reporter-friend from the *New York Times* asking him to arrange their meeting. Quite happily the couple's spontaneous love affair had matured into an enduring affection. Lowe had come to realize his beloved wife was not only his most intelligent companion and willing helpmate, but also an enthusiastic sharer of his dreams. He would discover that among all the disappointments and perplexities that would fall on his life, nothing would contribute more to his happiness than his choice of Leontine for a wife.

As soon as they had arrived back in New York, Lowe began work on his first balloon, made from plans in John Wise's book *A System of Aeronautics.* The airship was completed in April 1857. Spending all his free time, and most of their small savings, Lowe had assembled it with his own hands in a farm shed he rented from the Stevens family in Hoboken, New Jersey, just across the Hudson River from their New York City residence. Lowe and his wife had studied Wise's text thoroughly and then drawn out the patterns on wrapping paper laid out on their kitchen table. Leontine had helped her husband cut the twilled muslin from the patterns so as not to waste any of the expensive material. She had taught him how to sew strong seams, and he had shown her how to make a leak-proof valve. Together they had pinched pennies so there would be enough money to build the aerostat.

Nevertheless, Leontine, who at the time was pregnant with their first child, had become apprehensive when her husband returned home one evening and announced over dinner that he had applied the final coat of varnish to the gas bag and that his balloon was finished. Moreover, weather permitting, he intended to test fly it the next day.

This was a rather sudden disclosure in a life, which despite the impending arrival of a child, had become somewhat routine. When Lowe had left in the morning, Leontine had assumed her husband would return for supper with the usual news that there was still a great deal left to be done on his balloon. She had been silently hoping the work would go on forever, or until he had abandoned the project. Leontine had been taken aback by this pronouncement of such great consequence.

"Are you sure the balloon will go up in the air, and stay there as it should?" Leontine asked her husband apprehensively, pointing out he had never made an airship before. But Lowe reassured her, casually sipping the thin soup that had become their regular diet to save money for the balloon, that he had followed Wise's instructions carefully and even made some improvements of his own.

Leontine's fears, however, caused her to persist with the conversation. She reminded her husband that he had never been up in an airship before, not even one of someone else's construction. Leontine suggested that perhaps he should get some instruction in the handling of balloons or maybe get an experienced aeronaut to take his craft up for the first time to see how it performed.

As husbands thought that they always knew more about everything than their wives, Lowe attempted to put an end to his wife's concerns by reassuring Leontine he had read all there was to know about handling a balloon and that he was confident in his new airship. Lowe promised that the next day's flight would be the beginning of a brave new future for the two of them. He told her not to worry, as he would return from his first flight alive and hearty, and moreover all his ideas would be vindicated.

Placing a hand on her stomach, Leontine speculated that perhaps it was the baby coming that was making her so nervous. She urged him not to mind her, but finish his supper while it was still hot. After a few tenuous mouthfuls of her own meal, Leontine spoke to her husband again and asked if would it be all right if she came along to see the balloon go up for the first time. This was the response Lowe had secretly been craving. A smile lit his face. That night he went to bed exceedingly happy.

Although the weather the night before had seemed rather doubtful, the next day dawned bright and clear. Birds sang outside his window as Lowe stretched his head out to watch high cirrus departing over the East River. He felt no wind on his face, then stuck his head out further and still felt none. Leontine was apprehensive as she laid out the table, knowing that her husband would soon be venturing into what for them was a strange new realm.

Lowe always took a full breakfast, so they sat down to dine on their meal of bread, potatoes, eggs, and strong tea. Seeking to engage her husband in conversation, Leontine ventured to ask how he liked the tea. Lowe did not reply. She volunteered it was a different brand from what they usually drank, purchased from a new shop that had just opened on Vesey Street called the Atlantic and Pacific Tea Company. Lowe still did not respond, but rustled the papers and graphs he had laid out in front of him. Recognizing his mood, Leontine said no more and the rest of the meal was passed in silence.

After breakfast, Leontine, who ignored the dictates of fashion for her own look, carefully dressed in her finest outfit as befit the momentous occasion. Then the couple hailed a hackney to take them to a nearby Hudson River pier, where they got the ferry to Hoboken.

Leontine took a bench on deck for the short trip, thankful for the brief respite of fresh air during the passage across the river. The streets and avenues of New York were thronged with four-in-hands, broughams, and driving vehicles of every kind, which often caused Leontine to choke from the dust and the reek of horse droppings. She found especially offensive the stench of the pigs that were allowed to roam the city's parks and streets, including Broadway, to eat the garbage left out. These pigs sometimes numbered in the thousands, and "hog reevers" were employed to round up the more ill-mannered. Nevertheless, these free-roaming pigs were a boon to the city's poor— for whom Leontine felt a profound sympathy—who often caught the porkers and butchered them for their dinner.

The instant the boat began to pull from the dock, Lowe jumped from the seat at his wife's side and gingerly made his way to the bow. He deplored wasting time and put these daily ferry trips to good use. As was his habit, Lowe stood on the foredeck taking notes, carefully observing the patterns the currents made as the wind blew ripples across the water.

When the Lowes arrived at the Stevens farm, the balloon was already out of its shed and was being inflated from a nearby gas main by Lowe's assistants. The huge bag, made from twilled muslin that had been sealed with varnish to make it air tight, was tugging at the restraining ropes, its wicker gondola swinging freely below. Lowe climbed cautiously into the basket. His crew, three farm hands normally employed by Edwin A. Stevens, who not only owned the shed but was an inventor and patron of scientific experiments as well, began to remove the sandbags attached to the rigging.

After about a half hour more of inflation, the balloon had achieved its full shape and floated easily above the ground, bobbing to and fro on the slight breeze, held down only by the ropes in the hands of the crew. The broad smile on Lowe's face showed he was pleased with the lift his new balloon was achieving. He stood up straight in the basket and saluted his wife, his palm to his forehead in the military style. Leontine returned his salute. Placing her left hand on her chest, she felt her heart beat, and then, she was sure, the echo of another, smaller heart beating just below hers.

The fledgling balloonist reached up and began to untie the neck of the bag, which was connected to the gas main during inflation. Her mind in a muddle, Leontine secretly held out hope her husband would decide the whole thing was too risky and let the matter drop. But it was too late. She was deafened by a loud hissing noise. The acrid smell of coal gas filled the air as the excess gas escaped from the neck. Bending to his task, Lowe, one by one, tossed out three bags of ballast from his supply in the bottom of the basket.

A startled Leontine jumped backwards, at the same time protecting her nose from the biting scent of the gas with a handkerchief. The action served to muffle her panicked cries as the balloon carrying her husband slowly lifted itself into the sky. Seeing this, Leontine's body trembled with apprehension. The thought entered her mind that her husband might keep rising, right into the high clouds, and never return. She stretched out her arms, a living crucifix embracing the sky, as if to draw him back down to earth.

Floating calmly above her, Lowe looked down and, seeing Leontine's upraised arms, thought she was waving. He waved back. Putting the megaphone he had brought along to his mouth, Lowe shouted to his wife that he was having great fun. He could see everything from up there. Then, bellowing in a sonorous voice, on this most public stage, Lowe boldly repeated his prediction of the previous night that this was only the beginning of great things to come. The balloon crew in the meantime, although pleased with the success of the event, had been looking from one to the other with expressions on their faces that indicated they might be wondering if they weren't dealing with someone who was not quite mentally all there, perhaps even a madman.

The positive sound in her husband's voice reassured Leontine. She realized that he was only a few hundred feet above her, securely fastened to the ground by a tether, and not about to go anywhere. It was, she reminded herself, his first ascension. In contradiction to his original impulse to allow the winds to carry him where they might, Lowe had prudently decided that free flight would come later, when he had gathered more experience. But she had better get used to her husband's new madness for flight, Leontine told herself, watching him bobbing overhead, shouting and waving wildly, the balloon straining to break free of its tether rope. She suspected he would be going aloft quite often now. She was a good wife, who would do anything to help her husband through what she sensed might be a critical period. He was young, just approaching twenty-five years of age, overflowing with confidence, and in good health. With care he should have a long life ahead of him—that is, if he didn't do anything foolish.

At last, after many sleepless nights and morning sicknesses, Leontine gave birth to their first child, whom they named Louisa. The new baby occupied her time and gave her a good excuse not to have to travel over to New Jersey to watch her husband's frequent ascensions. In addition she was kept busy managing the family affairs, as Lowe more and more was adopting the profligate habits of his father Clovis in matters of money. It was up to Leontine to make sure they did not live beyond their means as her husband spared no expense when it came to maintaining his balloon.

The months that followed were a time of intense activity for Lowe as he continued to make practice tethered flights to perfect his ballooning skills. Often the balloonist spent the entire day in no other activity than to-ing and fro-ing at the end of his tether five hundred feet above the entrance to his shed. But even the brain of a perfectionist like Lowe eventually grew tired of such repetition. After much consideration he felt confident enough to risk a cross-country flight. Once he had escaped the restraints of his tether, even though some of his early flights ended up a tangled confusion a scant half mile or so from where they began, Lowe always found something to learn from his errors, something to add to his next flight. After considerable experimentation and some mishaps that he did not tell his wife about, Lowe mastered the free-flight technique.

The balloonist grew to love the silence that accompanied being in the air, the apparent motionlessness while the airship, carried by the wind, moved without effort far above the surface of the earth. Lowe was fascinated by the sight of even the highest hills appearing to flatten when his balloon passed over them. He enjoyed the many colors and the neat orderliness of the landscape when viewed from on high. During climbs and descents, Lowe found great satisfaction in experiencing the way in which the air currents, true to his prediction, changed at different altitudes.

Despite the joy he took in these pleasures, it did not take Lowe long to realize that his present balloon was too small to operate at the altitudes he required to investigate the upper air currents or to conduct meteorological studies as he had planned. He decided, therefore, much to his wife's agreement, to commercialize it. Lowe would use his first balloon mainly as a source of income, taking passengers aloft to earn the money he would need to construct a larger balloon. For a tethered ride the balloonist charged what was then the sizable sum of a dollar per person. To his more adventurous clients, Lowe offered the opportunity of a free-flight, or as he termed it, a "real sky ride." For these flights, which rarely lasted more than a half hour, he asked and received what was at that time the rather princely sum of five dollars.

Lowe had begun to write letters to his father about his work. They had been very close when he was a child, but had fallen away in recent years. For a time an unbridled conflict had raged between them. Lowe felt that his father disapproved of him for three things: first, was his giving up his job as boot and shoe maker with his brother in Boston; second, was giving up a successful career as a "scientific lecturer" to take up his mad experiments with balloons; and third, was marrying Leontine, rather than some nice girl from Coos County, New Hampshire, where he had grown up.

It was without his father's blessing that T. S. C. Lowe had married Leontine, who was not only someone who had been a "professional actress," but also a "foreigner," a French refugee. Lowe could not make his father see that Leontine Gachon was a unique and special person with whom he was in love, not just as his father referred to her—some immigrant woman frog.

Lowe's letters to his father about his free-flight activities had begun to intrigue the man. Clovis Lowe decided to visit his son in New York and find out what this balloon business was all about. Clovis' other motive for the long trip was meeting Leontine and his granddaughter Louisa for the first time, which he hoped might prove to be a pleasant experience.

As it was, the father was well received by his son, each man bending over backwards insisting that he was to blame for the controversy that had separated them all these years. They joked with each other in the rough and jocular way that had given young Thaddeus so much comfort when growing up. With Leontine and her daughter, Clovis was warm and sympathetic, behaving in a way more humane than Lowe thought he was capable of. All in all it was a pleasant situation, with the group passing many happy evenings together in front of the fire, reading, and playing checkers and card games.

The senior Lowe, however, preferred to spend the days with his son at the shop in Hoboken, sitting on a bench watching the work on the new balloon as it took shape. He also eagerly monitored his son's practice ascensions and went out with the chase crew to retrieve the balloon after a free flight. To Lowe's surprise his father was taking an inordinate interest in the activity of ballooning. Soon Clovis was no longer content to sit and watch, but was poking into every aspect of airship construction, even lending a hand when he was allowed. The day Clovis arrived, he had announced that he was only planning to stay a short time. But his visit stretched into weeks and then months. T. S. C. Lowe's father was now working in the shop on all phases of the fabrication and, more amazingly, making practice ascensions of his own. Though Clovis rose slowly and cautiously, and stood a little shaky on his feet while attempting to affect an air of casual nonchalance, he was going aloft. One must take these things as they come, Lowe told himself, as his father soldiered on, using up large quantities of gas in order to make ascensions almost daily. Much to his son's delight, Clovis Lowe, who had never shown any previous interest in flight, did not return to New Hampshire until he had become an accomplished aeronaut in his own right. Lowe could not imagine how useful his father's newly acquired skills would be to him in the war that was surely coming and that would engulf them as well as the rest of the nation. When cannon balls and grapeshot rained from the sky, Thaddeus would be in his father's debt, as Clovis would be to him.

4

A New Balloon, an Ascension in Canada, and a Boast of Flying the Atlantic

Since the middle of the 1800's the attention of the American public had been focused on the balloon as it never had been before. The newspapers were full of exploits of balloonists such as Eugene Godard, who not only made ascensions taking along his lovely wife, but also performed stunts on a trapeze while hanging below the basket. The 1858 season held a great deal of promise for the ever-growing corps of American balloonists who were riding the crest of a wave of balloon enthusiasm that would later be called "The Golden Decade of Ballooning." Most of the country's aeronauts were rushing to take advantage of this situation as each attempted to outdo the other with more and more spectacular flights.

A demonstration ascension by a young aeronaut, T. S. C. Lowe, at Ogdensburg, New York, on the Saint Lawrence River, had caused his name to become known to balloon enthusiasts in Canada. Planning a large festival for the summer, some enterprising Ottawa citizens decided to write to Lowe to see if the American would come to their city to make a flight. Thaddeus excitedly showed the letter to Leontine. Here was tangible proof his reputation as a balloonist was beginning to spread.

Having begun work on his larger balloon in the spring of 1858, Lowe was nowhere near to completing the project when he received the invitation to go to Ottawa to make an ascension. A festival was being held to celebrate two events: Queen Victoria's designation of Ottawa as the seat of Dominion government and the laying of the Atlantic telegraph cable, which was now expected to be finished in late August. The successful completion of the cable, faced with considerable difficulties, was still very much in doubt.

In 1856 an American company headed by Cyrus W. Field had laid an undersea cable across Cabot Strait, from Cape Ray, Newfoundland, to Cape Breton Island, Nova Scotia. The success of this venture prompted Field to organize the Atlantic Telegraph Company and begin plans to lay a cable from Newfoundland to Ireland. His first transatlantic cable, begun in 1857, had broken 360 miles from shore. His second attempt in June of 1858 also failed. What was bad luck for Cyrus Field was turning out to be good fortune for Lowe as it gave him the additional time he needed to complete his balloon.

Lowe planned that his new balloon be twice the size of his first. Because of the scale, he chose not to use twill, but rather the finest Indian silk, heavily starched with a rice-and-water mixture. The netting was also made of silk twine, much lighter yet stronger than the cheaper cotton twine used on his first balloon. Lowe and his men put in long hours at the shop in Hoboken, rushing to complete the new balloon in time for the Ottawa event. It was almost as if he and his crew were racing against the cable-layers working aboard the U.S. warship *Niagara* and the British warship *Agamemnon* out in the choppy Atlantic.

When asked to christen the new balloon, Leontine did not hesitate but immediately chose the name *Enterprise.* She did not reveal her reasons for the name. Perhaps she sensed that, though it would take a tremendous effort to complete, the new balloon promised the brave adventures and the hope of things to come, which her husband had so boldly predicted on his very first ascension.

Because the Atlantic telegraph cable had been heralded as one of the modern wonders of the world, its completion in September 1858 became an occasion for much celebration. Fairs were held, and huge fireworks displays shot off throughout Great Britain, Canada, and the United States. Called the "Nuptials of Old Europe with Young America," the impact of the cable on civilization was likened to the introduction of the steam engine. Her Majesty Queen Victoria had the honor of sending the first transatlantic wire message. In the streets of London newsboys hawked papers with headlines of the event, and vendors sold all-day lollipops in the shape of twisted cables.

Spirits were considerably let down on both sides of the Atlantic when, only ten days after its inception, the cable that had been so painstakingly laid developed technical difficulties on account of careless handling when installing the insulation. The magnificent underwater cable crackled and sputtered for three more weeks, its signals becoming weak and distorted, and then fell silent forever.

Despite the disappointment over the failure of the cable, Lowe's exhibition flights at Ottawa were a personal triumph. His first major public appearance as an aeronaut afforded him considerable publicity. Also, he had the occasion to met Samuel F. B. Morse, inventor of the telegraph, and Cyrus W. Field himself. Lowe was especially impressed by Morse, who was a well-known painter as well as an inventor, and who had supported himself by his art while working on his telegraph. For all his admiration, Lowe fancied himself cut from the same cloth as Morse, considering them both to be kind of present-day Renaissance men.

On the long train trip home from Ottawa, Lowe began working on the design for his next balloon. Immediately upon returning to New York, Lowe started construction of his third airship. He planned to equip this balloon with every instrument known for study of the upper air. A firm believer in the existence of constant air currents, Lowe hoped to discover if the movements of these upper winds, which he liked to call "the rivers of the sky," might not be used to propel airships, just as they moved great masses of air about to create weather.

A few years earlier the balloonist John La Mountain had accidentally discovered one of these "rivers." Intending only a short demonstration flight, La Mountain, accompanied by the newspaper reporter John Haddock, departed Watertown, New York, about 5:30 in the afternoon. Because of some unusual atmospheric conditions, La Mountain's balloon immediately ascended to fifteen thousand feet, where the two passengers evidently encountered an unknown wind phenomenon, now known as the jet stream. This wind pushed them along at such a great rate that they soon passed over what they recognized to be the city of Ottawa, Canada. Three hours later the men came down in a tree somewhere in the middle of the Canadian wilderness. When they finally managed to get to the ground, it took the pair four days of steady hiking to get back to civilization. Amazingly La Mountain's balloon had flown over three hundred miles in a little less than four hours. Although they had not flown in a straight line, but drifted around a bit, their ground speed for the distance was an unheard of seventy-five miles per hour.

Lowe's early findings about the direction and velocity of winds had convinced him that his basic suppositions were correct. He began to send his data on wind and weather to the Smithsonian Institute in Washington, D.C. The balloonist was trying to encourage the Smithsonian to organize a national weather bureau, with a system of forecasting, which would issue weather warnings to aid not only the aeronaut, but also farmers and mariners as well.

At the same time, Lowe worked constantly on improving the design and operation of his airships. He was also kept busy experimenting with numerous instruments of his own design, one of which was intended to measure latitude and longitude while aloft. The balloonist successfully developed a device, which he called an "altimeter," which used an aneroid barometer marked in feet to ascertain height above sea level. This instrument differed from modern altimeters only in that it lacked a Kollsman window, a means whereby the aviator could adjust his gauge to compensate for the changes in atmospheric pressure.

Not satisfied with the rice starch mixture he used to seal the balloon's fabric, Lowe perfected a new varnish to coat the envelope that prevented rapid dissipation of the gas, a major problem when attempting long distance flights. Tests showed him his new mixture would allow balloons to remain inflated for more than two weeks.

With the interest in his balloons growing, Lowe saw a way to make a profit out of what heretofore had been a rather expensive hobby. He opened a factory for manufacturing versions of his design to sell to the general public. The attention to detail and craftsmanship displayed by Lowe and his staff on these aerostats brought him many orders. Soon the factory was working at full capacity, and new employees were hired. With his newfound flow of capital, Lowe bought a piece of the Stevens farm, next to the shed he had been leasing, and erected a larger building. Even with this increased output he remained a perfectionist. Lowe constantly supervised all aspects of the construction of his balloons, which were now being shipped to all parts of the country. Also, he personally trained the dozens of new workers he had taken on.

The enormous financial success of his balloon factory, plus the birth of a second daughter, which they named Ida Alpha, convinced Lowe it was time to bow to his wife's wishes to leave their small, rented New York apartment and purchase a sizable townhouse. In addition, Lowe now had the means to employ a cook and maid, as well as a nurse for the children. Leontine managed the new residence, and her husband's private affairs, as wisely as she had done when he was earning little money. Her goal was to preserve Lowe from the need to occupy his mind with anything other than his balloons.

Having grown up in a house appointed with furnishings of the plainest kind, Lowe spared no expense at decorating his new townhouse, fitting it out lavishly and in the latest fashion. The Lowe's stylish drawing room became a meeting place for scientists, journalists, businessmen, and outstanding people from all walks of life. These guests, who represented the cream of Gotham society, were attracted not only by Lowe's work with balloons, but by his wife's gracious poise and intelligence. Conversations at these gatherings inevitably turned to the possibilities for new modes of travel. Everyone lamented the slowness of communication between America and Europe. People complained of the failure of the much ballyhooed Atlantic telegraph cable. No one anticipated it being repaired in the near future, and transatlantic surface vessels were too slow to be useful for sending important documents and letters.

It was at just such a friendly gathering, with some of the foremost travel experts of the time present, and everyone throwing their weight around predicting the future of transportation, that Lowe revealed his project for a transatlantic airship. His disclosure immediately flabbergasted the group. The next day, to Lowe's great surprise, he would find his idea much maligned in the nation's newspapers.

Lowe boasted to his guests that travel by balloon would be the means of the future and that it would be he who would first cross the ocean in an airship. Furthermore, he affirmed, he would not make the crossing as a publicity stunt or to attain a record, but to prove that commercial transatlantic airship travel was a practical way of transportation. Lowe estimated that his balloon trip would take much less than a week, at a time when the fastest ships from New York to England took up to two weeks. Even the highly anticipated *Great Eastern,* a fast new steamship currently being completed in England, was expected to take more than a week to make the crossing.

At the gathering in his New York townhouse, a function which often turned into a rowdy session with many wild ideas being bandied about, Lowe had proclaimed a transoceanic airship was the only answer to a faster crossing. He maintained that buoyancy was limited only by size. If one could make the gas envelope of a balloon large enough, then passengers, and even freight, could be carried. Lowe confidently predicted his giant airship, given favorable conditions, could easily waft across the Atlantic Ocean.

The group of experts had looked from one to another in amazement. They opined that no airship had ever stayed aloft for that long a period; the envelope would just not retain the air. Questions came thick and fast, everyone wanting to know the extent of Lowe's seriousness. Someone asked how the airship would be propelled. Another man questioned Professor Lowe as to the means of navigation he intended to use.

A newsman sitting in a corner sucking on his pipe and fishing for a story speculated that perhaps Professor Lowe was planning a larger version of the Frenchman Henri Giffard's steam-powered dirigible airship. He refreshed the group's memory of the fact that Giffard had accomplished a successful flight across the breadth of France as far back as 1852.

Lowe assured his interrogators no steam engine had yet been made that could push so large an airship as he was planning to build against even the lightest breeze. Leaning forward in his chair, the balloonist's eyes widened and his voice took on an almost mystical air. Lowe revealed that he planned to ride the uncharted currents of the upper air just as a sailing vessel rides the surface wind. The balloonist waved his hand smoothly through the air as his airship floated over the Atlantic. He explained that properly understood, the currents aloft were steady and moved regularly in the same direction. Higher up the winds would be strong enough to propel his balloon across the ocean at an undreamed of speed.

Skeptical, yet fascinated, the down-at-heel newsman returned home and wrote up a small article on Lowe's speculations about a transoceanic airship. The next day, as he had covered nothing of any greater importance the day before, the reporter walked to the *Tribune* office on Printing House Square and handed in his copy. His editor pulled his spectacles down from his forehead, read the article with some incredulity, and put it aside. Later in the day, needing something to fill up space, the editor read the piece again. Rewriting it to seem even more fantastic than it originally was, he decided to run the article on one of the inside pages.

A story on such an outrageous idea as a transatlantic flight by a balloon in a prestigious New York newspaper would not go unnoticed. Lowe's fanciful concept was immediately picked up by the rest of the nation's press. A profusion of newspapers latched onto the story and assailed the public with fact, opinion, rumor, and speculation. All over the country journalists and cartoonists had a satirical field day, heaping derision on the balloonist's wild scheme. Drawings appeared that were supposed to be Lowe, although none bore much resemblance even as caricatures as his face was not that well known, riding behind or below, or in some cases astride, airships that looked like they were taken from early designs by Leonardo da Vinci or the Jesuit Priest Francesco de Lana. In any case, while the art was less than accurate, the captions were even less flattering.

Lowe's rivals, and there were many as he was not the only man to be experimenting with airships at the time, were gleeful. Even John Wise, generally acknowledged to be the "King of the Aeronauts," denounced Lowe in the newspapers as a publicity-seeking showman rather than a true scientist. He made much levity of Lowe's origin as a one-time cobbler and magician with a traveling science show.

This chorus of harsh criticism was a bitter pill for Lowe to swallow, especially coming from as prominent an aeronaut as John Wise, whom Lowe admired greatly and with whom he had hoped to work on his transatlantic project. The balloonist, however, should have anticipated Wise's reaction. At the time of his negative assessment of Lowe's proposed ocean-crossing venture, Wise was also working on an airship of his own for a transatlantic flight. His airship, named the *Atlantic,* was to be the largest balloon yet constructed, having a spherical bag sixty feet in diameter, with a capacity for fifty thousand cubic feet of gas.

Lowe understood that timing was inevitably important to everything. He was aware that he was not the first balloonist in the United States to propose extensive cross-country travel by airship. Soon after the development of the balloon in France, a number of venturesome Americans, inspired by the visit of the French balloonist Jean-Pierre Blanchard, began experimenting with the building and flying of balloons. As far back as January 9, 1783, Blanchard had flown a balloon from the yard of the old Walnut Street Prison in Philadelphia, an event witnessed by most of the city's population as well as President George Washington, with John Adams, Thomas Jefferson, James Madison, and James Monroe.

By 1822 balloon activity had progressed so far that a congressman from Philadelphia petitioned Congress to grant one of his constituents, the mathematician James Bennett, a forty-year monopoly "for the right of steering flying machines through that portion of the earth's atmosphere which passes over the United States or so far as their jurisdiction may extend." The petition was referred to a special committee, tabled, and then forgotten.

Even Lowe's chief critic, the widely known aeronaut John Wise, had made his first public announcement of a proposed transoceanic flight as far back as June 1843, when young Thaddeus Lowe was still a student at the Common School in Jefferson Mills, in his free moments lying in the fields behind his house watching the movements of the clouds passing overhead.

Now, sitting contentedly in his favorite leather chair by a crackling fire in his opulent drawing room, surrounded by his loving wife and his two pretty little daughters, Lowe felt confident he was on the verge of success. For him abuse in the press was an old story. Rather than be deterred by the great laugh the nation's newspapers and John Wise had had at his expense, the mocking comments only urged him on. Lowe was determined to prove his critics wrong; he would be the first person to fly across the Atlantic Ocean.

On July 15, 1859, inventor, entrepreneur, flamboyant showman, and balloonist Professor Thaddeus Sobieski Constantine Lowe called a meeting of the press to formally announce to the world that he had started work on an immense hot-air balloon, measuring 130 feet from valve to neck, having a transverse diameter of 104 feet, and having a gas capacity of 725,000 cubic feet. This giant airship would be what Lowe would use for his ocean-crossing attempt.

Criticism of any kind was always intolerable to Lowe, but the public scorn he had endured was painful to the extreme. He was sure that now was his moment and determined to rise to the fame he had so long desired. However, at the time of his brash and overconfident announcement, the balloonist could not have imagined the hours of despair and anguish his bold project would provide him. Nor could he foresee how the growing conflict between the North and the South would soon involve him, altering his plans, as well as the shape of the nation. As he sat in his shop looking over the scattered materials that were to become his great airship, Lowe realized he was only at the beginning of a long road he had yet to travel.

Self-defense being the primary canon of the law of nature, John Wise naturally felt threatened by Lowe's boasting. His scornful comments in the newspapers notwithstanding, Wise considered Lowe a potential challenge to his own leadership in aeronautics. The elder balloonist wondered if he might not have been too long absent from the public's eye. He rushed his mammoth aerostat *Atlantic* to completion.

The trial flight of the *Atlantic* was announced for early July 1859. Despite the remarks Wise had made about his project, Lowe secretly admired Wise and harbored the fantasy of being asked to fly with the master. To Lowe's dismay one of his chief rivals, John La Mountain, a man with only two more years experience, was chosen by Wise to be his assistant. A Mr. Hyde, a reporter for the *St. Louis Republican*, and O. A. Gaeger, a millionaire balloon enthusiast who had put up the money for the trip, were to be the passengers.

For several days prior to the Fourth of July 1859, Lowe had been on route to Portland, Maine, with his balloon for a scheduled exhibition ascension. Travel was slow and communications difficult, so Lowe was not immediately aware of the result of Wise's cross-country flight. Arriving in Portland, Lowe was met by an old friend, the mayor Neal Dow, who handed Lowe a newspaper with the details of Wise's voyage.

On July 2, 1859, despite frightful conditions, John Wise and his passengers, John La Mountain and O. A. Gaeger, had set a distance record, traveling 826 miles, actually covering 1,150 miles as they were blown about. Although no one could foresee it at the time, the record would stand for another fifty years.

The *Atlantic* had departed from Saint Louis, Missouri, and landed in upstate New York near Henderson in Jefferson County nineteen hours later. According to the article, Wise and his passengers had a wild ride. After a hair-raising flight over Lake Erie, they were caught in a thunderstorm over Lake Ontario, where they were almost forced down in the raging water. The waves had been too high for them to safely use the small lifeboat tied under the gondola, so they cut it loose to gain altitude. Then the balloon had been blown along for miles, just skimming the tree tops, before finally plunging into the woods. The newspaper story concluded by saying it was just pure luck they had landed in one piece after all.

When asked by the mayor what he thought about the flight, Lowe replied facetiously he supposed that's what ballooning was all about—just pure luck. Then the balloonist went on to remark that luck wouldn't be such a factor if one could forecast the weather. He stressed it was imperative to continue to gather knowledge of the air currents aloft, which was what he had dedicated himself to doing.

Lowe's Fourth of July exhibition in Portland consisted in going aloft and releasing thirty-three small hydrogen-filled balloons he had fabricated, one for each of the states which at the time made up the Union. As he anticipated, the miniature aerostats were immediately blown eastward by the prevailing west winds heading out over the ocean. During the next week, ships arriving in America from Europe reported seeing the multicolored balloons as far as six hundred miles at sea. This was all the confirmation he needed, Lowe announced triumphantly. If these small paper balloons, treated with his special varnish, could remain aloft so long and fly so far, the airship he had in mind to build could surely cross the Atlantic. He would make his new balloon five times the size of John Wise's. Eager to gain favor in the metropolis where he lived, Lowe decided to call his great airship *City of New York.*

Lowe poured all his years of study and work into the building of the *City of New York.* He was determined that it would not only be the largest, but the most perfect airship ever conceived. Throughout the summer the balloonist put in sixteen-hour days, sweating beside his workmen in the shed in Hoboken, overseeing every detail of the construction. Seventeen sewing machines hummed constantly in the workroom, stitching together with triple seams the six thousand yards of fine cotton twill that had been cut into narrow panels to form the gas bag. In the next room a dozen men, working with deliberate urgency and rarely stopping for a break or bothering to converse with one another, painstakingly wove by hand miles of fine flaxen cord into the intricately patterned web that would encase the envelope. Calculating that the casing would need to withstand a strain of up to 160 tons, Lowe had substituted the stronger flaxen cord for the silk used on the *Enterprise.*

Lowe realized the open wicker gondola of his previous airships, in which the aeronaut was exposed not only to the wind and elements, but also to the nauseous smell of coal gas, was not suitable for the long trip over the Atlantic. The cab the balloonist and his transoceanic crew would ride in needed to be comfortable, completely enclosed, and heated. Consequently Lowe spent considerable time and effort planning this feature of the *City of New York.* He decided the compartment should be round and as large as possible, about twenty feet in diameter, about the floor space of an average drawing room. As he anticipated taking six men and considerable equipment, even as large an area as this had to be carefully designed for maximum use.

The basic structure of the gondola was a rattan basket that was woven to the height of Lowe's chest. Stretched canvas wrapped the sides and continued up, over stays, to form the roof. A leather-upholstered bench circled the interior. Above this seat, windows were cut in the canvas and glazed over. All remaining wall space was lined with shelves and pegs for the instruments. Lockers were built in below the bench to hold the provisions.

From O. A. Gaeger, the wealthy balloonist who had helped John Wise with his *Atlantic* and flown with him on the record flight, Lowe received a small lime stove to heat the interior. This flameless heater was especially designed for use in airships, where a coal or gas heater would be too dangerous in such proximity to the highly flammable gasses in the envelope.

Most nights there would be a light burning in Lowe's townhouse study as, after having spent a long day at the Hoboken shed, he sat up late, planning for the trip and inventing new instruments for navigation and meteorological observation. The heat that summer was excessive, and more often than not the balloonist would have to soak his nightshirt with cold water before retiring to be able to sleep.

On weekends Lowe found the time to give lectures describing the airship he had in progress and explaining his goals. The balloonist felt that it was important that the public be made aware that he was no mere showman, but a serious scientific experimenter and that the *City of New York* was not a stunt. He used these platform appearances to assure his audiences that he was neither rash, insane, nor a seeker of fame, although numerous cartoonists, journalists, and certain of his rivals had painted him as such. Lowe wanted to make it clear that he was giving this matter of a transatlantic crossing very serious consideration and that if he succeeded it would be because of careful planning and not just good fortune. These lectures also helped refill Lowe's bank account, which his grand construction project was constantly draining.

Gas lights flickered in the dank hall as Lowe unfurled one of his large parti-colored diagrams. All talking ceased as he began to explain his theories. He pointed out that over the past few years tremendous progress had been made in the design and construction of balloons. Despite the unkind things Charles Green and John Wise had said about him in the press, Lowe acknowledged the pioneering work of these two men in establishing the existence of upper air currents, thereby leading to increased understanding of their nature and movements.

Lowe continued by paying tribute to the safety record of ballooning, emphasizing there were now more than three thousand aeronauts who had taken to the skies. Then he added with a smirk that he doubted that fewer than ten percent of these fliers were truly competent. At this point the assembly usually rewarded Lowe with a hearty laugh. They, for the most part, were ready to accept the fact that all balloonists were incompetent. Many in the audience would unfailingly turn to one another and begin whispering tales of aeronauts they had known and of their misfortunes. Whereupon Lowe, raising his arm to restore silence and staring down from his lectern, would announce confidently that statistics proved air travel to be less hazardous than any other form of transportation. The people in the hall gasped incredulously.

Lowe pulled the figure of eight thousand from the air, claiming that eight thousand people made aerial voyages during the past fifty years—with only one loss of life. One! Lowe emphasized, holding up one finger on his right hand, solemnly displaying it round to the audience. Fortunately for the balloonist no one in the gathering ever questioned his figures or for that matter the source of his statistics. Although a man of science, Lowe had no scruples when it came to furthering the cause of ballooning and his own career.

The balloonist was ready now to pitch his agenda. Rapid progress in aeronautics was not being made, Lowe maintained, because most of the present-day balloonists were not scientific investigators, but exhibitors intent on making limited ascensions for money. The balloonist did not deny that exhibition ascensions had their place. He acknowledged that through them he had financed all his scientific projects to date, including his present and greatest project. Then he paused, running his eyes around the room to be sure he had the audience's undivided attention.

Raising a fist in the air, Lowe announced in a loud voice the time for talk and theory was past; aeronautic art must progress beyond its present state; someone must make a bold push forward; and that someone would be him! A person in the back immediately shouted

Lowe's name, answered by a second person, then a third. In an instant the whole hall was clapping and chanting, "Lowe! Lowe! Lowe!" The initial chorus was usually begun, on cue, by several of Lowe's workers, who received extra pay for coming out on the weekends to help him set up the easels for his charts and drawings.

Bowing modestly, Lowe acknowledged the applause. He rapped his stick on the lectern for silence. Pointing to the diagram behind him, Lowe began the serious part of his talk, the theory behind his giant airship. Buoyancy, he explained, was largely contingent on the amount of gas contained in a balloon's bag. He anticipated the *City of New York*, fully inflated, would have a lifting power of twenty-two tons if hydrogen was used or eleven tons if filled with the more readily available coal gas. He reminded the audience that these figures added up to a lot of passengers or freight.

Unraveling two large pieces of cloth, one soft and delicate, the other stiff and tough, Lowe extolled the virtues of his special varnish mixture. He explained how the fabric sealed with his varnish reduced gas loss to the minimum. Smaller pieces were passed from hand to hand among the audience, prompting much finger-squeezing and comment.

These small pieces were highly sought-after souvenirs that rarely made their way back to the boxes they had come from. And no one seemed to notice that the men distributing the samples were the same men who laughed the loudest at Lowe's attempts at humor and had started the shouting and clapping in the back. After the passing and murmuring had died down, Lowe held up a piece of his fabric stretched on a frame and hit it several times with a hammer without doing any apparent damage. He proudly proclaimed that because of his special varnish the *City of New York* would be able to remain aloft much longer than the three days he had estimated it would take to cross the ocean. While telling his stories Lowe often gazed around wildly into the air, as if seeing things the audience could not see. Looking off into the distance at the back of the hall, Lowe added with an air of finality the belief that his airship would cross the ocean.

A row of shiny copper and brass objects had been arrayed on a table next to Lowe, specially placed by him to catch the flickering gas light in their bright metal, and so capture the audience's attention and interest. He began to hold these up, one by one, describing with loftiness the mechanical appliances and navigational aids he had invented. The final item, and the one in which the balloonist took most pride, was the long anticipated propeller wheel. With this elaborate mechanical device his airship could be raised or lowered without having to release precious gas or toss out ballast.

Even the most skeptical person came away from one of Lowe's lectures admitting that his ideas were basically sound. But would they work? That passengers could traverse the sky as easily as the land or sea was an idea that most people of the time found too revolutionary to comprehend.

With their curiosity aroused by the article "Description of the Airship the *City of New York*" in the September 24, 1859, issue of *Scientific American,* uninvited visitors began showing up at the construction shed in Hoboken to see the balloon for themselves. Their growing numbers hampered the workmen, but Lowe was smart enough to know that their presence was good publicity and did not discourage the parade of curious. He knew that the article published in the prestigious magazine *Scientific American* had established him once and for all as a serious scientist.

The August heat lay heavily on the New Jersey fields on the day the writer from *Scientific American* had arrived to interview Lowe at his sheds in Hoboken. He found Lowe in a room even hotter than outside, as the balloonist was in his working clothes stirring a boiling vat of his special varnish. Lowe declined to answer the reporter's question about the ingredients in the varnish, revealing only that the substance needed to reach a temperature of six hundred degrees to boil.

Crossing over to the cooler construction shed, the first thing Lowe showed the reporter was the Francis Metallic lifeboat. The journalist noted down in his pad that the boat was thirty feet in length and had a beam of seven feet. Although the mast was not in place, Lowe explained the craft could be fitted with a large sail, if needed, to propel it. Despite its size, the cockpit appeared rather small. This was because the hull had been fitted with several watertight compartments. Its designer pointed out that the boat was as unsinkable as possible, as more than half of the compartments would have to be damaged and take on water before the ship would go under. He had named the lifeboat *Leontine* in honor of his wife.

The stern of the *Leontine* was fitted with a four-horsepower Ericsson caloric engine attached to the propeller wheel. On first glance it appeared as if the engine was there to drive the boat. But this was not the case. Lowe explained that engine and propeller were to actually be used to provide steerage to the balloon while it was underway. The propeller would provide a steadying influence in situations that would normally have made the airship difficult to control. The pitch of the fan wheel was adjustable, so the angle could be changed to drive the balloon up or down as was necessary to find the proper wind current.

It could also be used to stabilize the airship and keep it from spinning around in a high wind.

Picking up what looked like a ball of string, Lowe demonstrated to the reporter the simple device he had invented for determining the proper level for the most advantageous wind current. A cord of a mile and a half long, with a lead weight at the end, was to be hung from the airship at all times. Small flags of different colors would be attached at intervals, each denoting a specific level, not unlike the kite string with which he had flown the cat back in Hingham. If he was to find himself mired in an adverse current, Lowe could discover, by looking through his telescope, which flag was being blown in the proper direction. Then he would have his crew start the fan wheel and adjust its angle to push the airship down to the proper current. Going up, the balloonist would, by necessity, need to rely mostly on guesswork. Lowe revealed that he planned not to fly too high, despite the favorable currents higher up, preferring to remain low, where he would be able to see people and communicate with them as the airship passed over.

On the Atlantic crossing the lifeboat's cockpit would be enclosed with an India-rubber cover and extra provisions stowed inside. The rockets and Roman candles used for signaling were also to be carried in the lifeboat to avoid the risk of them going off in the gondola. Access to the provisions in the boat while the balloon was in flight would be via a rope ladder. The boat also contained suits for the crew made out of the same India rubber as the cover. These suits could be inflated and would keep their wearers afloat for an indefinite period of time as well as protect their bodies from the cold Atlantic water.

Besides the usual megaphones used for communication, Lowe proudly pointed out that the *City of New York* would also have on board a hundred small bags made of the same India rubber. In these bags, attached to silk parachutes, copies of the ship's log and other information could be dropped down on towns and ships as they passed over them to keep in touch with the people on the ground. This would be a running record of the airship's progress should it become lost.

If they did get lost, the aeronauts would not go hungry, at least for a while. Lowe revealed to the *Scientific American* reporter that he intended to carry enough food and wine on board to sustain him and his crew for six months if need be. Although Lowe had boasted he would deliver a copy of the Monday *New York Times* to London on Wednesday of the same week, he was realistic enough to prepare for the eventuality of being blown off course and ending up in the Moroccan desert or some other uninhabited place. His backers had already invested twenty thousand dollars in this project, and Lowe was doing everything in his power to ensure the trip's success.

Moving from item to item, the balloonist and the writer toured the rest of the shops. Lowe was beginning to show signs of fatigue caused by the long days he was putting in. He had given a similar tour to a reporter and artist from *Harper's Weekly* the previous week. His words were becoming a repetition of so many lectures he had given on his grand endeavor, none of which the *Scientific American* writer had bothered to attend. Lowe gave an indication that it was time for the interview to end. He was restless and needed to be getting back to his own work. The reporter, realizing the conversation was over, thanked Lowe for his time and wishing him good luck with his venture took his leave.

While Lowe concentrated exhaustively on putting together his balloon, the nation around him was rapidly dividing itself. The eighteen states in the North opposed to the institution of slavery and fifteen states in the South where slavery was accepted were continuously at each other over the issue. In 1857 the Supreme Court had attempted to resolve the question with the Dred Scott Decision, a case involving a slave who claimed freedom because he had been taken into a territory where slavery was illegal. The court ruled that Congress could not exclude slavery from the territories. Southerners rejoiced over the decision, but became angry when Northern leaders refused to accept the judgment as legally binding.

The Whig party broke up over the slavery question. In its place the Republican Party was formed, its main platform being to prevent slavery from expanding to the territories. Sensing the possibilities, Abraham Lincoln quickly joined the new party. Shortly thereafter, Lincoln and Stephen A. Douglas engaged in a number of debates centered on the question of slavery in the free territories. These spirited discussions were widely followed in the newspapers and made the relatively obscure Lincoln into a national figure. The not-too-distant future would find "Honest Abe," whom many considered to be nothing more than an ungainly prairie lawyer, ensconced in Washington, wheeling and dealing to heal the rift in the Union that his very election had played a large part in creating.

At the time no one could anticipate the fury of the coming storm that would see brother rise up against brother, champing to kill one another, while in the sky above, Lowe floated in his balloon, not across the Atlantic, but over the battlefields of Virginia.

5

A New York Failure, a Move to Philadelphia, a Death in the Family

In October 1859 Lowe and his wife were preparing for his greatest adventure yet, the inaugural flight of his new airship, *City of New York.* In order to accommodate the large crowds that were anticipated to turn out for the launch, the balloon had been moved from the Stevens farm in Hoboken to the Fair Grounds, an open area in New York City at the corner of 42nd Street and Fifth Avenue. The Fair Grounds had been the site of the Crystal Palace, that soaring, glittering wonder of iron and glass, which had opened to much fanfare in 1853. This massive structure, said to be the finest building erected in America up until that time and built to rival the Crystal Palace in London, burned to the ground five years later, on October 5, 1858, when a fire broke out in one of its storerooms.

Filled with the excitement generated by the presence of Lowe's balloon, merchants in the area decorated their stores with flags and bunting to attract the spectators that arrived by carriage, omnibus, or on foot to view the wondrous airship that was expected to be the first to fly across the Atlantic Ocean.

All the world waited. Every newspaper and magazine focused its attention on Lowe's activities, anticipating his departure. *Harper's Weekly* declared the *City of New York* to be "an engineering triumph in any age." And the normally circumspect *Scientific American* couched Lowe's work with uncharacteristic enthusiasm: "The dimensions of the *City of New York* so far exceed those of any balloon previously constructed that the bare fact of its existence is notable. Whether successful or not, it merits mention for the magnitude, energy, and fertility of resource displayed in its execution. The introduction of valuable improvements leads to the conviction that the general arrangement is greatly superior."

In the middle of it all was Lowe, bustling about reviewing the details, and especially checking and rechecking with the Manhattan Gas

Company to be sure that it could produce in twenty-four hours the necessary five hundred thousand cubic feet of gas required for inflation. The balloonist had explained to a gas company official that, due to the porous nature of the materials used, it was normal for a certain amount of gas to escape during the inflation. Even with Lowe's special varnish, this loss of some gas was unavoidable. Therefore, the longer it took to fill the bag, the greater would be the quantity of gas dissipated. Unless the mains could produce Lowe's required amount in the specified time, so much gas would escape that the airship could not be able to rise from the ground. The Manhattan Gas Company representative assured Lowe that his main, located near the 42nd Street and Fifth Avenue site, could provide the needed amount of coal gas without any problems. In order to have the balloon filled on time, inflation was scheduled to begin on the afternoon before the day of the trial flight.

With his usual thoroughness, Lowe arrived the next morning to prepare for the inflation. The pipe from the gas main was hooked to the balloon's neck and the balloon began to fill. However, after more than three hours of gas flowing into the envelope, it had not begun to take even the vaguest shape. The bag still lay strung out on the ground looking not unlike a sausage casing waiting to be stuffed. Lowe inquired of the gas men what the problem seemed to be. They replied that there was no problem; the main was delivering the required flow. Professor Lowe would have his fifty thousand cubic feet within twenty-four hours.

With the press and the public, which had gathered from all points of the world, already watching, Lowe suddenly became aware that the gas company had made an error. Someone, somehow, had misunderstood his specifications. The gas company was only prepared to deliver fifty thousand cubic feet in twenty-four hours, considerably less than the five hundred thousand cubic feet he required. And the main his balloon was presently attached to did not seem to be capable of producing even that. A quick calculation by the balloonist revealed that the gas was dissipating only a little slower than it was being pumped in. There would be no inflation. The trial would have to be postponed.

Lowe was bitter. Winter was approaching, and he could not make any immediate arrangements for a greater volume gas supply. The trial flight and the subsequent attempt at an Atlantic crossing would have to be put off until the following year. He feared the public's reaction.

Lowe, however, need not have worried; his reporter friends thoughtfully covered for him, placing convincing articles in their newspapers that laid the blame squarely on the gas works. Hundreds of persons, who had come out to witness the flight of the *City of New York* and been disappointed, vented their anger by writing letters to the editors of the various papers roundly denouncing the inefficiency of the Manhattan Gas Company.

Moreover, all the publicity about the insufficient gas flow brought an unexpected turn of good fortune for Lowe. A few days after he had canceled his flight, he received a letter from Professor John C. Cresson, president of the Franklin Institute in Philadelphia. On behalf of a group of prominent businessmen and scientists, Cresson had written to Lowe inviting him to bring his mammoth airship to Philadelphia. The group offered to pay all transportation costs. Cresson also promised Lowe that he would have no problem getting the gas flow he needed. This was guaranteed by the fact that Cresson was also the chairman of the board of the Point Breeze Gas Works of Philadelphia.

Lowe eagerly accepted the Philadelphia offer and began to make plans to move his operation and his family. However, as he would not be able to attempt a flight from Philadelphia until spring, the balloonist decided to spend the winter in the somewhat warmer climate of Charleston, South Carolina. There he could pass the colder months giving lectures, observing weather patterns, and making demonstration ascensions in his smaller balloon. The *City of New York* was packed up and left in storage at the sheds in Hoboken.

The Lowes settled in for a pleasant stay in this charming city, laid out along the wide harbor where the Ashley and Cooper rivers joined the Atlantic Ocean. At the time, Charleston was one of the richest cities in the South, with a fine theater, good restaurants, and many interesting things to do. As Lowe and his family stood on the waterfront, passing a balmy day enjoying the sights of the harbor, including Fort Sumter across the way, the balloonist had no way of imagining the events that would take place there in the coming months and how these events would drastically change the course of his life.

Lowe heard little talk in Charleston of holding the Union together as he had back in the North. The country was growing and the population was shifting westward. Many of the people in the new territories were in favor of slavery. Some of the more outspoken in the South maintained that the country had no tradition of union. Indeed, as far back as the Revolution, Americans had been more accustomed to putting the interests of their region or state ahead of those of the nation. The new Constitution had been heatedly opposed as a threat to the rights of the states. Two sides had formed, the Federalists, who wanted a strong federal government, and the Anti-Federalists, who felt the less a central body interfered with the rights of individuals and states, the better it was. At the time there were many who wished that once the war with England had been won the states would go their own separate ways. One Southern gentleman even went so far as to point out to Lowe that the proof the Constitution was a perfidious Yankee document could be found in its very first line: "We the people, in order to form a more perfect union." *Union* was the word found to be offensive.

With the first break in the weather in April, Lowe returned to New York to oversee the moving of his massive airship. Two full freight cars were required to transport the crates holding the *City of New York* from the sheds in Hoboken to the new home that had been promised for it near the Breeze Point Gas Works in Philadelphia.

When Lowe arrived with his train cars full of folded airship, he was pleased to discover that, true to his word, Professor Cresson had already prepared a mooring spot for him near the gas works. However, while Cresson was anxious for Lowe to begin the preparations for his Atlantic voyage, he had to admit that the committee backing the flight was having second thoughts. The group had seen letters printed in the newspapers and had been receiving letters from various self-appointed experts asserting that the committee had been "hornswoggled" by Lowe. Many writers asserted that his huge airship would never get off the ground. Others predicted that if the *City of New York* did rise into the air, the crew would not be able to manage it because of its great size. The balloonist assured the committee that they had nothing to worry about. He had worked out his ideas thoroughly and planned for all contingencies.

To reassure his supporters, Lowe boldly announced he would conduct a trial flight, weather permitting, sometime during the last week of June. To those who scoffed at his plan to cross the Atlantic, the balloonist had an answer he had often given, asking if the oceans of the globe were so worthy of exploration, what of the ocean of air around us in which we lived, in which the earth itself had moved in her eventful career for millions of years. Why not investigate that as well?

Since his huge balloon no longer had anything to do with the City of New York, and in an effort to please his new sponsors, Lowe decided to rename his airship. After considerable discussion, Lowe chose the name suggested by the newspaper editor Horace Greeley. The *City of New York* was rechristened the *Great Western,* a name considered appropriate for the world's largest airgoing vessel, since the world's largest seagoing vessel, the *Great Eastern,* would also be making her maiden voyage the coming spring.

There was yet one more thing Lowe would have to do to please his Philadelphia patrons. A delegation of Japanese dignitaries had been sent by their government to the United States as a gesture of appreciation for the historic visit to their country by Commodore Matthew C. Perry. In 1853 Perry had sailed the first Navy ships into Tokyo Bay, opening Japan to trade with the United States, an act that ranked as one of history's most significant diplomatic achievements. Commodore Perry had passed away in 1858.

When the Japanese tour reached Philadelphia, the city's newest attraction was trotted out for their visitors. Lowe was asked to participate in the welcoming festivities with a balloon ascension. Ever the consummate showman, Lowe began his performance by sending up one of his smaller balloons with a light-weight assistant in the basket to demonstrate how rapidly his airships could ascend. After his well-received prelude, the balloonist saluted his guests by going aloft himself in a much larger balloon festooned with Japanese and American flags.

The Japanese delegation, which included a prince and several of his noblemen, was very impressed. When Lowe was hauled back to earth, he was greeted by the prince, resplendent in a brocade silk robe, who kept bowing and gesturing. Through a translator Lowe learned that the prince was declaring he would never forget the vision of American ships that sailed in the air.

Lowe was ecstatic over the effect his balloons had on his distinguished audience. Describing his impressions, Lowe later wrote, "Philadelphia desired to impress them, and as I had something which the Japanese had never heard of, I was invited to entertain them with an aeronautic fete and an ascension which gave me much pleasure, and I created an impression which lasted for generations."

The balloonist was also mindful of the more practical aspects of the success of his aeronautical display: "All this, of course, was excellent publicity. The greater the interest of the public, the greater my hope for realizing the means necessary for my cherished plan, for I found the project more costly than I had first anticipated, and the long delay of winter had eaten into my capital. I was still several thousand dollars short of my requirements."

The balloonist's demonstration for the entertainment of the Japanese notables was widely covered in the newspapers. Once again Lowe became the talk of Philadelphia, and he and Leontine were sought after as guests for dinners and parties. As a result, several new sponsors came forward for his transatlantic project. But despite all the hoopla that the balloonist's spectacular ascension for the Japanese created, it would be but a modest rehearsal for the first flight of the *Great Western*.

Immediately after the stunning success of the *Great Western*'s inaugural flight from Point Breeze, on which the newsman Garrick Mallery and Captain John B. Dickinson had gone along as passengers, even though the mammoth airship had not reached it's goal of the Atlantic shore but come down in the middle of New Jersey, Lowe began bravely planning for his transatlantic attempt. The balloonist spared no effort nor expense, and final preparations for the *Great Western*'s epic ocean flight were completed by the first week of September. The vessel had been fine tuned, a crew assembled, and the lockers in the gondola copiously stocked with provisions.

The funds for this new venture had come from a fresh group of subscribers who, reassured by Lowe's June 28th flight, had been added to the list over the summer months. Contrary to anything the balloonist could have anticipated, in the midst of all his good fortune a letter arrived from the his old rival John Wise. Full of flattery, the elder aeronaut's communication congratulated Lowe on his successful flight. Furthermore, Wise had the boldness to volunteer to join the crew of the *Great Western* for its attempt at a transatlantic voyage. Lowe read the letter several times, considering how Wise's vast experience might be useful to him. But Lowe had soured on his former hero after Wise had been credited in the newspapers with a considerable number of negative statements discrediting his efforts. Lowe discussed Wise's offer with Leontine, who also read the letter a number of times, attempting to ferret out his old rival's true motive. The couple spent considerable time sitting on the bench in front of Lowe's shed dissecting Wise's correspondence, weighing the pros and cons of his offer. Many things seemed to point to the fact that although he professed friendship, Wise was indeed a determined adversary, whom Lowe could not believe so ready to capitulate. They suspected Wise's motives. After considerable discussion Lowe and his wife decided the best course would be to simply discard Wise's letter without responding.

Praise for Lowe's airship was coming from all quarters. Professor Joseph Henry, head of the Smithsonian Institution in Washington, D.C., and an outstanding scientist in his own right, wrote, "The Smithsonian Institution has long been aware of the work and theories of Professor Lowe, and we have found his statements scientifically sound. It is with a great pleasure and satisfaction that we welcome proof of his genius. We shall follow the outcome of his plan with interest."

By Thursday, September 6th, Lowe felt confident to match his airship against the perils of the Atlantic Ocean. With great fanfare he

announced that he would launch the following day. This delighted
his public. Early the next day, crowds of people, some who had been
there before and some who had not, had made their way out to Point
Breeze to "see the elephant." The enormous boodle milled about in
a festive mood as the airship, filling with gas, continued to grow.
Unfortunately for Lowe, around eleven o'clock the zephyr that had
been gently wafting over the site suddenly turned into a strong wind.
Concerned for his airship's safety, the balloonist ordered the inflation
temporarily halted. The partially filled envelope collapsed. Seeing his
balloon lying there, Lowe wondered if his decision to stop the inflation had been brought on by stage fright, or if it was the consequence
of his sudden realization of the vessel's inadequacies. The balloonist
perceived that, despite his hyperbole, he was apprehensive about his
chances for success, mainly because he saw clearly how many chances
there were for failure.

Lowe's crew worked to keep back the crowd, which, annoyed by the
delay, now pressed in on all sides to get a better view of the curious
thing that presently resembled, with its bright orangish-yellow color,
a giant summer squash that had fallen from a farmer's cart on the way
to market.

Around four o'clock the air began to cool and the wind died down.
Considering the immense consequences of not going forward with
the flight, Lowe ordered the gas turned back on, and the inflation
resumed. Most of the onlookers, amid much disappointed grum-
bling and assuming the balloon was unfortunately not going up, had
already left. Probably they had taken an early start, wanting to be sure
to arrive home in time for their supper.

Seeing the gas turned back on, an elated Garrick Mallery, who
had prepared a special "aerial edition" of the *Philadelphia Inquirer,*
began to load the newspapers into the gondola. As the wind danced
the balloon against its moorings, a nervous Lowe assured Mallery
they would leave as soon as the inflation was completed. Anticipating
their departure, the Reverend Doctor Newton of Saint Paul's Episco-
pal Church took the occasion to present the aeronauts with a Bible
and address the crew and the few remaining enthusiasts. The priest
concluded his brief talk with the words: "I commend the voyagers to
Almighty God, and beg Him to look graciously on their undertaking."
Lowe, who was not especially religious, thanked Doctor Newton and
got on with his preparations.

The time was now 5:30. As Lowe and his crew were about to enter
the gondola, a brisk wind came up again, blowing with almost gale
force, bouncing the *Great Western* against its rigging. Sensing that

nature was not about to accede to his wishes, a disappointed Lowe acknowledged it would be too great a risk to continue with the inflation under the present conditions. He ordered the airship secured and announced the flight postponed until the next day.

Sleep did not come easy for the Lowes that night. Outside the windows, the street lamps fluttered as a violent wind chased itself across the glittering sky. Startled from her rest by what she thought to be the banging of the shutters, Leontine sat up in bed. Her husband let out a muffled shout. Then she realized it had been her husband's cry she had heard. He gave out another. Reaching over to shake him from his dream, she found his body bathed in sweat. Awake now, Lowe paced the floor in his dressing gown. In an almost trance-like state, the balloonist described a dream in which he watched the *Great Western*, torn and crumpled, being blown across the ground by fierce gusts of wind, while he chased after it, unable to catch up. They took to analyzing the dream and tried to laugh about it, but, sensing a forewarning of some misfortune to come, neither could go back to sleep. With the first cold light of dawn, the couple rose from the damp and rumpled covers of their bed and prepared for the journey back out to Point Breeze.

Inflation of the *Great Western* began again early on Saturday morning. The weather was clear and calm, save for the occasional strong gusts of wind, which flapped the bag about in its netting. As considerable gas had leaked from the envelope overnight, it was not until the sun was at its zenith that the airship was full and pulling at her mooring ropes, ready to take flight. Lowe ordered the crew to attach the gondola. The party would leave as soon as the cabin was securely in place.

Talking incessantly through every stage of the preparations, Lowe had lost sight of his wife. He looked around to bid her a final farewell. The balloonist found Leontine standing discreetly off to the side of the crowd, the former actress not wanting to upstage her husband in this his biggest scene. As he held her tenderly in his arms, their mouths melded in a kiss, Lowe was startled by a loud rending sound behind him. The expression of horror that registered on Leontine's face gave him an indication of what had happened. The balloonist quickly turned to see that a sudden, strong gust had severely battered his airship. The wind was now dragging it across the ground, tearing a huge gap in the varnished fabric. The torn piece, over fifty feet in length, fluttered absurdly on the side of the lacerated envelope. For a moment the massive airship shuddered and staggered to one side. Then, deflating with a mournful hissing sound, the balloon collapsed.

Lowe rushed from his wife's arms and ran toward the dying brute. The launch site was a scene of confusion, like a dance during which the music had suddenly stopped. People were everywhere, running every way. The suffocating smell of the expelled coal gas quickly expanded over the area. In a panic, someone shouted that one of the workmen was buried under the fallen envelope. In an instant spectators and crew began clawing and tearing at the pile of crumpled canvas. Lowe leapt up crying for calm, concerned that more damage was being done to his balloon by the chaotic rescue operation. Shortly, to Lowe's and everyone else's relief, the worker miraculously emerged from under the rent fabric, quite unharmed, and laughing at his own predicament.

Ruefully Lowe recalled his nightmare and his conversation with Professor Cresson recommending that the committee install a high wooden fence to protect the *Great Western* from sudden shifts of wind during the inflation. The fence, however, had not been installed, and he had not insisted. Now it was too late; the damage was done.

After hurriedly assessing what remained intact of the *Great Western,* Lowe—ever the showman—held a press conference. Waving a torn piece of the envelope's fabric over his head, he announced confidently that the day's events had proven his balloon capable of enduring any strain it might ordinarily be subjected to. The balloonist auspiciously predicted that he would make the necessary repairs and be off again in less than three weeks.

True to his word, less than three weeks later, on the 29th of September, Lowe did try to launch the *Great Western* one more time. Blessed with favorable conditions, Lowe and his crew watched hopefully as the inflation neared completion. They were not without concern, however, as an enormous bulge had begun to appear at the point where Lowe had made his hasty repair. As the fabric stretched more and more, it became apparent that the fix would not hold. The balloonist woefully called for a halt to the gas. At that moment Lowe understood that this year would not see the fulfillment of his dream of an ocean crossing. He would have to devote his winter to giving the gas bag of the *Great Western* a complete rebuild.

A more unpleasant realization for Lowe was that not only had he run out of time, but also he was running out of money. More often than not these days, when he pulled out his wallet to look inside, it was empty. He was very near having exhausted his funds, and Leontine was pregnant again. Taking all this into consideration, the balloonist decided his only recourse was to pack up his gear and go back to touring the country as he had, giving lectures and exhibitions. In addition, Lowe was hopeful he might create enough interest in balloons to pick up a few orders for his factory, which was still in operation, but with a greatly reduced labor force, in the sheds on the Stevens Farm in Hoboken.

The balloonist was also optimistic that his traveling would allow him time to continue his experiments and enable him to gather valuable data about weather phenomena from the different areas of the country he visited. Lowe was galled that he had not been able to forecast the appearance of the sudden, strong winds that had so violently ripped his balloon at Point Breeze. He resolved to devote more time to coordinating his studies and observations in the hope it would be possible to more accurately forecast such potentially disastrous occurrences in the future.

Sadly, Lowe's most recent failure, despite all his careful planning, had made him realize that fame was as unpredictable as the weather. No man could foretell when, or if, his moment of greatness would come. It was fate, or what some people called the times, that predestined the role, if any, a man would play in history. Lowe, however, had taken up the challenge and was determined to have his bit, however short.

An indefatigable Lowe was putting in long hours in the shop working on the *Great Western*, hoping to be finished with the repairs to the torn envelope before going on tour. He had replaced the blown-out section and reinforced several of the gores that had been weakened by the accident. One evening, with the hint of snow in the empty winter darkness, Lowe returned home late and found his wife seated in her favorite chair, her head down and in tears. The children were tightly gathered around her, not sure what had overcome their mama, nor what to make of it. The mother gently stroked their little heads as she sobbed. Consumed with grief and anger, and in a voice that trembled, Leontine confided to her husband what she had learned of the death of her father, recounting the gruesome tale of how he had been murdered on the streets of Paris by Royalist sympathizers.

The previous summer, leaving his wife alone in New York, Pere Gachon had returned to the country of his birth. France was ripe with rebellion as Royalists and Republicans alike plotted the overthrow of their unpopular leader, Napoleon III. A man with no military training, who longed to win great victories like his uncle, Napoleon III had made many enemies with the Franco-Austrian War in 1859. Gachon, the former royal guard, had come back, vainly hoping he could serve the cause of the Republic. However, it was not to be. During one of the numerous riots, Leontine's father had been shot down in the streets of Paris. Just another troublemaker, Gachon had been left to bleed to death in a gutter.

Now Madame Gachon was a widow in Manhattan, and his daughter was here in Philadelphia expecting a child. Leontine wanted to go to New York to comfort her mother. But Lowe advised against traveling in her condition. He suggested that she write her mother and invite the woman to come here. Leontine's mother had not seen her grandchildren since they had left Gotham, and she would be good company, as Lowe was leaving soon on his tour. Leontine agreed it was a splendid idea and set about writing the letter to her mother in New York.

The next evening Cresson and several members of his committee, having heard of the death of Leontine's father, called on the Lowes to express their sympathy. They were shocked when they learned of the conditions under which it had happened. The serious nature of their call notwithstanding, Leontine's revelations immediately prompted a discussion of the political situation of the times. One gentleman, who allowed as how he had never been "across the water," expressed the opinion that the unsettled conditions in Europe had gone on long enough, since even the United States was beginning to be affected by the unrest.

Bringing the matter of unrest home, someone remarked, slavery was indeed a difficult issue; however, he could not understand what the Abolitionists really wanted. The Abolitionists had been very much in the news lately and were a popular topic of conversation. Agreeing that slavery was immoral and unchristian, a mutton-chopped speaker pointed out that the whole economy of the South was based on slaves and that he couldn't imagine what they would be able to do without this system.

On October 16, 1859, a little over two weeks after Lowe's third attempt to set off on his transatlantic voyage, the Abolitionist John Brown captured the Federal arsenal at Harper's Ferry, in what was then western Virginia. Brown and his followers planned to make off with the munitions stored there and to encourage the slaves to stage an armed rebellion. The group failed, however, to escape with the weapons, and were bottled up in the fort by the local militia. Two days later a troop of soldiers commanded by a then unknown commander, Colonel Robert E. Lee, retook the fort and captured John Brown. The Abolitionist was tried and convicted of treason. He had been hung a few days earlier on December 2. For weeks the newspapers had been filled with the story of John Brown's trial. There was much talk in the streets about the growing friction between the North and South.

People were beginning to discuss the possibility of a real war.

Absorbed in his work, Lowe no longer followed the news as closely as he had when he was a young boy back at his father's store in Jefferson Mills. He backed away from the conversation. Leontine, however, more than made up for his lack of interest. She was in the habit of reading several newspapers daily. Leontine described what the conflict between parties with different points of view had done to her native country, France. She was concerned, she said, that the same thing was going to happen to her adopted country.

Leontine had heard rumors of war last winter when they stayed in Charleston. She was worried that the problems between the two regions were so vast that they might come to a fight. Lowe was more optimistic. He expressed his firm belief that differences between the states would be solved by legal and peaceful means. Moreover, the scientist in him made him feel that the invention of new machines would soon make the system of slavery uneconomical, and the South itself would abandon the institution without having to be forced to.

Besides the kind gesture of expressing their condolences on the death of Leontine's father, the men had come on other business. After the political conversation had worn down, and Leontine had retired to take care of her children, Professor Cresson presented Lowe with a letter the committee had drafted. It read:

> To Professor Joseph Henry, Secretary of the Smithsonian Institution, Washington D.C.
>
> The undersigned citizens of Philadelphia have taken a deep interest in the attempt of Mr. T. S. C. Lowe to cross the Atlantic by aeronautic machinery, and have confidence that his extensive preparations to effect that object will greatly add to scientific knowledge.
>
> Mr. Lowe has individually spent much time and money in the enterprise, and in addition the citizens of Philadelphia have contributed several thousand dollars to further his efforts in demonstrating the feasibility of transatlantic air navigation. With reliance on Mr. Lowe and his plans we cheerfully recommend him to the favorable consideration of the Smithsonian Institution, and trust such aid and advice will be furnished him by that distinguished body as may assist in the success of the attempt, in which we take a deep interest.

The letter bore a group of signatures from some of the most distinguished citizens of Philadelphia, including businessmen Fairman Rodgers and J. B. Lippincott.

The evening had ended splendidly. The next day, Leontine, her spirits somewhat revived by the committee's visit and the letter they had written to Professor Joseph Henry, encouraged her husband to leave for Washington at once. But for a change it was Lowe who was in no hurry, content to be working on the overhaul of the *Great Western* and awaiting the arrival of their fourth child. A few days later a letter arrived from Leontine's mother. She said she could think of no better way to relieve the grief over the loss of her husband than to visit her daughter and grandchildren and perhaps be there for the birth of another. Content that he would be leaving his wife in good hands and that no drastic changes would be made in his absence, Lowe began to make plans for his trip to Washington.

Despite the committee's glowing letter of recommendation, Henry responded to Lowe that he was sorry, but unfortunately the Smithsonian had no funds they could appropriate for balloon experiments. He did, however, encourage the balloonist to come to Washington to meet with him to discuss his proposed ocean crossing. A statement about investigations Henry personally had made, which he included in his letter, was very encouraging to Lowe, as it supported the balloonist's own theories about upper air currents. Henry, who not only was the secretary of the Smithsonian Institution, but was considered the country's unofficial chief scientist, had written:

> It has been fully established by continuous observations collected at this Institution for ten years, from every part of the United States, that, as a general rule all the meteorological phenomena advance from west to east, and that the higher clouds always move eastwardly. We are, therefore, from abundant observation, as well as from theoretical considerations, enabled to state with confidence that on a given day, a balloon elevated sufficiently high would be carried easterly by the prevailing current in the upper or rather middle region of the atmosphere.
>
> I do not hesitate, therefore, to say that, provided a balloon can be constructed of sufficient size and of sufficient impermeability to gas, in order that it might maintain a high elevation for a sufficient length of time, it would be wafted across the Atlantic. I would not, however, advise that the first experiment of this character be made across the ocean, but that the feasibility of this project should be thoroughly tested and experience accumulated by voyages over the interior of our continent.

Filled with high hopes, Lowe traveled to Washington. As he stepped from the hackney in front of the red brick Smithsonian Institution building, he paused for a moment to look down the Mall at the Capitol building standing majestically at the other end. The massive dome was undergoing extensive renovations, and he understood that it was to be extended quite a bit higher. Wasn't it a strange time to be adding to the magnificence of the country's grandest symbol, Lowe pondered, when the very nation itself seemed on the verge of crumbling.

Henry greeted the the balloonist in his small and tidy office. Unlike Lowe, who had adopted his honorific, Henry was an actual professor. He had taught natural philosophy at Princeton, then known as the College of New Jersey, before coming to the newly founded Smithsonian as its first secretary and director. Noted for his work in the physical sciences, especially electromagnetism, the highly respected scientist had done much to establish the Smithsonian as a scientific institution of the highest rank.

As Henry rose from his chair to shake Lowe's hand, the balloonist realized that the red-headed secretary was his equal in height and breadth. Lowe had been expecting to meet a frail academic, but the large man had a powerful grip and wasted no words. Henry began speaking with his slight Scottish accent as soon as they sat down. Coming straight to the point, he immediately put Lowe off his guard by asking the balloonist what made him think that he and his airship were capable of flying across the Atlantic Ocean.

Not anticipating such a direct first question, Lowe leaned back in his chair and paused a moment before responding, studying Henry's face for any hint of disparagement. Lowe was accustomed to attacks of derision, even sarcasm, from people initially encountering his idea. He had thought that Henry was someone who believed in him, and who did not need to be convinced that his plan was possible.

Before Lowe could answer, Henry held up his hand to stop him. Henry repeated what he had written in his letter about meteorological observations confirming that all weather phenomena usually move from west to east and that the higher clouds generally move eastward. The professor reiterated that he was also of the opinion that an airship, provided its skin was sufficiently impermeable to retain the gas to stay aloft the required amount of time, could easily float across the Atlantic. Continuing, he agreed with Lowe that his *Great Western* was aeronautically sound. Henry, however, suggested to Lowe that perhaps a better plan would be to prove his methods by making a long overland flight before attempting an ocean crossing. He again stressed that the Smithsonian Institution had no finances to back such a flight. Nevertheless, Professor Henry volunteered, if Lowe was willing to start his endeavor from Cincinnati, Ohio, he could put him in contact with a good friend there, Murat Halstead, editor and part owner of the *Cincinnati Daily Commercial,* who would be willing to arrange the pertinent details of a long cross-country flight. Lowe considered the idea for only the briefest moment—he needed to make some practice flights anyway—and accepted Henry's offer. He would begin his flight from Cincinnati.

The journey from Washington took longer than usual, as the train service seemed to be disintegrating along with the health of the nation. When he finally arrived at his home in Philadelphia, Lowe found his family in a festive mood. He no sooner had set his suitcase on the floor when his wife held up a small bundle for his approval. Lowe studied the spitty mouth, the nervous play of the tiny hands, and the white baldness. Delighted, he smiled and applauded, and then took the infant in his arms. Rocking the baby, he beamed proudly; his family had grown by one. Lowe was further pleased to learn his wife was well and had given birth to their daughter without complications. That evening, after a family caucus, it was decided to name the child Ava Eugenie.

The next day, when the excitement of his arrival had settled down, Lowe revealed he would be going away again soon, perhaps for as long as a month. The balloonist told his wife of the plan suggested by Henry to make a long flight from Cincinnati. Secretly Leontine was disappointed with the news, but agreed that if the proposed flight was successful it would greatly enhance his chances of finding backers for his transatlantic flight. Leontine knew well her husband more often than not had his own program, which rarely coincided with hers. Her mother was still there, and she would keep herself busy with the new baby as well as her other two girls.

Although Leontine managed the money, Lowe spent the next day carefully checking his potential income to be sure his wife and family would be secure during his absence. Then the balloonist went to Hoboken, took his old airship *Enterprise* out of storage, and set about preparing it for a flight. As repairs had not yet been completed on the battered *Great Western,* Lowe's plan was to use the *Enterprise,* a steady and reliable airship and only slightly smaller than Wise's *Atlantic,* for the overland passage from Cincinnati.

A friendship had grown between Lowe and Henry. They corresponded regularly over the winter of 1860–1861. Besides the usual bits of news, the pages of their letters also contained a gathering of meteorological observations each had made in their respective region. This exchange of weather data prompted Lowe to make several trips to Washington to discuss with Henry ideas for a "national weather bureau" they hoped could be established. Preoccupied with his own plans most of the winter, Lowe gave scant notice to the fact that during this same period six Southern states, led by South Carolina, had seceded from the Union.

In March, Lowe left for Cincinnati to prepare for the overland flight he hoped would prove him capable of a transatlantic crossing. On the way he stopped in Washington to see Henry to get any last bits of advice the scientist might have for him. Henry, relying on his experience with public relations, told Lowe, if possible, to start with everything apparently against him. He recommended that the balloonist pick a day when the surface winds were from the east, although the winds aloft would be surely from the west. Then if he did succeed people would not say that it had just been a matter of good luck. Therefore, Henry advised, if all Lowe's years of effort were to come to naught, at least he could say he had conducted himself with focus and aplomb.

On the crowded train from Washington Lowe found himself sharing a car with a motley group from a traveling theater company. The actor in the seat next to him, who introduced himself as a Mr. John Wilkes Booth, asked Lowe what he did. Lowe hesitatingly responded that he was kind of in the entertainment business himself, being a balloonist. Lowe, however, confided to Mr. Booth that the part he was now proposing to play would take him well out of amusement and into transportation.

After some discussion between the two over the merits of entertainment, Lowe speculated to Booth that he had no doubt the actor would admit that in his profession the applause of the audience was more important to the player than his own scruples. Yet, on the stage of life, the balloonist continued, if one's compunction disapproved, what worth was the loudest applause of the world? Conversely one's conscience may clap enthusiastically, whereas the whole world hisses. Presently, Lowe explained, while many thought it to be folly, he was attempting to prove the Atlantic Ocean could be successfully transited by an airship.

Booth concurred that Lowe's was indeed an interesting endeavor, adding he must agree that a man must follow his will no matter where it took him. Likewise, Booth added, if an actor believed his role in life more important than his part on the stage, a grievance he must address perhaps, he must pursue that drama whatever the consequences.

Booth excused himself and got up to go to the dining car, leaving Lowe to ponder the implications of his statement. In the not too distant future the balloonist would have cause to remember his conversation with the actor John Wilkes Booth.

6

From Cincinnati to the Atlantic Ocean, Perhaps

On April 12, 1861, rebel forces began the shelling of the United States garrison at Fort Sumter in Charleston, South Carolina. Two days later the nation's newspapers reported that the fortification's commander, Major Robert Anderson, had surrendered his men and the fort. The capitulation had actually been made to a U. S. senator from Texas, Louis Trezevant Wigfall, who had returned to his native state to feed the fires of rebellion. Having no authority to do so, Wigfall had rowed out to the fort in a small boat with a private and two black oarsmen, with the shells from the bombardment passing overhead, and convinced Anderson to give up by pointing out the folly of continuing the engagement.

Busy preparing in Cincinnati for the start of the long cross-country flight in the *Enterprise,* Lowe did not give the action at Fort Sumter much attention. The same could be said for the majority of the 161,000 citizens of the "Queen City of the West." Despite the fact that the city's famous suspension bridge linked it with Kentucky, a state trying to maintain its neutrality in the face of strong secessionist sentiments by resident slave owners, the feeling of Cincinnati's populace, like most people throughout the North, was that the rebellion of the Southern states would be of no consequence. The conflict had been slowly simmering for more than ten years. Verbal skirmishes between the two sides were common; now there might be a military skirmish or two. Everyone expected the Union Army would head south to "put those rebels in their place," and it would all be over soon. No one was prepared for the overwhelming convulsion that would soon overtake the young nation, nor for the violent end in the offing for the whole of the South.

Reading about the impending conflict in his paper over breakfast in the hotel dining room, Lowe recalled the huge controversy surrounding the Compromise of 1850, the series of acts that Daniel Webster,

Henry Clay, and Stephen A. Douglas had put before Congress hoping to settle the dispute between opponents of slavery in the North and slave owners in the South. In that year a younger Thaddeus Lowe had been traveling the country with Professor Reginald B. Dincklehoff's magic show. While he had given up his trade of journeyman cobbler for the stage, Lowe had not yet adopted the title of "Professor of Science."

Now Lowe was in the landlocked city of Cincinnati, attempting to prove to the world that he could be the first person to cross the Atlantic Ocean in a balloon. After several unsuccessful attempts to launch the *Great Western* from Philadelphia, the last of which had caused considerable damage to the envelope, he had taken up the suggestion put forth by Henry that perhaps it might be wiser if he proved his balloon in a long flight overland before venturing out across the water.

True to his promise, Henry had put Lowe in touch with a friend of his, Murat Halstead, editor of the *Cincinnati Daily Commercial.* Besides the wonderful copy he foresaw Lowe's flight generating, Halstead himself was very interested in ballooning. He had readily agreed to provide all the advance publicity and arrange the details for Lowe's project. By the time of Lowe's arrival, several articles had already appeared in the *Commercial.* Consequently the balloonist found the citizens of Cincinnati displaying more excitement over his forthcoming flight than the possibility of an impending war.

Lowe was growing restless. Only in his late twenties, the tall and handsome Lowe, with a dashing black moustache, had already been in Cincinnati for two weeks giving speeches and attending luncheons and banquets as well as studying the weather and preparing the *Enterprise* for the cross-country voyage. Currently the toast of the town, he had lectured the previous evening, at the gilded Cincinnati Opera House, in front of a capacity crowd.

While the balloonist was anxious to get started, the main obstacle to Lowe's departure continued to be the weather. Despite it being the middle of April, winter was reluctant to give up its grip on the middle of America. The temperature continued to be rather cold, and the April showers frequently turned into light snow. Lowe was also impatient to get back to his lovely wife and children at home in Philadelphia. She too was eager for her husband's return and they exchanged telegrams daily. Nevertheless, despite Lowe's constant staring at the sky when he was outdoors, so much so that he often accidentally ran into people walking on the street, weather conditions had not been favorable for flying for several days.

Tonight would be what Lowe hoped was his last public event in Cincinnati. The date was April 19th; just two days earlier the State of

Virginia had seceded from the Union. A Mr. Potter, the owner of the *Commercial,* and his editor Halstead were giving a banquet in Lowe's honor, to which they had invited all the civic leaders and other important people of the area.

Having accomplished nothing all day, Lowe sat there impatiently as the late dinner dragged on. The time was now almost eleven o'clock. The balloonist was tired of banquets, the foul odor of cigar smoke, and having to constantly listen to idle chatter from boring people. He wanted to be away from it all, in the sky floating in the free air above. The sound of his introduction being given startled Lowe from his musings. There was a round of applause. In the silence that followed, people coughed. Slowly sliding back his chair, the balloonist gamely rose to say the same things he had said on previous evenings all over again.

The laughter at his opening remark came rather subdued, causing Lowe to wonder if many of those present that evening might not have heard it before at one of his other performances. The balloonist paused a second, considering how he might put a fresh twist on things. Then he was saved. One of the members of his balloon crew rushed in the back door and handed him a note. A smile came to the balloonist's face. The weather had cleared. He ordered the man to assemble the rest of the crew and begin the inflation as soon as possible. Lowe announced the good weather to the audience and excused himself. He was finally on his way. Amid much cheering, clapping, and well-wishes from the guests, Lowe, Halstead, and Potter hastily fled the hall.

The three men stopped first at the *Commercial* offices. While Halstead was ordering a special flight edition of the newspaper put on the presses, Lowe telegraphed Henry in Washington to tell him he was about to take off. Halstead proposed that they go by Lowe's hotel so he could change into his flying clothes, then stop back at the office for the first copies of the paper. Lowe replied he wanted no more delay. He was ready now and would go as he was, dressed in his banquet clothes of black top hat and long black frock coat.

As Lowe ordered, the crew had immediately rushed to the launch site at the west end of the Commercial Hospital lot. When the balloonist and the two other men arrived at the field, the inflation was well underway. Shortly thereafter a messenger brought the freshly printed newspapers and a telegram from Professor Henry. The message read: "Fair weather prevailing to the coast. Good Luck!"

By three o'clock in the morning the *Enterprise* was nearly inflated and straining at her mooring ropes. The banquet guests had spread the news of Lowe's impending departure. A small crowd had gathered in the luminous circle of torches surrounding the nervous balloon.

Someone had thoughtfully made up a picnic basket of food left over from the banquet table and wrapped a jug of hot coffee in a blanket for the aerial traveler.

Murat Halstead helped Lowe into the basket. The balloon swayed and then descended slightly with the balloonist's weight. Halstead hesitated, his eyes questioning those of Lowe. The editor had previously asked to go along. Lowe, considering all the favors Halstead had bestowed on him, had been reluctant to say no. Lowe told him he would give his decision just before the launch. The balloonist measured the probable dangers of this flight and the state of his balloon. Lowe was inclined to think that the weight of another passenger, added to the load of ballast he was required to take, would not be consistent with his own safety. Lowe shook his head at Murat, saying he was sorry but must, of necessity, make this a solo excursion.

Halstead, bemoaning the fact that he could not go along, held on to the gondola. The balloonist dwarfed the passenger basket as he leaned on the wicker sides. Lowe stood there, in the flickering glow of light from the lanterns and torches held up by the crowd of spectators, looking strange and out of place in his top hat and formal attire. The scene had taken on a sense of high drama, no doubt heightened by the dark night and the intense silence of the gathered onlookers.

At last the awaited moment came, every remaining cord was loosened, and the stupendous globe began struggling to get free, eager to leave the smoke of the flaming firebrands and to float in purer regions. The crew, aided by a group of strong-armed admirers, held on to the ropes and basket of the gently rocking airship, as if reluctant to allow Lowe the freedom of the air—or perhaps to meet his death. The balloonist gave the signal to let go. Then, to the delight of the hundred or so onlookers, the bold adventurer floated safely up into the atmosphere, buoyed up by a gas lighter than the air itself.

The sight was truly exhilarating. The watchers were all eyes, their throats choked with emotion. Their last clear view of Lowe was the look of confidence and composure on his aquiline face as the *Enterprise* climbed into the darkness. As one the group suddenly broke its silence, letting out a loud hurrah, and everyone waved. Acknowledging their cheer, Lowe removed his top hat and, placing his right hand to his forehead, held a military salute as he slowly disappeared into the black night. Lowe could not help wondering if at that moment he had not gone from the frying pan into the fire.

The balloonist could no longer see the circle of flickering lights he had ascended from. Lowe only now noticed, by their looming dark shadows, how perilously close he had come to some of the neighboring buildings in the excitement of his departure. The balloon was oscillating in all directions as it climbed out, rising so rapidly that Lowe felt a ringing in his ears. Then, as Henry had suggested, the *Enterprise* began moving off swiftly on a westerly heading. The balloonist laughed to himself, positive that at this very moment doubters on the ground, who had witnessed his departure, were gleefully predicting that his airship would probably come down somewhere in Kansas, not at the Atlantic Ocean. Indeed, reporters of rival newspapers were already at work preparing stories ridiculing the flight, concluding, perhaps all to willingly, that Lowe's theories of the upper atmosphere were wild and unfounded.

Lowe waited patiently, and in a short time the balloon began moving definitely toward the east. The balloonist was elated; he had found the current he needed. His barometer told him the *Enterprise* was at seven thousand feet. The thermometer indicated the outside air temperature had fallen to fifteen degrees. Lowe tugged down his top hat, turned up the collar on his frock coat, and wrapped himself with the blanket and oilcloth he had brought along. The early delight of his ascension had passed. The balloonist was becoming aware of the precariousness of his situation. He struggled his hands into the second pair of gloves Halstead had thrust into his pocket. Lowe wished he had not been so cavalier about his attire, and in such a hurry to take off. The balloonist accepted now that he should have changed into something more substantial than the clothes he was presently wearing.

The *Enterprise* wafted along smartly on the fresh breeze. The night surrounding Lowe was uniformly black, doused and without contrast. He appeared to be passing down the basin of a heavy and unlit valley in which the vast wooded landscape seemed arranged like theatrical scenery, the many rows of trees, one behind the other, becoming ever darker and more distant as they descended the gentle slopes on his left and right. The whole landscape, empty and grave, seemed almost imperceptibly to float, to shift slightly underneath the motionless billowing clouds. For an instant the moon broke through and painted a white road winding dramatically through that bleak and woody terrain. Then the world returned to its many shades of black, the color of self-denial, resignation, numbness, yet the benevolent color of restful sleep.

It was completely dark below now. Lowe hung on to the basket, staring blindly over the side, crouching on the bags of ballast. Moist when they had been loaded on, they were now frozen solid. His feet were extremely cold, and he began to worry about frostbite. Huddled up, rubbing his arms for warmth, Lowe heard a strange rattling noise in the gas envelope above him, the sound of walking on soft pine needles. The balloonist stood up and listened. He thought at first that an unfortunate bird might have gotten trapped in the bag during the hurried inflation. Then he perceived that the rapid climb from the damp but warm temperature at the surface to the winter-like temperature at his present altitude had caused the moisture in the bag to condense, and then to freeze into crystals.

The underside of the balloon diminished in circumference until it compressed into a narrow hose called the neck. This was usually kept open in flight so that excess gas could be blown off as the envelope became heated and the gas expanded. Now tiny, frozen crystals were forming on the inside of the bag and falling out this opening. The airship hit a gust of wind and Lowe's feet slid out from under him. He grasped the side of the basket for balance. The balloonist looked down, where the moon reflected off a sheet of white. The floor of the gondola was totally covered with bits of ice, appearing to Lowe as if the balloon had just flown through a snow storm.

The discharging of the frozen particles caused the gas to expand. causing the balloon to begin climbing again. The gust of wind that had dislodged the ice crystals had also blown his lantern out. Lowe was unable to read his instruments. He took off his gloves and rubbed his fingers on the raised markings of the barometer. The balloonist estimated he was at ten thousand feet. During the recent ascent the balloon had been rocked about, and driven from its course, but seemed to be settled on an easterly heading once again. From the occasional tiny pinpoints of light that he could see on the earth below, Lowe guessed his airship was moving along at a great rate of speed. Yet in the basket there was no sense of motion as he moved along in deathlike silence through what he himself had called "the mysterious region of the upper air."

Kneeling down, the balloonist drew his oilcloth over his head and lit a candle. He began to write in his diary. Later he would transcribe the hastily scrawled notes:

As I rose rapidly and to the west my feelings can hardly be analyzed. I had reached another pinnacle in my scientific career. I knew that this was the test and that my reputation was in a sense at stake. Not only this, but Professor Henry and the scientific men of America had accepted the upper east wind hypothesis as practical; their eyes, as well as those of the entire country were on me, and when at an altitude of a mile and a fifth I shot out of the lower westerly current, entered the great easterly river of the sky, and began to travel toward the Atlantic coast, I could have cheered in my elation.

The lack of oxygen at the altitude he was at, plus the odious smell of the gas leaking from the neck of the bag, was causing Lowe to become light-headed. The heat of his excitement had expired, now he was shivering, and suffering from the weariness of his ordeal. All he wanted to do was sleep. Lowe was not sure if this was a wise idea. He fidgeted helplessly, squinting in the darkness at his instruments, inventing tasks to keep him awake. He stood up, his hands shaky on the rails. He could not let himself fall asleep, worried he would never wake up. Eventually his eyelids became heavy. The balloonist could fight no longer. Giving in to his exhaustion, Lowe lay down and curled up on the floor of the gondola.

Lowe was just beginning to nod off when he felt the temperature drop dramatically—the cold chill that signaled the arrival of dawn. Crawling to his knees, the balloonist peered over the edge of his basket and watched in awe as the first rays of light emerged in the east. These first faint promises were soon followed by an enormous golden globe that appeared to be climbing out of the mountains that lay ahead of him. The time was 5:05, and he was on the Kentucky side of the Ohio River. From up here the myth of Orpheus seemed to him real enough. The earth was indeed being born all over again, Lowe jokingly consoled himself. He was, however, careful not to look back in the direction from which he had come.

As the sun rose its heat began to warm the *Enterprise* causing the gas in the envelope to expand further, sending the balloon lofting to eleven thousand feet. In the light of day the earth expanded in a parti-colored relief before the balloonist's delighted eyes. The ocher checkerboard of Ohio had given way to the green of the Cumberland Mountains. Infinite rows of trees marched in orderly procession across the ridges. The fluid strips and bands of forest seemed to rustle and grow beneath him, rising like a tide that was swelling him gradually to the New Jersey shore.

The day had begun clear enough, but now, as far as his eye could sweep the horizon, masses of threatening clouds were beginning to ascend to immeasurable heights. Unlike the level appearance they took when seen from the earth, the cloud's entire monstrous dimensions were visible in profile, seeming to Lowe to be tumbling headlong toward him. In a short time one colossal cloud mass pressed down on him, encompassing the airship on every side. The balloonist threw out ballast, and the balloon began to rise, helped by the upward ascending currents of air that bounced off the mountains like water off of rocks.

Soon Lowe was soaring just above the tops, the clouds rolling beneath him like the foam on a sea that had been churned up by a storm. The landscape below was now obscured from his view, except through the holes in the clouds; although even at this altitude he could still hear the occasional locomotive whistle, and the barking of dogs set off by the hissing of the strange object passing overhead. At intervals one of the cloud abysses might be illuminated by a ray of sunshine to reveal the continuous carpet of trees, or a more ominous outcropping of rocks. Committed to his southeasterly leap of faith, Lowe stood holding on to the side of the basket, as the airship, left to the whim of the winds, rushed on in wild confusion.

The updrafts and downdrafts off the mountains had turned the *Enterprise* into an intractable monster. Soaring over a cloudy cliff, Lowe felt his balloon dragged down as if by a giant unseen hand. He was falling at over a mile a minute. Fearing a crash was inevitable, the balloonist bent over to begin throwing out ballast, but no sooner had he lifted one of the heavy sacks than the airship was hurled frantically upward. More angry at his inability to control the situation than afraid of the consequences, Lowe hung on as the *Enterprise* rocketed up and down, at one point ascending as high as twenty-two thousand feet. As suddenly as it had begun, his wild ride was over; he was beyond the mountains.

Unknown to Lowe, telegraph dispatchers on the ground below, in cities such as Falmouth and Lexington, Kentucky, had tracked his initial progress and transmitted reports back to Halstead in Cincinnati. This information confirmed Lowe's predictions, and several newspaper writers were already retracting their earlier negative stories.

On top of the clouds, the ground obscured from his view, Lowe himself had no clue as to where he was. The balloonist suspected he might be nearing the Atlantic coast. He decided, as the balloon was descending, the wisest thing would be to continue down and take a look before he was blown out to sea without even knowing it. As he got lower, the balloonist began to vent off gas to continue his descent. Then he entered the blinding whiteness of the cloud bank.

Lowe knew he was descending, but his mind had lost all sense of dimension. Deprived of any image beyond the edge of his basket, the balloonist's inner ear began to dominate his equilibrium. He alternately felt as if he was climbing, then spinning, then turning in a circle. For a moment he thought he was hanging upside down. He resisted the urge to tug on the ropes, throw out ballast, or vent more gas. There was nothing he could do but believe that his balloon, left to its own devices, would bring him out of the thick cloud bank. Then the *Enterprise* broke out of the overcast.

The balloon had emerged from the clouds quite low. Lowe seemed to be in a shallow valley, with the cloud bases lying ragged on the surrounding ridges. The low clouds hid the hilltops. The space between the land and the thick gray ceiling was wet and misty, creating an atmosphere where everything was indistinct, muffled, and murky. The solid overcast blotted out the sun, giving the landscape a uniformly gray appearance, and causing it to appear later in the day than it actually was. The balloonist squinted to catch a sight, a sound, a smell, a feeling of something tangible, but clarity was elusive.

Through the haze Lowe thought he could make out a small group of men wielding hoes, working along the rows of a field. Apparently they had not seen him, but, as his balloon was wafting in their direction, he decided he would give them a visit. Approaching the group Lowe took out his megaphone and called down in a stentorian tone asking what state this was. The men looked around, confused by this question from a voice with a strange hollow ring, and apparently coming from nowhere. They swiveled their heads in every direction but up. Seemingly terrorized by some unseen being, no one replied. The balloonist, amused by their befuddlement, called out again.

"Virginie," someone shouted back guardedly, but still no one thought to look up.

Lowe was suddenly aware that his balloon expedition had taken him much farther south than he had planned to travel. In the excitement of his departure from Cincinnati, and his flight, he had completely forgotten about the secession of the Southern states. Was he now in enemy territory? Not sure whether the group he was presently interrogating was friendly to the North or the South, Lowe pondered how to phrase his question. As he was a practical man, who usually took the most direct solution, Lowe sang out again, asking what country this was.

The surface wind chose this moment to pick up, gently drifting Lowe's balloon in the direction of some tall pines at the edge of the field. Alerted to the danger, the balloonist quickly threw out some ballast to gain altitude, being careful not to hit the men below. The sand bags landed on the ground with a splatter, causing the group to finally look skyward. Shocked by what they saw, the men gawked wide-eyed at the huge globe hovering above them. No one bothered to answer Lowe's question, as the bewildered men let out the scream of a banshee and took off running. The balloonist deduced, from the breakneck speed at which the group departed, they had never seen a balloon before his unexpected appearance in the sky, and this had frightened them out of their wits. He would not wait around for their return.

Since the wind that had come up seemed to be propelling him in the right direction, Lowe dropped out ballast until he was above the height of the treetops, and continued to drift south along the stem of what he imagined must be the Blue Ridge Mountains. He was seeking a gap where he might cross over to the sea. Going along for some time and finding no such space, the balloonist jettisoned more ballast and used the ridge lift to climb up and over to the other side. He was again quite high. As it was almost noon, and he had not eaten since the banquet the previous night, Lowe decided to have some food. He dug into his hamper but discovered, to his dismay, the water, sandwiches, and fruit he had brought along were all still frozen from the previous night's cold temperatures. He would eat later.

Borne on a fresh breeze, the *Enterprise* was now moving at full tilt toward the east. The clouds had cleared, and in a short while Lowe imagined he could distinguish the blue of the ocean on the horizon. Knowing that the land below, from where he presently believed himself to be to the sea, was mostly uninhabited swamp, Lowe decided to descend and look for a place to set his balloon down. He also hoped it would be possible to land somewhere near a railroad station so that he would be able to ship his balloon back home without too much difficulty.

Lowe's balloon was continuing its drift rapidly eastward. He began his descent, not aware he was presently over Spartansburg Township, on the border between North and South Carolina. He espied some workers bent over in a marshy field so wet it appeared more fluid than solid underfoot. The men were wading in mud, and tending a crop which he believed to be rice. The balloonist decided, since he had not seen anyone else for some time, to come down near them. As he approached, Lowe called to them for assistance.

For some reason these men looked up, and spotted him immediately. While they were as frightened of Lowe and his balloon as the previous group, they did not run. Their stares fixed on him, the workers stood their ground, showing no intention of coming to Lowe's aid. Nevertheless, several of the black men had taken hold of the balloon's trailing ropes, perhaps awaiting the order from their overseer to wrench the hellish contrivance from the sky.

Attempting to allay their fears, Lowe shouted down to the group, he meant no one any harm, introducing himself as Professor Thaddeus Lowe, departed from Cincinnati, Ohio, that very morning, on a scientific mission. This pronouncement was greeted with skepticism by the white man who appeared to be in charge. The overseer informed Lowe he would be most thankful if the professor would leave with haste, and then ordered the slaves to let go of the ropes. Noticing the long-barreled pistol hanging at the man's side, Lowe decided he was better off out of there, and dropped a bag of ballast in order to ascend. As the bag sailed earthward everyone instinctively ducked, even though they were clearly in no danger of being hit.

For years after, Lowe liked to laughingly tell the story of how one of the field hands, seeing the sandbag hit the ground, ran after him as he climbed out shouting for him to come back as he had lost his baggage.

Urged on by a brisk wind, the *Enterprise* continued to bob along quite close to the ground in a southeasterly direction for another twenty miles. During that time Lowe was startled from his admiration of the landscape by several volleys fired from nearby fields. To his distress he speculated the shots to be muskets firing minie balls in his direction, although even at this low altitude he was well out of range. Nevertheless, he waited until he was clear of the area from which he believed the shots had come before beginning another descent. The balloonist was determined to land this time for good, come what may, as the *Enterprise* had little lifting power left and his supply of sandbags was exhausted.

Lowe found himself being slowly blown toward a small settlement. Not wanting to take anyone by surprise lest they begin firing at him, the balloonist attempted to signal the people there that he was benign. He waved a white handkerchief and bellowed through his megaphone that he was Professor Thaddeus Lowe, friendly, and meaning no harm to anyone. Although he was sure he could be heard, no one seemed to comprehend the meaning of his shouting and flailing. All his efforts managed to accomplish was to rout a great flock of crows which, perhaps taking the *Enterprise* for a huge hawk or some other predacious bird, scattered into the sky amid much screeching and crackling. This further frightened the local inhabitants, who had been regarding the airship's approach with considerable suspicion. Imagining themselves to be in great danger, the residents ran for the cover of their huts, many screaming in terror as they went.

Arriving at the settlement, Lowe leaned outside the gondola and threw down a heavy anchor, which thankfully caught, and held, in a small scrub oak. Then, with muscles only a little more willing than not, he pulled the basket down to the dusty red soil and dismounted, quickly tying a line to a nearby stout fence. A sense of relief came over him. He was back on the earth after nine hours in the air.

Lowe strode a few shaky circuits around the *Enterprise,* visually checking the condition of his balloon, while getting his legs used to being on the ground again. The envelope was wrinkled and underinflated, flapping slightly in the light breeze. Although he had not exactly snuck into town, no one from the burgh seemed inclined to greet him. Not a single soul had reemerged from inside the shacks.

Lowe dug into a pouch, unfolded his map, and began to make some quick calculations. By his own reckoning, he made himself to be somewhere in South Carolina. The balloonist would later write in his memoirs that he had traveled eight hundred miles in nine hours, or "a speed of almost a hundred miles per hour." Such were the tricks memory could play on a human being when he was not in complete harmony with his present. Since the straight line distance from Cincinnati to where Lowe actually landed in South Carolina was closer to four hundred miles, he either miscalculated, allowed for a considerably circuitous route, or his deduction was pure hyperbole.

The alarm and hostility shown by the locals to Lowe on his previous two attempts to land would prove to be relatively mild when compared to the reception that was eventually in store for him here. His balloon tied fast behind him, its gentle rocking to and fro giving it the appearance of a living creature, Lowe ventured out to see what had become of the people. Two little curly heads peered around the corner of a log hut that stood nearby. The balloonist called to them. The children did not move until Lowe made as if he was going to run after them, then they gave him what he took to be an obscene gesture and quickly disappeared.

Shortly thereafter, a group of two white boys, three old ladies, and three black men, came forward from behind the buildings, stopping within twenty feet of Lowe. At that precise moment a gust of wind chose to rock the balloon, causing it to swing over on its moorings and almost touch the ground. The up-to-now brave group took off in a panic. However, they returned in a few minutes led by a large and lusty-looking young woman. Emboldened by the woman's presence, the group came closer. Some even risked peeking in the balloon's basket.

The *Enterprise* was swaying nervously back and forth on its moorings, as if getting ready to leave. Nevertheless, Lowe had no intention of going anywhere. Despite what he suspected might be the grave consequences of remaining here, the balloonist decided to valve out the remaining gas. The curious group held their noses as the foul smelling fumes filled the air. Before their very eyes the giant thing began to gurgle and shudder. Then they jumped back in horror as the mammoth globe tumbled to the earth .

With the crumpled balloon now lying dead at their feet, the scene took on an ominous stillness. The group stood there in silence, almost as if at a funeral. The lusty woman was the first person bold enough to speak to the strange visitor.

Without questioning Lowe, or ascertaining his motive for being there, she began to scold him, telling the balloonist he had terrified the old people. They took his arrival as a sign that Armageddon had begun. They were all cowering in their huts, afraid to come out, and praying mightily for their salvation. The woman also warned the balloonist she heard the shots fired at him earlier, and suspected the men who had done the shooting saw him come down, and would be arriving here any moment.

Hearing this, Lowe began to hurriedly pack the balloon and his other equipment into his sacks. A crowd was gathering. People were converging on the landing area by horseback, wagons, and on foot. Most of the new arrivals were simple, uneducated farmers, with grim expressions on their weathered faces, and shotguns in their arms, ready to repel any threat "the devil that could travel through the air" might offer. They stood around the balloonist in a circle, their grim faces silent and watchful, their minds devoid of any comprehension of who, or what, had suddenly appeared in their midst.

Although his balloon was now out of sight, Lowe realized that he himself must still present a strange appearance to these rough folk, clad as he was in his top hat and long black Prince Albert coat. He studied the faces in the crowd surrounding him, and saw fear mingled with their curiosity. The balloonist sensed these people were unconvinced he was not some agent of the devil, or perhaps a creature who had descended to Earth from outer space. The anxious fingers ready on triggers of shotguns told Lowe he must act quickly to convince the crowd that he was not the evil demon they thought him to be, but a fellow human being, and a friendly one at that. It was apparent to the balloonist that he must provide them with some sort of common reference point.

Seizing on an idea, Lowe took from his gondola the hamper containing the sandwiches, cakes, fruit, and other delicacies hastily packed for him on his departure from Cincinnati. Forcing a big smile on his face, he offered these to the young children standing down front. But they shyly backed away, taking refuge behind their mothers' aprons and skirts. To show them the food was good, the balloonist began to eat some himself, making overly loud smacking sounds. Seeing grins appear on faces that just before had menacing frowns, Lowe held out his offerings again, with a "Here, try some of this."

A brave few came forward, took the proffered fare, and tasted it. Finding the treats had considerably more flavor than they were used to—they had come after all from a banquet prepared for the finest citizens of Cincinnati—some people asked for more. Soon almost everyone was sharing a small sample of the food.

Forever the showman, Lowe could not restrain himself from enlarging on his success. Taking out his water bottles, he showed them the frozen liquid and attempted to explain how it had gotten that way. He even cut one of the rubber bottles open with a knife, holding up a block of ice the same shape as the bottle it had been in. Then he took the jug of coffee from the blanket it had been wrapped in and poured out the still hot fluid.

All at once a cry went up from his audience. Lowe knew then he had made a mistake. The circle of people drew back from him, their eyes wide with fear. He had not foreseen his actions would be taken as a vulgar intrigue, the amazing machinations behind some secret force.

One old man shouted that only the devil could pull frozen water and hot coffee out of the same basket. Another suggested it would take the hands of Satan to force a large piece of ice into a bottle through such a small hole. People began to murmur over the apparent contradictions. They found a sinister meaning in the fact that some of the food was frozen, while some was not. A woman who had been happily munching on a piece of lemon cake suddenly screamed, and spit out the offending morsel, grinding the remains into the dirt with her bare foot.

The stranger wasn't the devil, but a Yankee who had fallen from the skies, a grim-faced farmer, in bib overalls decorated with the blood of a hog he had butchered earlier in the day, declared of Lowe. If the Yankee was capable of doing all those impossible things he had done, another man argued, he was too dangerous to be set loose. Someone shouted that Lowe should immediately be put before a firing squad .

Despite the now blazing sun, the balloonist felt a cold chill pass through his body. He heard a band of rough-looking fellows at the back voice their support for the firing-squad suggestion. There were other shouts as the proposal to kill the stranger won more support. But a few calmer heads called for a debate, wanting to learn more about the Yankee before summarily condemning him to execution. Lowe listened apprehensively while his fate was discussed, considering what desperate action he might take if it should become necessary.

The circle of people had closed in around the balloonist again, their presence, and the heavy scent of their bodies, masking any relief the slight breeze might have given to Lowe's profusely sweating brow.

Listening intently to the speeches, in accents so thick he might be hearing a foreign language, the professor sensed the discussion was going in his favor. A feeling of reprieve was slowly coming over him when he heard the vicious cry that he was a damn Union spy—that's what he was—and ought to be hanged. The balloonist knew now that he was in a situation where his fate might be resolved more by his presence of mind than by his courage.

Determined to allay the crowd's growing fear, and realizing he had not been properly introduced, Lowe stood up straight and, using his most shining voice, announced he was Professor Thaddeus Sobieski Constantine Lowe, a person engaged in scientific research. Then he began, with methodical precision, to unload his scientific equipment—the barometer, altimeter, and other things from the gondola—intending to carefully explain the use of each as he went.

Unfortunately this action had an effect on the crowd opposite of what he had hoped for. A man rushed forward, grabbed the altimeter from Lowe, and shook it in his face. Turning to the crowd, the accuser held up the instrument and shouted that what they had all heard the stranger saying was lies—this was some kind of Yankee secret weapon. The group began an angry clamor, calling for the destruction of the Yankee spy as well as his infernal weapons. As one, they moved menacingly toward the balloonist.

Lowe stepped back and quickly drew his Colt revolver, which had heretofore been hidden in the holster underneath his long black coat. Holding the gun up in the air, he fired off a shot, announcing he was prepared to use it if they should press an attack. The surprised group suddenly was still. Perceiving the danger of the situation, the large woman to whom Lowe had spoken first, pushed her way through the crowd. She assured Lowe he was in no danger and should put away his pistol. The woman told Lowe, loud enough to be heard by the group, that the men there were cowards, all the brave men of the neighborhood having gone off to the war to fight. Then she ordered two of the more sober louts to go and fetch a wagon. It had been decided, by what means Lowe was never able to ascertain, that he and his balloon were to be handed over to the authorities in the nearest town, which, ironically enough, was named Unionville.

7
Two Close Calls, Heading Home, the South Mobilizes

As she led him into her log shanty, the large and rather compelling woman told Lowe the place where he had landed was called Pea Ridge. She was not sure if that was the real name; everyone just called it that because peas were the only thing that would grow in the poor soil round there. Gracious in a shy and backward way, the woman offered to prepare some supper for the balloonist while they waited for the men to bring the wagon to drive him to town.

Taking a battered tin of snuff from the shelf, the woman passed it to Lowe and asked him if he wanted some. The balloonist handed the can back without taking any. She took a pinch and sniffed it into her nose before putting the tin back. They were alone in the semidarkness of the hut, the light from the fire flickering on the rough-cut logs of the puncheon floor. Lowe studied the young woman as she prepared the simple meal. It was extremely hot in the air-less one room, made hotter by the cooking fire, a kitchen with a bed in the corner. The woman's worn-thin cotton dress, moist with sweat, clung to the ridges of her body as she moved back and forth at her work. She had a full figure, and Lowe observed that she was rather attractive in a rustic way. He looked at the single bed and wondered what she was doing out here all by herself. Had her man gone to fight in the war? Then the improbable tricks that memory, or perhaps guilt, played on one caused the image of his wife Leontine to fill Lowe's mind. She was about half the size of this woman, and would never be seen in such a thin and dirty dress. What was she doing now, in her luxurious townhouse ten times the size of this shanty, with her mother and children, and cook, maid, and nanny?

Turning to Lowe, the woman, who for some reason had not revealed her name, announced the supper was ready. She removed a large pan of cakes about the size of ducks' eggs, which she called corn dodgers, from the Dutch oven over her fireplace. Lowe stared at the full pan, wondering if the two of them were meant to eat all those cakes, when she called to the guards who had been stationed outside the door. Two foul smelling, rather unkempt men eagerly crowded into the small room. They squatted down, elbow to elbow with the Yankee, on the three-legged stools gathered around a table that had been fashioned from a split pine log. As the woman bent over to place the pan of corn dodgers on the table, her dress gapped open at the top. Lowe's gaze flashed to the deep crevasse defining her ample breasts. Having a strong suspicion that he was not the only one who had been giving the lusty woman's figure discreet looks, he glanced around at the other men. To Lowe's surprise the men's hungry eyes were all fixed on the just arrived cakes.

The corn dodgers were passed around. Seeing they were about to eat them plain, Lowe said if they allowed him to go outside, he would get some jars of spread left in his hamper. Accompanied by the guards, the balloonist went back to his sacks, where he produced a container of peach jam and one of honey. The group was happy to see the spreads. One of the men remarked it sure was hard to get things like that around there. There's no store nearby, he explained, so most people ate only what they grew themselves. One of the guards laughed, then spat on the ground, saying he heard tell that Abe Lincoln was planning to blockade the Southern ports. He reckoned it won't make much difference around there as no one ever got anything from anywhere anyway.

Lowe, who was sitting there quietly eating his corn dodgers, made no response. Noticing Lowe's reticence, one of the guards ventured to wonder if the prisoner really was a Yankee. He had met Yankees and observed that they always talked very fast and had a great deal to say about everything, even if they didn't know anything about what they were talking about. This comment brought a hearty laugh to everyone, even Professor Lowe.

Shortly after their supper was completed, the wagon arrived, drawn by six mules. The teamster apologized for the delay, revealing it wasn't easy to find so many mules at such a short notice. Staring incredulously at the elaborate rig, Lowe asked why the need for all the mules. The teamster looked at the Yankee and spat his out his tobacco juice as if to show disdain at such a foolish question. He related as how he had seen the balloon come down and figured that it would take at least six mules to handle such a big load. Then he watched in amazement as Lowe bundled the collapsed bag into the wagon by himself. The lusty young woman helped him load the basket and his instruments as everyone else seemed afraid to touch them. Then she smiled, giving the balloonist's hand a discreet squeeze as he climbed up in the wagon. Lowe put on his top hat and waved. The teamster cracked his whip and the wagon rattled off, accompanied by a guard of nine rough-looking men, riding mangy horses bareback and armed with shotguns.

The guards were in no hurry to get Lowe to town. Everyone appeared in a festive mood, laughing and joking, and passing around a bottle of "shine," as if they were out on an outing. Lowe wondered if perhaps they did not get to town that often and if this was somewhat of an event. The balloonist was beginning to tire of the journey. Although he had been told Unionville was only three miles, the trip seemed to be taking forever in the spring-less wagon, which bounced and swayed freely on the grooved road. In addition, the party had to stop several times for crisis visits to the nearest bushes as the shine, combined with the woman's undercooked and greasy corn dodgers, had caused a few cases of the "Virginia quickstep."

Lowe was exhausted, and his clothes were covered with a layer of fine red dust, when he finally arrived in front of the town jail with his convoy of guards. In the dim lamplight he observed that the boodle had grown considerably. News of the strange intruder had preceded him, and he had picked up new followers at each intersection they passed. He was now being accompanied by a wild-eyed mob of bearded and slovenly locals, some riding shaggy ponies, but most walking, carrying shotguns, muskets, and pitchforks along with their torches. An especially turbulent fellow, in tattered bib overalls and a crumpled slouch hat, kept pace alongside the wagon laughing, while swinging a length of stout rope that he had fashioned into a noose.

Lowe's guards had intended to deliver him to the town jail, where he could be held until they received instructions from officials higher up as to what to do with their prisoner. Unfortunately the jailer was less than cooperative, positively refusing to allow "the Yankee devil" into his building, perhaps fearing that despite the guards' assurances, Lowe was indeed Satan in disguise. Claiming his cells were all full, the jailer suggested that the balloonist be taken to the town's only hotel and kept there under guard until morning.

This turnabout was a stroke of good fortune for Lowe. As the hour had become quite late by small-town standards, when the party arrived at the hotel the landlord had already retired and needed to be roused from his bed. Annoyed by the commotion, the man came bustling downstairs and raised his lantern to the stranger's face to see what it was all about. Startled by who he saw, the rotund little innkeeper quickly jumped back in surprise. Recognizing Professor Lowe, he apologized and extended his hand in a warm greeting. The proprietor then introduced himself as Flynt, saying he was an enthu-siastic follower of ballooning and very familiar with Professor Lowe's scientific work. He was, in fact, present at one of the balloon ascen-sions that Lowe had made the previous year in Charleston.

The guards, who apparently knew Flynt well and respected his judgment, stood looking on in amazement as the innkeeper recounted his enjoyment of the balloonist's exploits in Charleston. The guards' appreciation of this strange Yankee was growing with each word from Flynt's mouth. Soon they too were all apologies to Lowe for the rude way in which they had treated their distinguished guest.

Overjoyed by the feeling that he had just been plucked from the edge of some fathomless abyss, Lowe rose to the occasion by an-nouncing he would stand everyone in the party to a round of "flip." A non-drinker himself, Lowe did not take any of the drink composed of beer, rum, and sugar, but joined them with a cup of cider. Continuing his generous mood, Lowe even presented the driver of the mule team with a tip he learned later was more than the ride would actually have cost. Checking his purse that evening, the balloonist realized that his impulsive gesture had subtracted a good amount from the modest sum he had been able to raise from his sponsors in Cincinnati, and brought with him on the trip. Lowe vowed to be more frugal in the future, as such largess was something he presently could ill afford, uncertain as he was of the duration of his stay in the South.

A loud pounding on the door rudely awakened Lowe from his sound sleep. With a moan, he pulled the pillow over his face. The early light of dawn was beginning to define the pine-covered ridges visible through his window. The balloonist shook his head, taking a moment to recall where he was, which was in a small room, in a small hotel, in the small town of Unionville, South Carolina.

Lowe felt as if he had just gone to sleep. The hour had been after ten o'clock when his party reached town, and several more hours had passed, in confusion and then revelry, before the balloonist finally got to bed. Despite the circumstances, he had slept well, exhausted from having been awake for the previous thirty-six hours.

"Professor Lowe! Professor Lowe!" The pounding on the door be-came more insistent. Someone was shouting his name. He rubbed his burning eyes. Who was knocking at this early hour when he had es-pecially given instructions last night that he was not to be disturbed? Lowe reluctantly rose from his bed. It was then he heard the sound of belligerent shouting coming from the street. He opened the door to Mr. Flynt, who told him a threatening crowd had gathered in front of the hotel demanding something be done about "that damn Yankee spy." The innkeeper also informed his distinguished guest that the local sheriff and some other officials were downstairs looking for him.

A bit of a dandy, vanity being one of his failings, Lowe did not hurry with his dressing. Glancing in the mirror to groom his luxurious moustache, he was surprised by the face that greeted him. His skin was red and swollen, burned from the wind and sun encountered on the previous day's flight. He had felt a tingling on his cheeks last night when he came in, but had not seen himself clearly in the room lit only by a small candle. The balloonist put his hands into the cold water in the basin. They were stiff and discolored. Burns showed on his palms where the ropes had dug in deeply as he hung on to the rigging during his wild ride over the mountains.

When he finally arrived in the lobby in his "bang up" attire, Lowe was immediately confronted by a trio of angry men that included the sheriff, the local newspaper editor, and a Mr. Thompsen, a representative to the South Carolina legislature. Smiling politely, Lowe suggested they not stand out there awkwardly in the lobby, but move into the privacy of the hotel parlor for a discussion. The innkeeper brought them coffee in the ornate room now decorated with the new Confederate Stars and Bars.

Apparently the "biggest toad in the puddle," and therefore the spokesman, Representative Thompsen introduced himself first, shaking hands, before introducing the others to Professor Lowe. Lowe noted the other men did not offer him their hands, but only nodded politely when they were introduced. Reaching in his pocket, Thompsen offered everyone a "long nine," the cheap nine-inch cigars usually sold in the North for a penny an inch. Everyone declined, but he lit one up himself and, puffing on it hardily, began to present their case.

Looking very stern, and attempting to sound official as befit the occasion, Representative Thompsen informed Professor Lowe, that a state of war currently existed between South Carolina, the state he was presently in, a member of the Confederate States of America, and the Federal Union. And in so much as Lowe was without a doubt a Yankee, he was hereby declared to be in enemy territory. Having arrived in the township clearly in an unusual manner, the three officials, and the rest of the local citizenry, assumed that Lowe's intentions might not be entirely friendly. Moving aside the curtains, the sheriff pointed to the unruly mob gathered outside in the street, stressing to Lowe that there were many thereabouts who considered him to be a Union spy and who felt that he should immediately be dealt with as such.

Lowe countered that such allegations were absurd, maintaining that he could easily prove that his motives for making this flight were solely scientific. He had no quarrel with the Confederacy and no desire to be in South Carolina. He had departed from Cincinnati the previous night, ostensibly headed for the Atlantic Ocean, which he hoped to meet somewhere near the coast of New Jersey. It was only by accident and by chance of the winds that he had arrived in what they were now calling enemy territory.

Thompsen asked Lowe what proof he had of his statements.

Offering to pay the cost, Lowe suggested they telegraph Murat Halstead, editor of the *Cincinnati Daily Commercial*, who would verify his story.

The men hesitated, considering Lowe's proposal. Then the balloonist remembered the stack of fresh newspapers Halstead had put in the gondola before he departed. Asking the men to follow him out back, Lowe announced he had another way of proving his story.

The group aocompanied Lowe to a shed behind the hotel where his balloon and basket had been stored overnight. To Lowe's great relief nothing had been tampered with; the newspapers were still there. The balloonist carried a sack back into the parlor, where he tore it open and handed each man a copy of the *Cincinnati Daily Commercial*, dated April 20, 1861, hoping it would prove that his flight was purely scientific, not the one-man infiltration of the Confederacy they imagined it to be.

The sheriff took one hasty look at the newspaper and immediately handed it back to Lowe as if the pages were on fire, warning that this writing was "Abolitionist propaganda, the possession of which was punishable by death." Then, making a sound that fell somewhere between a cough and a hack, the sheriff let fly a considerable portion of tobacco juice in the direction of a spittoon crouching in the corner, missing it by about six inches, and adding to the ring of moist brown splotches that encircled the dull brass receptacle.

The newspaper editor, who impressed Lowe as being rather a bit of a "lick finger," was less panicked at the thought of reading the forbidden literature. Putting on his pince-nez, he proceeded to carefully study his copy of the *Daily Commercial*. Here was a real big city newspaper. He admired the quality of the paper stock and the printing, the well-written articles, and the preponderance of advertisements, all things he could never hope for in his small local paper. He rubbed the printed letters and a faint smudge of black appeared on his fingers. Sniffing the ink, the editor remarked that the newspaper indeed had yesterday's date, and it smelled as fresh as if it had been printed only the day before. Then he added he could not imagine how the newspaper had arrived from Cincinnati in such a short period of time.

Only Mr. Thompsen bothered to concern himself with the text of Murat Halstead's article, which read:

A Night Balloon Ascension!—Prof. Lowe, who has been in this city some time, silently perfecting his arrangements for an aerial flight, was to ascend this morning at 4 o'clock. We visited the Hospital lot at 12 1/2 A. M. and found the process of inflation going on smoothly—not a leak discovered, nor anything wrong. The balloon has a diameter of 42 feet, is 44 yards in circumference, 55 feet from top to valve, and will hold over 30,000 feet of gas.

The sky is almost cloudless, moon shining, and not a breath of air stirring. A prosperous voyage to you, Professor.

The representative finished the article, shook his head, and reread it out loud to the others. Thompsen was convinced of the truth of Lowe's story and conveyed his opinion to his colleagues.

The three asked Lowe to leave the parlor while they held a brief discussion. Called back in, the balloonist was given back his revolver, but no bullets, and told he was free to return home. Lowe was informed, however, that he first must be paraded through the streets in Mr. Thompsen's cabriolet, so that the townspeople could see him and be reassured he presented them no real threat. Lowe protested his being put on exhibition, a curious objection from a professional showman, perhaps fearing some bodily harm might come to him from the hostile crowd outside.

Thompsen and the editor took Lowe's arms, while the sheriff preceded them out the door. The mob stepped back quietly to let them mount into the carriage. Comfortably seated in Thompsen's cabriolet, the four were driven through the streets for the better part of an hour waving to and acknowledging the crowds, while Thompsen passed out cigars and stumped for votes. The bystanders were for the most part curious, and somewhat impressed at seeing a "real Yankee celebrity" in their own hometown, although a few did shout derisive remarks.

As they rode in circles around the small town, traversing many of the rutted thoroughfares several times, the conversation turned to the coming conflict. The three Southern gentlemen were convinced it would only be a short while before their brave Confederate Army would be parading triumphantly through the streets of Washington, D.C.

Lowe, realizing he was still in effect an enemy prisoner, was somewhat circumspect. He did, however, point out that he was a scientist and, as such, was inclined to believe that wars were not won by bravery, but by the army that could bring the most men, most matéri-el, and most sophisticated weapons to the places of encounter. Asked what he was getting at, Lowe reminded his overconfident compan-ions that the North's population outnumbered the South's by seven million, or a three to two margin. In terms of resources, the North had twice as many railroad tracks, three times the bank deposits, and five times more industrial potential. Speaking from his own experience, Lowe could even confirm that Northerners produced ninety percent of the nation's boots and shoes.

The three prominent citizens of the Confederacy were becoming annoyed with this large and loud-mouthed Yankee. Sucking hard on his cigar, Thompsen asked Professor Lowe just what was his point.

Lowe replied that with more boots, and more shoes, and more cloth, and more iron, and more railroads, and more locomotives, and more ships, and more rifles, and more cannon, and more people, and more fighting men, it would appear to him that the North could easily defeat the underpopulated and under-industrialized rebels.

The sheriff spat another chew on the floor, this one landing threat-eningly close to Lowe's dusty congress boots. Then he looked the bal-loonist in the eye and announced, for the Yankees to win the war the South would have to surrender, and he was damn sure, no matter how badly they might be whipped, the South would never surrender.

When the carriage ride was finally over, and the group returned to the hotel, Representative Thompsen signed a certificate of safe conduct for Lowe's passage home. The balloonist was eager to leave, but as it was Sunday there were no trains running. Thompsen, seem-ingly in need of the intellectual companionship this small, rural town denied him, extended an invitation to Lowe to dine with him and his wife and to stay the night. Remarking he was impressed by the kind offer, which he considered a display of genuine Southern hospitality, Lowe graciously accepted.

Wearing smart jackets and white gloves, several black servants bustled in and out of the spacious dining room bringing in the courses on silver trays as Professor Lowe and his hosts enjoyed a pleasant meal. The conversation was polite, both sides avoiding any mention of the impending war. Afterwards, as it was still light outside and warm, Lowe was given a tour of the family garden. Although only early spring, and the balloonist recalled the snows of last week in Cin-cinnati, the vegetation was already showing signs of growth from the abundant South Carolina sun. As they crunched along on the well-tended gravel paths, Lowe gave lavish praise to the plants, especially the budding beans, cabbage, and squash. Mrs. Thompsen allowed as how she had her servants set them in for her son who, she proudly announced, was at this very moment on his way to Manassas Junction with his Confederate regiment. She was confident they would be ready to harvest in a month or so when Washington was captured and the war was over—and her son returned home.

On Monday morning Professor Lowe inquired at Unionville's small train station and learned that there was no longer any service to either Washington or Cincinnati from that part of the Confederacy. The station master was not really sure what lines, if any, were still open to the North. He suggested that Lowe take a train south to the capital city Columbia, where he might find a train to the west as far as Louisville. From there he could take an Ohio River ferry up to Cincinnati. If the balloonist was going to get back home, he would have to make a long end-run around the armies that were massing in Washington and Virginia.

After Professor Lowe had arranged his ticket, the balloonist went to the telegraph office to send a number of telegrams he hoped would get through to his wife and friends up north. He wanted to tell them the results of his flight, and what happened after he landed, and that he was not sure how, or when, he would be returning. The telegraph operator was reluctant to take his messages since they were being sent to Yankees, and so Lowe had to rewrite them, being very circumspect with his wording, and avoiding anything that the suspicious operator might have construed as having a secret double meaning. Lowe wanted no more risks of being accused of spying.

The "short" train ride had taken six hours, due to delays, changing engines, and a great deal of what appeared to be military movement. Lowe, removing his top hat and mopping his brow, stepped from the car into the heat of the capital city. He walked briskly, happy to be heading home, if even by a roundabout way. With Thompsen's letter in his pocket Lowe was reasonably confident he was no longer in any danger merely because he was a "Yankee." Stopping in the office of the Adams Express Company, Lowe arranged to have the large sacks containing the balloon and the basket, which had been off-loaded from the baggage car and were presently lying on the platform, transported to Cincinnati. Concerned about possible damage to his delicate instruments, he decided to hand-carry them himself.

As the balloonist walked inside the depot, his instruments under his arms and a small satchel in his hand, but with the large and unwieldy barometer slung over his shoulder, he found the waiting room swarming with people. He assumed the crowd was there to see off a group of departing Confederate soldiers. But as he started toward the gate to catch his next train, the boisterous throng pressed after him. A man pointed at Lowe shouting that a stranger there had a gun on his back and some infernal machine in his hands.

The balloonist felt someone grab his arm. He turned to see a large bearded man wearing a sheriff's badge and brandishing a revolver. Lowe, not a small man himself, shook free of the man's grasp, demanding to know what was going on. He was told he was under arrest as an enemy of the Confederacy. For Lowe it was *déjà vu*, Unionville all over again.

The crowd was angry. The people were becoming extremely bold, as they usually did when in groups. Someone shouted out a cry to tar and feather the damn Yankee. A more strident voice hollered that was too good for him and demanded Lowe be hanged.

Sensing the mood of the mob, the sheriff whispered to Lowe that for his own safety, he must accompany him to the sheriff's office. The angry mob was reluctant to let go, but the sheriff brandished his badge and his pistol, and the two men pushed their way through the crowd without incident. Once outside the station they quickly headed for the lockup. The balloonist was placed in a cell, and his "dangerous instruments" left on a table in custody of the jailer. Lowe watched with concern as the guard, chomping hard on his plug of tobacco, fingered the strange devices with curiosity, blowing into the barometer to see if it made a noise. The balloonist was obliged to wait for the mayor, who was supposedly on his way to look into Lowe's situation, having been summoned by the sheriff.

After a considerable time had passed, the mayor and several councilmen finally arrived, dressed as if for official business and wearing top hats. Lowe was brought before them in a dim room with a large table. When they were all seated and cigars were passed around and lit by everyone but the nonsmoker Lowe, the mayor introduced himself as W. H. Boatwright. The prisoner was then asked his name and what business he had there in Columbia, South Carolina.

Lowe explained who he was and what he had been doing, stressing the scientific nature of his balloon flight. He also presented the safe-conduct certificate Representative Thompsen had given him back in Unionville.

The cigar smoke hung thick in the closed room as the city fathers mulled over Lowe's tale and his certificate. Growing impatient with the delay, the balloonist interrupted them to ask if anyone was acquainted with members of the faculty at South Carolina College. Lowe assured them he was known to several of the professors there, and to the president himself, who would vouch for the truth of his story. The group still seemed skeptical so Lowe added he had been working with Professor Joseph Henry of the Smithsonian Institution in Washington, D. C. At the mention of Washington, D. C., several of the members of the committee made a noise and spat, causing Lowe to realize that he had not helped his situation by asserting this additional fact. There followed another lengthy discussion and much cigar puffing; thereafter the group agreed to give Lowe an opportunity to prove he was not the spy they suspected him to be. A messenger was dispatched posthaste to the faculty at South Carolina College.

In a short time the president of the college appeared, accompanied by two faculty members. Fortunately for Lowe, all three men were familiar with the balloonist's work. The president even knew Lowe by sight, having attended one of his lectures in Charleston the previous winter, and was also a fellow of the Smithsonian Institution and a personal friend of Professor Henry. The educators were elated to find "Professor" Lowe there, albeit under rather embarrassing circumstances. They immediately began a conversation about Lowe's recent flight and then inquired about the progress of his proposed Atlantic crossing. The ties of science had proven stronger than the men's apparent political differences.

As had happened in Unionville, the mood of the town fathers immediately shifted in Lowe's favor. Cigars were again passed around, and apologies were made to the balloonist for the mean treatment he had received at their hands. Professor Lowe was told he would be detained no longer. Furthermore, the mayor announced he would present Lowe with a passport that would assure his safe passage through any and all Confederate lines. The document, which Lowe saved, and often produced when later relating this story, stated:

> Columbia, S.C., April 22, 1861
>
> This is to certify that Professor T. S. C. Lowe, now accidentally in our midst, is a gentleman of integrity and high scientific attainments, and I bespeak for him the courtesies of all with who he may come in contact, and trust that this letter, to which I have affixed the seal of the City of Columbia, S. C., will answer as a passport for him through the Confederate States of America.
>
> (signed) W. H. Boatwright, Mayor

The group accompanied Professor Lowe to the door of the jail only to discover that another mob had gathered in the street outside. The mayor suggested, as it was now too late to catch a train and Lowe would have to stay over, to avoid possible trouble he and the rest of the group would walk to the hotel with the professor. As had happened with his carriage trip in Unionville, Lowe's public appearance in company with the mayor, his councilmen, and several distinguished professors seemed to reassure the citizens of Columbia that "the damn Yankee spy" meant them no harm. Chatting cordially as they strolled along, Lowe and the group passed through the streets of Columbia without incident.

That evening Professor Lowe dined at his hotel with the professors he had met from the college. They sat talking until quite late about a wide variety of subjects, the least of which was the impending conflict between the two regions. Then the balloonist accompanied the party to the door, and everyone shook hands and said good night. Passing through the lobby on the way to his room, Lowe encountered an attractive red-headed woman, wearing a black velvet dress cut quite low, who caught his eye and smiled at him, giving him a clear indication she was ready for a night of frolic.

The balloonist had not been in his room more than a few minutes when he heard a soft tapping on his door. Thinking it was the strumpet, and wishing to send her away quietly, he opened his door a crack to speak to her. Instead he was greeted by a pair of scrawny "plug uglies," carrying clubs, intent on venting their anger on the Yankee. The crackers stood there with their mouths open, revealing a considerable shortage of teeth, apparently confused by the formidableness of Lowe's size, as he was more than a match for both of them. Looking the men squarely in the eyes, Lowe shook his fist and, using his firmest voice, commanded them to leave. Cowed, the two men turned and, without saying anything, ran off rapidly down the hall. He recalled the statement the woman in Unionville had made when the crowd there threatened him—that all the brave men had gone off to war, the only ones left behind being cowards.

The next morning Lowe found that his baggage had not been sent on, but was still waiting at the station. He stuffed his instruments into what space he had remaining in the sacks, willing to accept a little damage to avoid an incident such as he had just escaped from. After a thankfully short wait, during which no one seemed to notice him, the balloonist boarded a train for Louisville, Kentucky.

As the train crawled slowly across the western portion of the South, the scenes of mobilization revealed to Lowe's eyes made him realize that a war was indeed underway. The balloonist considered, with conditions as they were, that he might be wise to postpone his plans for a transatlantic flight. At each stop long lines of young men in gray uniforms, carrying weapons of every description, including the new muskets with rifled barrels, filed into the coaches.

The crowded station platforms were quenched with activity: politicians gave jingoistic speeches; bands played "Dixie," and other martial music; tufted bankers and businessmen cheered and waved flags; while mothers, daughters, wives, fiancées, and sweethearts, wearing their best dresses, cried and said good-bye. Off to the side, half-naked black men sweated as they loaded and unloaded bales, boxes, and barrels. Civilian passengers were shuffled back and forth between the cars, or made to disembark entirely, to make room for the grizzly farmers and beardless youths who had suddenly become soldiers.

The number of recruits that Lowe observed was staggering. It appeared to him as if the entire white male population of the South was going to war. The South's land mass, as large as that of Western Europe, and ten percent more extensive than the North's, was yielding up the flower of its manhood, hoping to make up in bodies what it lacked in railroads and factories. Lowe wondered where the North would find the army large enough to occupy its breakaway half, even if it could be successful in conquering it.

Swept on by their victory at Fort Sumter, the South was awash in a fervent wave of chauvinism. The war actually seemed to be welcomed, like the evil, anvil-headed thunderstorm that promised relief from the unbearable heat wave. Whatever the conflict might bring, at least the years of doubt and indecision were over. The grim horrors of war would come home soon enough, but first the unsophisticated folk would surge out, waving flags with glad shouts, as if the scourge that had come upon them was a cause for celebration.

8

Back in the U.S.A., on to Canada, Still Hopeful, an Invitation From the President

On April 28, 1861, Lowe arrived back in Cincinnati on an Ohio River ferry from Louisville. Stars and stripes now fluttered from many of the wharves and buildings along the riverbank. He was glad to be back in the Union after a combined train and boat trip that had taken five days. The travel had been less than agreeable, crowded as the cars were with Confederate troops moving in every direction. At one stop a string of rather ragged and filthy lads, apparently on their way to join a Rebel regiment somewhere, had streamed into his car. Finding no place to sit down, and perhaps sensing he was a Yankee, they had stood in the aisle next to him chewing tobacco and spitting, decorating not only the floor, but also the ceiling, wall, and window with their noxious juices.

One of Lowe's more bizarre moments came while changing trains in Nashville. Walking through the station, the balloonist had come upon a group of tufted politicians, excitedly engaged in discussions, who, assuming by his top hat and frock coat that he was one of them, invited him to attend a session of a special group of legislators meeting to determine if Tennessee was to secede. Lowe was tempted to join them, but did not, although he did fantasize being there and casting the deciding vote to keep the state in the Union.

Gone less than a week, Lowe returned to find the public interest in his historic balloon flight had all but faded. All talk was now about the Rebellion and the effects it was going to have on people's lives and fortunes. This was brought home to the balloonist on the evening he accompanied Murat Halstead and some of the other backers of his balloon flight to a meeting of businessmen concerned with how they were going to recover large sums of money owed to them by Southern plantation owners. They feared that if the war was to continue, their claims would probably evaporate.

Some voiced the belief that the government should muster a large force of troops and end the conflict quickly. Others were of the opinion it might be reasonable to recognize the Confederacy and bring about peace, despite the consequences to the nation as a whole. Jingoist speeches for both sides were given far into the night. A thick veil of cigar smoke clogged the air when the last whiskey glass was emptied and the vote was finally called for. A consensus was reached. It was unanimously agreed, amid much whooping and hollering, the vote being binding on nobody anyway, that the war should be pursued to the final victory, regardless of how long it might take and how great the losses in human life and property.

The balloonist returned to his hotel that night swept up by the patriotic zeal. He also realized that his dream of a transatlantic voyage would have to be put aside. As a practical man he knew that it would be impossible to raise interest, and especially money, for his project with the country in the war mood it was now in.

Lowe had seen enough of the South's preparations to know that President Lincoln's call for the states to place seventy-five thousand militia at the disposal of the Federal government to "restore order to combinations too powerful to be suppressed by the ordinary machinery of peacetime government" would not be enough. What the balloonist did not know was that the Union's regular army at the time consisted of a mere sixteen thousand men. This was a force spread out over the frontier, Indian Territory, and the coastal fortifications. An idea had gotten into Lowe's head that kept growing stronger. Remembering his boyhood readings about Napoleon's observation balloons, Lowe decided, since he had chosen to postpone his transatlantic voyage, to offer his services to President Lincoln for the purpose of organizing an aeronautical corps attached to the Federal army.

Sitting in the office of Murat Halstead drinking a coffee, Lowe revealed his plan to the editor. Halstead was excited by Lowe's idea and agreed to write a letter of recommendation on the balloonist's behalf to Lincoln's secretary of treasury, Salmon P. Chase. Recognizing that it might take some time to convince the War Department of the value of balloons for military observation, and that a lengthy stay in Washington could be quite costly, Lowe proposed to raise the necessary funds by making another demonstration flight from Cincinnati.

On May 8, 1861, Professor Lowe, with Junis Brown of the Cincinnati *Daily Press*, W. W. Hare, and Jacob C. Freno, whom he had known in Philadelphia, climbed into the crowded basket of the *Enterprise*. After a short flight to the village of Bethel in Clermont, the group landed and Ware and Freno left to return to Cincinnati. During the flight Lowe, who was usually quite tolerant of other people's idiosyncrasies, developed an intense dislike of Freno. He did not know why; perhaps it was the man's rather vulgar attitude. While Lowe was aware of the commercial possibilities of ballooning, more often than not he went aloft for the pure joy of flying. Freno, however, hopped about the gondola like a turkey in a cage, grabbing the ropes from Lowe and attempting to make the balloon go here and there, all the while describing one or the other of his moneymaking schemes. When Freno announced he had to return to Cincinnati, the balloonist was more than happy to be rid of him. Unfortunately Lowe would come to regret his relationship with Freno, who would reappear in his life again in not too many years, bringing him much grief when he least needed it.

Several weeks later, Lowe, accompanied once again by Brown, attempted another long voyage. The balloonist was hoping to use this flight to convince the War Department of his skill and experience. Blown north by unusually high winds, the pair drifted far off their expected course and ended up in Canada, near the city of Hamilton, Ontario. Already known in Canada from his ascensions at Ottawa, Lowe contrived to turn an unfortunate situation to his benefit.

Reading in the newspapers that he had arrived by chance a few days before Queen Victoria's forty-second birthday, Professor Lowe arranged a meeting with the mayor of Hamilton. As he was already there, Lowe argued, the city should invite him to stay and make a series of ascensions in honor of the Queen's birthday. The mayor agreed and funds were found to pay for the flights. Lowe's ascensions went very well and received a tremendous response. The Canadians were delighted by the balloonist, who had literally fallen from the skies into their midst. Paid generously for this exhibition, Lowe now had the money he needed to set up the demonstration flights he planned to make in Washington, D.C., for President Lincoln.

Lowe packed up his balloon and took a train from Canada to his home in Philadelphia. During the long ride, as the train rumbled across barren upstate New York, he took out his notepad and began to write down all his ideas for the presentation, positive the War Department would be most impressed with his ideas. What Lowe did not know was that he was not the only balloonist anxious to volunteer his services to the Union cause. The well-known aeronauts John Wise, John La Mountain, James Allen, and William Paullin were already in Washington pleading their own cases.

At the time, ballooning was widely regarded by the general public as merely a showman's art. Lowe was well aware of the fact that few of his colleagues aspired to anything beyond flying before carnival crowds. He realized it would be difficult to impress the politicians in power that ballooning came from the realm of science, the same as guns and gunpowder. As a scientist, Lowe was ready to have his balloons serve the cause of the military. He was confident that not only could his observation balloons help the Northern effort, but also that they would greatly reduce the duration of the war.

Back in Philadelphia, Lowe was disappointed to read in the newspapers that his friend and competitor, John Wise, called by many the "Father of American Aeronautics", and who had made his first flight when Lowe was only three years old, had already been in Washington for several weeks petitioning the War Department. As a schoolboy, Lowe had read of Wise's offer to use his balloon to bomb the Castle of San Juan de Ullos and end the siege of Vera Cruz during the Mexican War. His plan had been rejected, but Wise's name had become known to many influential people in the capital. If Lowe was to convince those in power that he was the one to set up the new aeronautical corps, he would have to lay claim to a superior knowledge of science. Moreover, Lowe knew he would have to be the better salesman, if he could get to the right people.

While Lowe was in Canada, his friend Murat Halstead had been active on his behalf. When he arrived at his home in Philadelphia, the balloonist found among his letters one from Halstead, stating that he had received an answer to his letter to Salmon P. Chase, the secretary of the Treasury. Chase wrote that he had spoken to the Secretary of War about Lowe's ideas, and they had been well received. But Chase cautioned that there was some difference of opinion as to what aeronauts were to be employed. Nevertheless he had assured Halstead that he would give his support to Lowe.

Halstead's letter to Lowe stated he was fully convinced that he should be the person to set up the aeronautical corps and volunteered to write another letter to Secretary Chase. Halstead wrote that it was "time science were employed to do away in a great measure with the embarrassments, difficulties, and dangers of sending out scouts who bring little information and that little very far from reliable." He encouraged Lowe to proceed immediately to Washington with his balloon and "there present a series of convincing demonstrations of aerial observation."

That evening, sitting by a roaring fire with Leontine and his two young daughters, Lowe discussed his plan for a balloon corps with his wife. He described what he had seen during his travels through the South. Leontine was convinced—from her experience in France and despite all the optimism in the newspapers for a quick Union victory—that the coming war would be long and bloody. Her husband had been away for more than a month, and perhaps almost twice been killed. Their time together was all too short. Now he was proposing to go away again; there was, however, nothing she would do to stop him.

Following Halstead's advice, on June 5, 1861, Lowe returned to Washington with the *Enterprise*. The capital was a bedlam of activity. From his train window on the way to Washington, the balloonist had seen bivouacs and military encampments in every surrounding field. The station was a spectacle of disorder. None of the trains arrived or left on time. Troops, hundreds of officers, and men wearing the varied uniforms of their regiments jostled off the cars. These were the factory workers and farm boys, led by lawyers and shopkeepers as untrained as they were, who had responded to Abraham Lincoln's call for volunteers.

In three months it was all going to be over, or so they were told, so they didn't want to miss anything. The men and boys poured into the streets like sightseers on holiday, smiling at the scattering of strumpets who eyed them boldly. If this undisciplined mob of citizen soldiers was the North's answer to the determined Rebels he had seen mobilizing in the South, Lowe mused, then the Union would surely need the advantage his observation balloons had to offer.

After first seeing to the storage of the sacks containing the *Enterprise,* and then settling into his room at the National Hotel, Lowe made a call on his friend Professor Henry at the Smithsonian Institution. Henry was glad to see the balloonist again and took him to his office. Wasting little time on pleasantries, Lowe immediately began explaining his plan for an aerial observation corps to the scientist. Henry quickly understood the balloonist's idea and asked pertinent questions about the details. When they parted, Henry assured Lowe of his complete support.

Lowe's next visit was with Secretary Chase. Chase greeted him warmly, indicating he was extremely interested in the professor's plan for a balloon corps. After a lengthy conversation, during which the secretary seemed astonished by many of Lowe's ideas, Chase agreed to bring up the matter with President Lincoln, warning he could not guarantee anything would come of it as he had heard there were already several other balloonists in the capital pursuing their own agenda for an aeronautical corps.

Lowe was pleased that at the least the wheels had been set in motion, even though he knew he still had a long way to go. The very next day Professor Henry brought Lowe's proposal to the attention of the Secretary of War, Simon Cameron, who also expressed interest and asked the professor to prepare an official report on Lowe's system of aeronautics. Secretary Cameron pointed out to Henry that he had already spoken to the Allen brothers and to John Steiner in April and found their aeronautics to be sound. More recently he had been contacted by John Wise and John La Mountain. Cameron confided that several of these men and their balloons were already in action. The Allens were on their way to Falls Church to join up with Burnside's Brigade, while the navy had jerry-rigged a barge into a kind of balloon carrier to take La Mountain down the Chesapeake Bay to Fort Monroe. The secretary made it clear, however, that none of the balloonists were actually commissioned in the army, but working as independent contractors under any regiment that was willing to sponsor them and, hopefully, see that they got paid. He also showed Henry plans that had been submitted for things like portable generators and balloon carriers and all sorts of other items for which the government had no money.

Shortly after his meeting with Secretary Cameron, Professor Henry met with Lowe in his office at the Smithsonian. Henry briefed Lowe on the results of his meeting with the secretary of war. Lowe sensed that Cameron had not been too encouraging and wondered if his request for Henry to prepare an official report on Lowe's system of aeronautics wasn't merely a dodge. When Lowe had his suspicions confirmed that other balloonists, his very rivals, were already engaged as aerial observers, he became very irritated and resentful. Lowe expressed the fear that he had perhaps arrived too late. He went on to argue that these other aeronauts were using wornout balloons and obsolete operating techniques. Moreover, they were attempting to prove the worth of aerial observation, and not even being paid for their services. If something should go wrong with one of these free lance operations it would cast doubts on his plan to organize an aeronautical corps as an official branch of the army.

Growing more angry by the minute, Lowe questioned Henry about the method his rivals were using to inflate their balloons. Henry replied that he understood that they were inflating them at gas mains on the streets of Washington and transporting the inflated globes to the front lines using whatever help and means they could find.

Lowe expressed astonishment at this, wondering how his rivals had not damaged, even destroyed, their balloons, towing them under such awkward conditions with inexperienced crews.

Henry informed Lowe that both Wise and La Mountain had presented plans for portable generators capable of inflating balloons in the field, but both designs had proved unwieldy and too expensive to build and operate. At this news Lowe allowed as how he had a design for a light, compact, and inexpensive generator, which he was ready to produce as soon as he could sell the government on the idea of setting up an aeronautical corps—with him in complete charge.

The balloonist left his meeting with Henry disappointed, but still hopeful of getting his opportunity to set up an official balloon corps. Nothing he ever achieved had come easy to him, Lowe reminded himself; he would not give up, but pursue this new goal with renewed vigor.

The afternoon of June 11, 1861, was especially steamy, even for Washington in the summertime. The humidity hung heavy in the air. What faint breeze there was only served to stir the dust that ran along the street gutters. Retired from the heat to his hotel room, Lowe was aroused by a knock at the door. Could it be the message he was waiting for? A room clerk handed him an envelope. The letter inside was from Secretary Chase instructing Lowe to "go up to the President's House, this evening as early as you can after getting this note." In the matter of a moment the balloonist's spirit shifted from depressed to elated.

Lowe quickly scribbled his own note and sent a messenger running to Henry at the Smithsonian, asking him if he would come along with him when he met with President Lincoln. Lowe wanted Henry there to assure the president that he was "a man of scientific standing, and the recognized authority in the field of aeronautics." Henry sent the messenger back to the balloonist with a positive response—he would be happy to accompany the balloonist on his visit to President Lincoln.

That evening, dressed in their top hats and frock coats, the two men presented themselves at the door to the White House. They were immediately shown in to the president. Professor Henry, being a well-respected Washington figure, was known to Lincoln. For Lowe, however, it was his first meeting with the tall, angular, self-taught lawyer from Illinois who was now, at age fifty-two, the sixteenth president of the United States, and the man who had been called on to "unite this house divided."

They rolled out Lowe's designs on Lincoln's large mahogany desk. Without saying anything, the president bent over his tall frame and studied them carefully. From the tired expression on Lincoln's face Lowe could tell that these were not the first set of plans, the first ideas, that he had been shown promising his armies the advantage, or perhaps even a speedy end to the war. Yet President Lincoln carefully examined the papers, displaying thoughtful interest, making comments, and asking questions. While most people, on both sides of the conflict, were presently rushing at each other blindly and unprepared, Lincoln's patient, rustic nature allowed him to proceed with a reassuring calmness that allowed him to accomplish things where others could not.

After what seemed to Lowe like an extremely short time, Lincoln turned away from the designs and asked Lowe what his next step was. A bit at a loss for words in the president's presence, the balloonist had his answer given for him by Henry, who asserted that Lowe would perform, completely at his own expense, a series of demonstration ascensions from the grounds of the Smithsonian, sending his balloon up under many different atmospheric conditions. The ascensions would be witnessed by distinguished scientists and military men, who would evaluate the balloon's practical value as an observation vehicle during battles. The balloonist agreed; he could not have said it better himself.

Lowe left the White House that evening convinced that he was now a "huckleberry above a persimmon," or a cut above the other balloonists he was vying with for the position of head of the aeronautical corps. While they were out conducting their free-lance operations at various unimportant postings, he had gotten the ear of the president. Lowe was sure that it was only a matter of time before he would be given a budget and told to organize a balloon unit for the army.

To pitch his program, Lowe convinced some of the more venturesome of Washington's government and army men to go aloft with him on his demonstration flights. Tethered half a mile above the Mall as the gondola swung with the wind, Lowe's more often-than-not terrified passengers usually clung bare-knuckled to the sides of the fragile wicker basket. The balloonist, accustomed to the swaying, cut a brave figure as he stood there, balanced, looking through his telescope, pointing out the Federal fortifications along the river from Chain Bridge south to Alexandria.

Soldiers could be seen digging breastworks into the dull red clay of a flowering countryside. From below, the sounds of drums floated up as companies of infantry drilled with military precision between the long rows of tents. Lowe knew that no matter how frightened the man in the basket next to him might be at the moment, that night at a fashionable dinner party he would tell a different story, speaking only of the wondrous vista he had seen, and of the clear advantage the balloon presented as a vehicle for military reconnaissance.

As successful as these demonstration ascensions were, they were mere rehearsals for the flight Lowe planned as his *pièce de résistance*. He proposed to take aloft a telegraph operator, with a long wire attached to the ground. From his high altitude, supposedly overlooking hostile territory, the balloonist planned to demonstrate how he could telegraph back to headquarters a description of the enemy's position. This information could be used by draftsmen on the ground to create a virtual map of the foe's deployment.

The morning of June 18, 1861, dawned bright and clear with a calm wind. Larks fluttered in the branches of the trees, as the clouds slowly dragged their shadows across the Mall. It was the perfect day for the spectacular ascension Lowe was planning from the Columbian Armory (now significantly the site of the National Air and Space Museum). This was the flight that he had announced would be dramatically different from all his previous ones. In the basket with the balloonist was Herbert Robinson, a telegraph operator who would transmit Lowe's message, and George McDowell, in charge of the equipment lent for the occasion by the American Telegraph Company. A half-mile of telegraph wire trailed down the *Enterprise*'s tether rope to another operator on the cool green lawn.

Carried on the lips of the curious, the news rapidly spread throughout Washington that a telegraph message was to be sent from Lowe's observation balloon to the ground. Crowds gathered in the street to witness the event. With the naked eye, onlookers could just make out Lowe in his basket, surveying the enemy entrenchments laid out beyond the Potomac River, his spyglass sweeping in a wide arc across the landscape with a grand showman's gesture. Then the balloonist began to dictate.

The people on the ground had become silent. Suddenly an excitement spread through the crowd as the spectators down front heard the first tentative clicking of the Morse code signal transmitted down from the balloon being received by the operator in front of the armory. The ground operator rapidly tapped out an answer on his own keys. A shout went up. The experiment was a success. This became the first time in history that a telegram had been transmitted from the sky to the ground. Professor Lowe sent the following message to President Lincoln:

Balloon Enterprise, in the Air

June 18, 1861

To His Excellency Abraham Lincoln, President of the United States

Dear Sir:

From this point of observation we command an extent of county nearly fifty miles in diameter. I have the pleasure of sending you this first telegram ever dispatched from an aerial station, and acknowledging indebtedness to your encouragement for the opportunity of demonstrating the availability of the science of aeronautics in the service of the country, I am your excellency's obedient servant.

T. S. C. Lowe

The ground operator sent up a message that the reception was perfect. A formal announcement of the successful link up was made, and everyone cheered again. Encouraged by his accomplishment, Lowe and his assistants stayed aloft for the better part of an hour, sending and receiving messages that were relayed to various points, including the War Department, General Winfield Scott, Alexandria, Virginia, and Leontine back in Philadelphia. For Lowe it was a masterpiece of public relations, greatly strengthening his position as chief candidate for the yet-to-be-created position of head of the aeronautical corps.

But there was yet much more to be gotten out of this show. Signaling his crew, Lowe had the *Enterprise* hauled closer to the ground. Then, with the three men still in the basket, and enthusiastically waving small U.S. flags, the balloon was towed, bobbing in triumph, through the streets now lined with wildly cheering crowds to the White House. There President Lincoln received the balloon group from out a second-story window. After shaking hands with the president, Lowe had the basket lowered to the ground, and the still inflated balloon moored on the White House lawn. Upon disembarking, the ebullient Lowe found a personal note of congratulations waiting for him from Abraham Lincoln, and an invitation to supper.

That evening a triumphant Lowe, trying his best to restrain his hyperbole, dined with the president and several members of the cabinet. When the meal was finished, the president remarked that he was extremely interested in Lowe's scheme for organizing a corps of observation balloons. Lincoln requested that the balloonist remain after the others had departed. The president indicated that he wanted to discuss the time it would take to get the corps operational and details of its employment. He was especially intrigued by Lowe's plan to direct the fire of artillery from the air, thereby enabling gunners to shell targets they could not even see.

Lincoln and Lowe talked well into the night. As the hour was rather late and, despite all the military presence, Washington was not the safest town; the president suggested to Lowe that he was welcome to stay at the White House. Honored to be the president's guest, Lowe readily accepted the invitation. Wearied with the cares of the nation, Lincoln showed the balloonist to his room and said good night. Although the bed was larger, and more comfortable than the one in his room at the National Hotel, and he was tired from the toil and excitement of the day, Lowe did not sleep well. He lay in bed staring at the ceiling excited by, and yet fearful of, the prospect of becoming the founder, and head, of a new branch of the military service.

In spite of his fitful night, bright and early the next morning Lowe was in action again, taking advantage of his balloon's mooring place to make several more ascensions from the lawn of the White House, demonstrating his balloon's capabilities, and campaigning to members of the cabinet and the military. Thaddeus Sobieski Constantine Lowe was now the man of the hour. The day's newspapers all carried front-page articles about Lowe's balloon ascension and his pioneering telegraph message to Lincoln. The same newspapers which had given little attention to the activities of the Allen brothers and John La Mountain in the preceding weeks now heralded Lowe's accomplishment as if it were a secret weapon about to change the course of the war.

The editor of the *Boston Transcript* predicted that the balloon-telegraph combination would enable a Union general to remain "accurately informed of everything that may be going on within a long day's march of his position in any direction." The *New York Herald*'s headline read "War as a Science—the Important Combination of the Balloon and Telegraph." The local *Evening Star* reported that "the aeronautical telegraphic enterprise in Washington has proved, so far, to be a complete success," and another article predicted that Lowe and his "telegraphic balloon" would "help to equalize the advantages gained to the Confederacy and lost to our side by the perpetual reports of their spies and the blabbering of super-serviceable newspaper reporters."

Wise, La Mountain, and the other American aeronauts who had been involved in demonstrating the balloon's potential were jealous of the attention Lowe was receiving and were quick to point out to the public that his idea was far from original. They cited a long list of precedents, beginning with the French Corps d'Aerostiers organized in 1794 and not disbanded until 1799; the balloonist Jean Margat, who had made ascensions during the Algerian campaign of 1830; and Louis and Eugene Godard, who flew French military balloons just two years earlier, during the Italian campaign of 1859.

Lowe's detractors called attention to the fact that many other nations had previously experimented with the use of balloons during war. The Russian Army had sent observers up in balloons during the siege of Sebastapol. The Danes and the Milanese had scattered political leaflets from balloons at various times. And the Austrian forces had sent balloons bearing explosives into the air during the siege of Venice in 1848.

As with most innovations, it was not usually the person originally conceiving the idea who was remembered; more often than not it was the person who most fully exploited the concept that was honored. Completely overlooked amidst all the hoopla over Lowe's showy demonstration was the fact that over twenty years earlier, in 1840, a Floridian named Frederick E. Beasely had proposed to then Secretary of War Joel Poinsett that balloons, in combination with a telegraphic network, might be used to track the movements of the Seminole Indians who were then waging a guerrilla war against the U. S. Army in the Everglades.

Apparently the idea was never tried. As far as anyone knew, Beasely's plan had been dismissed because of lack of funding, and the belief, probably correct, that once the Indians realized what the balloon was all about, they would have quickly devised a means of camouflage to conceal their activities from the Army's aerial observers.

Lowe was more than aware of all that had gone before him. Standing in his balloon looking down on the streets of Washington, he rubbed his hands together; all that his critics had thrown against him had been a blessing, only making him more determined to succeed.

9

Called to Action, Competition, the Army Runs Away

When an exuberant Lowe finally prepared to depart the White House lawn with his balloon and other paraphernalia, President Lincoln handed him a letter he had his secretary draft to Winfield Scott, the general-in-chief of the Army, asking the man to meet with the balloonist to discuss the possibilities of organizing an aeronautic corps.

By that time General Scott was a rather old man. With fifty years of distinguished military service behind him, he was still greatly esteemed by the nation. But he was not the same Winfield Scott who, on September 14, 1847, had cantered into the Plaza de Armas in Mexico City astride a magnificent bay charger, tall and resplendent in full-dress uniform with gold epaulets and white plume chapeau, while the military band played "Yankee Doodle." Even the humiliated Mexicans had applauded, as General Scott dismounted to accept the formal surrender of the Halls of Montezuma, thereby enlarging the territory of the United States by one-quarter and reducing that of Mexico by half.

Lowe found the country's "Grand Old Man" to be "very infirm, pompous and with many of the affectations which sometimes go with extreme age." The balloonist discovered it difficult to engage Scott's interest, finding the general's mind centered on the make-up of an army as he had always known it, and not interested in any innovations. In fact when Lowe first arrived at Scott's headquarters, the general refused to see him at all. And when he eventually did, he dismissed the balloonist and his ideas after a very brief hearing by pointing out the window at the rows of tents and drilling soldiers and saying he was busy "turning that bunch of rag-tag rabble into an army." In truth Scott was hoping that his hastily thrown-together army would never have to fight.

General Scott, a Virginia Unionist, disfavored a war of conquest that even if successful would produce "fifteen devastated provinces . . . not to be brought into harmony with their conquerors, but to be held for generations, by heavy garrisons, at an expense quadruple the net duties or taxes it would be possible to extort from them." Instead of invading the South, Scott proposed that the Union's supremacy at sea be its key to victory. He hoped that the war could be won mainly by the navy. The general planned to install a choking water blockade around the eastern Confederacy. The Union navy would capture all the Southern ports on the Atlantic Ocean and the Gulf of Mexico, thus sealing off the Confederate States from any possible aid it might receive from European nations.

The Federal army, on navy boats, would seize control of the Mississippi River, splitting the western states of Louisiana, Texas, and Arkansas from the rest of the Confederacy. Scott anticipated that a surrounded and isolated Confederacy would not want a war and quickly rejoin the Union. The idea of a conventional land campaign appalled him. The general warned that if we have to "conquer the seceding States by invading armies" the "waste of human life" would be "enormous" and the destruction of life and property . . . would be frightful."

Scott's plan would take time. But in the North people were growing impatient. Public opinion demanded an immediate invasion to punish the Confederate States. The newspapers fanned the flames of conflict; battles sold papers, not blockades. The journalists scorned Scott's strategy and derisively named it the "Anaconda Plan." Editorials asked why a general who had taken an army of only eleven thousand men to Mexico, invading a country of eight million people, and returned victorious was reluctant to engage a raw and untrained Confederate Army only twenty-five miles away. Other papers picked up Horace Greeley's cry, "On to Richmond!" suggesting that Scott's Anaconda Plan was a traitorous reluctance to invade his native state.

Aware of the controversy swirling around Scott's plan to blockade the South, in which his balloon was seen as playing no part, Lowe left his meeting with the general holding the man in little regard. Feeling especially put upon, the balloonist wrote in his papers, "It is almost impossible to realize to what extent ignorance sometimes finds lodgement in high places, and doubtless every inventor, every man who has a new idea, is destined to make a desperate fight for the life of his special ambition."

Lowe felt that he had demonstrated successfully that he was a master of airships, not only being able to fly them but to build them. He had ascended to the highest altitudes at which it was possible to live, and found the various air currents that allowed him to control the direction of flight of his balloons. He had also proved his ability to make long, rapid, and continuous journeys at high altitudes. His reputation as a scientific student of aeronautics was fully established. Yet he was frustrated that, despite having the most powerful influences behind him, he had not been able to convince the commanding general to accept his services. But where a lesser man might have given up, Lowe left determined to return, and to prove to the army that his system of balloon observation would be of great value to the war effort.

On June 21, 1861, Lowe received a telegram from Captain Amiel Weeks Whipple, of the Topographical Engineer Corps, instructing him to "proceed as quickly as possible to Arlington, Virginia, with his inflated balloon, his telegraphic apparatus, and other equipment he might need to make an ascension." Lowe was excited at the possibility of perhaps finally being able to demonstrate the value of his balloon under actual battlefield conditions.

Several problems remained, however, the least of these being how to inflate the balloon. The Washington Gas Company was not able to supply a main until the following afternoon. Once inflated, the enormous globe would have to be transported through the narrow streets, and over the Long Bridge to Arlington. It would not be a simple matter. However, after scratching his head a bit, the balloonist soon had the *Enterprise* inflated and ready to go.

With Lowe riding in the swaying basket scant feet off the ground, shouting orders to the inexperienced handlers, members of the 8th New York Infantry, the procession departed for the war. The strange parade made quite a sight as it moved at a snail's pace through the crowded streets of the city. The soldiers holding the guy wires tugged the bobbing airship around trees and fought to keep sudden gusts of wind from damaging the fragile envelope on corners of buildings. Helplessly watching from the basket, Lowe was made less confident by the knowledge that the Allen brothers had destroyed their balloon only the week before in a similar operation.

Finally, after much marching and maneuvering, to Lowe's relief, the group finally arrived at Arlington House with the *Enterprise* intact. Lowe and his tired men were happy to receive Whipple's orders to remain there overnight. At 4 A.M., however, the balloonist and his crew were roused from a fitful sleep and told to immediately move their balloon on to Falls Church.

In the predawn light the globe took on the appearance of some unearthly creature, swaying and bobbing just above the treetops, as the caravan of handlers silently marched down the highway. Hanging on to the guy ropes as the group walked along, one of the sweating soldiers was heard to complain that he had volunteered to fight Rebs, not be part of some damn circus parade.

Upon arriving at the Alexandria and Loudoun Railroad, Lowe was warned by the guards that it was unsafe to proceed any further as there were no Union pickets out in the direction he was heading. Not wanting to lose his opportunity to prove his balloon in combat, the importance of his mission having been stressed by Captain Whipple, and unable to find an alternate route to Falls Church, Lowe devised an ingenious plan. He ordered the guy ropes loosened, allowing the balloon to take him up to a height that would enable him to make an observation. As the *Enterprise* rose through the ground fog in the faint early light, Lowe strained for a sight of any Confederate troops that might be in the vicinity. Observing none, he had the balloon hauled lower and ordered the party to move on. With Lowe aloft in the basket, scouting with his spyglass from just above the tree tops, the group safely traveled the remaining two miles to Bailey's Crossroads,

When Lowe and his small unit, towing their large balloon, finally marched into the center of Bailey's Crossroads, he found the inhabitants there milling about in the square in a festive mood, laughing and clapping their hands as if some great joke had been played. A Confederate cavalry troop had been occupying the village for several days previous. While Bailey's Crossroads was technically in Rebel territory, the troopers had been freely helping themselves to the local's chickens and vegetables. When the Rebel troops had sighted the huge balloon on the horizon, they assumed that a vast Union army was arrayed behind it and ready for a fight. Fearing they were greatly outnumbered, the cavalry had hastily departed the area. Lowe had planned only to pause briefly to give his men a rest at Bailey's Crossroads and was at first mistrustful. However, at the insistence of the town's citizens, who had pulled out all the stops for his entertainment, his "brave band of liberators" was not allowed to leave for Falls Church until they consumed the lavish banquet which was promptly prepared for them.

Although no action occurred on this his first military outing with his balloon, Lowe did remain "in the field" at Falls Church for two full days. During this time he was able to make numerous ascensions without any problems. General Daniel Tyler, the commander of the First Division, which was occupying that area, sent an officer up with the balloonist, who observed the enemy's movements and drew an accurate map of the surrounding terrain. Captain Whipple and several of the other officers also went up in the *Enterprise.* The staff officers all concurred with Lowe's analysis that the balloon would provide a very useful means of observation during a battle.

On June 26, 1861, Lowe met with Captain Whipple at his request. The captain informed him that the Bureau of Topographical Engineers had concluded that it wished to immediately adopt the balloon for military purposes. Lowe was understandably pleased by this unexpected news. Filled with gratitude, the balloonist did not hesitate when Whipple asked him for a full account of his methods of operating balloons in the field, and for a cost and time estimate on balloon construction. During the conversation, the captain carefully made notes of all Lowe told him, and asked the balloonist to call on him again the next day.

When they met again, Lowe asked Whipple what conclusions his office had reached regarding the construction of a balloon for the army. The balloonist was informed that the government had decided to give their order to his old rival John Wise. Anger rose on Lowe's face when he learned, disregarding all the information he had provided the day before, the army's decision had been based solely on the fact that Wise's estimate for balloon construction had come in two hundred dollars lower than his. Sensing Professor Lowe's pique, and hoping to accommodate him, Whipple suggested that perhaps Lowe might be employed to operate Wise's balloon when it was completed. This offer had the opposite effect, throwing Lowe, currently the toast of the Washington dinner party set, into a callous rage. Filled with fury, the balloonist replied, "I would not be willing to expose my life and reputation by using so delicate a machine where the utmost care in construction was required, which should be made by a person in whom I had no confidence." Lowe assured Whipple, "I have greater experience in the balloon business than any other aeronaut, and would guarantee the success of the military observation corps if I were put completely in charge." Lowe's boasting of his greater experience rang a bit hollow in view of the fact that he was only a lad of three years when John Wise had made his first balloon ascension in Lancaster, Pennsylvania.

Feeling confident of his ultimate vindication, and not willing to abandon his cherished plans, Lowe continued to make regular balloon ascensions from the grounds of the Smithsonian. Lowe did not deny his self-esteem had been damaged. He remarked in his journal: "It is difficult for a man to give the details of his own work without conveying the impression of egotism, yet since my whole success lay in my ability to adapt original thought to operation, I speak of it not in a spirit of self-laudation but to be informative."

It was obvious that Lowe had little regard for the skills of his chief rivals, Wise and La Mountain. While conceding that Wise "had won a considerable distinction in his profession," Lowe considered La Mountain "simply a balloonist," contending that "neither had the least idea of the requirements of military ballooning nor the gift of invention which

... made it possible for me to achieve success." Going on to castigate his two rivals, Lowe claimed they had "assiduously courted the attention of whatever officer happened to be in charge of the Topological Corps." This was a paradoxical statement from a man who had used his friendships with Murat Halstead and Joseph Henry to gain access to Washington's inner circles and ultimately to the White House itself.

In the meantime, James Allen and John Wise had returned to the capital to present their case for becoming head of the Army's aeronautical corps. A confusing situation had now arisen in that Captain Whipple's superior, Major Hartman Bache, having been convinced that the formation of a balloon corps was inevitable, had refused to take responsibility for its organization and structure. His inactivity had further affected Captain Whipple. Lowe was sure there was a conspiracy against him and wrote in his papers: "Without a doubt there were some kind of influences holding back the decision of Captain Whipple. These delays were maddening. History was being made every hour, and I was chafing to get into action."

In truth, Major Bache, a weak person unable to make a decision when confronted by men with such strong egos as the aeronauts, had merely decided to wait, in the hope that Allen, La Mountain, Lowe, and Wise would play off against each other, the strongest aeronaut emerging from their self-induced competition.

The first week of July 1861 passed hotter and drier than any other in Washington so far that year. Thousands of marching feet turned the Mall into a gritty dust bowl as troops paraded up a massive, choking haze that oftentimes obscured the sky all day long. The main streets were clogged with troops passing through the capital on their way to Virginia. A few units were clad in the new blue "shoddies" of the Union Army, but most of the soldiers still wore the multicolored uniforms of their state regiments. There were the Garibaldi Guards in their dashing feather caps, the 79th New York "Highlanders" in tartan kilts, and the Zouaves in baggy red breeches, short blue coats, yellow sashes around the waist, and fezzes or turbans for headgear. Underneath their garb many of the men secretly had on a gray flannel belly band in the mistaken belief that it prevented dysentery.

In the shady parks officers strolled with their ladies, while martial music, popular tunes like "Yankee Doodle" and "John Brown's Body" wafted on the heavy air. Battle cries rang down the avenues as cavalry regiments rushed along at a trot in the hot powder, not intending to stop until they got to Richmond. The newspapers and the public clamored for action. Bawdy houses with names like the Blue Goose, the Haystack, Hooker's Headquarters and Mother Russel's Bake Oven did a thriving business. Meanwhile, the encamped men of the "three-month militia" roasted meat on their bayonets and grew nervous that the mayhem might end before they had their chance to become heroes. Everyone was sure that Johnny Reb would turn tail and run at the first sign of the Federal forces. Confederate skirmishers had been seen as close as the other side of the Potomac River. The men were ready to go—as soon as the big wigs made up their minds what to do.

Lowe had given the outside of the *Enterprise* another coat of his secret varnish and oiled the inside, and was continuing to make demonstration ascensions from the Smithsonian grounds. These flights were supposedly "scientific experiments," but were in fact pure public relations designed to keep his name in the front of influential members of the government and the military. The novelty of a balloon flight, however, was beginning to wear thin and the balloonist's audience was diminishing with each passing day.

Nevertheless, Lowe was more content than he had been in some time. Leontine had left their children in Philadelphia and joined him at the National Hotel. She had been reluctant to travel, as the train had to go through Maryland, a neutral state. Secessionists, opposed to the "Yankee army" passing through their state, had caused a riot in Baltimore and continued to sabotage the trains: Travelers to Washington, from most cities in the North had to change trains in Baltimore. There were several railroads and each had its own station in the city, which were not in close proximity. Passengers had to transfer either by carriage or on foot, through a rough section of town at the risk of being plagued by mean gangs of street thugs.

On April 19, 1861, the first volunteers to answer President Lincoln's call up, seven hundred men of the 6th Massachusetts, had detrained at Baltimore's President Street Station, where they were loaded on to wagons to be transported to Camden Street Station. As the convoy of horse-drawn wagons slowly lumbered down Pratt Street, some of the pro secession locals began to take objection to this apparent invasion by Yankee troops. Catcalls were shouted, and paving stones pulled up and hurled about. Soon a large crowd had gathered, and barricades of overturned wagons were hastily placed in the troops' way. People started pushing and shoving. A riot broke out. Shots were fired from somewhere, and several of the soldiers fell. At that the green and panicked regiment quickly piled from the wagons, resolved to make their way on foot. The troops ran, then turned and stopped to fire at their pursuers, running again and repeating the maneuver until they reached the safety of the station. Even after clambering into the shelter of their cars, the soldiers continued random firing out the windows.

When the pandemonium was over, nine soldiers and twelve civilians lay dead. To avoid a further incident, as troop movements from the North continued, the train no longer passed through Baltimore, but had been rerouted via Annapolis.

Worried about traveling alone on a train loaded with soldiers that might even be sabotaged, Leontine had taken advantage of a visit by their old friend Murat Halstead. The journalist had stopped in Philadelphia on business before coming to Washington to cover the war for his newspaper. The two had traveled on the train together.

Lowe was overjoyed to see them both. For a time he felt as if the war and his battles with the military bureaucracy were over as they wandered about Washington seeing the sights, dining and catching up on recent events. However, after only three days in the capital, Halstead announced he was leaving to join the troops at the front. Lowe went silent, dumbfounded. Halstead's revelation piled on agony for the balloonist, who anguished everyone was getting into the action but him. Leontine, on the contrary, was happy that her husband was where he was. She reminded him that war was a dirty and dangerous business, which he would do well to stay out of as long as he could. When the war was over she would be happier to have him with her and their children than to have him dead and remembered as a hero.

Turned out in their finery, the Lowes sat graciously sipping lemonade and eating pastries in the elegant front parlor of their hotel. It was cool for the 7th of July. The previous week had passed quietly, with no sign of the widely predicted Confederate attack on the capital. Lowe was complaining to his wife that to his dismay, on the previous day, Captain Whipple had detailed his subordinate, Lieutenant Henry Abbot, to muster the services of James Allen for a reconnaissance of the Confederate positions. This order had been given despite the fact that he was almost daily in the air in the same area. Lowe could not hide his glee when he related to Leontine, to Whipple's alarm, Allen's attempt to inflate his large balloon failed on account of a malfunction of his gas generator and an inexperienced crew. Nevertheless, Allen had attempted an ascension with a half-filled balloon, but the underinflated craft bobbed about so violently that he was unable to make any observations.

Lowe was pleased to learn that in his written report on Allen's failure to his superiors, Lieutenant Abbott had observed that balloons "may be useful in the coming campaign," but he felt a formal organization was required. The lieutenant recommended that "each balloon have, in addition to the aeronaut, a skilled officer/observer, and a permanent unit of men trained as balloon handlers." Moreover, Abbot concluded, the generation of hydrogen under field conditions was too difficult. He advised "inflating the balloons by city gas and moving them by wagon to the points where they are needed." Acting on Lieutenant Abbot's recommendations, Captain Whipple ordered Allen's two balloons back to Alexandria, where they would be attached to General Daniel Tyler's division as it moved toward the Confederate forces gathering at Manassas, Virginia.

On July 14 the smaller of Allen's two balloons burst during inflation. His larger balloon, in which he had made all his flights so far, managed to hold its air. The task of towing the craft to Tyler's headquarters at Falls Church, Virginia, had been handed over to sixty gaily dressed soldiers from the 11th New York Zouaves. The spirit of the troop was as bright as their attire, and they began the trip with enthusiasm, if not skill. The party had been on the road only a short time when a sudden, furious wind struck the balloon. Lieutenant Abbot described the ensuing scene in his report: "The detail, struggling and shouting was slowly pulled to the river in spite of their efforts, until the balloon in one of its stately plunges struck a telegraph pole. There was a puff of gas, and our work was ended."

Also ended was James Allen's hope of obtaining the post of head of the aeronautical corps.

Two days after the destruction of Allen's aerostat, on July 16, 1861, John Wise completed work on his new balloon. As requested by Major Bache, Wise had altered some of the details of his earlier balloons to better adapt the new design for military service. Fabricated with a double thickness of silk, the envelope's capacity had been increased to twenty thousand cubic feet. The rigging and netting had been modified to accommodate the need of observers and mapmakers. Also, the willow and cane basket had been covered with iron to protect the occupants from Rebel sharpshooters. John Wise and his brother, with the new war balloon in hand, reported to Major Bache as ready for service two days later, on July 18.

All this time Lowe had been occupying himself with reinforcing weak spots on the *Enterprise*'s fabric, especially in the area around the valve, and replacing some frayed ropes. He was just cleaning a paint brush after having applied another thin coat of varnish to the envelope when he heard more than the usual activity passing in front of his shop. The balloonist took a break from his work and went outside. Lowe stood there in surprise as he watched carriages and broughams loaded with top-hatted senators, congressmen, and businessmen, accompanied by well-dressed ladies, rush past him in a holiday mood. He shouted to one of the passing carriages, asking them where they were going. The driver slowed and hastily replied they were on their way to Virginia to witness the coming battle. He could not delay, as they wanted to get there before the Federals had won the day. The passengers, who were in high spirits, expected it would be a short battle, with the rag-tag Rebels being sent back to where they had come from.

Lowe hurried back inside and rushed his repairs to completion; if a big battle was finally to be fought, he did not want to be left out. The balloonist checked and double-checked his preparations. He wanted the *Enterprise* to be ready if his nation should need him to take part in the great dash that everyone said was coming, the battle that would quickly end the war.

Meanwhile, a mere twenty-three miles to the southwest of the capital, in the vicinity of Manassas Junction, General Irvin McDowell and a force of thirty thousand Federal soldiers were moving toward a sluggish, tree-choked river named Bull Run. McDowell, a former officer on Scott's staff had no previous experience in field command. Unlike most of the other officers in the army, McDowell was a teetotaler, who compensated for his lack of liquor by consuming huge quantities of food. General McDowell's mission was to find and destroy the twenty-thousand-man army lead by his former West Point classmate, the dapper, voluble Creole who had commanded the attack on Fort Sumter, General Pierre Gustave Toutant Beauregard.

The Confederate plan was for Beaureguard's army to move up the northern end of the Shenandoah River Valley and attack Washington. A Union force of fourteen thousand under General Robert Patterson commanded the Shenandoah Valley, believing they were holding in check the eleven-thousand-man Confederate army of General Joseph E. Johnston. Unknown to McDowell, on July 18 and 19 Johnston's army had slipped away from Patterson, doggedly marching from Winchester to the railroad at Piedmont, where they entrained for Manassas to link up with Beauregard. With the arrival of Johnston's men the Confederate forces at Manassas were now equal in size to the approaching Union Army. In the face of this, McDowell had only one brigade he could put his trust in under fire, the rest of his force being composed of poorly trained volunteers armed with smoothbore muskets.

At a strategy meeting at the White House on June 29, McDowell had pleaded for a postponement of the offensive until he could train regular "three-year" men. But public pressure was making it impossible to delay action on the Virginia front. Quartermaster-General Montgomery Meigs was of the opinion, "It is better to fight the Rebels here than to follow them into their own country, and it will be cheaper to stage a battle in Virginia than further south." Always a practical man, Lincoln agreed. As for the question of untrained troops, President Lincoln responded: "You are green, it is true, but they are green also; you are all green alike." He ordered the offensive to begin. And so the stage had been set for the first major battle of the Civil War.

Since the first week in July numerous isolated, but bloody, skirmishes, had occurred between McDowell's and Beauregard's forces. Neither side, however, had been able to ascertain the other's full strength. McDowell, who was awaiting reinforcements, suspected that Beaureguard may have received additional troops. However, his agents and spies had been only able to supply information that was spotty at best, and in the main contradictory. On July 19th, and again on the 20th, McDowell, who had made an ascension with Lowe in Washington, and was therefore convinced of the value of aerial reconnaissance, requested an observation balloon be sent to his headquarters.

Unsure that Wise's balloon was fully operative, and knowing that Allen's balloons were no longer in service, Major Bache requested that Lowe inflate his balloon and proceed to Centreville, near Manassas Junction, to join up with General McDowell's troops. On Saturday afternoon, July 20, a jubilant Lowe, excited to be part of the action at last, began to inflate the *Enterprise* at a gas main near the Columbian Armory. The balloon was nearly half full when an agitated Wise came running up and, waving an official looking sheaf of papers, ordered Lowe to remove the *Enterprise* from the main so that he could inflate his new war balloon. Major Bache and Major Albert J. Myer, Chief Signal Officer, had arranged for Wise and his balloon to immediately be transported to McDowell's position by a wagon team, accompanied by a squad of hand-picked men.

Lowe was furious. There was nothing he could do, however, but comply with the orders. The hour was well past midnight when a smug Wise, standing in his balloon's armored basket, was towed off in the direction of Chain Bridge. Despite the lateness of the hour, Lowe prevailed on the men at the main to finish inflating his balloon in the event that he might also be called up.

As dawn rose on Sunday July 21, reports began drifting back to Washington that a major battle was underway near Bull Run. Citizens of the capital awakened to the rude realization that rather than the anticipated Federal victory, an apparently stronger Rebel force appeared to be turning the tide of battle in their favor. This turnabout might lead to the capture of their city and a swift end to the war in favor of the Confederate States.

Tension mounted as new reports of Union losses trickled in. Too nervous to even sit down, an agitated Lowe paced back and forth beneath the tethered *Enterprise* awaiting his call. At last the moment came. Around noon an exhausted messenger galloped up, his horse lathered from hard riding. He presented Lowe with a packet of orders, and the news that in this morning's predawn hours, despite the efforts of his hand-picked crew, Wise's war balloon had become hopelessly entangled in some trees just past Fairfax Court House. Attempts to remove it from the branches had caused the bag to develop a large tear. Wise and his son Charles were forced to return to Washington to make repairs. They had come so close to the battle that they were able to hear the the noise of the cannon through the trees, but had been forced to turn back.

Lowe had no sooner finished reading his orders when a dusty detachment of engineers hurried up ready to transport the *Enterprise* to the battlefield. This was the call to action he had been waiting for. The balloonist was to proceed across the Aqueduct Bridge, past Fort Corcoran toward Falls Church, and then down the Warrenton Turnpike until his group made contact with McDowell's army near Centreville.

Not wanting a repeat of Wise's misfortune, Lowe exhorted his men to proceed carefully with the huge globe. The balloonist elected not to ride in the gondola, but marched ahead, carefully checking out every threat to the *Enterprise*'s progress. Even though there was little wind, he had the engineers give a wide berth to the many overhanging trees and sharp corners of houses lining the route. In contrast to the eagerness with which they had arrived, the engineers marched along slowly with their charge, hanging on to the balloon's guide ropes, sweating in the excessive heat. To keep out the choking dust, they wore their bandanas across their faces like outlaws .

Having successfully crossed Aqueduct Bridge, Lowe's balloon squad had advanced but a short distance into Virginia when they began to meet ragged groups of Federal soldiers streaming from the other direction. The troops were a ghastly mass of wretches running in fear, who had no intention of stopping until they were back in Washington. At dawn they had heard the chill scream of the "Rebel yell" reverberate across the battlefield, and seen the lines of the enemy streaming across the fields. Too frightened to even fire their muskets, they had run away.

Most swore, as they hurried past, that they were not deserters. When President Lincoln called, they had signed on for three months. Now, no matter if there was a battle going on, their enlistment time was up. Fast behind them, and clogging the roads, came the carriages of panic-stricken civilians: congressmen and their ladies, business-men in top hats, "parlor women," and newspaper journalists. Hun-dreds of people had come out from Washington in a festive mood, with picnic hampers filled with food and drink, to witness the battle from the slanting hills east of Manassas Junction. Lowe saw a con-gressman, fleeing himself in his fancy carriage, audaciously brandish-ing a heavy revolver at the exhausted soldiers, cursing at the men and calling them yellow cowards, urging them to stand and fight or he would shoot if they did not.

With this ever growing, chaotic tide moving against them and slowing their progress, it was not until 4:30 that Lowe and his balloon crew finally arrived at the village of Falls Church. The sounds of can-non and gunfire in the distance, which had been growing louder, and more frequent with each step they had taken toward Manassas, were now more isolated.

An officer in charge of pickets at Falls Church ordered Lowe and his balloon unit to a halt. As the crew rested in the shade of some trees, the moored *Enterprise* gently rocking in a field, few sounds could be heard from the direction of the battlefield. Although there were several hours of daylight remaining, and Lowe was eager to go on, the picket officer returned and ordered the balloonist and his men to bivouac. They were to remain where they were for the night.

Though disappointed, Lowe and his engineers were tired, so will-ingly set to erecting their tents alongside the road. Darkness was be-ginning to fall as the men gathered around the cook fires to eat their is-sue of beans, salt horse, hard tack, and coffee. The engineers watched anxiously from their circles as the steadily growing stream of wounded and stragglers tottered past them toward Washington, their uniforms caked with dust, and stained with sweat and blood. More than one of the balloonist's men was seen to put aside his meal, such as it was, his appetite gone. Wide-eyed and shaking, a younger soldier, who looked to Lowe like he could be not more than fifteen, darted behind a bush where his stomach hastily let go what he had just put into it.

Unlike the hurried panic of the earlier groups, the retreating men marched silently now in a slow, ominous procession. Gone was the joking and bonhomie that had marked their confident departure from the capital; how the roads had rung with song on their way out.

Occasionally an "avalanche," or two-wheeled ambulance cart, would rattle by loaded with bleeding wounded stacked like cord wood. The incessant jostling, which these spring-less vehicles pro-vided their passengers with, could do nothing but compound their injuries. The less fortunate died on the way. Those, however, who did make it to the field hospitals had to survive physicians who, knowing little of the need for sanitary conditions, simultaneously dressed and infected gaping bullet wounds with their dirty hands, and sawbones surgeons who indiscriminately hacked off wounded limbs with whiskey, or nothing, for anesthesia, while the next patient in line watched.

Lowe had gotten his wish; he was now "in action." As he lay in his tent on the hard ground Lowe realized that he would not sleep well that night, as he suspected would be the case with most of his men. It was not that he was missing the comfort of the National Hotel. The balloonist knew that although his corporal had posted guards, his engineers were no match for any Confederate cavalry troop that might come riding down the road on patrol. As Lowe pulled his blanket over him he was embarrassed to discover he was shaking. He thought at first it was the cold. Then the balloonist recognized the morbid fear he was experiencing at the thought of the savage and fantastic violence wrought that day on the battlefield he and his men had been headed for.

The next morning, at first light, a still tired Lowe pushed open the flaps of his tent to find the sky muddled with low gray clouds. It had begun to rain. The corporal in charge of the engineers, seeing Lowe awake, advised him that as it was bad weather each man in the unit was entitled to a ration of "anti- fogmatic," commonly known as whiskey. The corporal had read this somewhere in the rules. Never before having been "in the field" himself, the corporal, who had been given his rank when it was discovered he could read a bit, did not know that, despite what the rule book said, the officers kept all the whiskey for themselves. The usual way for a soldier to get whiskey, besides stealing it, was to be wounded. Lowe informed the corporal, as he had no commission, that he had no knowledge of the rules and, although he was not a drinking man himself, was sorry he had no whiskey to give them.

The rain, which had turned heavy, kept falling on the pitiful procession of wounded and frightened soldiers that continued to file past Lowe's encampment. The falling-back men were exhausted, their mouths hanging open, their lips cracked and blackened from the powder in the cartridges they had bitten off during the battle, their dilated eyes staring straight ahead in fear. The rain water had drenched the dust on their uniforms to a timeworn shade of gray. In the pale predawn light the grim, retreating column had taken on the appearance of a ghost army.

There were few officers in the line of march who would stop for Lowe's hail. Those the balloonist did question smelled heavily of alcohol, and claimed not to know the whereabouts of General McDowell, every officer being concerned mainly with keeping his own troops in orderly retreat. Having been provided with no uniform of any kind, Lowe must have looked out of place, causing the officers to wonder what a civilian was doing out there near the battlefield with a large balloon and apparently in charge of a squad of engineers.

In addition, the picket officer who had ordered them to remain there the previous day had completely disappeared, as had his men. A few of the officers whom Lowe had asked speculated McDowell was still at Centreville attempting to rally his forces. No one had the authority, however, to tell Lowe and his balloon crew to go there, remain here, or return to Washington. The balloonist considered moving forward on his original orders until he found McDowell, but he realized that his men and balloon would not be able to proceed up the road, sloshing in the deep mud, and against the huge landslide of troops, wagons, horses, and cannon moving at him.

Although the rain had not let up, about mid-morning, Lowe contemplated making an ascension, as he had done at Bailey's Crossroads, to ascertain the nearness of the Rebel patrols. However, as he had no orders allowing him to make such a flight the balloonist decided against it, not wishing to jeopardize his chance of eventually being put in command of the aeronautical corps. As the flow of marchers to the rear seemed to be diminishing, Lowe concluded it was only a matter of time before the Confederate cavalry appeared in hot pursuit.

In the days leading up to the battle, the balloonist had read newspaper stories written by enterprising writers, perhaps true or perhaps exaggeration to sell papers, about the terror produced by the Confederate's fearsome, saber-wielding "black horse cavalry." Having no desire to test the veracity of these stories first hand, Lowe realized his only alternative was to return with his men to the nearest secure Federal position. He decided to head for Fort Corcoran, the large, earthen fortification that had been established on the Virginia side of the Potomac, across from Georgetown Heights, to protect the access to the Aqueduct Bridge.

Lowe's group fell in with the retreating column, and began towing the balloon through the driving rain, the task made more difficult by the ankle deep mud that had been churned up by the hundreds of troops that had gone that way ahead of them.

10

A Rash Decision, a Crash, to the Rescue

After a painful four-hour march, during which the *Enterprise* nearly collapsed from the weight of water it had absorbed, the balloonist and his twenty engineers finally arrived at Fort Corcoran. Greeted with considerable confusion, Lowe was told to meet with the fort's commander. Not knowing what to do with Lowe or his balloon, the commander gave permission for the unit to remain there and to establish operations until they received further orders.

The next day, July 23, the weather cleared somewhat and Lowe, anxious to demonstrate his balloon's usefulness, began making tethered observation flights from Fort Corcoran. From his lofty vantage point, the balloonist could view the scattered remnants of the Union Army still retreating eastward. Pursuing Rebel patrols, however, seemed to be few and widespread. Lowe wondered if the Confederates might not have pulled back their forces to mass for an attack on Washington. The balloonist conveyed his suspicions to McDowell, who was now back in his old headquarters nearby at Arlington House. The rest of McDowell's staff agreed with Lowe's analysis, wondering why General Beauregard had not pressed on when he had the advantage. They did not know that the Confederate President, Jefferson Davis, had arrived at the rear by train from Richmond during the battle and upon hearing from General Johnston of a Southern triumph had urged a vigorous pursuit of the beaten enemy. However, after the Confederate Army had gone but two miles beyond Manassas, Beauregard and Johnston had called off the pursuit since, in Johnston's words, "Our army was more disorganized by victory than that of the United States by defeat."

Determined to further display his balloon's value by obtaining information about the Confederate Army's intentions, Lowe decided, although he had no authorization, to make a free flight from Fort Corcoran. The balloonist's plan was to cross over the Rebel lines, complete his reconnaissance, and then find a current that would blow him back to safety. This would indeed be a most critical test of his "rivers of the sky" theory. Failure, however, might cause him to be caught and imprisoned, or maybe even executed as a spy.

The evening's fiery sunset gave hint of improving weather conditions for the next day. Taking this as a good sign, Lowe decided to attempt his first ever free flight over Confederate territory in the morning. Before retiring he left orders for his men to prepare for a launch at dawn. The next day, July 24, shortly after daybreak, the balloonist stepped into the swaying basket. He would be all alone in the *Enterprise.*

When he arrived at Fort Corcoran, Lowe was able to send a telegraph message to his wife. Leontine had been relieved to learn he had missed the slaughter at Manassas. She decided to accept a ride from Washington with some military personnel and come out to visit him. Now, Leontine stood with the crew in the moist dawn air, feeling not unlike she had felt when she was pregnant and watching her husband prepare for his first-time ascension at Stevens Farm. The tiny woman tried to show a brave face, but concern was deeply inscribed on her features. Seeing her expression, Lowe attempted to reassure his wife that he would be in no danger, too high for the Rebel gunners to hit. Somewhat unconvincingly he announced he would be back in time for supper.

Leontine answered him with a sad little smile. Leaning over the side of the basket, Lowe placed a kiss on her forehead. Then he stood back up, checked his lines a final time, and shouted to the men to release the mooring ropes. The *Enterprise* rose slowly into the cloudless sky. As the balloon climbed out, remembering his first flight, Lowe put his hand to his brow and gave his wife a snappy salute. Seeing their commander's gesture, and not sure if he had received his commission or not, Lowe's crew of engineers jumped to attention and smartly returned his salute.

At about a thousand feet, a brisk wind began driving the balloon to the west. Startled Confederate pickets looked up in wonder as the strange globe floated over their lines. They fired a few shots, but knew it was useless as the balloon was well above the range of their guns. A true "Yankee spy" now, Lowe floated westward on a river of air, following the Warrenton Turnpike to Stone Bridge.

Below him the landscape was a scene of devastation. Farm houses and bridges were charred ruins. Corn that had been shoulder high lay trampled by the charge of cavalry and infantrymen. On a knoll in front of him lay the burned-out remains of Henry House, the home of a convalescent widow who had refused to leave during the battle, and been killed by a shell arriving through her bedroom window. The scorched fields were filled with the detritus of war: discarded wagons and cannon, and the bloating carcasses of men and horses. Crows and turkey vultures competed with the Rebel scavengers picking over the dead bodies. The hastily fleeing Union soldiers had abandoned enough guns, ammunition, and other gear to equip several Confederate brigades.

Like a malicious force the wind that had been propelling him ever so gently suddenly stopped, leaving Lowe hanging motionless over the scene of carnage. The balloonist sniffed the breeze. Even at this altitude the pungent stench of death wafted up from the killing ground below. His stomach began to turn, to tie itself into knots. The wind refused to move. It was as if he had been thrown into some clear space in the sky, from which he was not going to be allowed to be set free.

When Lowe was three he had found a rotting raccoon under the shed behind his father's store, the first dead thing he had ever seen. He remembered the smell and the circle of flies buzzing around the black mass where its eyes should be. He had screamed, and then ran, and thrown up where he fell. He couldn't run now; all the balloonist could do was lean over the side of the basket and release his undigested breakfast into the clear air. He watched as the grubby pieces raced each other to the ground.

Then the wind rose, still soft and gentle, but he accepted it as if it were brutal and fierce. It kneaded the air, got it moving again, pushing his gigantic globe along, its worn fabric flapping like a giant canvas sail.

Henry House Hill was below Lowe now. He had been told that this was the center of the action. Here, for several hours during the afternoon of July 21, Rebel and Union forces had mounted furious, but uncoordinated, attacks and counterattacks across this low mound. The balloonist drifted on, trembling with tension. He wanted to climb up to a higher atmosphere, out of this tortured air, where he could too clearly see the bloated bodies lining the entrenchments both sides had dug in the hard clay. Anonymous commanders had led their regiments into battle the previous day, but those who had not died, whether victorious or not, were part of legend now, and history: Ambrose E. Burnside, William T. Sherman, J. E. B. Stuart, and Wade Hampton. At Manassas they had faced each other in battle for the first time. And it was at Manassas that a former professor from the Virginia Military Academy, Thomas J. Jackson, got his legendary nickname, "Stonewall."

The wind stiffened its velocity and Lowe began to drift rapidly south and west, leading him over the enemy's positions, while he made copious notes on their strengths and movements. Numerous Confederate patrols spotted him and stared, but no shots were fired. In the silence of his passage the balloonist could clearly hear the oaths being hurled up at him by the frustrated Rebel pickets .

As it was late afternoon, and he had not observed the suspected massing of troops that would indicate a planned attack on Washington, Lowe decided to drop ballast, hoping to rise and find an easterly current that would take him back to Union lines. His flight seemed to be going perfectly. After a short ascent, he had caught a breeze that appeared to be heading him directly for McDowell's headquarters at Arlington. In his mind's eye the balloonist envisioned himself landing in triumph in McDowell's front yard and personally handing the general his report. While his rival John Wise was back in Washington repairing his damaged balloon, he had proven the worth of aerial observation. Lowe was confident now that he would be named to head the aeronautical corps. Convinced of his success, Lowe began to release gas for the descent.

Federal guards, seeing a strange craft in the sky approaching from the west, the direction of the Confederate lines, sounded an alarm. A skirmish line was set up to shoot down the weird intruder. Then one of the soldiers shouted to hold fire. He recognized the balloon as the one he had seen making ascensions when he was camped on the Mall in Washington. The captain of the guards yelled up to the balloonist to show his colors. A startled Lowe looked down at the nine muskets he was drifting over and sadly realized he had not thought to bring along a flag, nor was he dressed in a military uniform. Not wanting to take out his megaphone less the guards mistakenly think that he was producing a weapon, Lowe cupped his hands and yelled down that he was Thaddeus Lowe and had business with General McDowell. Without warning, the wind abruptly shifted direction, becoming a giant hissing lasso. An invisible lariat ensnared Lowe and his balloon. The *Enterprise* was being briskly pulled westward again, back behind the Confederate lines, and there was nothing he could do to prevent it.

The balloonist was now headed toward a burning orange sun sinking splendidly behind the line of low hills directly in front of him. It was a magnificent sight, but Lowe was not in a mind to appreciate the beauty. Not only was he facing a landing behind enemy lines, but also the prospect that it would be a hard, crash landing. He had valved off so much gas, and thrown out the last of his ballast, that there was no possibility his balloon would be able to lift him over the ridge he was now coming up on.

As he got nearer, Lowe could see that the deeply shadowed slopes were covered with an infinite carpet of trees. There was no place to land. Then, as if guided by the benevolent hand of fate, his balloon began drifting down in the one clear spot in the thick woods. Just when Lowe was about to thank the Lord for his kindness, the descending bag caught on one of the trees, spinning the balloon around, and tumbling the balloonist out of his basket at a considerable height above the ground. An astonished Lowe landed hard on the roots of the tree. He felt a sharp pain as his leg buckled under him. Holding tight to his ankle, the balloonist crawled into some nearby bushes and waited, breathing softly, listening for any sounds that might indicate that his descent had been seen and that he was being searched for.

After a half hour of crouching there, hearing nothing but the noises of crows and crickets, Lowe came out of his hiding place and hopped about exploring the immediate area around him. Finding nothing and no one, Lowe set about dismantling the *Enterprise.* Moving painfully in the fading light, he deflated the bag and managed to untangle it from the tree with only a few small tears. Carefully folding the fabric, which looked like parchment in the dull glow of the pale sky, the balloonist put the envelope and the lines in a neat pile next to the basket, then sat down on the pile to rest. By now it had become completely dark, and a swarm of mosquitoes clustered around his face.

Save for the shrill cry of the crickets and the occasional call of a night bird, the only other noise was the rumbling in his stomach telling him he was hungry. Fishing blindly in his haversack, the balloonist pulled out a ration of "desiccated vegetables." With no water to cook this in, he began munching on the compressed, cake-like form, his free hand fending off the insects.

Lowe wondered if his wife was aware he had not returned. Was she still waiting at Fort Corcoran or had she gone back to Washington as she said she might do so as not to miss her ride? Gazing up at an opening to the star-lit sky, Lowe cursed the trees for having snagged his balloon, but he secretly blessed the woods for the shelter it had provided him. Apparently no one on the Confederate side had seen him come down, or if they had they didn't know where to look for him.

The balloonist guessed he was less than three miles from the Union lines, but he would not be able to walk there with his bad ankle; and, with darkness having fallen, he had no idea in which way to head. Then there was the *Enterprise.* It was the only balloon he had left, and he was not about to leave it there and forfeit his chance at becoming the leader of the aeronautical corps. Lowe worried that if he should have to construct another airship, the war would be over before he was done.

Pondering all this and the other activities of the past day, Lowe became aware that he was extremely tired. As the hour was getting late, the balloonist wrapped himself in the stiff, wrinkled fabric of his balloon and lay down to sleep. He shivered. The night was cold. Lowe huddled in a ball and wrapped his arms around himself. The owls and night birds had begun a steady cacophony of sound in which he imagined he could still hear the distant noise of battle. He wanted desperately to sleep, but the day's scenes of violent destruction kept passing real and horrific before his closed eyes.

Lowe had been curled up only a short while when he was aroused. Awake, he listened to the ringing in his ears. He shook his head; he thought he heard something. The balloonist, afraid to move, listened to what appeared to be tramping sounds moving in his direction. It could be deer or a Rebel patrol searching for him. He lay still, hoping that whatever it was, it would not find him in the dark, wishing he had crawled into the bushes instead of under his balloon bag. Peering out from under the fabric, Lowe could see three shadowy human figures, almost on him. His time was up. Lowe was about to raise his hands and surrender when he realized, not having on a uniform, and not being officially in the military, unlike at Unionville this time he really was a spy. He would probably be given a perfunctory trial by a Confederate military tribunal, the judge sitting over a drumhead no doubt, and then be either hanged or shot.

The balloonist's heart beat faster as the men came closer. They were probing the bushes with the barrels of their muskets. Leontine, probably still at Fort Corcoran, came into his mind. Maybe the Rebels, carrying a white flag, would bring his body to the fort in a wagon and dump it out at his wife's feet, as her father had been dumped on the streets of Paris. Then Lowe imagined his beautiful little daughters sitting comfortably in their bedroom in Philadelphia playing with dolls. They would have to grow up without him; he knew there were no pensions for spies.

The balloonist's thoughts were flowing backward into oblivion. One of the dark shapes spoke in a hushed whisper. Lowe couldn't make out what had been said, but the voice could have been a shout; it did not appear to have a Southern sound. The figures circled his hiding place. Lowe was considering a pact with the devil, when another voice spoke, and the balloon fabric was slowly lifted from his body. He had been discovered. A panicked Lowe attempted to slide back into the folds, but he hesitated. The soldiers were speaking with an accent the balloonist recognized. A man, who appeared to be in charge, asked him if he was Professor Lowe, then introduced himself as Corporal Dokes of the 31st New York Volunteers.

The corporal told Lowe that his wife had watched the free flight from Fort Corcoran and seen the balloon go down. Standing guard duty, Dokes had also observed the *Enterprise* go in and remarked that the end seemed strangely dignified. There had been some disagreement as to where the balloon actually descended. The guards at McDowell's headquarters thought that Lowe had landed somewhere south of Arlington, near Long Bridge. They sent a telegram to Fort Corcoran, apologizing for almost shooting down his balloon, but explained that no one had notified them them Professor Lowe was going to make a free flight. A search party had been immediately dispatched to Long Bridge, but found no sign of Lowe or his balloon. Although she had never traveled the area, Leontine had been most positive about where her husband had gone down, and indicated exactly where to look for him.

As best he knew, Corporal Dokes figured they were only two and a half miles west and north of Alexandria on a farm called Mason's Plantation. Although this area was known to have many Union sympathizers, it was presently covered with roving Rebel pickets.

Seeing they were on foot, Lowe asked the soldiers where they had left their horses, assuming their mounts were tied somewhere outside the woods. Corporal Dokes replied that they were infantrymen, and had been sent because their commander thought a cavalry patrol would be too noticeable. This gave Lowe cause for concern. He questioned how they intended to get him back, pointing out that not only had he sprained his ankle on the landing, but also he did not mean to leave his only balloon behind. Dokes revealed to Lowe that his wife had worked out a clever plan, which had been approved by the fort's commander, but of which they presently could not give him any further details.

Working swiftly, one of the men fashioned a splint from a branch with his bayonet and tied it to Lowe's swollen ankle for support. Then he helped the balloonist hobble down the hill and out of the woods. The two other soldiers followed behind with the balloon bag and made a second trip for the basket. Lowe and his gear were hidden in a cornfield alongside a farm road. The balloonist was told to remain out of sight until shortly after dawn when a farm wagon would come for him. Heedless of any obstacles, as if obeying some inner rhythm, Lowe crouched there watching silently as the three soldiers from the New York Volunteers disappeared in what appeared to him to be an inexorably straight line down the road into the dusty darkness.

The balloonist waited in the field between the rows of corn. Above him the dark sky glittered with stars. Lowe had been thrown into a kind of transport in which the night seemed to him to be endless. Despite his rapture, he felt ill at ease. Unlike the dry woods, the bottom land had a cold dampness that crept into his bones and made his turgid ankle throb. He slid between the folds of his balloon and tried to sleep, but could not. The golden light of predawn brought the coldest hour and the fog. In his half-sleep the balloonist caught the sound of horsemen coming from the direction the sun was rising, the way to the Union lines. As they got nearer, Lowe staggered to his feet and moved to the edge of the corn. He would wave, not wanting to risk his rescuers passing him by in the mist.

Straightening up, the balloonist suddenly remembered the corporal's words. He had specifically said the plan was for a farm wagon to come for him. Lowe lunged back into the cover of the corn just as six riders rounded the bend in the road. He could see the gray color of their uniforms now, as dismal as the sky overhead. His hiding place was so near the roadway that the cloud of dust kicked up by their horse's hooves made Lowe want to sneeze. Choking as they went by, he held his breath, watching the feathered plumes on their slouch hats bobbing above the dust and fog. He had no quarrel with these men, yet he knew the consequences if they had found him here. In his head he reviewed the angry history of a nation's hatred for itself, then returned his mind to the oblivion of the cornfield.

The morning again sunk into stillness, until a flock of crows announced their arrival in the field. No one had traveled down the road since the six Confederate riders. Lowe was beginning to think he had dreamed the part about being found by the three men from the New York Volunteers. The dust, or the corn, or the cold night had caused his sinuses to run. He wiped his nose. Then he heard the faint clip-clop of a single horse, moving slowly, and the creaking of a wagon. The crows took flight, screeching, as a battered Owensboro drove into sight on the road. The balloonist peered from his cover, the sound of cicadas loud in his ears. With his hand he parted the corn and cleared the circling flies from his face.

It was indeed a farm wagon, but driven by an old woman, Lowe observed, obviously not the soldiers returning for him and his balloon. The woman wore a ragged dress with a shawl over her head, and kept her eyes down on the left side of the road as if searching for something. She was not looking left and right, only left, as though she was not randomly exploring, but seeking something she had been told was there, but not exactly sure where. The hag probably lived thereabouts and was collecting wood for her fire. He couldn't let her see him; she could be a Rebel sympathizer, or if not, might just offhandedly mention him to the next patrol that stopped her. The balloonist retreated farther into his cover as the wagon rattled toward him.

The woman was just about to pass when Lowe received one of those intuitive messages that a husband and wife seem to be able to communicate to each other. He looked up and their eyes met. It was Leontine. Seeing him, she gave no recognition. Her finger moved stealthily to her lips as a sign he should not speak. Then her palm told him to stay where he was.

Driving the wagon as if she had done so all her life, Leontine continued past her husband to the far end of the field, where she pulled off on to a dugway and into the cover of some bushes. Lowe had pressed after her, and no sooner had she tied up the horse, than he hobbled up to her side. As they embraced he whispered how impressed he was by her disguise, which completely concealed her pert and sprightly gaiety. Not only did she look like an old farm hag, but she smelled like one. Leontine explained that she had to mask her sweet scent of lavender with liberal helpings of cow manure. She reminded her husband that she had aspired to be an actress before she married him.

Lowe was happy to see his wife, but concerned that she had put her life at risk for him. He pointed out there was a good possibility both of them could be caught, and would be considered spies.

His wife told him she was well aware of this possibility and was sure if he had known about her plan that he would not have approved. This was why she told the soldiers who had been sent to find him not to reveal that it was she who would be coming to rescue him. The fort's commander had been reluctant to agree to her plan, but she convinced him it had to be her, pointing out that Rebel pickets would be less apt to notice an old woman in a farm cart, whereas a young man of military age would be immediately suspect—especially if he was stopped for questioning and responded with a distinct New York accent.

Perspiring in the now risen sun, the two hustled the basket and balloon through the corn and over to the wagon, and loaded them on board. Not able to be very helpful because of his injured ankle, Lowe was surprised by the strength and tenacity of his tiny wife. She unrolled a dirty tarpaulin, which she threw over the basket, balloon, and her husband. Then Leontine climbed up onto the seat and with a giddy-up and crack of the reins began down the road in the direction she had come from, aware that the slightest mistake on her part might deprive them of the possibility of escape.

Lowe lay on the floor of the bouncing wagon, unable to breathe under the heavy and filthy cover, sweating profusely, his ankle throbbing painfully. He recalled his last wagon ride, when he had been taken as a prisoner to Unionville, and hoped for a better outcome this time. As he was jostled along, Lowe's mind turned to Wise and La Mountain and the other balloonists. He wondered what they were doing back in Washington. President Lincoln needed to be convinced that had he and his balloon been able to reach Bull Run in time to make observations the outcome of the battle would have been completely different. Then his fatigued body surrendered to the deep lilt of sleep.

The wagon ride had suddenly become smoother, breaking the cadence of his slumber. Lowe's body was feeling less distress. He guessed they had turned onto a main road. The balloonist, wide awake again, kept hearing sounds that made him believe they were passing a considerable amount of traffic, most of it heading west, in the direction of the Confederate lines.

Leontine slowed down several times, which caused Lowe to hold his breath, but the Owensboro was not stopped and searched, perhaps because it reeked of cow waste. Each time she was hailed, he heard Leontine reply with the Southern accent she had affected, but yet with her slight touch of French. Lowe chuckled under his cover, as the sound reminded him of a speech he had heard in Charleston given by the Creole, Confederate General Pierre G. T. Beauregard. The balloonist could not remember a word of what the voluble general had said, but he could not forget the ease and grace with which he had said it.

Leontine had been stopped several times, and allowed to pass without her wagon being searched. Assuming she was headed in the right direction, each stoppage had caused Lowe, motionless and breathless under his filthy cover, to revise upward their numerical chance of a successful escape. As the wagon jounced along, Lowe had ceased to think of his imminent demise, but about the more practical need of a chamber pot.

It was not until late afternoon that the Lowes finally made contact with Union forces, Mrs. Lowe having wandered about the landscape not sure of her way, and sometimes retracing her route to avoid Rebel pickets. A cavalry patrol had been sent out to meet them. Transferring to a faster carriage, Lowe and his wife, now minus her disguise, were escorted by the patrol to Arlington House. There Lowe gave General McDowell his report, including not only all he had seen of the Confederate forces, but also the details of his forced landing behind enemy lines and his daring rescue by his wife. McDowell was relieved to have Lowe's information on the enemy troops, confirming his belief that the Confederate Army was not moving to attack the capital. More importantly for the balloonist, the general agreed with Lowe's assessment—that had a Union observation balloon been in the air during the Battle of Bull Run the outcome might conceivably have ended in a more favorable manner.

In subsequent weeks the Southern newspapers would have a field day seeking scapegoats for the Confederate Army's failure to "follow up the victory [at Bull Run] and take Washington." An indelicate row developed among the followers of each of the principals—Beauregard, Johnston, and Davis—blaming one or the other for the inaction, a controversy that continues to this day. However, the argument over the failure to pursue had not dimmed the South's hope for ultimate victory. The first major battle of the Rebellion had only strengthened the belief of many Southerners that "one Johnny Reb could lick any number of damn Yankees."

In fact, the disagreement between the two sides had become so pronounced that they could not even agree on the name of the bloody battle they had just fought. The Confederates called it Manassas, after the town that had been their headquarters, while the Union forces referred to it as Bull Run, the name of the sluggish river that meandered through their lines.

In view of the great battles yet to come, the casualties on both sides were small. The Confederates had about 400 killed and 1,600 wounded, of whom 225 would subsequently die. The Union losses were approximately 625 killed or mortally wounded and 950 wounded. More than 1,200 men were captured.

Although many in the South were dissatisfied with the strategic results of Manassas/Bull Run, the battle did postpone for a further eight months any Union attempt to invade Virginia's heartland.

In the North the news of the defeat was met with shame and grief. The day became known as "Black Monday." Horace Greeley, whose *New York Tribune* had done so much to incite the government to its untimely action, drafted a somber letter to President Lincoln: "On every brow sits sullen, scorching, black despair. . . . If it is best for the country and for mankind that we make peace with the rebels, and on our own terms, do not shrink even from that."

11

A Note From Lincoln, a Burst Balloon, McClellan

Immediately upon arriving back in Washington, the Lowes were surprised to learn that news of their exploits had preceded them. The description of their adventure had been circulated by Halstead, who peddled their story to all the newspapers. Lowe's daring flight and his wife's more daring rescue were the talk of the capital, a town desperately looking for any positive spin on the recent tragic events that had occurred at Bull Run.

Lowe's report that his balloon flight over Confederate territory had revealed no mass concentration of troops preparing for an immediate attack on Washington was even more welcome news. People stopped packing their valuables for a fast, and maybe permanent, trip out of the city. A round of parties was given to celebrate McDowell's "victory," at which Lowe and his wife were honored guests. The balloonist had no doubt now that he would be named head of the aeronautical corps.

On July 25 President Lincoln summoned Lowe to the White House. He congratulated the balloonist on his brave reconnaissance flight and acknowledged the nation's indebtedness to him for the valuable information he brought back. Frustrated by the defeat at Bull Run, the president speculated, "Knowledge of the enemy's troop movements, such as later had been supplied by observation from your balloon, might have turned the tide of the battle, had you not met with delays and been able to make a timely deployment." Lowe agreed and detailed to the president the chaos that had reigned as the three civilian aeronauts tried to operate free-lance under the loose control of Captain Whipple and Major Bache.

The president stated: "I wish to avoid such problems in the future, so am ready to set up a permanent balloon corps. I would like you to contact the head of the army, General Winfield Scott, and arrange the matter with him." Lincoln was aware he had sent Lowe to see General Scott once before and that the balloonist had been rebuffed. Now, fully convinced of the need for a balloon observation corps, the president asked Lowe to again present his plan. To that end the president took out one of his personal calling cards and wrote a note on the back: "Will General Scott please see Professor Lowe once more about his balloon?" It was a simple message, but there was no ambiguity about its intent, couched as it was in the plain language so characteristic of Abraham Lincoln.

Armed with this note, Lowe went to Scott's headquarters in the War Department and presented himself to the general's orderly. The balloonist waited in the outer room, anxiously going over in his mind what he was going to say to the "Grand Old Man" when he was finally escorted into his presence. However, he need not have worried as the aide returned saying General Scott was too busy to see him now, and that he should come back in a little while.

When he returned a short time later, Lowe found a different orderly, but received the same reply. Returning a third time, the balloonist was told that the general was dining and could not receive any visitors. On his fourth visit Lowe was informed that the general was napping and did not wish to be disturbed.

Sensing he was being given the runaround, Lowe returned to the White House in a bit of a huff. The president had been anticipating the results of Lowe's conference with General Scott and had him ushered in to his office despite an anteroom full of waiting callers. Lowe related to the president the difficulty he experienced in trying to meet with the general. Lincoln, who was quite familiar with Scott's procrastinations, jumped up from behind his desk, clamped his tall silk hat on his head, and ordered Lowe to follow him, adding that he proposed to find out just what was wrong with General Scott.

With the balloonist in tow, the president exited by a side door to avoid being seen. Then the two strode to the the War Department at such a fast pace that Lowe, not a small man himself, had difficulty in keeping up with Lincoln's long legs.

When the two marched into Scott's outer office, the orderly, who had previously displayed a rather casual, almost annoyed attitude, leapt to his feet and saluted, calling out in a loud voice: "The President of the United States." The visitors were immediately ushered into Scott's presence. Appearing not quite awake, Scott gave them a befuddled look. Then realizing who had arrived, immediately stood and saluted.

Having gained Scott's full attention, President Lincoln immediately came to the substance of the meeting. He told the general, Professor Lowe, who was his friend, was presently engaged in organizing an aeronautical corps for the army, of which he was to become the head. He wished the general to facilitate Lowe's work in all ways possible. Lincoln also asked Scott to write two letters: one to Captain John Dalghren, the commandant of the Navy Yard; and a second to Army Quartermaster Montgomery Meigs, instructing them to provide Professor Lowe with the materials necessary to equip his new balloon corps to operate on land and water.

The old general nodded; Lowe was not sure if he was in agreement or simply falling back asleep. Then Scott stood and bowed graciously, saying he would be happy to comply with the president's directive. Going to the door, the general ordered his aide to call for his secretary.

As they waited Lowe went over the details of his plan, which seemed to interest the general less than the cigar he had just lit. When his secretary arrived, the general, with Lincoln helping with the particulars, drafted the orders to the men the president had specified. The two documents were completed and reread. Then the ink was blotted, and the letters folded neatly and handed over to Lowe to deliver. The mechanism had been put in motion for Lowe, although not yet thirty years of age, to become the commander of the nation's newest military branch, the Corps of Aeronautics of the United States Army.

An excited Lowe returned to his hotel room and showed the letters to his wife. Leontine was happy for him and suggested that as his new duties would doubtless keep him very busy, she would return to their children while the trains to Philadelphia were still running. Showering her with hugs and kisses, Lowe waxed poetically about how much he would miss his sweet wife, and how sorry he was to see her go. But Leontine could tell from the look in his eyes that, despite his love for her, his current passion was his new post and she would be better off out of the way. Lowe was filled with enthusiasm for the undertaking that President Lincoln had thrust on him, and eager to demonstrate what his balloons could do to support the Union cause.

The balloonist's zest, however, would be short-lived. Although his passion moved him more than he was willing to concede, in a matter of days Lowe determined that the difficulties he had experienced in arriving at his new position paled in comparison to the difficulties that now faced him as he attempted to carry out the tasks that accompanied this post. He was soon ensnared in the trap of military red tape. The problems the new chief aeronaut had to deal with were not only technical matters concerning the balloons, but also he was forced to deliberate on a considerable number of other things that he considered distractions, such as politics, finances, and even the idiosyncrasies of his personnel.

Despite the great complexity of Lowe's mind when it came to dealing with practical matters and inventions, he was on the whole lacking in the judgment of human nature. That so many disparate qualities could exist among the people he had to work with was a never-ending fascination to the balloonist. While he strove to understand them, most of the times he realized he did not even understand himself.

The Aeronautical Corps's operations were to be carried out under the command of the Topographical Engineers. Apparently neither Lincoln nor anyone else had directed a letter be sent to the highest ranking officers of this service officially informing them of Lowe's appointment. Or perhaps a letter had been sent, but reflecting the military's resentment at President Lincoln's intervention, it had been willfully ignored. Early on, an untenable situation developed between Lowe and some of these officers, who had supported La Mountain, and who freely expressed their disagreement with Lincoln's decision.

On July 29 Lowe received an order from Captain Whipple of the Topographical Engineers to report to Arlington with his balloon ready for duty within twenty-four hours. A crew of twenty engineers was to be provided to transport the inflated aerostat. The balloonist replied immediately in the affirmative, but not without protesting that the *Enterprise* was now too old to be used under combat conditions, and further, the damage from his forced landing behind Rebel lines had not been fully repaired.

Captain Whipple informed Lowe that the War Department believed that the Confederate army had moved uncomfortably close to Washington and was preparing for an attack on the capital. He impressed on Lowe the need for an observation balloon to be sent up as soon as possible. Wishing to serve his country, and unwilling to disobey Whipple's order, although he had received as yet no military commission, the balloonist hastily set about making the necessary repairs to the *Enterprise*'s envelope.

The special varnish he had applied should have had a second day to dry, but there was no time. The next morning Lowe inflated the balloon from the gas main at Columbian Armory and started his march toward Arlington. In the distance a line of thunderstorms could be seen mobilizing on the horizon. Scanning the sky, the balloonist studied the dark clouds converging on the area and urged his troop of engineers to be extremely careful. As the procession moved through the streets in relative silence, Lowe caught the breath of ozone in the steely air. The smell of rain came in on a moist fresh breeze. He watched from his swaying basket as the wind picked up and a black anvil drifted overhead. The storms were all around him now. Lowe considered the alternatives, and decided, on account of the urgency of Whipple's request for a balloon observation, that he had no alternative but to have his men continue on with their transport.

Halfway to Arlington the balloonist felt the temperature dropping rapidly and knew it would be only a matter of minutes before the fury of the storm would be on them. Jumping from the gondola, Lowe called an immediate halt to the march. As the wind whipped about wildly, the men struggled to hold on to the ropes in the heavy gusts. He gave the order to deflate the bag. But his decision was too late. The cloudburst broke with thunder, lightning, and torrential rain. Lowe could only watch as, despite the men's best efforts, the fierce winds ripped the partially collapsed balloon from the engineers' hands and flung it into some overhanging trees. Entrapped there, the *Enterprise* flailed about defenselessly as the intense downpour battered it on the limbs, ripping huge holes in the weary balloon's threadbare fabric.

When the storm finally passed, streaming out the last streaks of its power into the clear air, the balloonist and his men gathered the remnants of the battered *Enterprise* and carried it back to the shop. Lowe felt a great sadness at the loss of this balloon that had taken him so far. It was as if an old friend had died. He also had a sense of guilt at the hubris that made him take the balloon out in what he knew to be unsafe conditions. He had become nervous and unstrung, and carried on when it was clear that he should have aborted the mission. His better judgment had told him not even to attempt a flight until the *Enterprise* had been repaired properly. But he had persisted, unwilling to earn the disfavor of Captain Whipple.

Upon learning that Lowe's balloon had been destroyed, Captain Whipple became furious. On August 1 he sent a telegram to his superiors, Majors Woodruff and Bache, stating he had had enough, remarking erroneously, "Lowe's balloon filled at our expense has burst." Whipple claimed that despite "my honest attempts to work with three different balloonists, before, during, and after the Battle of Bull Run, I have been disappointed each time." The captain wanted nothing more to do with the balloon experiments. Whipple had come to the conclusion that the balloon was "too delicate and temperamental an instrument to operate under field conditions," and recommended totally abandoning the program. However, at the time he wrote his scathing analysis Whipple was unaware of Lowe's meeting with Lincoln and of the president's interest in the balloon corps. Nor was he aware of the measures General Scott had already taken to comply with Lincoln's directive. Also, Whipple had not counted on Lowe's friends in high places. Concerned that the destruction of the *Enterprise* and that his failure to make the observation ascensions might have fatally damaged the idea of a balloon corps, Lowe requested that Henry write a letter to Whipple on his behalf.

Professor Henry established that Lowe's failure to arrive in Arlington with his balloon as requested was due entirely to a severe and unexpected thunderstorm. He reaffirmed his continued belief in Lowe's ability by closing his letter with the following paragraph:

> Mr. Lowe came to this city with the implied understanding that, if the experiments he exhibited were successful, he would be employed. He has labored under great disadvantages, and has been obligated to do all that he has done, without money. From the first he has said that the balloon he now has was not sufficiently strong to bear the pressure of a hard wind, although it might be used with success in favorable conditions and in perfectly calm weather. I hope that you will not give up the experiments and that you will be enabled, even with this balloon, to do enough to prove the importance of this method of observation, and to warrant the construction of a balloon better adapted to the purpose.

Captain Whipple forwarded Professor Henry's letter to his superior, Major Bache, where it was put in Lowe's file, along with letters from a number of others from America's scientific leaders, including Dr. Cresson from the Franklin Institute, who opined that Lowe was "unsurpassed in the requisite qualifications for military aeronautics."

 In possession of a surfeit of such glowing letters, and faced with President Lincoln's clear wish to go ahead with the balloon program, Bache had no other alternative but to ignore Whipple's recommendation to do away with the aeronautical corps.

At Major Bache's request, on August 2, 1861, Lowe met with the major in his office. Lowe had been apprehensive as he headed for the meeting considering all that had gone wrong in the previous weeks. Lowe's fears, however, were unfounded as the major had some good news. Bache informed the balloonist that the army wished to contract with him for the construction of a new war balloon. In addition, Lowe would receive "five dollars per day during the time it takes to construct the balloon, to be raised to ten dollars, when the balloon is finished and you enter service as an official military aeronaut." Lowe's salary would be paid by the Topographical Engineers, as would all the costs related to the construction of the balloon and the purchase of the required supplies and equipment.

An elated Lowe rushed back to Philadelphia. He planned to construct the balloon at his facility there, as his Hoboken shop had been closed for lack of orders and the workers going off to war. But best of all, he was looking forward to spending some time with Leontine and his rapidly growing daughters. While he assumed an air of gaiety and bravado at home, Lowe's ever-increasing absences, the constant problems with his superiors, and the risks he was putting himself to, which he had to conceal, were making it difficult for him to know how to deal with his own family. Increasingly the subject uppermost in Lowe's mind was becoming himself. Waves of loneliness, feelings of discontent over his situation, and dissatisfaction with the progress of organizing a balloon corps seemed at times to overwhelm him. Lowe was painfully aware that such spells of despair were failings in and of themselves; however, he was at a loss as to know what to do about it.

Leontine too was faced with similar problems, but put on a brave face and did not reveal her fears to her husband, although she did confide that she often sobbed uncontrollably when he was away.

There were some days during his stay when the balloonist was calm and contemplative, and time passed happily with his family. These usually were days warm with sun, when the horizon swept golden in the gap between the houses. But such days were becoming fewer and fewer. Lowe would not stay long in Philadelphia, only long enough to finish his balloon. Once again his career would take precedence over his family. He was anxious to return to Washington, worried that in his absence someone else might be given command of the aeronautical corps. His home life would have to wait until the war was over to be straightened out.

Lowe put in long hours, feverishly working at his shop. While the time was short, and the work intense, Lowe was careful to maintain his standard of craftsmanship and detail. A group of women was employed to cut the silk into strips, from the balloonist's pattern, and sew them together with reinforced seams. When the envelope was completed, a team of men gave the outside four coats of Lowe's special varnish to make it airtight. Then the inside was scrubbed with a light oil to keep it flexible, a technique which the balloonist himself had perfected after considerable experimentation.

The cost of constructing the balloon was high for the period, but, as most often the case in times of war, cost was no object. Price for the silk used in the new balloon came to over $500, and the netting was another $200. The wicker basket, slightly larger than the gondola on the *Enterprise*, was woven by craftsman for $12. Sandbags, a considerable number of which were thrown out, and not retrieved, on each flight, cost 70 cents each.

By August 28, less than two weeks after receiving the order, Lowe would be back in Washington with his new war balloon which he had named the *Union*. With a capacity of twenty-five thousand cubic feet, the new balloon was somewhat smaller than the *Enterprise*. Lowe's plan was that it would be a prototype for a series of balloons that could be constructed in a shorter period of time and be more maneuverable in the field. The *Union* was also stronger, being made of the best India silk, with linen network, and three guy ropes of manila cordage fifteen hundred feet in length.

Hoping to avoid the confusion which saw him nearly shot down by his own side when he drifted back from the Confederate lines after his first free flight, Lowe hired an artist to decorate the pear-shaped bag in a clearly Federal patriotic motif. The tan silk of the envelope was covered over with red, white, and blue painted stars and stripes, with the name *Union* featured in large letters. The reinforced basket was painted red with white stars.

The timing of Lowe's return to Philadelphia could not have been better. In the weeks after Bull Run it was as if the two warring sides had taken a breather. The Confederate victory had left their commanders feeling as if the next move was up to the Yankees. In Washington the new head of the army, General George McClellan, filled with his own importance and beginning to have political ambitions, was attempting to create an efficient fighting force. The ninety-day militia regiments had been demobilized and sent home. President Lincoln had drafted an additional seventy-five thousand men for a three-year period.

George McClellan, who previously had left the army to work for the railroads and eventually become head of the Illinois Central, was an old acquaintance of Abraham Lincoln. On July 27 the president had assigned McClellan to replace the luckless McDowell as commander of what now was being called the Army of the Potomac. A West Point graduate, McClellan had resigned his army commission, but at the outbreak of the Rebellion he had returned to take command of the Ohio Volunteers. After a brief campaign, McClellan had successfully cleared western Virginia of what scant Confederate forces were there. It was a small victory, but a victory nonetheless, coming at a time when the Union was badly in need of successes.

General McClellan's new post, however, was not without its difficulties. By August 13, a little more than two weeks after he had taken over the Army of the Potomac, McClellan had been faced with a mutiny in three regiments that had threatened to spread to the entire unit. The insurrection had begun with the 79th New York Highlanders. They had become disgruntled after Bull Run. The unit had fought bravely in that bloody battle, losing nearly 200 of their 750 men, including their commander. As part of the retreating column in the heavy rain of July 22, they had taken shelter in a barn. When the brigade commander arrived, then Colonel William T. Sherman, the men of the 79th were ordered out of the barn to make room for the horses of Sherman and his staff. The men had been forced to sleep out in the rain on the damp ground.

The Highlanders had seethed over this and other grievances until August 14, when things finally fused. Standing on parade, the regiment was ordered to strike their tents and load them on the wagons for a move. Eight out of the ten companies did not obey the command. Most of the men, aware of the coming order the day before, had spent the night drinking whiskey. The mutiny soon spread to the 2nd Maine Regiment. Seeing his authority, and that of the government, threatened, McClellan acted quickly and harshly, making examples of the perpetrators. Sixty-six soldiers were arrested and chained to the hull of the U. S. S. *Powhatan,* which took them to the Federal prison at Fort Jefferson on Dry Tortugas, off Key West, Florida.

When Lowe returned to Washington with his new balloon, the Army of the Potomac was still boiling from the sedition and the stern measures used to put it down. As armies usually found, if there were no battles to be fought with the enemy, they would fight among themselves.

No sooner had the balloonist settled in when he received a dispatch from Major J. C. Woodruff of the Topographical Engineers instructing him to report with his balloon to the Columbian Armory, where he was to be assigned a crew of thirty men to aid him in inflating and transporting. The major also enclosed an authorization for gas. This was a blessing to Lowe, who had previously been paying the Washington Gas Company out of his own pocket.

Confederate forces had occupied Mason's, Clark's, Munson's, and Upton's Hills just across the Potomac from Washington. These were the very Virginia hills the balloonist had flown over before making his ill-fated forced landing. Fairfax Court House and the roads leading toward Arlington and Alexandria were also in Rebel hands. Batteries had been erected on the south bank of the Potomac that effectively blockaded the water approach to Washington. Lowe's assignment was to go aloft and observe the Confederate troop movements in these areas.

On the evening of August 28 Lowe began inflation of the *Union* from the gas main at the Columbian Armory. Troops camped on the Mall watched with interest and then chuckled as the balloon unit marched off with great ceremony. As many of these men were from the country and had never even seen a balloon before, they had difficulty imagining what this strange device was meant to contribute to the war effort. True to Lowe's design, the smaller balloon had inflated quickly. He also found that the crew was able to haul it with considerably less difficulty than the *Enterprise.*

The day had been dark and cloudy, so night had fallen early. The air hung heavy with the damp scent of summer gardens. With no wind to move them, the capital's flags dangled furled and darkened. At every corner, gas lamps flickered as the strange parade bobbed its way through the dimly lit streets. Coming upon the balloon quite by accident, the first dog to espy the monstrous globe was sent into a panic. Its shrill barking alerted Washington's many other stray dogs, who quickly joined in sounding the alarm. Their combined howling awakened a considerable number of the citizens who, looking out and seeing the red, white, and blue design on the huge balloon, turned out of their houses to applaud the patriotic procession. Enjoying it all from his basket swaying just above the roadway, the balloonist doffed the wide-brimmed black hat he now affected, and bowed and waved to the cheering bystanders.

As Lowe still had not received his formal commission, he was wearing civilian clothes. Nevertheless, the tall and handsome balloonist cut a stylish figure with his full mustache and broad hat. He was clad in a long, black frock coat over black trousers stuffed into high cavalry boots. While his men wore standard field service garb, their caps were adorned with a special metal insignia, which Lowe had designed. The brass emblem was shaped like a balloon and bore the letters "BC" for Balloon Corps in the center.

Early on the morning of August 29, Lowe's group proudly reported, with their new war balloon, to McClellan's aides at Fort Corcoran. Marching steadily through the night, Lowe and his crew had reached the fort just after sunrise. Shortly after his arrival, the balloonist was instructed to make his first ascension.

Although exhausted by the tension of the inflation, and the slow passage out from Washington, Lowe set about preparing the *Union.* By early morning he was ready to make his ascension. As the balloon rushed skyward with a lightness that denied the *Union's* great bulk, Lowe knew that his design was a success. His new war balloon was far superior to the *Enterprise* at the task it was conceived for, that of rapid deployment for military observation.

As the balloon stretched to the thousand-foot length of its tether, the sight that greeted Lowe took away some of the exhilaration he had been feeling over his new balloon. The Rebel fortifications he observed on Munson's Hill appeared formidable. In his haste to go aloft Lowe had forgotten to take along his spyglass; however, he did not need to look through a telescope to see that the Confederate entrenchments were as near as one quarter mile to Fort Henry. Rebel soldiers could be seen hard at work building breastworks on the side of the hills. Some of the completed fortifications mounted large batteries of cannon. He observed the scene for several minutes, until his presence caused the working soldiers to dive for cover. Nevertheless, no shots were fired at him. Lowe squinted at the cannon arrayed in front of him. To the balloonist's eyes something about a number of the Rebel artillery did not look quite right. He made note of the apparent incongruity of some of the guns, then signaled for the *Union* to be hauled down.

A short while later Lowe returned to the air with his spyglass and an officer observer in the gondola. The two men studied the Confederate batteries for some time through the balloonist's extra powerful telescope. They came to the conclusion, by closely comparing the muzzles of the various cannon, "while some of the guns were actually artillery pieces, a good number did not appear to be genuine, but looked like they had been fabricated from various nonlethal materials to look like cannon, and therefore serve as decoys." A report of their suspicions was dispatched to McClellan's headquarters.

On September 7 McClellan himself made a two-hour tethered flight with Lowe to observe the Confederate positions threatening Washington. The general grimaced as he looked long and hard at the Rebel fortifications. He did not quite accept the idea that some of the batteries facing him were fake. McClellan seemed almost offended by Lowe's notion. He wanted further reports from his spies on the ground to reassure him that the Confederate Army did not presently feel it was strong enough to mount an offensive, but was merely attempting to bluff him into taking a defensive stance. However, this Rebel tactic, if it was indeed so, suited McClellan's purpose as the general was positive he was presently in no position to mount an attack on the Confederates. He felt his new army was not ready for any kind of engagement and was primarily preoccupied with its training.

Allan Pinkerton, the founder of the detective agency that bore his name, was the head of McClellan's spy service. Pinkerton had the habit of supplying McClellan with inflated estimates of the Confederate forces facing the Army of the Potomac. While Pinkerton's men, who had been trained mainly as investigators, did a credible job of uncovering and arresting Rebel agents, they themselves were less successful as spies. Pinkerton espionage was confined, as a rule, to frequenting the taverns and bawdy houses in Richmond and elsewhere, hoping to pick up what bits of rumor and gossip that were available. The figures they acquired on troop concentration and movements were rarely accurate. By the time they made their way to McClellan, the numbers had transmuted into an enormously exaggerated figure, perhaps in a effort to please the general, who could then demand more troops to train before he would attack the huge army supposedly facing him. At any rate, McClellan was convinced of what he wanted to be convinced of and therefore was not about to mount an offensive until he was positive his army vastly outnumbered the enemy forces.

When McClellan first arrived in Washington, he had been greeted as a hero—the man who had come to save the Union. Although his campaign in western Virginia had been small, it had been a victory, which was what the nation needed. McClellan's statement that he intended to "carry this thing 'en grande' & crush the rebels in one campaign" had lifted the people's spirits. The press lionized him. Republican politicians were convinced the president had found the right general to end the war swiftly and decisively. But the man who had boasted, "I can do it all," soon began to drag his boots. A manifest lack of confidence had begun to creep into McClellan's manner, even while he drilled his men, riding Napoleon-like down his rows of troops who had been ordered to shout and cheer lustily as he approached. McClellan began to express fears that the Confederate general, P. G. T. Beauregard, was now in command of an army that numbered over 150,000 men, and was poised to attack the Union capital.

In late September, for reasons unknown, the Confederate forces withdrew from their more exposed fortifications on Munson's Hill overlooking Washington. During the five weeks they held the hill, their positions had appeared intimidating, even though Lowe had reported, "something does not look quite right about their cannon." Federal forces moving into the vacated breastworks found the suspicious guns the balloonist had spotted earlier and reported their presence to McClellan. The lines of formidable artillery that had been holding the Army of the Potomac at bay were discovered to be no more than decoys, phony cannon with barrels made out of stovepipes or tree trunks that had been painted black and propped in position to deceive Union observers. These bogus guns, which the under-equipped Rebel forces had used to hold the mighty Army of the Potomac at bay, were sarcastically christened "Quaker guns" by the press.

The "Quaker gun incident" was widely lambasted in the newspapers and greatly diminished McClellan's standing. Congress was beginning to question his constant reports of greater Rebel numbers.

The patience of President Lincoln and of the nation was being exhausted by McClellan's inability to take action against what now appeared to be a much smaller Confederate Army. The Quaker gun incident had created a leak in the once vast reservoir of endorsement and flattery that had swirled around the dazzling General McClellan.

For Lowe and his struggling Balloon Corps this public reaction against McClellan was extremely unfortunate as the general had become a close friend of the balloonist and a strong supporter of his activities.

12

A Quiet Time for the War, Lowe Prepares, a Deadly Experiment

As the leaves began to fall, the month of September giving way to October, whole bright weeks passed in explosions of sun, shadowed only occasionally by banks of clouds. Dizzy with this vast window of opportunity, Lowe continued to make daily tethered observation flights from Fort Corcoran. Meanwhile the Army of the Potomac was still undergoing training and was nowhere in the temper to advance. While Lowe was writing admiringly of McClellan, calling him "a genius at reorganizing the army into one of the finest and best equipped armies the world had ever seen," many of the Republicans in Congress were beginning to question the general's competence and even his loyalty. The rallying cry "All quiet along the Potomac," which had been a reassurance to the Union after the Battle of Bull Run, now was a phrase of ridicule targeted at McClellan. Popular opinion had it that "Young Napoleon," as McClellan had come to be called in the press, was going down as fast as he went up. The nation wanted action. The public worried that if the Army of the Potomac went into winter quarters without fighting a battle, England, France, and other foreign governments might recognize the legitimacy of the Confederacy and come to its aid.

McClellan's delay, however, was a blessing for Lowe, as it gave him the time he needed to develop some of the ideas he had been working on. Between August and September the balloonist made ascensions on twenty-three consecutive days, taking aloft, in addition to McClellan, the generals John H. Martindale, William F. "Baldy" Smith, and Samuel P. Heintzelman. Each of these officers remarked that they had been suitably impressed by the *Union*'s performance. Lowe also had used the duration to train a permanent ground crew and to set up procedures that would form the basis for the later operations of his Balloon Corps.

On account of Lowe's heavy schedule of daytime observations, a regular procession was made back to Washington every four nights to replace the gas that had seeped out of the *Union*'s envelope. When the days passed with cooler temperatures, and returning to refill the bag was not necessary, the balloonist made night ascensions. On these flights Lowe would slowly rise out of the darkness just in time to catch the sun disappearing below the horizon. When the balloon reached its zenith, the balloonist would crouch in the gondola and make a count of all the glowing Confederate campfires he observed. Back on the ground this tally multiplied by four gave a fairly reasonable estimate of the opposing troop's strength in numbers.

Despite Lowe's promising demonstration to President Lincoln, the use of the telegraph to transmit military intelligence from the balloon to the ground was proving undependable, largely on account of failures of the primitive equipment then in use and the vulnerability of the transmission wire. To provide immediate and concise information to the soldiers in need of it, Lowe devised a system of communication that used large sign boards with numbers painted on them. A code was set up between Lowe and his officer on the ground, an example of this being when a "2" was held up followed by a "4" the balloonist meant "marching toward" or "advancing." Holding up three boards in the sequence of "2," "3," "6," while pointing, was Lowe's way of saying, "I can observe infantry in the direction I am indicating."

Lowe developed numerous other methods useful for military observation. The balloonist could estimate the number of troops in a march by noting the time it took the column to pass a given point of reference. He determined the number of men in a camp site by counting the number of tents and multiplying it by the number of men each one held. The tents could be sighted through his telescope at a distance of six miles or more. The smoke from campfires could be detected from as far away as twenty-five miles. The movement of cavalry was revealed by the tall cloud of dust put up by the horses' hooves, even though the column might be hidden behind woods or hills.

Confederate generals, such as Beauregard, had become concerned with the effectiveness of Lowe's observations and went to great pains to thwart the balloonist, carefully covering their installations with trees and shrubbery. Beauregard also used blackouts, troop dispersal, camouflage, and false campfires to confuse the aerial observer. Lowe did comment that "a considerable number of campfires seemed to appear as soon after I went up."

The balloonist's "spying" tactics especially provoked General Joseph E. Johnston, commander of the Rebel troops around Manassas, who established a special group of sharpshooters with orders "to fire at the infernal balloon whenever it appears." Notwithstanding the hundreds of scarce rounds the group expended, they never did succeed in shooting Lowe out of the sky. Edward P. Alexander, a renowned Confederate artillery officer, was particularly fond of training his guns on Lowe's balloon. In a letter to his father Alexander crowed, "We sent a rifle shell so near old Lowe and his balloon that he came down as fast as gravity could take him."

In the fall of 1861, apparently inspired by Lowe's early success, the Confederate Army attempted to establish its own aeronautical corps. Northern newspapers had carried reports of Southern balloon activity near Fairfax Court House as early as June 18, but these were probably mistaken sightings of Lowe's balloon.

Beauregard and Johnston were believed to have had a balloon at their disposal. On August 22 Johnston wrote to Beauregard that "the balloon may be useful. . . . Let us send for it; we can surely use it advantageously." The origins of this balloon were not clear. Reports in Northern newspapers implied that "several aeronauts had offered their services to the Southern Government as early as May, a considerable time previous to the offers made to the Federal Government by Professor Lowe and others."

Southern newspapers, however, contained no mention of any aeronauts in the Confederate service during the early months of the war. One officer on Beauregard's staff did note that the general, unable to obtain a balloon through official channels in Richmond, had attempted to procure one through "a private source." Beauregard's balloon was apparently of poor quality and little used. However, on September 4 a manned balloon was sighted rising from the Confederate positions on Munson's Hill, a day and place at which it might have been confused with Lowe's aerostat.

Lowe's courageous flights had generated him a core of enthusiastic supporters among the staff officers of the Army of the Potomac. General Fitz-John Porter was an especially strong advocate of Lowe's activities, going aloft with the balloonist whenever his schedule permitted. Porter recommended that Lowe draft a plan for the organization of an expanded aeronautical corps. Lowe replied that he would be only too happy to comply with the general's request as he had been trying to persuade the army to do just that for many months. The balloonist revealed that he was so short of trained men that he had persuaded his father, Clovis, to come down from New Hampshire to help out the cause. Porter stressed that he found observation balloons too valuable a service to be run on its present hand-to-mouth basis. He agreed to review Lowe's proposal and pass it on to General McClellan with his strong recommendation. Porter felt sure that McClellan, who was known to have a vivid organizational sense, would want the balloons incorporated as a regular corps of the army.

Feeling he had found a critical ally in Porter, Lowe eagerly set about drawing up his proposal. His projection called for a permanent group of officers and men, to be trained by him in the flying and handling of balloons, and for increasing the number of balloons in the service to four. Lowe estimated that he could supply two aerostats of thirty thousand cubic foot capacity for $1,500, and two smaller ones of twenty thousand cubic foot capacity for $1,200. Pointing out that since the war would soon be fought far from Washington and its readily available gas mains, he would design a portable gas generator to enable the balloons to be inflated in the field. Lowe estimated he could provide these for around $300 each. In addition, his generators would inflate the envelopes with hydrogen, rather than coal gas, making the new war balloons more buoyant, thus allowing for observations from a higher altitude. Also requested in Lowe's proposal were funds for sundry smaller items such as calcium flares for night signaling, semaphore flags, sandbags, and extra powerful spyglasses.

Porter signed his approval to Lowe's plan on September 16, 1861. The next day the papers were sent on to McClellan's headquarters. Now all Lowe could do was wait while his proposal was moved and shuffled through all the mundane procedures that accompany a military bureaucracy.

In a war that at the moment was somewhat bereft of action, and therefore of heroes, Lowe had become a bit of a celebrity. Countless newspaper and magazine writers and artists were drawn to Lowe's balloon camp at Fort Corcoran. Arthur Lumley, an artist from *Leslie's Illustrated Weekly,* came and did numerous drawings. The photographer Matthew Brady took pictures of Lowe's activities and even made several ascensions. Among the more unusual visitors were a group of French noblemen who traveled with the army in August as observer aides. In the party were two childhood friends of Leontine, who had shared her escape from their native country: Philippe, Compte de Paris, son of the "Citizen King" Louis Philippe, and his uncle, the Prince de Joinville.

Lowe's observation flights had become rather routine. More often than not he took along some newsman or general who was mainly interested in seeing the view. The Confederate Army had dug in deeply and was not pressing the advantage it had gained at Bull Run. Although Rebel troops crowded the hills overlooking Washington, so close that through their telescopes they could observe the congressmen bustling about on the Capitol steps, McClellan was content to busy himself with drilling his army and in no hurry to drive the enemy off.

On September 23, 1861, Lowe was surprised to receive a message from General William F. "Baldy" Smith, battery commander at the forward post "Camp Advance." He was being asked to perform an experiment that, if successful, would forever change the way wars were fought. General Porter had wired the following request: "At about 8: 30 tomorrow morning, I wish to fire from here to Falls Church. Will you please send the balloon up from Fort Corcoran, and have note taken of the position reached by the shell, and telegraph each obsevation at once."

The next morning Lowe rose from his sleeping tent at first light to find the ground cloaked in a light fog. He rubbed his hands together against the unseasonable cold. Last night's clear sky had allowed the earth's heat to escape. Now the sun was attempting to make its presence known, although the moon could be clearly seen not yet departed from the steel-gray sky. Observing the sutler's cart open for business, Lowe walked over and bought a can of condensed milk. Then he joined his men at their mess for a breakfast of slapjacks and coffee. The balloonist shared his Borden with the soldiers, their pay, when it did come, not allowing them to purchase much from the sutler's overpriced stock.

The *Union* gently backed and filled against its mooring ropes, the warm sun burning the mist from around it. The heat was expanding the gas in the bag, but the envelope's wrinkled surface told Lowe that the next day the balloon would have to be towed back to Washington to be topped off. The balloonist's telegraph operator, Mr. Park Spring, was already crouching in the gondola adjusting his tapping key. Lowe unfurled the plain white flag he had fastened to a staff the previous evening, waved it idly in the air a few times as if testing it, then rolled it back up and put it in the gondola.

Union forces on the south bank of the Potomac were expecting an attack, so Lowe had been ordered to make an ascension above Fort Corcoran. Porter had wired Lowe this message: "Two mounted orderlies will be sent to you so that you can, with the assistance of your officer, report to headquarters during the time of fire. It is very important to know how much the shot or shell fell short, if any at all. . . . If we fire to the right of Falls Church, let a white flag be raised in the balloon. If to the left, let it be lowered; if over, let it be shown stationary; if under let it be waved occasionally."

The orderlies were waiting, the telegraph cable was attached, and the telegraph operator all hooked up in the gondola. His crew was hanging on the mooring ropes. The ground fog had burned off. Lowe took out his pocket watch; the time was 8:15. He climbed into the basket next to Park Spring. General Smith wished his batteries to begin firing at 8:30. Lowe gave the signal to release the ropes; and the war balloon, with the weight of two on board, began a slow ascent. As the *Union* climbed out, Lowe felt a chill run through his body. It was not the cold morning air, but a sense of horror at what he was about to do. Although he had thought often about this moment, when it finally had come the circumstances were making him uneasy. Directing fire during an attack by the enemy to save the day was how he had imagined it. But the Confederate soldiers he was about to rain death down upon were probably having breakfast, or perhaps still peacefully asleep in some battle-scarred meadow. Lowe knew that the main purpose of war was to kill your enemy, but somehow he had always thought of his role in a more abstract way, as if he were solving some scientific problem. This was the first time he had been faced with the reality that his mission was about destroying human life, not saving it.

Stretched to the full extent of his tether, the balloonist observed the presence of the Confederate troops no more than three miles away at Falls Church. Lowe had Spring telegraph to Porter that they were in position. Receiving the message, Porter ordered General William F. Smith's battery installed at Chain Bridge to commence firing.

Watching through his spyglass, Lowe could see the Union gunners ramming the shot down their barrels and then scrambling as the cannon were ignited. He saw the puffs of smoke first and then heard the loud report as the battery fired. Shifting the focus of his telescope to the Confederate position at Falls Church, the balloonist saw the first volley arrive. It was a miss. The landing shells kicked up the dirt in an open field to the right of the town. A lump formed in his throat, a simultaneous sense of guilt and relief, as he watched the now alerted enemy emerging from their tents and bough houses. Lowe raised his white flag.

Following the balloonist's signal, the Union batteries adjusted their aim to the left. The second round landed in the fields on the other side of the village. Then followed more flag waving and several telegraph messages. After much trial and error, the Union gunners found the range. Within minutes the woods were full of startled soldiers and civilians running for shelter like frightened deer. The officers, seeing no sign of the attacking Union troops, stood looking around in panic.

The bombardment went on. From his lofty vantage point Lowe continued to use his semaphore signals to convey the points of impact of the cannon fire. The Confederates were forced to abandon their positions. Many of the houses of Falls Church, hit by errant rounds, were ablaze. Wounded and dead littered the fields and roads. The Rebels soon realized that the devastating barrage from the unseen artillery was being directed by Lowe from his balloon. All their batteries in the vicinity of Fort Corcoran were directed to train their fire on Lowe's aerostat. Shortly musket and cannon balls were whizzing dangerously close to Lowe and his telegraph operator crouching in the gondola of the *Union*. Feeling he had accomplished his mission, and not wanting to take any further risk, Lowe signaled his crew to haul the balloon down.

This was the first time ever recorded in military history that the firing of an artillery battery on the ground had been directed by a spotter in an aircraft above the battle field. An English observer at the scene, Captain Frederick F. E. Beaumont, declared that "the artillery fire would have been completely ineffective without Lowe and his balloon." In his own papers T. S. C. Lowe would later write: "In accordance with [General Porter's] orders I ascended to a height of 1000 feet and carried on this simple system of signals, which worked in a very satisfactory manner. The battery marksmen, without seeing who or what they were firing at, by watching me made such an accurate fire that the enemy was demoralized."

Porter was ecstatic, greeting Lowe as soon as he and his telegraph operator touched down. He also handed the balloonist a congratulatory telegram from Battery Commander General Smith that concluded, "This demonstration will revolutionize the art of gunnery."

Discovering a musket ball lodged in the wicker of the balloon's basket, Lowe pointed out to Porter the closeness of the fire directed at him. The general was taken aback by how but for a few thin strips of wood this grand experiment might have ended in an abrupt failure. He recommended to Lowe, for his own safety, that when the new balloons were authorized they should have heavy metal plating on the gondolas.

That evening an exhausted Lowe returned to Washington to repair some of the balloon's frayed ropes and have the gas bag reinflated. The balloonist secured the *Union* at the Columbian Armory, where his father Clovis, whom the men under him understatedly referred to as being "somewhat eccentric," had set up a kind of shop to keep the new balloon and the old *Enterprise* in operating condition. After discussing the needed work with Clovis, Lowe retired to his hotel. He planned to take the next day off for some much needed rest.

Sleeping late the following morning, the balloonist was awakened by a loud rapping. One of Quartermaster General Meigs's aides was at his hotel door. The success of Lowe's mission the previous day had not gone unnoticed. Once again the balloonist's accomplishments were the talk of the capital. The stories in the newspapers of Lowe's innovative use of a balloon had served to grease the War Department's slow-moving gears. The orderly handed the balloonist a note from General Meigs that read:

> Quartermaster General's Office
> Washington City
> 25 September 1861
> On recommendation of Major General McClellan, Secretary of War has directed that 4 additional balloons be at once constructed under your direction, together with such inflating apparatus as may be necessary. It is desirable that they be completed with the least possible delay.
>
> Very respectfully,
M. C. Meigs

Lowe was ecstatic. Only nine days had passed since Porter had signed his proposal and passed it on to McClellan. He immediately telegraphed his shop in Philadelphia to begin work on four new war balloons.

Although he was still attached to Porter's division, Lowe commuted between Washington and Philadelphia supervising the construction of the new aerostats. Oil lamps burned long into the night as an army of women cut and stitched endless yards of silk to hurry the new balloons to completion.

Lowe decided a great show of patriotism was in order when naming the new aerostats. The four new war balloons were called *Intrepid, Constitution, United States,* and *Washington.* Two additional balloons would be built at a later date and named *Eagle* and *Excelsior.* Although there was an urgency to get these aerostats off to the war as soon as possible, Lowe's aesthetic side, and the desire to avoid any of the confusion that almost got him shot down by his own troops at Arlington, assured that none of the balloons left the shop until it had been elaborately decorated by artists. The paint schemes were, of course, red, white, and blue, featuring the craft's name in large gold letters, and some appropriate illustration, such as a rampant eagle or a portrait of George Washington.

While Lowe concerned himself with the rising cost of silk, rope, varnish, and the other materials needed to construct the balloons, the war, except for an occasional skirmish by opposing pickets, seemed to be still on hold. No one was quite sure what the Confederates were doing in the face of conflicting reports by Federal spies and the

Pinkertons. Nevertheless, McClellan was demanding that President Lincoln give him more men to drill.

When he was not supervising his shop in Philadelphia, Lowe was at the Washington Navy Yard. There a group of pipe fitters and shipwrights, under the direction of master joiner Henry Forrest, were attempting to fabricate the portable gas generators. Lowe had turned to his knowledge of chemistry for a solution to the problem of having to fill his balloons with coal gas from a municipal main.

Lowe's rival, John La Mountain, had experimented with a portable gas generator some time before, but had abandoned the project, concluding that the weight and cumbersomeness of the machinery necessary for gas generating made the idea impractical. Lowe decided to try using the reaction of sulfuric acid on iron filings to produce the hydrogen he needed. Lowe's design was actually a huge laboratory retort mounted on the frame of a standard army wagon. The balloonist's generator consisted of a strong wooden tank about eleven feet long and five feet high. The tank was coated inside to make it acid proof, and its sides were heavily braced to resist the pressure of the gas. In use, iron filings were dropped into the tank through a circular opening on top. Internal shelves distributed the filings evenly. Then sulfuric acid was poured into the tank through a vertical tube. When the acid began to attack the iron filings, hydrogen was generated. The resulting hydrogen was filtered through a limiter washer and a water cooler before a hand-operated pump was used to force the gas into the balloon. In total, twelve of the generators were constructed, six being in service by the spring of 1862. In actual field conditions the "iron filings" often became any scrap iron—broken wagon axles, cannon balls, grape shot—that could be found in the area of operation.

All through the fall of 1861 construction continued on the balloons, generators, and other needed apparatus. At the same time, Lowe was faced with the problem of finding men to fly the aerostats when they were finished. This would not be an easy task. Although Lowe knew almost all of the country's serious balloonists, he also was aware that most of them were intemperate and free-spirited individuals unwilling to take orders from anyone. Besides, about half of their number had been his rivals for the post he now held.

The army only offered to pay the balloonists $3 per day until the aerostats were completed. Lowe doubted he would be able to find anyone who would be willing to serve for such a small salary. He assumed the Balloon Corps would be made a regular branch of the army. Then the balloonists would be entitled to receive pay "according to the rank designated by the government" and be entitled to pensions and other benefits. Lowe had been promised the rank of colonel, with the other aeronauts holding the rank of major. However, until the commissions came through, Lowe was counting on his fellow balloonists to serve their nation as a patriotic duty.

William Paullin, a well-known balloonist who had flown with Lowe before the visiting Japanese dignitaries in 1859, joined the Balloon Corps on October 11, 1861. Unfortunately Lowe would have to dismiss Paullin from the corps after only three months service for refusing to give up a business as an ambrotypist, an early form of photography that he had been conducting while on duty.

An old friend of Lowe's from Boston, John B. Starkweather, signed on as a balloonist in the middle of November 1861. Starkweather would serve briefly with Brigadier General Thomas W. Sherman's troops at Port Royal, South Carolina, before resigning in the summer of 1862.

In December 1861 Ebenezer Locke Mason joined the Balloon Corps after a lengthy correspondence with Lowe. Originally from Troy, New York, where he had been an acquaintance of John La Mountain, Mason had pursued a number of careers in his life. When he had written to Lowe volunteering for the balloon corps, he was a harness maker in Philadelphia. Just prior to that, however, the colorful Mason had been a press agent for an Albany magician known as 'Wyman the Wizard." Mason's first assignment was to Lowe's shop in Philadelphia, where he was put in charge of overseeing the work while Lowe was away. Signed on at the same time as Mason was Ebenezer Seaver, a man with very little previous ballooning experience.

Eventually Lowe was able to enlist a number of the older, more experienced balloonists. John Steiner joined the Balloon Corps in December 1861. Realizing he was not about to become head of the army's aeronautical corps, Lowe's chief rival, James Allen was added to the Balloon Corps on March 23, 1862. His brother Ezra had signed on ahead of him in January.

A lawyer from Philadelphia, Jacob C. Freno, was recruited in January 1862. Freno, who had a taste for aeronautics, had made a previous ascension with Lowe on a Cincinnati free flight. At the beginning of the war, Freno had enlisted in the 66th Pennsylvania Infantry, but was soon drummed out of the service charged with cowardice, gambling, and a number of other crimes.

After several months of good behavior in the Balloon Corps, Freno, taking advantage of his previous acquaintanceship with Lowe, would lapse into his old ways. His patience exhausted, Lowe would eventually dismiss the lawyer "for repeated absence without leave, expressing disloyal sentiments, opening a faro bank for the purpose of gambling, and for the demoralizing effect he had on subordinates." But this, unfortunately for Lowe, would not be the last the balloonist would hear from Freno.

The ninth and final aeronaut hired by Lowe was the former sea captain John R. Dickinson. Dickinson had flown with Lowe in the giant airship *Great Western* on its first test flight from Point Breeze to Medford, New Jersey. The captain had also signed on for Lowe's transatlantic journey, prepared to sail the lifeboat *Leontine* in the event they had gone down in the Atlantic. Dickinson was put in command of the *Union* when Lowe was not in Washington.

All in all, Lowe's aeronauts were a varied group, some of whom could hardly be relied upon. The balloonist could only think abstractly about how these men would perform under actual combat conditions. Their presence did, however, fill the blank in the plan he was attempting to complete. He wondered, dizzily, how long he would last. Each time he volunteered to make an ascension, he contemplated that it might be this time one of the many musket balls hurled in his direction found its mark.

13
Chain Bridge, a Runaway Balloon, the Orphan Corps

On the evening of October 12, 1861, Lowe arrived back in Washington after an exhausting trip to Philadelphia. Despite the joy of being able to spend time with his wife and family, the frequent traveling was beginning to take its toll. He would be happy when all the new war balloons were completed and delivered to the army. The balloonist had just settled into his bed at the National Hotel and was lying there idly watching two enormous moths coupling in amorous frolic on the ceiling, when he heard an urgent knock on his door. He opened it to an orderly who handed him a message from General McClellan. Lowe was instructed to report, with his balloon, to General Smith at Johnson's Hill as early as he could the following day. As he refolded the note, the balloonist glanced back up at the ceiling. The moths continued their clumsy, vibrating fluttering for another moment, then flew past him, as if racing one another to escape the empty air in the room, and fled out the open window.

Lowe quickly rounded up his ground crew, who were bivouacked near the Columbian Armory, and ordered them to begin inflating the *Union*. It was 9 o'clock before the bag was full. Despite the lateness of the hour, the party set off in the direction of Chain Bridge, with Lowe directing from the basket. As heavy winds had come up, the balloon was being towed lower to the ground to keep it from swirling about. Concerned about the presence of the many trees, telegraph lines, and other obstructions that the balloon was normally floated over, Lowe decided to abandon his usual route along the streets and take a circuitous path through the fields. Even so his crew had to halt numerous times to trim branches from trees hanging in their way.

Because of these difficulties, it was not until 3:00 A.M. when Lowe reached Chain Bridge. Arriving there the balloonist found the bridge already heavily clogged with military traffic on the way to the front lines. Considerable numbers of men and equipment were lined up waiting their turn to cross. With no priority authorization to insert his balloon group in the line of march, Lowe was informed by the officer in charge it would be several hours before he and his men would be allowed to cross the bridge. Scratching his head, Lowe studied the situation, determined to avoid the delay.

Noting that a trestlework eighteen inches wide extended from the sides of the bridge, Lowe asked his men if they would be willing to walk this narrow path holding the guy ropes, while he floated over in the balloon. There would be a considerable risk to anyone who should slip and fall into the rocky river below. Since he was not an officer, he could not order the men to walk the trestlework, but only sit waiting in the glare of the torches as the men met to decide. Lowe was glad when the corporal returned and reported the men had agreed to his plan. Images had raced through his head of some great intrigue the men were planning against him, but their consent had served to reaffirm his faith in them, and of their faith in him and his notion of a balloon corps.

The night was moonless. The balloonist sensed a premonition of disaster as, with only the occasional flare or firebrand to guide them, his men straddled the column of marching troops and began to walk the *Union* over the bridge. Fortunately the wind had died down a bit as Lowe, in the swaying basket above, shouted instructions to his men hanging on to the guy ropes while balancing on the narrow stringers. As the men inched along, the turbulent Potomac swirling below them, an artillery troop rattled across Chain Bridge, the weight of its cannon causing the bridge to shake and sway. Lowe's crew stopped and hung on to the girders with concealed fear, while the bridge gyrated through its wild dance.

At several points the trestle was bisected by bridge supports, forcing the men to climb precariously out and around the broad beams. Hanging on to the basket, the balloonist felt the cold wind pick up, drying the sweat on his forehead. Then Lowe heard the barking of dogs greeting his party and its enormous globe; they had made the other side without a mishap. He could feel the sense of relief floating up from the men below. Once clear of the bridge, the balloonist ordered the *Union* hauled down lower for safety as they continued on their march.

The sun was beginning to rise in the east when Lowe and his balloon finally reached Lewinsville. He and the crew were exhausted and hoped to be able to have some rest before having to put the *Union* into service. Lowe set the men to securing the balloon in an open field as there was no protective cover thereabouts. They had not had breakfast, so a corporal was sent to forage for whatever rations were available. This was unfortunately common practice for Lowe when in the field, being handicapped by not having a commission, and therefore not able to requisition food for his men in the normal manner.

As the balloonist with his tired men sat eating a meager meal of hardtack and coffee, he suddenly felt the wind freshen. A stack of dirty cooking receptacles toppled over and rattled clumsily across the ground. Dust swirled around the water cans and buckets. Men clutched at their hats. The flames in the campfire leapt to and fro as if unsure what position to take, then gave up and went out altogether, leaving the resin-sented smoke to seek its own element. The breeze quickly turned into a gale. An enormous, black, moving amphitheater that had taken shape high above the Federal camp was beginning to descend in spiteful spirals.

Lowe could recognize the gale by its powerful effects. The sky was swept lengthwise by lines of energy, vast and silvery-white. One after another tents collapsed, leaving the occupants standing in embarrassed emptiness. The balloonist ordered his men to see to the *Union*'s mooring ropes, which had been lashed securely to tree stumps. As the wind increased in ferocity the balloon began to struggle against its restraints, the stretched netting giving it the appearance of a sea monster caught in a fisherman's net. Rows of tall pine trees surrounding the field swayed with their branches upraised and screamed a howling of disaster. Lowe's troop dived for cover as, in an explosion of madness, an uprooted tree sailed by in full flight.

The *Union*'s mooring ropes were now stretched taut. The netting drummed on the sides of the envelope as if its ropes were not made of stout hemp but of elastic. For three hours the men, grinding curses and blasphemies out of their dust-filled mouths, fought to restrain the balloon, which was now spinning like a top. Suddenly, with a series of sharp pops, which caused several of the men to duck thinking it was musket fire, the netting separated. Free of any restraints the *Union*'s gas bag shot skyward. Lowe and his men watched incredulously as it was carried away on the gusting, howling gale. All that was left of the the war balloon was the basket and an octopus mass of broken, tangled rope lines.

Seeking out his telegraph officer, Lowe immediately had a tracer sent out on the runaway balloon. The wires hummed with reports, some true perhaps, and some so far to the west as to be completely improbable. The balloonist was concerned that the *Union* might have been blown south and fallen into Confederate hands.

After several hours Lowe finally received word that his balloon had landed in a field in Delaware, on the land of a farmer known to have strong Confederate sympathies. Pro-Union neighbors had seen the patriotically painted globe come down and rushed to claim it. A fight was in progress over the rapidly collapsing bag when a group of Federal cavalry arrived following Lowe's directions. The officer ordered the brawlers to cease and took possession of the balloon, which was now nothing more than a mass of tattered and wrinkled fabric lying on the ground. The troops quickly loaded the balloon on a wagon and took it away. Their arrival doubtless saved the *Union,* which surely would have been torn into pieces by both sides had the squabble continued.

A few days later the balloon, after a roundabout journey, was returned to Lowe. Upon examining the bag, the balloonist found that, despite its wild flight of several hundred miles, the *Union* had suffered relatively little damage. After some minor repairs at Clovis' shop at the Columbian Armory, the first war balloon was soon back in service.

The last military action of the fall of 1861 would not be what the Federals had been hoping for. The Confederates occupied the town of Leesburg, Virginia, about forty miles upriver from Washington. Perhaps motivated by the public's cry for action, McClellan ordered a division led by General Charles P. Stone to make a "slight demonstration" against the Leesburg Rebels.

On October 21 the Union regiments that had crossed to Virginia on Chain Bridge the same night as Lowe's balloon were ordered to march against the Confederate flank to support General Charles P. Stone's attack from the Maryland side. Stone's lead group was to be commanded by Colonel Edward Baker, a former Illinois politician and close friend of Lincoln, who had named his youngest son after the president. The inexperienced Baker foolishly sent most of his brigade directly across the river, where they ran into Confederate forces entrenched in the woods at the top of a hundred-foot bank called Ball's Bluff. The Rebel positions would have been easily spotted by aerial observation, but Lowe and his crew were not at the scene of action; rather they were back in Washington waiting to be called up.

Finding themselves in poor position, the Federals put up a brave, but brief, skirmish during which Baker was killed. The troops bolted. Volleys of Confederate fire rained on the leaderless brigade fleeing in disorder down the steep bank and into the river, where those who managed to escape the bullets were drowned. More than half of Colonel Baker's brigade of 1,700 men were killed, wounded, or captured.

The humiliating defeat moved Lincoln to tears of grief and the Republicans to look for a scapegoat. Congress set up the subsequently notorious Joint Committee on the Conduct of the War to investigate inefficiency in the army. Its first victim was General Stone, who among everything else was attacked for his early proslavery reputation. It was even hinted that there had been contacts between Stone and Confederate officers, and that he had purposely sent his men into a trap.

McClellan tried for a time to shield his subordinate. However, when he realized that Stone was a surrogate for the committee's real target, which was himself, McClellan quickly threw Stone to the wolves. Although no formal charges were ever brought against him, Stone spent six months imprisoned at Fort Lafayette. In the end he was released and restored to minor commands, but his career had been ruined.

The cold of winter was beginning to settle into northern Virginia. There was little military action and Lowe was making relatively few ascensions. Rumor was that McClellan was planning a large offensive for the spring. With his new war balloons arrived from Philadelphia, and his corps of aeronauts hired, Lowe was eagerly looking forward to being part of the campaign. Unfortunately his Balloon Corps was being transferred from bureau to bureau like an orphan child.

Originally under the Bureau of Topological Engineers, the balloonists were soon given over to the Quartermaster Corps, which passed them on to the Corps of Engineers, which finally handed over their supervision to the Signal Corps. Lowe's activities were controlled by a number of different field commanders, in addition to his Washington administrators, so the head of the Balloon Corps was often unclear as to whom he was actually responsible. Consequently, Lowe more often than not operated as best as he saw fit, an attitude that did not gain him favor with the officers in charge of regulating his organization. Moreover, Lowe's attempt to justify the value of his Balloon Corps was now being clouded by the recent activities of his old rival, the aeronaut John La Mountain.

La Mountain had chosen not to become part of Lowe's official Balloon Corps, nor any other military unit, but remained an independent contractor. He answered only to the man who had hired him, General Benjamin F. Butler. The aeronaut was based at Fort Monroe at the tip of the Virginia Peninsula, where Butler was in command. La Mountain had served well with Butler's unit while flying a balloon he had cobbled together from salvaged pieces of his giant aerostat *Atlantic.* This was the balloon he had flown from Saint Louis to upstate New York, and which he had subsequently abandoned in the Canadian wilds after being blown over the deep woods by a freak air current. Having established himself at Fort Monroe on July 31, 1861, La Mountain thereafter made numerous ascensions to reconnoiter Confederate positions. By August 3 he was also making tethered flights from the deck of the steam tug *Fanny.*

La Mountain continued to observe Rebel shipping on the James

River and monitor Confederate forces in the area. Butler himself flew with La Montain on several occasions. He and his staff made frequent use of the aeronaut's maps and sketches of enemy positions. La Mountain also was attempting to sell the general on his idea to construct a large balloon that could be used to "shell, burn, or destroy Norfolk or any city near our camps." However, despite all his good service, for reasons which were never understood, he failed to give warning of the Confederate troop advance toward Hampton Roads on August 7.

On August 10 La Mountain made what would prove to be his last flight from Fort Monroe, a night ascension. As he had used up his supply of acid and iron used for generating the gas, General Butler gave the aeronaut leave to return to his home in Troy, New York, to obtain his specially built hydrogen generator that worked on the principle of the decompression of water. La Mountain also planned to bring back his large balloon *Saratoga* to be used as a bomber. Prior to his departure the aeronaut submitted an invoice to Butler for $1,200 to cover the cost of the use of the *Saratoga*.

By September 12 La Mountain had returned to Fort Monroe with his generator and the *Saratoga*. He was surprised to learn that General Butler was no longer in command, having been replaced by General John E. Wool. La Mountain was further perplexed when he was informed by Wool that he had no knowledge of any aeronautical program under his command, and had not been passed on the invoice for $1,200 the aeronaut claimed to have left with Butler.

Having spent a month of his time and a good deal of money in going to New York and returning, La Mountain was considerably upset by the turn of events. He demanded that Butler be contacted to clarify the situation. Wool resented being told what to do. He refused to wait for any response from Butler and immediately sent La Mountain packing. The aeronaut was told to return to Washington and request instructions from Secretary Cameron at the War Department. Although technically a civilian, La Mountain, seeing no employment at Fort Monroe, had no choice but to comply with Wool's order. La Mountain reported to Cameron in Washington. The secretary had recently received a request for a balloonist from General William F. "Baldy" Smith. La Mountain was assigned to Smith's division.

Foreseeing a possible conflict between the two strong personalities La Mountain and Lowe, General McClellan, "Baldy" Smith's superior, ordered General Fitz-John Porter to arrange a discussion between the two balloonists to determine if they were prepared to cooperate. The meeting was arranged to take place in Lowe's tent at Fort Corcoran, a fact which the head of the Balloon Corps regarded as clearly weighing things in his favor.

La Mountain arrived at the occasion dressed in what for him was splendid attire. He, like Lowe, had as yet no commission and therefore could not wear an official uniform. Nevertheless, La Mountain had adopted a rather showy outfit, which Lowe felt made his rival look rather like the captain of a volunteer fire brigade. Although Lowe remained pointedly courteous to La Mountain, he considered him to be a profane and impertinent fool, smart but not too deep.

After greetings, which could hardly be described as friendly, the dialogue began. The three men sat on folding camp stools at Lowe's table drinking coffee. Porter and La Mountain both lit up cigars. Lowe, a non smoker, did not join them and, being a teetotaler, did not produce any whiskey. The more the men talked, the more they disagreed and the more scathing became Lowe's assessment of La Mountain. As tensions increased, Lowe surprised himself by holding his ardent, disputatious nature in check, proving to himself that when the need arose he could be a model of civility and self-restraint.

Aware he was facing an overzealous adversary Lowe avoided taking the lead, even though it was not in his nature to stand back. After considerable discussion, during which tempers several times came close to getting out of hand, an agreement was reached. Porter hastily wrote down the details. La Mountain would remain an independent contractor, not subject to Lowe's control; however, the aeronaut would coordinate with the Balloon Corps if and when that became necessary. In addition, La Mountain would be put on the payroll of the Bureau of Topological Engineers at a salary of $10 per day. This amount, much to Lowe's chagrin, was equal to his own pay. He argued that as La Mountain had no administrative duties he should receive less, but this was not to be the case. Finally La Mountain would not be assigned to "Baldy" Smith, who had been a firm supporter of Lowe since their successful experiment with artillery spotting at Falls Church, but to General William B. Franklin's division at Cloud's Mill, Fairfax County, Virginia.

The meeting was about to draw to a close when La Mountain casually, and with an air of bravado, let drop his plan to begin free flights over the Confederate lines. Lowe jumped up, immediately expressing his disapproval. He was adamantly opposed to this idea. The balloonist reminded La Mountain and Porter that although his only free flight, that of July 24, had brought back much useful information, he had gone down behind enemy lines. Only the daring rescue by his wife had saved him and his balloon from capture. Lowe trenchantly maintained the risks of making free flights far outweighed the advantages gained.

Porter sensed the reopening of hostilities. In a conciliatory gesture, he allowed there was merit in conducting experiments using both systems. Porter recommended that Lowe's Balloon Corps continue with their tethered observations, while La Mountain explored the possibility of free flight. Lowe, who had gone to the meeting anticipating a victory, came away with a sense of defeat. The balloonist felt he had lost ground in that Porter had sided with his rival on most of the key issues.

In early October, Lowe returned to Philadelphia to check on the progress of the new war balloons. On October 4, taking advantage of Lowe's absence, La Mountain made his first attempt at free flight using the *Saratoga*. The aeronaut wisely did not undertake to cross Rebel lines, but flew east and north over Washington, coming to a landing about twelve miles away in a field near Beltsville, Maryland. La Mountain returned to the capital with his balloon and, after making some minor repairs, spent the next ten days conducting tethered flights. Feeling he was ready to chance another free flight, the aeronaut made his first foray over Rebel lines on October 15 near Camp Williams. This short flight, which went without incident, did not reveal much useful information. La Mountain's confidence, however, was buoyed up enough that three days later he again took the *Saratoga* aloft for a free flight. This he planned to be a much longer voyage starting from General Franklin's base at Cloud's Mill.

Safely above Rebel fire at 1,400 feet and drifting with the winds, La Mountain passed over a considerable bit of Southern territory observing "every Confederate position between the [Potomac] river and the Blue Ridge." He had floated over troop concentrations at Fairfax Station, Manassas, and Centreville, and gun batteries on Aquia Creek without a shot being fired at him. However, not unlike Lowe's free flight, his return home was to become a fiasco. Descending over Union lines, La Mountain was "disagreeably saluted" by a volley of rifle fire from General Louis Blenker's troops. Bullets cut out whole sections of the balloon's netting and pierced the lower half of the bag in several places. Shots whizzed by the aeronaut's head. Rather than be a flying target, La Mountain vented gas and quickly brought the *Saratoga* to the ground. As he hopped from his basket, eager to secure the mooring ropes, the aeronaut was surrounded by a squad of Union soldiers with bayonets fixed to their muskets. Before La Mountain could explain who he was, several of the men jabbed the sharp points of their bayonets into the sagging envelope, releasing what gas yet remained.

When he finally arrived back at Cloud's Mill with his tattered balloon, La Mountain wrote a letter of protest to General Blenker about the action of his soldiers. Blenker insisted that his men were guilty of no wrongdoing, and had assumed La Mountain was a Confederate spy. When McClellan learned of the incident, the organizer that he was, he set about drawing up strict guidelines designed to prevent his balloonists from being accidentally fired on by their own side.

Over the next few weeks La Mountain, who unlike Lowe usually flew alone, made numerous free flights. His daring exploits were widely covered in the newspapers, and the aeronaut's reputation was growing rapidly. His two balloons, *Atlantic* and *Saratoga,* were purchased by the army, and he was given a permanent detachment of forty men. In mid-November La Mountain did consent to take a reporter with him, who included in his written account the fear that they might not return:

> [La Mountain], satisfied with the reconnaissance, as well he might be, after noting down the strength of forces and their position, discharged ballast and started for that higher current to bring us back. Now I acknowledge I looked anxiously and (I am sure I was excusable) nervously for a backward movement, conscious that to come down where we were was death, or at least the horrors of a Richmond tobacco prison. Up, up we went, but still bearing west and south. I looked at [La Mountain's] face. It was calm and confident, so I felt assured that all was right. That assurance became a settled thing, when in a few moments we commenced passing gently back to the east.... Back, back we went, as though a magnet drew us, until our own glorious stars and stripes floated beneath us.

Nonetheless, La Mountain's winning operation was not without its misfortunes. On November 16 the *Saratoga* was carried off by a high wind when his inexperienced crew allowed it to get away from them. Knowing he could not risk making free flight observations with his battered *Atlantic,* La Mountain inquired about the fleet of war balloons Lowe had stored in his warehouse in Washington awaiting assignment to his new aeronauts. He requested one of these from General Franklin. La Mountain's request was also accompanied by a caustic letter charging that Lowe "was hoarding scarce materials necessary for the war effort."

The degree of cooperation between Lowe and La Mountain previously had been minimal at best. Having bested the challenge of all the other balloonists seeking the job as head of the Balloon Corps, Lowe was in no mood to deal with a truculent La Mountain. He refused La Mountain's request, pointing out the balloons in storage had already been assigned to the other aeronauts of his corps. Franklin passed the controversy over to McClellan's headquarters, with the conciliatory notation that La Mountain "would be of little value to the army without a new balloon."

In the meantime La Mountain persisted making free flights using his old and battered *Atlantic.* His activities continued to generate considerable interest in the newspapers of both the North and South. Several Southern commanders publicly expressed the opinion that La Mountain's free flights posed a greater risk to their activities than the tethered flights of Lowe's new Balloon Corps. General James Longstreet demanded that "measures be taken to prevent the reconnaissance advantage gained by the Yankees floating balloons over our heads."

On December 18, 1861, a heated Lowe forwarded to General McClellan's office a selection of newspaper clippings that portrayed La Mountain's aeronautical activities in extravagant terms. The head balloonist also included a letter of complaint he had written about his rival's lavish claims. Lowe stated unequivocally, "I am not about to turn one of my war balloons over to La Mountain." Lowe was particularly incensed by an article that had appeared in the *New York Herald,* with the headline "The New Aeronautic Department under Professor La Mountain." The article touted the contribution of the new "Balloon Corps" that had been set up under the command of the Bureau of Topological Engineers. The writer went on to say that La Mountain was "the most daring and successful of the Federal aeronauts" and implied that General McClellan with Major John Macomb of the Topological Engineers "were about to put Professor La Mountain in charge of the entire aeronautical program." Lowe's name as well as his numerous contributions to the war effort had not been even mentioned. Lowe argued, "Articles such as these damage my reputation and raise the public's expectation of the Balloon Corps to an unrealistic level." In his correspondence to McClellan, and in similar letters he addressed to Colonel A. V. Colburn of the adjutant general's office, as well as the numerous other generals he had worked with, Lowe stressed "the importance of having all aeronautical endeavors under my exclusive control."

As the winter weather closed in, the controversy between the two balloonists, which was nothing more than a continuation of their prewar conflict, slowly ground on. A disappointed John Wise had been able to overlook their disagreements and work with his young rival when Lowe was made head of the Balloon Corps. It seemed, however, as if it was not possible for Lowe and La Mountain to patch up their squabbles and work for the good of their country.

Growing tired of the controversy, as he had enough of his own, McClellan took the matter into his hands and came to Lowe's aid. He wrote a letter to General Franklin offering to replace La Mountain with one of the other aeronauts who had been recruited by Lowe. Franklin, perhaps not wishing to offend his superior, did not respond strongly in La Mountain's defense. He transpired to damn the aeronaut with faint praise, commenting that La Mountain "appears to work energetically" and had "done as much and as intelligently as any balloonist could." McClellan recognized that in effect Franklin was cutting La Mountain loose. The general of the Army of the Potomac wrote a letter to La Mountain informing him: "Henceforth all balloons shall be under the superintendence of Mr. Lowe. Upon this basis if you can come to an understanding with Mr. Lowe, it may be of interest to yourself and the service."

In February 1862, not to be deterred, John La Mountain initiated another attempt to obtain one of Lowe's war balloons. Unable to find support among either Franklin's or McClellan's staff officers, the aeronaut petitioned directly to Major Macomb, who had replaced Major Whipple as the officer in charge of balloon affairs at the Bureau of Topological Engineers. Macomb, ignorant of McClellan's letter to La Mountain informing him he must come to an understanding with Lowe, ordered the head of the Balloon Corps to supply La Mountain with a war balloon from his inventory.

Lowe wrote Major Macomb a strong letter stating his reasons for refusing a war balloon to La Mountain. Annoyed by the balloonist's response, Macomb replied with an even more trenchant letter, stressing that "this matter admits of no further delay." A few days later a determined La Mountain showed up at Lowe's warehouse with some men and a wagon and demanded his balloon. Just as stubborn, Lowe would not be dissuaded. After a fierce argument, during which Lowe barred the door to his warehouse, La Mountain went away empty-handed, whereupon La Mountain returned to Major Macomb and reported that "Mr. Lowe refused to recognize authority and would not obey."

Lowe called on Macomb to discuss the situation that had developed between him and La Mountain, but the major refused to see him. The head balloonist attempted to arrange a meeting on several other occasions, but got no response. When it became clear to Lowe that Macomb was not about to engage in a conversation, he sent the major a lengthy letter. In it Lowe explained that the two war balloons he had yet remaining in his warehouse had been promised for service elsewhere, a fact he had repeatedly made known to Mr. La Mountain. The head balloonist related, "I would have been happy to comply with the Major's order, but given the present circumstances it just was not possible." Then Lowe went on to spill out all the resentment he had stored up against his rival:

> [La Mountain is] . . . a man who is known to be unscrupulous, and prompted by jealousy or some other motive, has assailed me without cause through the press and otherwise for several years . . . he has tampered with my men, tending to a demoralization of them, and, in short, has stopped at nothing to injure me . . . so much so that it is impossible for me to have any contact with him, as an equal in my profession, with any degree of self-respect. . . .
>
> This man La Mountain has told my men that he is my superior, and is considered to be the Commanding General . . . he says that he is paid by Lieutenant Colonel Macomb two hundred dollars a month more than I am paid. . . . I do not think that I should serve this man by giving him possession of my improved balloons and portable gas generator for his examination . . . yet if it is the desire of the General that I should do so, I will most cheerfully comply. . . . Without the improvements that I have made in the manufacture and management of balloons, they could be of little service to the Government; add to that my invention of the portable gas generator, which I am using for the benefit of the Government Service. I submit that I should not be interfered with in the management of this matter, at least until I have instructed men in the use of my invention.

Major Macomb was not persuaded by Lowe's dithyrambic arguments. He ordered that a war balloon immediately be released to La Mountain. Not a person to be intimidated, Lowe appealed his case to McClellan, who on February 19, 1862, overruled Macomb's decision and furthermore ordered La Mountain dismissed from the Army.

During the time the controversy between Lowe and La Mountain had been simmering, unknown to Lowe, the Army generals had been entertaining yet another challenge to the head balloonist's authority. In October 1861 William H. Helme, an aeronaut from Providence, Rhode Island, and friend of James Allen, contacted McClellan with the proposal that hot air, rather than gas, balloons might be more useful for aerial reconnaissance.

Helme indicated that a large Montgolfier could be inflated considerably faster, and for much less cost, than Lowe's hydrogen balloons. He also argued that hot air balloons cost less to construct and had fewer maintenance problems. They themselves would be easier to transport, and there would be no need for the bulky gas generator wagons. Helme offered to construct a prototype balloon for the modest sum of $500, or one third the cost for Lowe's war balloons.

McClellan was intrigued by Helme's idea and instructed Macomb to fund Helme's project. Perhaps exhausted by the money squabbles with his other aeronauts, Macomb warned Helme to stay strictly within his budget and to have all bills approved beforehand.

In little more than a month the self-proclaimed "amateur aeronaut" had completed the envelope. An inflation was scheduled for late November. On his first attempt, using an alcohol burner to heat the air, Helme's ground crew failed to lift the balloon high enough on its support structure and the bag was badly scorched. He took three more weeks to make repairs.

By mid-December, Helme had completed the fix and made two successful inflations. He calculated that seven to eight gallons of alcohol had been consumed on each occasion. The aeronaut wired Macomb, informing him of his success, and predicted that, with the improved burner he was working on, ten gallons of alcohol would be sufficient to inflate and maintain the balloon. He advised the major that he would be ready for a demonstration flight by December 20.

Unfortunately there was no record of Helme's demonstration flight ever being made. Nor was there any mention of the Army giving any further consideration to the purchase of hot air balloons for observation.

Having expended as much time and energy infighting with his rival aeronauts as he had observing the enemy, by March 1862, Lowe had attained his ambition. He was now the sole commander of the Balloon Corps, a unit that consisted of seven war balloons, six gas generators, and eight trained aeronauts. While none of the aeronauts had yet received their commissions, and the status of his unit in the organizational structure of the Army of the Potomac was not clear, Lowe was confident that the Balloon Corps would provide a useful service in McClellan's long awaited spring offensive.

14
The Balloon Boat, Camp Lowe, on the Move

Although the envelope had been found virtually intact, the runaway of the *Union* during the gale at Lewinsville had left Lowe particularly feeling devastated. While the loss had been declared an unavoidable accident, the balloonist blamed the incident on himself and on the hesitation by the War Department to provide him with orders authorizing the purchase of proper equipment. He wrote to Captain Whipple: "This, the first accident of my life of the kind, prevented me from being of service on this important occasion. . . . With the facilities that will soon be at hand, the accident would not have occurred."

The accident, however, was proving a blessing of sorts. With the *Union* down for repair, Lowe was freed from making observation flights, allowing him to concentrate on the construction of the new balloons and the training of his men. The head balloonist had no time to waste though as the Confederates were now attempting to blockade the Potomac River, cutting off shipping between Washington and the Chesapeake Bay, and a balloon was needed to make observations in that area.

When General Winfield Scott had resigned, citing age and physical infirmities, Lincoln had appointed McClellan general in chief of all the armies. McClellan was now filled with boundless self-confidence. Nevertheless, while things were quiet on the Potomac, the war had been shaping up in the West, where Kentucky had ceased to be neutral and cast its lot with the North. Battles of lasting significance would be fought in the Mississippi Valley before McClellan even got his army going.

At last, by the first week in November 1861, McClellan felt he was ready. Washington and Richmond, the two capitals, were separated by only one hundred miles. The armies that defended or attacked there got the greatest attention and the biggest headlines in the newspapers. McClellan prepared to take his place on that stage. To sustain

173

any equivalent of delay now was impossible. Knowing his hour had come and that he must rise to the occasion and play a leading part, he would play it with all that was in him.

Several divisions of the Army of the Potomac had been moved down along the river. General Joseph Hooker was camped with his men near Budd's Ferry, Maryland, close by Mattawoman Creek. The general sent a note to McClellan asking for a balloon for mapping and reconnaissance. McClellan approved the request and forwarded it to Lowe, who assigned the new war balloon *Constitution,* with William Paullin as aeronaut, to the task. Paullin was to make several observation flights at Budd's Ferry with General Daniel Sickles and then move the balloon overland to work in conjunction with Hooker's command. Captain Dahlgren, the commandant of the Navy Yard, was to provide the means to transport the balloon and gas generator down the Potomac.

The many delays and complications notwithstanding, Lowe was pleased with the work the Washington Navy Yard had accomplished during the past several months. Not only had they constructed from scratch six portable generators to Lowe's design, but Navy Yard carpenters had also refitted the coal barge *George Washington Parke Custis* for use as a balloon boat. Lowe's Balloon Corps had been assigned the *Custis* by Secretary of the Navy Gideon Wells. The barge, which had a length of 122 feet and a beam of just over 14 feet, was towed by a steam tug. The ship had been elaborately modified to Lowe's specifications. He had the hull completely decked over flat to avoid the balloons fouling on any rigging or funnels. Hooks for mooring were firmly mounted in the center, and a small structure was erected on the stern for the generator and other equipment.

On November 10, 1861, under cover of darkness, the tug *Coeur de Leon* gently pulled the balloon boat from the dock and steamed down the Potomac. In tandem, the two ships hugged the tree-lined Maryland bank to avoid the Confederate batteries on the Virginia shore. They reached the mouth of the Mattawoman at dawn, where they had to lay by until the next evening before unloading for fear of Rebel gunners.

The next morning, Lowe, who had accompanied Paullin and the balloon down to be sure everything was in order, made an ascension with General Sickles. The *Constitution* was magnificent to behold as it floated skyward in its red, white, and blue colors. Many of the soldiers watching let out a loud whoop at the sight. Mostly farmboys, few of the men had seen a balloon before. When the balloon reached the height of the tether, Lowe pointed out to the general the Rebel batteries at Freestone Point, just three miles away. The weather was fine with visibility being almost unlimited, so the two men spent an hour aloft, the balloonist briefing the general on the basics of aerial observation.

Next, Lowe took Paullin up for a similar session, which lasted three hours. Doubtless Lowe had good intentions, but the experienced aeronaut Paullin was rather annoyed by the head of the Balloon Corps chaperoning him down the Potomac to give him a check flight before turning him loose in the *Constitution.*

Unfortunately Lowe had a long record of obsession with the minutiae of whatever he was working on. He was a detail wizard, with a scientist's grasp of the smallest items of the most complicated issues. Whether this constituted true engagement or merely a boyish pleasure in achieving mastery of the abstruse was unclear. That night the balloonist, apparently satisfied that everything was in order, sailed back to Washington on the steam tug *Coeur de Leon.*

When Lowe returned to the capital, he found the Allen brothers had arrived. Also there were Ebenezer Seaver and J. B. Starkweather, both from Boston. John Steiner came later in the week. Although these men were experienced aeronauts, they had to be indoctrinated into Lowe's system before being assigned: the handling of the new war balloons, military spotting and observation, the operation and care of the generators, and how to pack the balloon and other equipment quickly and compactly. The aeronauts also had to learn how to deal with their complement of troops. Although still civilians, they were technically in command of fifty enlisted men, as each balloon unit included that number of soldiers trained in inflating, towing, and the ascension procedure. These men not only functioned as a ground and maintenance crew, but were armed with muskets to protect the detail in the event of an attack.

The Union army had suddenly taken a serious interest in balloon reconnaissance. A scant two weeks after Lowe had begun to train his new aeronauts he began to receive requests for their services.

On November 27 J. B. Starkweather, the balloon *Washington,* its generator, and a detail of men were loaded on board the steamer *Mayflower* and sent off to Port Royal, South Carolina. There they joined General Thomas W. Sherman, who had requested that an observation balloon be attached to his division, which was occupying the port. But before Starkweather and his balloon could get to Port Royal, Sherman found himself facing an unusual situation that had nothing to do with the need to observe the Confederate army.

Sherman and his troops soon discovered all the white citizens had fled the area, which included not only the port, but also the nearby Sea Islands and the local "metropolis" of Beaufort. No abolitionist, Sherman grudgingly found himself the guardian of thousands of abandoned slaves, dependent on him for food, shelter, and employment. Sherman turned the problem over to his quartermaster, Rufus Saxton, a New Englander, and a man relatively free from preconceptions and prejudices.

Saxton worked out a system for employing the newly freed blacks on the abandoned land. Saxton's plan, now called the "Port Royal Experiment," soon caught the public's attention. A group of Northern teachers and missionaries showed up in the territory and founded "Freedman's Schools." The former slaves soon began to prosper, growing more crops than they needed on the abandoned properties. Saxton had great faith in his experiment and even established a bank for the blacks' savings. He had hopes of the former slaves being able to buy the land they were working.

President Lincoln shortly issued an executive order decreeing the sale of the abandoned properties to recover back taxes. Twenty-acre plots were to be sold to loyal citizens for $1.25 an acre. However, freedom, prosperity, education, and the promise of economic independence all were brushed aside by the Treasury Department tax commissioners who rescinded the president's order and auctioned the land off in a bidding war won by white real estate speculators.

Although airships were now posted with several commands, the next action for the Balloon Corps did not occur until mid-December 1861. The balloon ship *Custis* provided support for the *Intrepid* and the *Union,* which were used by Lowe and Ebenezer Seaver in a very minor operation with General Charles P. Stone's command at Edward's Ferry.

The day after Christmas, traveling in the snow and cold, some of the men and equipment of the Balloon Corps were moved to Edward's Ferry, where a permanent balloon camp had been established. This key spot, high in the mountains between Harpers Ferry and Poolesville, near where the states of Virginia and Maryland, and the newly formed state of West Virginia met, provided the aeronauts a clear view of any army that might be approaching Washington from the northwest. Not known for his modesty, Lowe declared he would take this opportunity to name this first ever United States aeronautical base "Camp Lowe."

Lowe spent only a few days at the new camp bearing his name at Edward's Ferry. Huddling by a hot stove rubbing his hands together, the balloonist watched glumly out a drafty window as the freezing rain and snow swirled over the mountains. Finding the weather and the primitive conditions not to his liking, he quickly returned to Washington.

Back in the capital, Lowe continued to fly the now refurbished war balloon *Union,* in conjunction with Porter's brigade west of the City. The head balloonist also on occasion shared the duty of flying the balloon the *United States* with Ebenezer Mason. During the same period, the Allen bothers were keeping the *Eagle* in operation from the deck of the balloon boat *Custis,* which was now anchored in the Potomac near Alexandria. Of all the aeronauts, only Seaver remained at Camp Lowe, in the cold, damp mountains, with the *Intrepid* and a small complement of men.

With Lowe's new war balloons now operating in a number of areas, several different generals took the opportunity to explore the possibilities of aerial observation. Hooker, however, found his initial experiences with Paullin to be less than convincing. On November 30, 1861, Hooker wrote to Lowe expressing his dissatisfaction:

> The history of the balloon here is one of accidents and failures. I most despair of being able to turn it to any account at this season of the year. Hitherto we have been prevented from taking satisfactory observations from the windy or smoky state of the atmosphere, and now we have no gas. In the bonds of its present manager I apprehend that we will find it of little or no service.

The head balloonist immediately dispatched his father Clovis with a supply of acid and iron so Hooker's gas generator could be put back in service. Clovis remained with Hooker's command for a time to help Paullin with the operation of the *Constitution.* With Clovis there, things began to go much better, so much so that by early December one of his advisers, General William F. Small, wrote to Hooker, "Mr. Paullin, the aeronaut in charge of the balloon, is entitled to much credit for the skill and zeal displayed in the ascensions and seconding my efforts to comply with your directions."

Unfortunately Clovis was needed back in Washington and had to return. William Paullin, who was not a young man, was finding it difficult to keep up with the rigorous schedule demanded by Hooker. Having a stomach that did not take kindly to army food, nor the foul-drinking water at the post, Paullin was spending less and less time in the air.

Lowe made the decision to send John Steiner to Camp Lowe and to transfer Ebenezer Seaver, who had found the mountains there also too cold for his liking, to assist Paullin. Shortly after his arrival at Budd's

Ferry, a strained relationship developed between Seaver and Paullin. Despite being younger and less experienced, Seaver demanded to be put in charge of the whole balloon operation.

Seaver's behavior became extremely aggressive. Hooker reported this to Lowe, who came down to look into the situation. In the course of his inquiry the head balloonist unearthed the fact that Paullin, to supplement his meager pay that often did not even arrive, was devoting most of his time to his side business of photography.

Lowe was furious. He had just fired his old acquaintance Jacob C. Freno for "operating a faro bank on an army post for the purpose of gambling." He could not afford to lose Paullin as there were not that many experienced aeronauts available. At his meeting with Lowe, Paullin promised to give up working at his photography while on duty.

After carefully considering the matter, the head balloonist decided to merely reassign Paullin to Washington, where his schedule would be less demanding. After Paullin left, things went much smoother at Hooker's command post. Even Hooker himself began making regular ascensions with Seaver, often making key strategic decisions based on his own observations from the airship.

Meanwhile, things were not going well for Starkweather at Port Royal, South Carolina. He was having serious problems with the *Washington* and kept writing to Lowe, plaguing him with questions about everything from rations to wrenches, and especially about his commission. Starkweather, like the rest of Lowe's balloonists, had not yet received any official military designation, a fact which did not encourage the aeronauts to function with amicable proficiency. Whether the *Washington* flew seemed to matter little to his commander, General Thomas W. Sherman, who, although he had requested a balloon, seemed to have lost interest in the project and not asked for any flights to be made. As a consequence Starkweather made no ascensions until April 1862, when Sherman was replaced by General Henry J. Benhorn.

Meanwhile, in the foggy and storm-swept mountains at Camp Lowe, Steiner was experiencing the same conditions that had driven away Seaver. The winter snow and freezing rain continually eroded the *Intrepid*'s outer coating of varnish, causing the gas to seep out much faster than normal. So much gas escaped that the balloon, even with its own generator going most of the time, was rarely in flight. Steiner wrote Lowe asking for an additional balloon and an assistant. In that way he hoped to be able to keep one balloon in the air while the other dried out. Lowe responded by sending the recently completed *Excelsior,* along with Ebenezer Mason, the foreman of the repair shop who had requested active duty.

Within two weeks of the arrival of Mason and the *Excelsior* at the balloon camp, Lowe received another request for a deployment. Mc-Clellan ordered the head balloonist to send one of his aeronauts to General Henry W. Halleck, commander of the Department of Missouri. Halleck and Brigadier General Don Carlos Buell were engaged in a campaign to clear the Confederate forces from the Mississippi Valley.

Along with the Mississippi, two other rivers, the Cumberland and the Tennessee, were military objectives of prime importance as all were potential highways to the South. The Cumberland led to Nashville, and the Tennessee led all the way to northern Mississippi and Alabama. The Confederates had constructed a series of makeshift forts along these two rivers and several more substantial ones on the Mississippi.

Aiding the Union Army in their offensive against these forts was a fleet of seven shallow-draft gunboats under the command of Flag-officer Andrew H. Foote. Flat-bottomed, wide-beamed, and paddle-wheel driven, these boats were protected by a sloping casement sheathed in iron armor 2.5 inches thick. Looking not unlike a giant tortoise, these strange craft were nicknamed "Pook's turtles," after their designer Samuel Pook. Although bizarre looking, these boats were formidable weapons, each mounting thirteen cannon, and more than capable of going up against the few converted steamboats the South had operating on the rivers. Aeronaut Steiner had been assigned to Foote's gunboat flotilla.

On February 17, 1862, standing in a driving snow squall, Lowe said good-bye to Steiner as he left for the West with the balloon *Eagle.* Ezra Allen replaced Steiner at the balloon camp, and Lowe went back to Philadelphia to see his family and have a rest. Moving from crisis to crisis was taking its toll on the balloonist, who had been made somewhat melancholy by his repeated absences from home. His normally ruddy complexion appeared rather pale. Although tall, Lowe was never stout, and a loss of weight was beginning to show on his angular frame.

Travel to the West was difficult for John Steiner and his balloon. Few trains were running, and winter had made the roads all but impassable. It took Steiner a week to finally arrive at General Halleck's headquarters in Cairo, Illinois. After all his hardship the aeronaut found, when he reported to Halleck's chief of staff General George W. Cullum on February 24, he was all but ignored. This was perhaps because before Steiner got there two significant and bloody battles had been fought, and Foote was presently repairing his battered gunboats, while the war in the West continued by conventional means.

On February 5 Foote's ironclads had protected a landing of fifteen thousand Union troops, commanded by the then little-known Ulysses S. Grant, seven miles down river from the poorly constructed and under-defended Confederate Fort Henry. The next day's heavy rains turned the roads into a quagmire, slowing down the progress of the Federal forces. The rains, however, also raised the level of the river, flooding the low-lying fort's first level. Only nine of Fort Henry's guns were out of the water and able to fire when Foote's flotilla of "Pook's turtles" hove into sight.

For two hours the Confederate cannoneers battled it out with the flotilla, while the fort's 2,500 man garrison beat it out the back door and escaped to fight again at Fort Donelson. The one artillery company left to execute a delaying action performed well. The ironclads took a total of eighty hits. One boat suffered a direct hit on its boiler and was put out of commission when twenty of its men were scalded to death. With half their men wounded or killed, the men of Fort Henry surrendered to Foote's gunboats before Grant and his men even arrived.

Rip-roaring after the victory, Grant telegraphed Halleck saying: "Fort Henry is ours. I shall take and destroy Fort Donelson on the 8th." But bad weather again intervened and slowed the resupply and marching of his troops. And Foote, whose ironclads had steamed down the river after the battle at Fort Henry all the way to Muscle Shoals, Alabama, shooting up everything in sight, was refitting his battered gunboats.

On February 12 Grant's confident fifteen thousand soldiers launched a probing attack against Fort Donelson, which was not really a "fort" but a wooden stockade enclosing fifteen acres lined with huts for soldiers and their equipment. The main defenses were two batteries of twelve heavy guns dug into the side of a hundred-foot bluff. These cannon repelled attack from the Cumberland River, while a semicircle of three miles of trenches protected the land side. When his probing attacks were repulsed, Grant was convinced that Fort Donelson would not fall without a fight.

Grant waited. Two days later an additional ten thouand men arrived, accompanied by four of Foote's ironclads and two wooden gunboats. Seeking a repeat of the Fort Henry victory, Grant ordered the gunboats to bombard the fort while his men attempted to surround the trenches. An overconfident Foote made the mistake of bringing his flotilla in too close. His gunners overshot their targets, giving the shorter-range Rebel cannon a chance to rake the ironclads with devastating shots that found their mark, knocking down smokestacks, shooting away rudders, piercing armor, and blowing through pilot houses turning the men inside to burning flesh. One by one these crippled "turtles" abandoned the fight and drifted slowly downstream. Some vessels had taken as many as forty hits. Fifty-four Union sailors lay on the decks dead or wounded, while not a man nor gun in the Confederate batteries had been lost. A demoralized Foote withdrew to lick his wounds, leaving Grant to press the attack with his infantry.

Two days later the Confederate General Simon Bolivar Buckner, realizing the hopelessness of his situation, surrendered his garrison of twelve thousand men to General Grant, to whom he had once lent money for a train ticket home when the down-and-out captain had resigned from the army in 1854 because of a drinking problem.

With the news of the surrender of Fort Donelson, Grant's second victory in as many weeks, the man who only eight months earlier had been a disgraced ex-officer of dubious reputation became a national hero. The name Ulysses S. Grant and his exploits could be read in all the newspapers. In every city church bells rang and cannon fired salutes. A grateful President Lincoln promoted Grant to major general, placing him second in command to General Halleck in the West.

By the time Steiner had reached Cairo on February 24 the Union Army felt the situation was well in hand. The last thing it needed was this man and his balloon. Just the day before General Johnston's forces had abandoned Nashville, making it the first Confederate state capital to fall. There was little Rebel activity in Tennessee or Kentucky except for sporadic guerrilla and cavalry raids. Confederate forts still stood on Tennessee's western border along the Mississippi, but the Union generals knew their time was limited. The *New York Tribune* was now heaping praise on the war effort with the same degree that it had heaped scorn after Bull Run: "The cause of the Union now marches on in every section of the country. . . . Every blow tells fearfully against the rebellion. The rebels themselves are panic-stricken, or despondent. It now requires no very far reaching prophet to predict the end of the struggle."

Thus not only did Steiner find himself with nothing to do, but he could find no officer responsible to see he got his pay and supplies. Days passed while the disgruntled aeronaut cooled his heels and inundated Lowe with letters written in his broken English and asking for help: "I can not git any assistance here. . . . They say they know nothing about my balloon business, . . . they even laugh ad me. . . . Let me hear from you as soon as possible and give me a paper from Headquarters to show theas blockheads hoo I am." Steiner had been languishing in Illinois for over a month when he wrote Lowe, "All the officers here are as dumb as a set of asses."

At one of his meetings with McClellan, Lowe brought up Steiner's problems on the Western front. McClellan drafted a set of orders for the aeronaut and had them sent to Halleck. Lowe wrote Steiner informing him of McClellan's action. However, even this was apparently of little help as Steiner wrote back: "I came here but I finde that no such papers arrived here. I told the General here how I was situated and under wot sircumstands I bin send out here. He loack ad me a moment and then sed I can doo nothing for you and waif off; and such has bin my treedment every where."

Steiner was finally able to get the *Eagle* into the air in March with the help of Commodore Andrew H. Looe, who was in charge of the mortar boats attacking the Confederate fortifications on Island Number Ten in the Mississippi River. Looe provided the aeronaut with a flat boat from which he could launch his balloon to make observations of General Pope's advance and adjust mortar fire against the defenders.

Between March 25 and 27, 1862, Steiner made numerous ascensions, taking artillery spotters aloft with him. Despite being exposed to enemy fire, and playing an important role in the attack of Island Number Ten, Steiner was still ignored by the Department of Missouri. Shortly after this engagement he wrote to Lowe, "I am here like a dog wisout a tall and I dond know ware I will be abel to draw my pay, for no one seams to know eny thing abought this thing." In another letter to Lowe, Steiner complained, "I am treed wis contempt and if I had the means to return to Washington I would strait today . . . now that I can git no payout here."

In spite of McClellan's letter, and numerous suggestions from Steiner as to how he might be of service, Halleck continued his refusal to deploy the *Eagle.* Steiner would eventually write Lowe: "I am satisfied that General Halleck is no friend of the Aeronautics Corps. I could have bin of grade servis at Cornis [Corinth] and explained it all to General Halleck at Pittsburg Landing, but he told me to stay ad Cairo ontill he woulde send for me."

Lowe later speculated that Halleck's disregard of Steiner and his balloon was, in all likelihood, not so much caused by his lack of appreciation for the value of the Balloon Corps, but rather a stubborn response to his superior, McClellan, imposing the aeronaut on him without his consultation.

During the time Starkweather and Steiner had been struggling with their commanders in the South and West, Lowe and the other aeronauts of the Balloon Corps had not been idle. They had been quite busy in Washington and at Camp Lowe, preparing for the part they hoped to play in McClellan's much anticipated spring campaign.

However, for all his men's best efforts, the head balloonist was not content with what was being accomplished, and almost every day had something to say about the activities of the Balloon Corps. Lowe was exhausted by the importance of what had to be done. His sense of urgency was growing greater by the day. Sometimes he felt total despair at the corps ever coming up to the standards he measured it against. He knew the future was exceedingly dangerous, and given his experience with human frailty, his mind was full of eventualities. Nevertheless, Lowe had confidence in the things he stood for and encouraged his men to greater exertions. Half measures would not do.

After considerable urging from President Lincoln, McClellan had finally devised a plan for an offensive against the Confederate Army occupying Northern Virginia. Instead of attacking the Rebel forces head-on at Manassas, McClellan proposed to transport his army by boat down the Potomac to the Chesapeake and thence to the mouth of the Rappahannock, eighty miles to the south. Using this point as a staging area, McClellan hoped to advance up the Virginia Peninsula, putting his army between General Joseph E. Johnston's Confederate army and their capital at Richmond.

McClellan hoped to capture the Confederate capital before Johnston got his army back to defend it, or if they did fight, to have the advantage of the battle being on a field of his choosing rather than having to assault an entrenched Rebel force at Manassas. Lincoln was reluctant to agree to this plan as he realized it would leave Washington dangerously unprotected.

The president did not share the popular suspicion that McClellan, as a Democrat, was "soft" on Rebels and did not want to attack them. However he had lost faith in his general, and had taken to staying up late reading books on military tactics. Lincoln had come to believe in the strategy of attacking and defeating the enemy's army rather than maneuvering to capture their territory. He told McClellan, by "going down the Bay in search of a field, instead of fighting near Manassas, [you are] only shifting and not surmounting a difficulty. . . . [You] will find the same enemy, and the same or equal, intrenchments, at either place."

In early March, Johnston somehow became aware of McClellan's plan. Before McClellan could move his troops, Johnston withdrew his forces from Manassas to a more defensible position forty miles to the south. This action angered the Confederate President Jefferson

Davis, who felt the retreat was not necessary. Moreover, Johnston had departed Manassas in haste, destroying vast stores of precious supplies because his men could not haul them over the mud-clogged roads.

Lincoln was angry too. Federal forces occupying the abandoned Rebel entrenchments at Manassas found them to be not as formidable as they seemed. The newspapers played up the fact that more Quaker guns were discovered at Centreville. It appeared that there had been no more than forty-five thousand Rebel troops in the area between Manassas and Centreville, less than half of the number McClellan had claimed.

Aware that he could no longer outflank Johnston via the Rappahannock, McClellan decided to ship his forces further down the bay to Fort Monroe, a Federal fortress on the tip of the peninsula formed by the York and James rivers. The troops could then march the seventy miles to Richmond, needing to cross only two rivers on the way. Lincoln still favored an overland invasion that would keep the Army of the Potomac between the Rebel forces and Washington but impatient for any action, he agreed to McClellan's plan, provided the general left behind enough troops to defend Washington from a sudden Confederate attack.

Lowe stood shivering on a dark quay in Alexandria, Virginia, watching by the light of flares as his balloons and generators were loaded aboard the *George Washington Parke Custis.* A brisk wind banged the barge against the dock. Freezing rain dampened the chill night air, hung with the odor of the horses and mules and the gunpowder being loaded on the boats at adjacent slips.

The weather had been bad for weeks, as Lowe remarked, "It was a season of terrible storms and incessant rains and never before or since in my long life have I known a worse one." Nevertheless, the Army of the Potomac was on the move, and the Balloon Corps was going with it. Weeks of boredom making regular tethered observations from the fortifications surrounding Washington were at an end. The moment they had honed themselves for had come; they were going into battle as part of an army on the attack.

Lowe, James Allen, and Ebenezer Mason were to sail aboard the balloon boat *Custis,* along with the *Intrepid* and two generators. Ebenezer Seaver, who had gone to the peninsula earlier in the month to serve with Hooker's command, would meet them at Fort Monroe. The enlisted men and their wagons were packed onto other transports, as were the horses and mules, which went on boats with the other animals. Lowe despaired of ever seeing his favorite horse again as he watched it being coaxed up the gangplank and then disappear into the hold of the barge at the next slip.

As the balloon boat was slowly tugged from its mooring, Lowe reluctantly informed his comrades they were all still civilians. Despite his weekly letters to the head of the Topographical Engineers, his balloonists, as well as the telegraph operators and signalmen, had not yet been given their military commissions, a condition his men were finding increasingly difficult to tolerate. They would still have to go into action without wearing uniforms, facing the possibility of being shot as spies if they were captured. Lowe questioned why their appointments were taking so long to accomplish, and told them he had high hopes that the newly appointed head of the Topographical Engineers, General A. A. Humphreys, would soon rectify their situation.

Quartermaster-General Montgomery Meigs had assembled a mighty flotilla of 400 ships and barges to transport McClellan's army of 125,000 men, 25,000 animals, 300 cannon, and various other impedimenta, such as ambulances, wagons, rations, ammunition, and pontoon bridges the two hundred miles to Fort Monroe. However, this magnificent display of the Union's logistical powers, that took three weeks to complete, almost had not gotten underway.

Having lost confidence in McClellan, Lincoln reduced his authority, demoting him from general in chief of the whole army to commander only of the Army of the Potomac. The president also had withheld several divisions from McClellan when he discovered that the general had left behind fewer troops than he promised for the protection of Washington.

McClellan claimed he had assigned seventy-three thousand soldiers to the capital's defense. However, a count ordered by Lincoln could turn up only twenty-nine thousand men. Apparently, by accident or design, McClellan had counted some troops twice, and included General Nathaniel Banks's army of twenty-three thousand bivouacked in the Shenandoah Valley as part of the capital's watch. Consequently Lincoln removed General Irwin McDowell's entire thirty-five-thousand-man corps from McClellan's command and ordered them to remain guarding the capital. An embittered McClellan would arrive at Fort Monroe with only 90,000 of the 130,000 men he expected to have.

Storm clouds threatened over the Chesapeake as Lowe and his Balloon Corps arrived at Fort Monroe on April 2. Union flags fluttered on the gunboats that lay at anchor all across the tip of the peninsula off Hampton, Virginia, charged with protecting the operation. Overhead, squadrons of geese honked across the gray sky as Lowe and his

aeronauts stood on the deck of the *Custis,* awaiting their turn to disembark. Staring in awe at the vast array of the Army of the Potomac
spread across the fields and roads in front of them, Lowe, turning to
Allen, was moved to remark, "I wonder if ever before in history there
has been such an immense movement of men and equipment?"

The very next day, Lowe was ordered to depart Fort Monroe with
a balloon unit and join Porter's division on its advance up the peninsula. The head balloonist had been assigned a new sergeant by
General Humphreys. Unlike the conscripts that made up the bulk of
Lowe's unit, Sergeant Charles Eaton of the 22nd New York regiment
was a regular army man who had seen service in the West as an Indian
fighter. Observing the efficiency with which Eaton set up bivouac on
their first night at Fort Monroe, Lowe was quickly aware that the sergeant knew more about things military than he ever could. Thus the
head balloonist felt confident turning over the responsibility for the
unit to Eaton and Wagon Master Robert Collins when the troops had
to be sent on ahead since he had lost his horse. Searching through a
corral full of animals, while dozens of flies swarmed around their faces, Lowe and Allen had been unable to pick out their own fine mounts
from among the vast and nervous herd.

The next day their horses were found mixed in, by chance or by
design, with those of a cavalry brigade. Lowe spent most of the morning dealing with the endless paperwork needed to get their horses
back. As a consequence it was not until afternoon that he got around
to the details of assigning balloonists Mason and Seaver to remain at
Fort Monroe. By then it had begun raining. The rain continued and
had become rather heavy by the time Lowe and Allen finally set off,
almost a full day behind their balloon unit.

Wrapped in waterproof slickers, the two rode on in the persistent
deluge, water draining off the rim of Lowe's broad-brimmed black
hat. The two balloonists had only gone a few miles when they came
upon the first of many army wagons wallowing in the heavy mud. The
teamsters cursed and whipped their mules, but the poor creatures
could not move the bogged-down wagons. On orders from their commander, the soldiers began unloading the supplies and putting their
shoulders to the task of freeing the wheels from the muck.

As the aeronauts rode along the stalled wagons, they became the
subject of curses and derisive comments from the men who, seeing
them on horseback, mistook them for officers. Lowe shivered at the
thought of the many stories he had heard of officers being shot from
behind by the wretched soldiers they had sorely mistreated.

Coming upon yet another mired column, Lowe began to look ap-

prehensively for the wagons from his own unit. Whole regiments doggedly marched along in the mud and pouring rain, their clothing heavy
with the water it had absorbed, their boots sliding in the sticky muck
swirling with the dung of horses and mules. Lowe and Allen were generously splattered with the liquid filth, their boots and pants, and their
horses flanks completely covered.

They had only gone a short distance past the village of Big Bethel
when the two aeronauts began finding overcoats, blankets and even
boots scattered along the roadside. At every rest stop, even veteran
soldiers found things in their knapsack they could leave behind to
lighten their load. The tired troopers would miss these things later
on. But at the moment they were thinking only of the straps digging
into their sore shoulders. A canteen of water weighed three pounds;
sixty rounds of ammunition, a cartridge box, and belt, five pounds;
musket, nine pounds; haversack, five to ten pounds; knapsack, rations, and blanket, twenty pounds; even a lightened load could easily
total forty pounds.

The rain continued to pour down. Laden with moisture, the air was
difficult to breathe. Lowe and Allen rode on without stopping to rest
their horses. With a solid overcast overhead, darkness would be arriving early. The two balloonists passed columns of soldiers staggering
forward; they had been, hour after hour, completely tired out, like
oxen in a furrow, not knowing when their misery would end. Seemingly more dead than alive, the men continued slogging on, one foot in
front of the last, because that was what they had been ordered to do.

15

On to Yorktown, Lost, General Porter Goes for a Ride

Just after dawn on April 5 an exhausted Lowe and Allen, their horses lathered and drawn from having been ridden all night, finally arrived at the Union lines. The *Intrepid,* two portable generators, and four army wagons of supplies were aiready there. Lowe reported immediately to General Porter's headquarters, which had been set up at Howe's Sawmill, a mile behind the front lines and two miles from the York River. With their flanks protected by the Union gunboats on the James and York rivers fifty-five thousand of McClellan's men had advanced to the historic Revolutionary war battlefield at Yorktown.

As the rain had stopped, and the weather was beginning to clear, the general asked Lowe how soon he could get his observation balloon into the air. Responding that it could take between four to six hours, the weary head balloonist hurried off to begin the inflation of the *Intrepid.* He had no time to lose as McClellan was eager for a reconnaissance to be made, and it appeared the weather would soon go bad again.

At 5 o'clock one of Porter's staff officers arrived at the balloon station located on a piece of high ground near the sawmill. The aide explained that the general was occupied with other matters and could not come; he would take his place. Lowe checked his watch. It was 5:20 when the balloonist and the officer rose skyward in the *Intrepid.* A slight breeze had cleared the sky considerably, although the visibility was far from perfect. The artificial colors of the overcast day were slowly giving way to a hazy late afternoon. Standing rigidly next to the man he had heard of, but only just met, the young officer gripped the sides of the swaying basket as he stared in amazement at their unimpaired view of the nearby Confederate fortifications. Through his spyglass the Union officer could observe the wretchedness of the wasted crews digging breastworks, the second-rate anatomy supporting misshapen heads with rotten teeth and matted beards, some men even barefooted. In sharp contrast behind them, splendid astride their mounts, he could see the Confederate officers.

Eager to expand on his previous observations, Lowe went up again the next day at first light with another observer. The clouds had departed and the visibility was much improved. "What do you make of that?" an astonished Lowe asked pointing across the river. As they peered disbelieving through their spyglasses, they could clearly see, spread out for about five miles along the Warwick River, a vast chain of earthworks and spiked log, cheval-de-frise, defensive positions. Although they studied the Confederate positions long and hard through their telescopes, what the two men could not detect was that these apparently formidable defenses were manned by only about thirteen thousand Confederate soldiers under the command of a cagey general named John Bankhead Magruder.

Lowe reported the discovery of these seemingly formidable fortifications to McClellan. The balloonist was surprised when the general appeared almost elated by the news. Which indeed McClellan was, as now he had a good reason not to attack, being unsure of the strength of the opposing forces. An amateur actor in his pre-army days, the showy Confederate General Magruder, nicknamed "Prince John," had contrived an elaborate performance to confound McClellan. In plain view of Lowe in his balloon, but out of range of Union guns, Magruder marched his men up and down the hills in an endless circle, while his artillery batteries covertly moved and fired from different fields, to give the impression that he had considerably more troops and cannon than he actually had.

McClellan eagerly took Magruder's bait. He wired President Lincoln: "The fortifications at Yorktown can only be taken by a siege." Having decided this, "Young Napoleon" bedded down his army and waited for the arrival of his sappers and massive guns. Lincoln was furious and wired McClellan about growing Republican doubts about his loyalty; he concluded, "I think you had better break the enemy's line . . . at once, by delay the enemy will relatively gain upon you. . . . I have never written you . . . in greater kindness of feeling than now, nor with a fuller purpose to sustain you. . . . But you must act."

Week after week went by while McClellan's engineers constructed "corduroy roads," hundreds of logs laid side to side, to get his large cannon across the Virginia mud. Some of the guns were so heavy they required as many as a hundred mules to haul them to the front. While these preparations were going on, Lowe was making several ascensions per day with the *Intrepid*. He had developed a program of regular observations with members of General Porter's staff. Draftsmen were taken aloft to sketch maps from the air as the army was using mainly maps they had bought in civilian bookstores. In addition, Major General Daniel Butterfield, as well as General Porter himself, both made numerous ascensions with the head balloonist, coming away exceedingly impressed by the merits of balloon reconnaissance.

Having established his operation in Porter's area, and sensing that McClellan was not about to attack anytime soon, Lowe placed James Allen in charge of the *Intrepid* and returned to Fort Monroe to prepare a second balloon assigned to General Erasmus Keyes at Warwick Court House. His final advice to Allen was to keep an eye out for Rebel sharpshooters who had taken to climbing tall pine trees to get a pot shot at him in the balloon.

Finished with his business at Warwick Court House on April 10, Lowe headed back to his balloon camp at General Porter's headquarters. Darkness overtook the balloonist while he was on his way. He had been confident of arriving before nightfall, but now seemed to have lost his way. Federal engineers had repaired several of the bridges destroyed by the Rebels in their retreat. Thus Lowe, traveling alone, found himself returning by a different route than he had used on the way down. He must have taken a wrong turn on the unfamiliar roads for it was now completely dark and he was not yet to his camp. In fact, he had no idea where he was as he had not passed a town or even a farmhouse in some time.

A pallid moon slid in and out of the thick clouds. Only his horse's intuitive sense kept them going forward and in the middle of the road. Up ahead, Lowe thought he saw the faint glow of a campfire. Not one to throw caution to the wind, as he had crossed the river several times and was now not sure if he was still behind Union lines, the balloonist dismounted and tied his horse to a tree. Staying in the shadow of the woods, Lowe slowly worked his way toward the dim light. He stopped a safe distance away and crouched in the weeds. Frogs croaked in the damp ditch at his feet, and mosquitoes swirled around his face as he listened for some noise from the barely discernible figures gathered around the flickering fire.

The sound of a harmonica being played drifted to Lowe's ears. He strained to hear the tune, hoping it would give a clue as to the allegiance of the men. The unknown musician was playing "Home Sweet Home." It was a song popular with both sides. The balloonist shifted his weight and a twig cracked loudly under his foot. The music stopped. A man stood up and looked around. Taking a burning brand from the fire in one hand and a pistol in the other, the soldier began to advance in Lowe's direction.

The balloonist slipped silently back into the trees. The man kept coming. Now Lowe could see the faded gray color of his kepi and uniform. Motionless in the darkness, Lowe held his breath as the man walked past, but he knew he had another problem. If the Rebel picket continued down the road in the direction he was going, he would surely discover his horse and confiscate it. Lowe would have to hike back from wherever he was. Or the alarmed Confederate soldiers might even probe the woods and perhaps find him. Without a doubt they would hold him as a spy.

The Johnny Reb continued on a few more feet; his firebrand was smoking, burning out. He stopped and listened while considering his options. Then he turned around and walked back to the campfire. After waiting for several minutes and seeing no more movement from the encamped group, Lowe crept back to where he had left his horse. Mounting up, the balloonist rode off in a slow trot in the direction from which he had come.

The sun was just beginning to appear through the tree tops when fortune delivered Lowe to a familiar looking road. Continuing on, by 6:30 the balloonist sensed he was almost in sight of his camp, anticipating that he would get a good breakfast and perhaps sleep away the rest of the morning. Suddenly he was astounded by the sight of a massive form floating overhead. He reigned up his startled horse. Sailing by in free flight was the *Intrepid.* Lowe, shielding his eyes from the sun, regretted not having his telescope as the balloon was too high for him to determine who the occupant was. The person in the basket appeared to be observing the enemy fortifications through a spyglass. Lowe was furious, his heart pounding, convinced that James Allen had taken advantage of his absence from camp to attempt a free flight over Confederate territory, when he had specifically forbidden such actions.

As he watched, Lowe's frame of mind shifted from furious to terrified; the balloon seemed to be in imminent danger of coming down behind the enemy lines. He knew that the Balloon Corps had too few balloons and too few balloonists to take such a foolish loss so early in the campaign. Lowe urged his horse on in the direction that the *Intrepid* was descending, now being wafted back toward him and the Union lines.

Abruptly the balloon began losing altitude, coming down with such speed that the lower half of the envelope was being forced into the upper hemisphere forming a parachute. This was a stroke of luck for the occupant as this slowed the descent rate considerably. Lowe galloped on after the run-amuck *Intrepid.* As he watched, it disappeared behind the top of a ridge directly in front of him.

The balloonist crested the hill to discover the balloon down and already surrounded by a mob of horsemen, soldiers, and reporters. Dismounting and working his way to the middle of the crowd, Lowe found Porter himself, looking slightly disheveled, standing in front of a puffy pile of varnished fabric, which still hissed and quivered as the last of the gas escaped.

Seeing Lowe emerge from the group prepared to vent his fire, a mortified James Allen, accompanied by General Porter, rushed up to explain what had happened. The aeronaut recounted he had come down from his regular dawn reconnaissance and was informed that Porter wished to go aloft with considerable dispatch. Therefore, he instructed the handlers to moor the balloon with only a single rope, instead of the three normally used. Then Allen hurried off to find the general who in the meantime had arrived at the balloon site, and was assured by the men he would be right back. The balloon handlers assumed Allen had gone to visit the latrine as he had not told them he was going in search of Porter. The general, not being a person to waste any time, had the two men who were holding the other two tether ropes help him into the basket. All this while the sun had been shinning directly on the bag, heating and expanding the gas.

The mooring line, which had been slack, was now taut. Allen was returning to the balloon station when he heard a loud pop. He surmised that the single tie-down rope had broken and started to a run. Allen had arrived at the launch site just as the balloon began to ascend. The handlers, having been knocked over by the sudden jolt, had let go their grip of the basket. They got themselves up and, taking little more than a moment to grasp the situation, grabbed for the trailing lines, but it was too late. Porter had started on his journey, the balloon providing him a rapid ascent.

While Lowe had an infuriated look on his face, Porter seemed to be hiding a smile under his full beard. He mopped his brow and asked to be allowed to continue the story. Porter maintained that he had not been overly concerned as he felt that he had made enough ascensions with the two aeronauts to be thoroughly familiar with the *Intrepid*'s operating procedures. He knew that releasing gas was the swiftest way to get the balloon down: The end of the rope one pulled to open the gas valve at the top was painted red, to distinguish it from the other guide ropes. This end was tucked into a separate little slot to keep it from being pulled accidentally, as opening the valve all the way by mistake could be disastrous. Porter was contemplating the venting of gas and coming down when he observed that the hasty ascent had caused his valve rope to whip around and become completely fouled in the balloon's netting. Well aware he was drifting over the enemy lines, the general endeavored to make the best of a bad situation. He had come to make a surveillance of the Confederate fortifications, and so he would.

The Confederates in the meantime, having recovered from the shock of seeing the Union balloon floating freely over their heads, had opened fire at it with every musket and cannon available. Realizing the danger of his situation, Porter hastily finished his observations. "I took good observations, some notes, but mainly instantaneous impressions like a photographic instrument, and had the enemy's position and defenses so grafted on my mind that when I descended I was able to give a good sketch of everything," the general later wrote.

Upon his sudden departure from the balloon camp, a cavalry troop had been mustered to find the general and bring him back, wherever he might come down. The patrol, however, was having difficulty following him as the *Intrepid*'s track was not confined to the roads and fields as they were.

Observing he had been blown back behind his own lines, Porter decided to descend as soon as possible lest the winds change again. He climbed up into the netting and, not without first slipping and nearly falling out, freed the tangled valve rope. As he jumped back down, the general must have accidentally pulled the rope opening the valve and releasing gas. The balloon lurched and then began to come down at a rapid rate. As Porter chanced to look upward, he was distressed to find the fabric of the envelope collapsing over his head. The neophyte balloonist had vented off too much gas, much too quickly.

Fortunately the netting had gathered the varnished silk into the shape of a parachute. Although the swooning *Intrepid* had returned to earth rather swiftly, it landed safely behind Union lines and General Porter happily escaped injury. Lowe would note in his papers, "I found it difficult for a time to restore confidence among the officers as to the safety of this means of observation."

One of Lowe's men who had watched the flight laughingly commented, "If the general had been reconnoitering from a secure perch at the tip of the moon, he could not have been more vigilant, and the Confederates probably thought this some Yankee device to peer into their sanctuary in despite of ball or shell."

While Porter had escaped being shot down, in the excitement of the moment the *Intrepid* was almost destroyed by another means. Having consistently failed to take out Lowe's balloons by artillery and rifle fire, the Confederates attempted to resort to sabotage. Among the boodle that swarmed around the *Intrepid* when Porter landed abruptly was a lame and seedy peddler of tobacco and notions who had been hanging around the balloon camp for the past week. The peddler had become so ubiquitous with his wares that the soldiers no longer took notice of him. As Sergeant Eaton and his men were folding up the *Intrepid* to return it to camp, the peddler watched from a bit too close. In a seemingly harmless gesture he took out a match and began to light his pipe. Eaton, catching sight of the the rising white smoke, immediately grabbed the peddler and put his flame out, ordering his men to remove the civilian from the area. Two soldiers took the man by his arms and hastily frog-marched the recalcitrant peddler down the road.

Later that day Sergeant Eaton described the incident to Lowe. The balloonist felt the blood pound in his temples when he learned of how close his balloon had come to disaster. He questioned Eaton to determine if his actions might have been premature. The sergeant, however, was positive his instinct had been correct. As further proof, the unkempt peddler was never seen again near the balloon camp, nor anywhere around the Army of the Potomac, after the incident. Later a rumor circulated widely that the peddler had been a Confederate spy, sent out with the express mission of destroying Lowe's balloon.

Some years after the war, in 1886, an anonymous "ex-Confederate" would claim in an interview in the *Detroit Free Press* that he was one of five men who had volunteered when promised $1,000 in gold and a commission as a second lieutenant, if they could put a Federal balloon out of action. He stated that at the time the secrecy of the mission was such that none of the five volunteers knew who the other four were.

The men were kept completely unaware of each other's plans and traveled independently. When the "lame peddler" arrived at Lowe's camp, he learned that two of the other saboteurs had already been captured. They had been discovered working with a gang of contraband blacks building earthworks near the balloon camp. The *Intrepid* always had so many men around it that the peddler had been forced to bide his time. Porter's landing in a strange field seemed to him the opportunity he had been waiting for. The former Confederate spy related:

>   I had matches, and I had only to destroy the balloon in a flash. I meant to take every risk, but as I drew a match from my pocket, having a filled pipe already in my mouth as an excuse, a big sergeant who stood beside me seized me by the neck, and shouted at me: "You infernal idiot! Do you want to fire the balloon?" I did, but he had deprived me of the opportunity. Some of the men laughed. Some said I ought to be kicked out of camp, and prudence whis-

pered to me to take myself off while I had the chance. Only two of us out of the five got back to our regiments. What became of the others was a mystery I have never been able to clear up.

Records made public after the war revealed that the other would-be balloon saboteurs were captured and eventually shot as spies.

The *Intrepid* was soon refurbished, and Lowe resumed his regular observations along the Yorktown line. The value of these flights was becoming apparent to the Confederates as well as to the Union commanders. Distressed by the Yankee's ability to peer down into the very heart of their fortifications, Confederate gunners under the command of Edward P. Alexander trained their cannons on the balloon every time it went up. One war correspondent reported:

> It came at length to be our principal amusement in camp to watch the rebels fire at the balloon, as it sailed tranquilly above our picket line, and I have seen many a dollar staked by the "boys in blue" on the skill of the gray-coated artillerists. It was laughable to watch these bets, and I think I shall not go too far astray from the truth, when I say that some very good patriots would have been very glad to see the balloon struck, since it would have enabled them to win their wagers.

A great, undulating spring morning was unfolding its brightness as Lowe ascended over the Confederate fortifications at Yorktown in the *Intrepid* on April 13. He was on one of his regular observation flights. Below him lay the "Red Fort," a massive parapet of red clay constructed during the Revolutionary War by the British army under Lord Comwallis. Shot after shot whistled past Lowe and his balloon as if he were being sent up for the sport of the gunners. The balloonist knew that at his altitude he was safe; it was when he was going up and coming down that he became most vulnerable.

As Lowe looked out at the familiar landscape in front of him a new sight greeted his eye. He stared incredulously. Could it be that he was no longer the sole master of the sky in this sector? It was not his other balloon gone astray from Warwick Courthouse. Rather it was some strange, rather-ragged looking airship ascending from behind the Rebel lines, emerging cautiously like a shy school boy looking for a partner at the local dance. Lowe wondered if he might be seeing the same balloon that had made a brief appearance over the Confederate camps on Munson's Hill in northern Virginia the previous winter. Not yet ready to abnegate his command of the air, Lowe studied the airship carefully through his spyglass. The Rebel balloon was ascending so slowly it aroused more mirth than alarm in the balloonist's mind. It was apparent that this new arrival was no masterpiece of the airship art. As it was tethered at a considerable distance, Lowe determined that even if it did reach its height it would present him no harm. Back on the ground, the balloonist wrote in his notes that, as far as he had observed, the Confederate craft had "neither shape nor buoyancy," and predicted "it would burst or fall apart after a week."

At the time, the head of the Balloon Corps was not aware that his Confederate opposite was Captain John Randolph Bryan. The twenty-one-year-old former aide to General Magruder had volunteered to fly the rather fragile hot air balloon, which was inflated using the heat from burning pine knots soaked in turpentine.

Captain Bryan and his balloon had barely risen above the tops of the pine trees surrounding the field he had departed from when Lowe saw the Federal artillery below him rushing into action. Officers barked commands as the gunners struggled to elevate their field-pieces for a shot at the unfamiliar target. Bryan signaled his handlers to let out more rope, and he slowly rose out of the dangerous lower altitudes before the surprised Union cannonists could get off a shot. The small hot air balloon had barely enough force to lift the aeronaut and its lone tether line, let alone the three tether ropes Lowe used to keep his balloon from turning with the wind. As a result the Confederate balloon spun around constantly on its single tether.

Whirling slowly, Bryan quickly drew a map of the Union positions, noting concentrations of cavalry and infantry, and the location of artillery and supply wagons. It was a difficult task, made more so by the need to complete it before the hot air in his bag cooled. When Bryan was ready to descend, a team of six horses was used to pull the balloon down more rapidly to avoid Federal gunfire. After the first appearance witnessed by Lowe, the Confederate balloon would make several more flights over the next few days and then, for reasons unknown, disappear from the skies.

At the same time the Confederates were attempting to perform observations with their primitive aerostat, Lowe was facing increased enemy fire on his regular aerial reconnaissance flights. These flights had taken on particular significance as Lowe's daily reports on Confederate targets would form the basis for the siege that was soon to begin.

There had been little action in the previous weeks, most of the shooting that had occurred being done by Rebel gunners camped behind the red earthen walls firing at Lowe's observation balloon. No Federal unit relished being stationed in proximity to Lowe's balloon camp due to the heavy rain of incoming shells that had failed to hit the balloon. To avoid this fallout, the balloonist occasionally had reinforced structures constructed to protect his ground crews from the descending shrapnel. In April 1862 Porter had to ask Lowe to move his operation because of the heavy Confederate artillery fire. A New York sergeant recounted how shells aimed at Lowe's balloon fell on a cook shack at General Henry Slocum's headquarters, "scattering camp kettles and cooks, who were just then preparing breakfast."

Moving to yet another location, Lowe received a complaint from General Stoneman, who was upset because the barrages directed at the balloon were falling in a corral filled with valuable cavalry horses. Apparently the closest that generals Stoneman, Heintzelman, and McClellan ever came to being hit by Confederate fire during the Peninsula Campaign was when visiting Lowe's balloon sites. Recalling this danger in a letter to Lowe some years after the war, Union veteran Lieutenant Colonel W. J. Handy wrote:

> I was on guard duty opposite the "Red Fort" in the woods May 2, 1862, when we saw the balloon about to rise, then commenced a heavy cannonading from the Confederate woods, shots went over our head, tearing big branches from the trees. We were safer inside the line of fire than closer to our own camp. The balloon rose and firing was soon directed at this Air Target. Shot after shot, shells exploding way up, occasionally the sharp crack of a rifle would be heard when their sharp shooters took a chance shot, kept up the work for half a day. No damage was done as I remember, except the slaughter of fine old trees and great holes in the ground where solid shot struck."

One correspondent wrote that the appearance of Lowe's balloon sent the Confederate artillerists into "paroxysms of rage." Failing to hit it with rifle and shell fire, the thwarted Rebels often "cried at it in derision."

E. P. Alexander's cannoneers attempted to use shallow trenches dug behind their guns to gain a greater elevation. As guns of the period could be elevated on their carriage no more than a few degrees, Confederate Lieutenant Thomas Rosser had come up with the idea of digging a pit behind his field piece into which the trail could be lowered to elevate the muzzle and allow for recoil. He had first used this technique against Lowe at Centreville on September 2, 1861.

As there were no range tables for this unorthodox form of gunnery, the artillerists had to estimate anytime they aimed at a balloon. When Lowe appeared the Rebel cannon would be dragged back into the dug holes to raise the angle of their barrels. But even this did not work.

The gunners took to ignoring the *Intrepid* when it was at its height, hoping to catch it at a low altitude when it was taking off or landing.

While Lowe flew the *Intrepid* at Yorktown, James Allen kept the *Constitution* aloft as much as possible at Warwick Courthouse. General William F. Smith, now in command of the 2nd Division of Keyes's corps, had assigned a junior officer named George Armstrong Custer to part-time duty as an observer with Allen. Called "Cinnamon" by his friends because of the smell of the hair oil he used to control his flowing golden coiffure, Custer had already established a reputation among the officers and men as a flamboyant character.

Custer reported to Allen sometime around April 23, when he had moved the *Constitution* from Warwick Court House three miles closer to General Smith's headquarters. Known as a dashing horseman, Lieutenant Custer was less comfortable in the air. He would write in his memoirs: "Ballooning was a kind of danger that few people have schooled themselves against, and still fewer possess a liking for." Custer therefore accepted General Smith's order with "no little trepidation."

Although the fear associated with his first flight prevented Custer from standing up next to Allen and he remained seated on the floor of the basket firmly grasping the sides, he did later write a vivid depiction of the experience. In November 1876 the description appeared in Custer's "War Memoirs," published in the *Galaxy Miscellany and Advertiser:*

> To the right could be seen the York River, following which the eye could rest on Chesapeake Bay. On the left, and at about the same distance, flowed the James River. . . . Between these two extended a most beautiful landscape, and no less interesting than beautiful; it being made a theatre of operations of armies larger and more formidable than had ever confronted each other on this continent before . . . I endeavored to locate and recognize the different points of interest, as they lay spread out over the surface upon which the eye could rest. The point over which the balloon was held was probably one mile from the nearest point of the enemy's line. In an open country balloons would be invaluable in discovering the location of the enemy's camp and works. Unfortunately, however, the enemy's camps, like our own, were generally pitched in the woods to avoid the intense heat of a summer sun; his earthworks along the Warwick were also concealed by growing timber, so that it would have been necessary for the aeronaut to attain the highest possible altitude

and then secure a position directly above the country to be examined. With all the assistance of a good field glass, and watching opportunities when the balloon was not rendered unsteady by the different currents of air, I was enabled to catch glimpses of canvas through openings in the forest, while camps located in the open space were as plainly visible as those of the Army of the Potomac. Here and there the dim outline of an earthwork could be seen more than half concealed by the trees which had been purposely left standing on their front. Guns could be seen mounted and peering sullenly through the embrasures, while men in considerable numbers were standing in and around the entrenchments, often collected in groups, intently observing the balloon, curious no doubt, to know the character or value of the information its occupants could derive from their elevated post of observation.

Custer's initial observation must have satisfied General Smith, for he ordered the lieutenant to continue making ascensions.

16

A Cannon Explodes, the Rebels Retreat, a Boat Trip

By the beginning of May, 1862 having finally dragged his heavy guns into position, McClellan was prepared to lay siege to Yorktown. However, as Lincoln had warned, the Confederates had used McClellan's delay to move General Joseph E. Johnston's entire army to the peninsula.

Inspecting the Rebel breastworks at Yorktown after he arrived Johnston had pronounced them, "hopelessly weak," stating, "No one but McClellan could have hesitated to attack." He recommended that the Confederates withdraw all the way to the defenses that had been prepared just outside of Richmond. But Jefferson Davis was opposed to his proposal and ordered Johnston to defend the Yorktown line. Hunkered down in the frequent rain and ever-present mud, Johnston bided his time.

On the afternoon of May 2 the weather cleared enough for Lowe to make an ascension above the "Red Fort." The balloonist, like his men on the ground, felt more nervous than usual. Everyone seemed to sense that the long-awaited offensive was about to begin. The usual barrages whistled by below him as Lowe began to make his observations. For some reason his eyes were drawn to the interior of the fort, where a large Armstrong gun had been propped up to an extreme angle. Lowe gaped down at the gun, which was pointed exactly at him, so accurately he could see directly down the muzzle. Lowe watched as if mesmerized as the crew packed the barrel full of powder, determined to bring him down once and for all.

Over the past month Lowe had observed this crew through his telescope so many times it was almost as if they had become old friends. The balloonist knew he was above their range. The barrel was angled higher than usual, and they seemed to be loading it with more than the standard amount of gunpowder. Lowe was about to signal to be hauled down. Then he thought better of it. The gunners could lower their aim and get him before he reached the ground. Though more exposed, he was safer where he was. Or was he this time?

Captivated by the clamor of confusion and the disorderly shuffle of feet as the men scrambled around the gun, Lowe watched as a gunner lit the fuse. He saw a bright flash, then heard the roar, as the cannon exploded in smoke and flames. Bits of debris flew wildly about, and with it parts of the gun crew—arms and legs. Through his lens Lowe followed a bearded head, its mouth moving, still apparently trying to be say something as it rolled across the red earth. Unable to control himself, the balloonist doubled over in the basket and began to throw up.

Clearly shaken, his complexion pale, Lowe sat on the floor of the gondola for some time without looking at the ground. The firing had temporarily halted while the Confederate artillerists considered the fate of their fallen comrades. The balloonist thought of his wife and daughters back in Philadelphia, these beautiful cherubs life had entrusted him with. Was it them he was fighting for? Lowe listened with growing anxiety to the screams still rising up from the fort below. After almost two years with the army, everything—preserving the Union, states' rights, slavery, and whatever other abstractions this war was being fought for—had all become meaningless.

Regaining his composure, Lowe peered at his own lines. Below him the "contraband," as blacks were called, were hard at work digging trenches, and building bridges and fortifications, any of the heavy work the soldiers were reluctant to do. The military's recent General Order's #3 denied runaway slaves sanctuary behind Union lines. Federal officers were supposed to return slaves to their masters, yet the rule was mainly ignored, with the fugitives put to work for little or no pay, often receiving only food and a place to sleep, and treated with not much more kindness than they had from the owners they fled.

Lowe took a folded handkerchief from his pocket and began cleaning the vomit from his frock coat as best he could. Then he wiped his hands, and gave the signal for the *Intrepid* to be pulled down. Normally the balloonist felt quite dapper in his long black coat and black felt hat; however, at that moment, Lowe felt more as if he were dressed for a funeral.

On May 3, as ordered by General Smith, Lieutenant Custer made an ascension in the *Constitution* at Warwick Court House. The novice aeronaut reported that everything appeared as it had been, observing no movements of troops or artillery. Later that same evening Lowe also conducted an aerial reconnaissance at Warwick Court House. Seeing nothing out of the ordinary, the head balloonist returned to his own camp at Yorktown.

Around midnight Lowe was awakened from a sound sleep by Captain Moses, General Heintzelmann's aide. Alerted by his guards to the bright glow of what must be a huge fire blazing behind the Confederate lines at the "Red Fort," the general wished Lowe to go aloft immediately to determine what was going on. Heintzelman had maintained all along that the Confederate stand at Yorktown was only a delaying action. He suspected that Johnston intended to slip out with his troops as soon as McClellan was ready to begin his siege.

Gripping the load ring, Lowe swayed in the basket of the *Intrepid* as the balloon rose rapidly into the cool night air. Above him the dark night was lit by only a few stars, but across the river the sky glowed with the light of a blazing inferno. From the location the balloonist knew the site of the fire to be the Confederate's vast supply depot. Lowe wondered what kind of fool with a cigar, or perhaps a lantern, had caused this apparent disaster.

Training his spyglass on the area, the balloonist noted the fortress was alive with activity. Men and wagons were moving everywhere, yet no one seemed the least bit concerned with putting out the roaring fire. He swept the earthworks with his lens. Several columns of marching troops, accompanied by supply wagons, could be seen disappearing down the road into the darkness. Alarmed by what he was seeing, the balloonist signaled his men to haul him down posthaste.

Lowe reported what he had observed to General Heintzelman. His information seemed to confirm the general's suspicion that Johnston was evacuating the fortifications. Heintzelman, himself, went aloft with Lowe, but by now the blaze of the fire had died down considerably making an accurate observation of what the Confederates were about difficult. As the two men watched through telescopes, a parade of wagons could be discerned in the dim light making their way out of the fort. What confused them was the line of wagons entering the fort at the same time.

Lowe studied the scene carefully. After a time he noticed that the wagons coming into the fort were moving easily, apparently empty, while the wagons leaving were moving slowly, their teams working hard to pull them, obviously heavily laden. Reluctant to wake up McClellan to give him this information, as Heintzelman was sure his superior would disregard any intelligence that contradicted his theory that the Army of the Potomac was facing a massive Confederate force dug in for a long siege, the two decided to wait until morning to make another ascension.

On May 4 Lowe went up alone before dawn. In the faint light his observation was inconclusive, but he did note a conspicuous absence of campfires on the other side of the river. Shortly after the sun had risen, Lowe ascended again, this time with Heintzelman. From a height of a thousand feet, the two men swept the Confederate defensive line with their spyglasses. They were startled to find the fortifications completely empty of soldiers and equipment. As far as they could see there was not a Rebel camp or moving column. Johnston, having become aware of McClellan's impending attack, had abandoned Yorktown and withdrawn his troops to the defensive ring around the capital at Richmond.

Finally out of bed, McClellan was apprised of the Confederate's stealthy departure. In an instant "Young Napoleon" was astride his horse riding up and down the ranks shouting orders. Soon the entire Army of the Potomac was preparing to march. However, even in their haste, the Union forces found it necessary to display extreme caution passing through the deserted fortifications as the Confederate sappers had generously littered the landscape with mines and booby traps rigged to explosives.

The men of the Signal Corps were among the first to go into the conceded territory setting up knocked-down poles and restringing wires. In a spirit of cooperation Lowe had volunteered his telegraph operators, and he and most of his other men had gone along to help. The work was proceeding with efficiency and speed. The balloonist watched as D. D. Lathrop, his chief telegraphist, descended from a pole on which he had just completed a connection. Lathrop reached the ground. With an air of pride and accomplishment the telegraph operator looked up, taking a step back to admire his work.

Without warning there was a blinding flash, and the man and pole disappeared in a cloud of smoke and dirt. Lowe stood there feeble at the destructive force he had witnessed, his face red, his eyebrows singed. The balloonist turned away, sick with horror. Lathrop had been killed instantly, having stepped on the primer of a buried mine. However, the telegraph operator's tragic passing would not go unnoticed by history, as would the deaths of so many others in this war. Lathrop would have the distinct honor of being the only casualty suffered by McClellan's Army of the Potomac while "taking the Red Fort."

It was a dejected crew that towed Lowe in the basket of *Intrepid* through the deserted streets of Yorktown later that day. If there were people in the houses, no one came out to watch his strange procession as normally happened whenever he passed down a road swaying above the housetops in the gondola of his brightly painted globe.

Although there was apparently no one anywhere, Lowe and his men kept alert for Rebel sharpshooters who might be hiding in the woods. The only sniper they did encounter presented them no threat as he was hanging from a tree, a bullet through his skull, a victim of one of the Federal soldiers that had passed through earlier. Lowe's slow and ponderous balloon unit was basically traveling alone, even behind the supply wagons. The main bulk of McClellan's army had galloped and marched off at a feverish pace early that morning.

The balloonist ordered the *Intrepid* to be released a little higher. At his new altitude Lowe was able to train his telescope on the York River. A flotilla of Federal gunboats lay at anchor just below Gloucester Point, a high jut of land on the north bank of the river opposite Yorktown. The gunboats had cleared the point of Confederate batteries, and were now awaiting orders to proceed upstream. Off to the east Lowe could see his balloon barge and its tug, and several small transports, steaming up the river from Chesapeake Bay. The balloonist shouted the news to the men, and pointed in the direction of the *Custis.* The slip where the balloon boat, its tug, and its escorts would dock was their destination.

Arriving at the pier, Lowe was hailed by a familiar and raucous greeting. The balloonist was surprised to discover his father Clovis had come down from the capital with the war balloon *Washington.* John B. Starkweather, having had his fill of the war and of red tape, had returned the balloon to Clovis at the armory in Washington, D. C. When Federal forces finally occupied Fort Pulaski and closed the Savannah River to blockade-runners, Starkweather felt his mission was over. In addition, he had not received any salary since leaving Washington and his family was in serious debt, so he had decided to leave the Balloon Corps to return home and find a paying job.

Although Lowe was sorry to hear of Starkweather's departure, he was happy to see his father and pleased when the man volunteered to stay on in Virginia with the Army of the Potomac. The balloonist warned Clovis, from what he had seen so far, that the campaign was going to be a rough one. Unshaken, and feeling that his son was probably exaggerating the dangers confronting them, the elder Lowe asked the younger if he ever knew him to flinch from a good fight. Then, producing a small bundle from behind his back, Clovis joked he had brought several letters of recommendation. With this he handed his son a packet of letters from Leontine. A delighted T. S. C. Lowe retired to the privacy of the tug's wheelhouse to read his correspondence. Clovis, already taking on duties, remained on the pier to await the arrival of James Allen and his balloon unit from Warwick Court House.

It took the entire morning of May 4 to stow all three balloons, their gas generator wagons, and all the men and animals on board the *Custis.*

Lowe, his father, the other aeronauts, and the telegraph operators were crowded onto the tug. The plan now was to sail with a small convoy of transports and gunboats up the York River to West Point, and then via the Pamunkey River to White House Landing, McClellan's proposed new base of supply. While most of the Army of the Potomac was traveling up the center of the peninsula by land, the balloons were being sent by water as the roads were heavily wooded around the old colonial city of Williamsburg.

Although it was getting late in the afternoon, and the balloon carrier and its tug were loaded and waiting, the transports were still embarking the troops that were to accompany them to the new base. Also remaining on the docks were the troops' baggage and rations, as well as an arsenal of weapons and ammunition that had not been used in the siege of Yorktown.

Concerned that his balloon unit always seemed to be the last in the line of march, Lowe was eager to get started. Assuming that the other boats would sail by evening, despite the possibility of rain, Lowe ordered his tug and barge to depart. As a precaution, one of the aeronauts was sent aloft in a balloon to keep a watch for any threat from Confederate forces that might be along the river. While the aerial observer did spy several cotton-bale fortifications lining the shore, for the most part the banks of the York seemed to be deserted.

By sundown the tug and its trailing barge reached the mouth of the Pamunkey River. The rain had begun again. As the tug captain had never been up the narrow and winding Pamunkey before, he did not want to risk running the river in the dark. Lowe agreed to the captain's suggestion that they anchor off West Point. They were well into Rebel territory and would doubtless not be welcomed by the Southern sympathizers on the shore. As night fell Sergeant Eaton posted several guards. Then the balloonist and his men settled down to try to sleep.

Within an hour the rain, which had begun as a drizzle, began falling heavily. Lightning flashes and the sound of thunder punctuated the damp night. Lowe and the aeronauts were squeezed into the small cabin of the tug with the captain and his crew. As the balloon barge had no structure, the enlisted men vied for space on the deck under the tied-down generator wagons to escape from the rain. The less-fortunate had to sleep out in the open, along with the animals, wrapped only in their rain slickers.

A stiff wind kept up all through the night, howling, whistling, and groaning, all the while violently rocking the boats up and down on the waves. Mostly landlubbers, a considerable number of the soldiers became sick to their stomachs. In the darkness oaths and curses could be heard as many of the sufferers, in their rush to hang their heads over the gunwale, accidentally stepped on their dozing comrades who lay shivering on the cold and wet deck. As the lightning glittered on the churning water, and the rain beat down on them, the men could do nothing but huddle together for warmth, listening to the sounds of the storm, waiting for daylight and for the safety of the rest of the convoy.

By morning the rain had stopped. Lowe's balloon unit woke to a wet and chilly dawn. A dense fog hung over the water, preventing a clear view of the land. The boats containing the army units, which were to have accompanied them up the Pamunkey, were nowhere to be seen. The balloonist decided to make an ascension to get above the mist and perhaps determine their situation.

Lowe's legs were unsteady as the *Intrepid* slowly rose out of the damp vapor. He had not slept well curled up on the pitching deck of the tug and was tired. At five hundred feet he could see little except the clouds of last night's cold front hanging on in the sky to the east. The balloonist signaled for the full length of the tether to be let out. Arriving at the apex of his line, Lowe swept his spyglass slowly in a complete circle.

To the west he could see isolated columns of what appeared to be Confederate soldiers, but his own army was nowhere in sight, neither on land nor water. The heavy rains had doubtless turned the roads into a quagmire, accounting for the delay of the marching troops. But where were the other boats? He motioned to be hauled down. His group would wait until the fog had lifted. Perhaps the convoy would arrive, but from where, he wondered, as he had not seen any sign of them. There were patches of dense fog on the river, however not enough to hide the large flotilla that had been loading on the docks back at Yorktown. Lowe signaled for a pause in the descent. He cocked his ear to the south. He thought he could hear cannon fire from the direction of Williamsburg, Lowe shouted down. He listened again, but realized he was too far away to be sure.

The balloonist and his men waited on the decks. The sun was rare in the sky, although the fog had dissipated. On the river bank at West Point crowds could be seen gathering, with the occasional Confederate army uniform spotted among the civilians. For the moment the group was safe on the river. The detachment of soldiers accompanying the three balloons included 150 men with muskets. Lowe doubted that the Confederates could muster enough men and boats to attack them where they were, but there was the possibility that an artillery unit had been sent for to shell them. In that case they surely would be "sitting ducks."

The captain of the tug paced the deck, eager to push on. He kept stressing his need to get the barge up to White House Landing and return before nightfall. Annoyed by the hours of idleness caused by Lowe's indecision, the captain kept pressing him to start. The balloonist decided to make another ascension. As he hung aloft listening, the booming of the cannon became more frequent, whole volleys replacing the skirmishers' isolated shots. He was sure now that he was hearing firing from the vicinity of Williamsburg.

Lowe was confused by the sounds because he was not aware of an impending battle. No one expected General Johnston's army to stop until he reached Richmond. Moreover, with the lead Johnston had, McClellan had not expected his army to catch up with the fleeing Confederates. Given McClellan's penchant for maneuvering, rather than engaging in head-on conflict, the Union commander had not given much thought to the pursuit, but had devised an elaborate scheme for outflanking his enemy with sea power, using the York and Pamunkey rivers.

Lowe brought the balloon down, and explained what he had heard to the captain. The two men discussed the situation. The balloonist was inclined to head back down river to see what was happening. The captain, however, pointed out his orders were to deliver the barge to White House Landing, which was what he intended to do. Lowe agreed to go on. He would keep a balloon aloft to watch out for any Confederate forces that might be lying in ambush along the shore.

The captain powered up his steam engine, and his tug began to tow the heavily laden balloon barge into the current of the Pamunkey. Low gray clouds crept across the landscape. It had begun to rain again. No one on board the two boats was aware that the "missing" army was now engaged in a battle at the colonial capital of Williamsburg, Virginia, which McClellan would term "an accident, brought on by the rapid pursuit of our troops." Also unknown to Lowe and his balloon unit was the fact that they now constituted the advance guard of the Army of the Potomac.

By mid-afternoon, having traveled up the Pamunkey without incident, the *Custis* and its tug arrived at White House Landing. A slight drizzle had replaced the heavy rain.The Richmond and York River Railroad bridge, which crossed the stream at that point, was a forbidding sight. Having been torched by the fleeing Confederate Army, its charred black structure was still burning in some spots, the smoldering creosote beams giving off on obnoxious odor. Lowe and his men were reluctant to disembark. No Federal troopers had appeared on shore to greet them. In fact, there was no supply camp there at all, only an empty beach, and an elegant white mansion, in the colonial style, which dominated the bluff above them. The balloonist asked the tug captain if he was sure this was the place. The captain showed him his chart. There was the house, the bridge, and the bluff; this was White House Landing.

The tug crew unhooked the tug and secured the barge to a small, sagging wooden pier, the only dockage available. The tug captain shook Lowe's hand and wished him good luck, then, without further ceremony, quickly departed. Professor Lowe, his three balloons, generators, supply wagons and mules, three aeronauts and 150 men with muskets were left standing on the damp and soggy shore. The captain had promised to tell anyone he saw down river that the balloon unit had arrived, and was waiting for the rest of the army.

It was only then that Lowe began to comprehend the gravity of his predicament. The sounds of battle he had heard coming from the vicinity of Williamsburg he guessed to have been caused by McClellan's advanced guard overtaking Johnston's rear guard. That was the reason no one was here, and no one would be coming until the battle was over. Whether it would be his own side or the Confederates, he had no way of knowing.

As Lowe was pondering this, Sergeant Eaton reported to him with the information that he had been surveying the terrain with a telescope and had discovered a Confederate scouting party along the bluff. Eaton pointed the group out to the balloonist, who trained his spyglass on the men sitting on their horses in the shadow of a stand of trees. It was a small party and they were keeping their distance. They seemed to be studying Lowe's group, trying to determine its strength. The scouting party presented no immediate threat, but Lowe and Eaton could only guess what size unit they were fronting for. The two men agreed that the best plan would be not to hide, but put on a show.

Eaton returned to the men and ordered the tents set up, wide apart, and in a line leading from the river to the woods. The plan was to convince the Rebel observers that there were more men bivouacked in the trees. Also, numerous camp fires were set up, not only along the river but in the woods as well. In the meantime Lowe had selected a party of six men and headed up to the mansion.

The White House was a imposing building, sitting on a bluff that commanded a wide sweep of the Virginia countryside, both up and down the river. Lowe had been told that the house was presently owned by William H. F. Lee, son of Confederate General Robert E. Lee. George and Martha Washington had lived there for a time, and the presidential residence in Washington had been patterned, and named , after this grand structure.

Lowe ascended to the front porch and watched his men surround the building as he knocked on the front door. No one answered. He knocked two more times, then tried the massive door brass handle. Finding the house unlocked, the balloonist drew his pistol and stepped inside. He called out, but there was no response. As he moved from the large hallway into the rooms, Lowe got the distinct sense that the house had just been vacated. In the first parlor there were clear indications that the family residing there had only recently departed, and in a hurry. There was knitting left, with the needles still in it, on a chair, and the ball of yam unraveled halfway across the floor. An open letter and spectacles lay on a table. He called again.

Cautiously pushing open a door, Lowe found himself in the large and well-appointed dining room. The table was set with spotless linen and sparkling silver, and a sumptuous evening meal laid out in ornate china servers. The food steamed in the covered dishes when he lifted the lids.

A flash of motion in the garden outside caught Lowe's attention. Through a curtained window he spotted his men crouching nervously behind a low hedge. Without warning, the soldiers jumped a white man and two black men who were skulking through the garden toward the house. The balloonist went back out on the porch, where the three men were frog-marched up to him at bayonet point. Professor Lowe questioned the captives, asking them what had happened to the occupants of the house, who appeared to have vanished in a hurry.

The three prisoners were reluctant to talk, perhaps wondering why they were being questioned by a civilian in a black felt hat and long black frock coat. Lowe did determine the men belonged at White House, the white man being the overseer for the plantation, while the two blacks were house servants. He didn't know where anyone had gone, the overseer maintained, claiming they were all there when he left. He and the two slaves had been sent to search for some cattle that had strayed, and only just now returned without finding the beasts.

When pressed by Lowe as to where the rest of the household might have disappeared to, the overseer insisted he had no idea. The two black men stood there in silence, nodding their heads in agreement. Then the taller of the two spoke up saying that his "boss" was telling the truth, and that he never lied.

Despite the war ostensibly being fought for their freedom, Lowe had been surprised to find that most of the slaves he had encountered, in the South and the North, were unusually loyal to their masters.

Grabbing hold of the shorter black man's arm and twisting it behind him, one of his men volunteered to work the captives over a bit, saying they would sing a different song when he was done with them. Lowe indicated to the soldier that he didn't approve of that in his unit and ordered the man to release his grip. Hoping to draw the prisoners out Lowe speculated out loud that perhaps these men didn't know anything worth telling. No one, however, took his bait. Deciding that he was not about to learn anything more from the three, Lowe let them go into the house. The startled cries he heard when the three men discovered everyone gone convinced the balloonist his observation was correct.

Gathering his men, Lowe returned to camp. Since the rain had stopped, the wind died down, and the sun was sinking; the area had become totally infested with black flies and mosquitoes. The insects circled and dived at the party's exposed hands and faces. Some of the more venturesome bugs even swarmed in their mouths, where they were ingested by the men's heavy breathing. The walk back had become as hazardous as if they were under Rebel sniper fire.

On the next day's regular dawn reconnaissance, Lowe observed that the Confederate scouts were still where he had seen them the day before. Apparently they had made camp and spent the night. Although his group was small, the Rebel patrol was considerably smaller and obviously had no intention of moving closer to the balloon camp until the rest of their troops arrived.

Two hours later the balloonist made another ascension. The enemy patrol was still there, in its original strength. Sweeping his spyglass in a circle, Lowe detected a trailing cloud of dust, an indication of a column of cavalry riding at a fast pace. The riders were coming from the south, up the peninsula. Arriving from that direction they could be either Union or Confederate, depending on the outcome of the battle he had heard yesterday. For half an hour Lowe studied the column from his swaying platform as it approached partially hidden by trees and ridges. Finally, as the horsemen crossed a large open space, the balloonist clearly saw their colors. They were Federals. A relieved Lowe waved to his men to bring him down.

A short time later Major General George Stoneman and his troopers thundered into White House Landing. Although Lowe still had no military commission, he greeted the general as would a subordinate officer turning over control of the base to his superior. After all, the chief aeronaut was nominally in command, the only person of any real rank being Sergeant Eaton.

Stoneman was surprised to see Lowe and his group as he had assumed his was the lead unit in the push toward Richmond. Lowe explained how he had departed early, while the rest of the flotilla must have been held back. He told the general how relieved he was to see him and his men, directing his attention to the Confederate patrol on the bluff, which now had disappeared into the woods. Stoneman immediately dispatched a patrol to reconnoiter the Rebels. The general seemed genuinely pleased to find Lowe and his balloon corps there, apparently having gotten over the row they had had when shells directed at the balloon had fallen on his horses. Learning from Lowe that the Lee mansion had been deserted except for the overseer and two slaves, who were now probably gone also, Stoneman decided to set up his headquarters there.

Over the next few days, by boat, wagon, horse, and on foot, the rest of the Army of the Potomac straggled into the camp at White House Landing, tired and dirty, and with many wounded. The Confederate rear guard, commanded by James Longstreet, had inflicted 2,283 casualties on the Federals, while suffering 1,560. More importantly he had delayed the Union army pursuit long enough to allow Johnston to get away with the bulk of the Confederate army, and its artillery and supply wagons.

Now McClellan's finest had hunkered down on the banks of the mosquito-infested Pamunkey to lick their wounds and deal with the miseries that would cause more deaths than the total on both sides to die from gunfire: diarrhea, typhoid, typhus, malaria, and pneumonia, maladies that would bring grief to the balloon unit as well, and Lowe himself.

17
Visitors From France, an Execution, on to Richmond

Shortly after his arrival at White House Landing, General McClellan set up his command post in a tent on the lawn of the Lee mansion, refusing to set foot in the "traitor's" house. While the generals sat on the porch of the White House, leisurely smoking cigars, drinking whiskey, and arguing over what should be the next moves of the campaign, a sea war was going on at the mouth of the James River on the southern most end of the peninsula.

The Confederate navy, realizing that Johnston's retreat had made their position untenable, abandoned the Norfolk Navy Yard on May 10, blowing up everything of military value and scuttling the *Merrimac,* which had been modified into the ironclad *Virginia.* With the *Virginia* no longer a threat, the Union gunboat captains in Chesapeake Bay dreamed of emulating the elderly but still vital David Glasgow Farragut, who only a month earlier had run a fleet of boats up the Mississippi, past two Confederate forts, and captured New Orleans. They hoped to sail their flotilla of boats, led by the *Monitor,* up the James River and seize Richmond. Learning of this, the Confederate government began packing up their papers in preparation to flee the city.

They needn't have bothered. On May 15 the Confederate batteries at Drewry's Bluff, seven miles below the city, repulsed the Federal gunboats. The dreaded *Monitor* tested ineffective as its guns could not be elevated high enough to hit the Rebel batteries dug in atop the ninety-foot bluff. Confederate artillerists punished the other boats with a devastatingly accurate rain of shells. And sharpshooters on the banks picked off any Yankee sailor careless enough to show his head. The Union fleet gave up and turned around. Upon hearing the news, crowds turned out in the streets of Richmond to celebrate the victory, while church bells rang wildly.

During the same week, three old acquaintances of Lowe's wife Leontine showed up at White House Landing. Visiting General McClellan were three French nobles, who were in America to observe the war. Louis Philippe Albert, Compte de Paris, and his brother Robert, Duc de Chartres, both held the rank of captain; although General McClellan would later write that they declined "any higher rank, though they had fully earned promotion before the close of their connection with the army." Accompanying them, without rank, was their uncle the Prince de Joinville, a talented amateur artist, who was recording America's Civil War in watercolor.

The prince, who was the third son of the deposed King Louis Philippe, had entered the French navy and risen to vice-admiral before his father's downfall. Now he was content to merely play dominoes in his spare time and paint his impressions of the conflict.

Lowe was pleased to see the Frenchmen again, and they him, as they had visited briefly in Washington. They joked with the balloonist and asked him if he was still flying his *montgolfier*. The prince, who was an excellent cook as well as a painter, prepared a fine pâté for their dinner, which they ate in the White House, while all around them the corps commanders bustled about drinking and smoking and making a tremendous racket, as if something important was going on.

Looking around him during dinner, the prince remarked he knew this was war, but thought it horrible what these men were doing to this grand old mansion. He could expect such conduct from mere soldiers, but these men were officers, whom he imagined should have some sense of tradition and cultural values.

The three other nobles agreed. As lovers of fine things, the Frenchmen were upset by the wreckage the officers seemed to be intentionally imposing on the interior of the house. Men ground out their cigars on the polished table tops and spit tobacco into the fine old rugs. The lovely sun porch stank horribly as the group had taken to urinating in the potted plants, and, if the need was urgent, directly on the floor.

After they had finished eating and sent the leftover pâté to McClellan, the prince showed Lowe his watercolors. The balloonist studied the colorful papers and pronounced them as fine as any of the works he had seen executed by the many "official" war illustrators who had visited his balloon camp.

As the Frenchmen had been observers of the battle at Williamsburg, Lowe was keen to know what actually happened there. The Compte de Paris was keeping a very accurate diary. Although the others gave stirring verbal accounts, he produced the pages he had written about Williamsburg for his American friend to read.

By candlelight in his tent that night, Lowe read the details of the horrific fighting in the rain and mud, and of McClellan's triumphant arrival at the front, too late to contribute anything to the Federal effort. Nevertheless, his troops had cheered him lustily as the general briefly reconnoitered the scene of death and destruction.

His candle was burning low when the balloonist reached the Compte de Paris's description of his party's visit to the makeshift hospital for Confederate prisoners that had been set up in the main building of the College of William and Mary. Lowe was tired and had intended to turn in, but the compte's compelling text carried him on:

> We dismount and enter the building. The scene that awaits inside is one that cannot be forgotten. Whatever one's impression of a dead man, the spectacle of suffering, of the desperate struggles to hold on to life, can be much more moving. These poor people lie in dilapidated rooms; most of them received no treatment from the enemy. They lie on a little straw, clothed as during the battle. No one has come to dress their wounds. Many are still on the same stretchers that brought them here. The floor is covered with blood and bits of clothing. A horrible stench lingers everywhere.
>
> I see a Confederate captain who stands out by the elegance of his uniform. His cap, embroidered in gold, is beside him on the stretcher and inside it are several letters. He died during the night. Other soldiers are in good spirits despite their suffering. In the midst of so much misery I do not hear any complaint. Most of the secesh soldiers are veritable children, some no more than fourteen. One was hit by a ball which struck his brain, yet he continues to live. I have never seen anything more frightful than the mixture of life and death in this unfortunate young man. He no longer has the strength to fight; his rigid hands and face announce that death has taken its prey. Yet the color of youth remains on his cheeks, now more transparent than wax. His chest still rises slowly and regularly as if it belonged to a man peacefully asleep. For two days, whenever I visited the hospital, I would always find this same immobility. Finally, on the last day before leaving Williamsburg, I learned that life had left him. It was a blessing.

The diary went on for several more pages, describing the setting up of the hospital and the arrival of Confederate doctors given leave to return to tend the wounded left behind. The meeting between McClellan and the Rebel surgeons was extremely cordial, giving an indication as to how close some of the combatants had been before the war: "The General [McClellan] asks him [Doctor Cullom] for news about all the secesh generals, his classmates and comrades in the army. Soon everyone surrounds him and inquires about a friend or relative in the rebel army . . . as if receiving news of friends after a long absence."

McClellan had set up his headquarters in the house of the richest man in Williamsburg, the same house used by Confederate General Johnston. The task of guarding the abandoned house had been left to:

> a Negress whom we immediately dub Aunt Sally and an old negro whom we simply call "Uncle." Uncle is over seventy years old, but for his white hair which seems even whiter because of his black scalp, nothing reveals his age. He says he has aged so well thanks to the good treatment of his masters. He is a "good negro" in the strongest sense: faithful to his masters, pious, talkative, zealous, and with a prodigiously limited intelligence.

The pages Lowe had been reading, struggling with his limited command of French, ended on a more positive note:

> A garden filled with flowers surrounds Mr. Vest's house. We find ourselves in the midst of roses, jasmines, and muguets. Their scent reminds us of other mornings spent in the midst of flowers, with no memory of the past, no fears for the future. The contrast between the bloody scenes we have just come through and this peaceful corner is so strong that each of us feels the need to immerse himself in it.

The next morning low clouds scudded across the leaden sky, bringing a light drizzle to the Pamunkey. Coming down from his chilly dawn ascension, Lowe was informed by Sergeant Eaton that he was to cease his observations, and he and the rest of the balloon unit were to immediately report to the "Parade Grounds."

The chief aeronaut and his crew hurried along the soggy river bank, the ground more liquid than solid, wondering what was occurring. Arriving at the normally barren parade ground, Lowe was surprised to find the entire division, three brigades, lined up in full regalia with muskets and sabers, two ranks deep forming three sides of a square. On the fourth, or open, side of the square down by the river, was a freshly dug grave. A flock of geese milled about the newly opened hole, as if they too were unsure of what was going to happen.

Lowe and his men were shown a place to fall in the ranks. They were informed that a soldier who had been caught deserting during the fighting at Williamsburg was to be executed. In order to give full

meaning and impact to the event, the entire division to which the unfortunate runaway belonged was being made to watch.

Protesting that he was a civilian and as such not bound to participate in these affairs, the head balloonist declined to get in line.
Whereupon Sergeant Eaton discreetly advised Lowe it was very unwise to agitate the provost marshals who went around orchestrating
these events as they were often mean fellows who did not like being
crossed. The veteran sergeant pointed out that desertion from the
ranks was quite common in an army now composed mainly of conscripts and substitutes who had been paid to take the place of draftees. With so many men running away the odds favored the deserter,
Eaton explained. So when one was caught, an elaborate and frightful
spectacle was made of it in hope of deterring the other soldiers.

No sooner had Lowe and his men taken their places than the
line in front was ordered to step six paces forward. Then that rank
turned to face the row behind, forming a long, dull blue aisle. Down
this lane, at a slow march, came the "funeral procession." First in line
was the provost marshal and his gang of assistants, sporting what
braid, medals, and decorations they had achieved, looking as stern
and self-righteous as one could look while sloshing along in freshly
churned mud. Following them came the brigade band, dressed in
all their tassels and finery, solemnly playing the somber notes of the
Death March. Behind the band were two firing squads of twelve men
each. Lowe counted the executioners, wondering aloud to Eaton if the
number twelve had been chosen at random or was meant to have a
biblical significance.

Eaton whispered that the second squad was needed if the first
should fail to do the job. The balloonist found it inconceivable that
twelve men with muskets shooting at almost point-blank range could
fail to kill a man, until the sergeant pointed out that oftentimes men
chosen for the execution squad had so little stomach for the detail that
they frequently missed on purpose, aiming wide or high, not wanting
to have the death on their conscience.

After the firing squad came four men carrying a plain pine coffin.
As the drizzle had increased slightly, the men bearing the box slipped
and slid, having difficulty finding a footing in the slop fomented by
the marchers in front of them. Immediately following the coffin, his
hands tied behind his back, came the condemned man himself. The
prisoner appeared not weak and tottering, but calm and resigned, his
only unsureness seeming to be caused by the sludge under his feet.
His head bowed only slightly, not in shame but rather because he had
no hat to keep off the falling rain. He glanced down the ranks as he

passed, even speaking cheerfully to those few comrades he chanced to recognize.

The prisoner's eyes met Lowe's; he looked at the balloonist's black broad brim hat and black frock coat, and hesitated for a second before continuing on without saying anything. Lowe wondered what he was doing here. This was not what he had anticipated when he had sat up late into the night with President Lincoln outlining his plans for a balloon corps.

Hard behind the prisoner came the chaplain and four guards. The chaplain's main concern at the moment seemed not to be the condemned man's soul, but rather the toll the wet slop was taking on his shiny new boots. Bringing up the tail end was another escort of twenty men with their muskets reversed for some apparently symbolic reason.

The morbid procession reached the open end of the square of men and drew up. The four pallbearers placed the empty coffin next to the freshly dug grave, scattering the geese. The prisoner was frog-marched to the center, and stood facing his division. An adjutant stepped forward, unrolled a paper, and read out the court-martial decision in a stentorian voice and with elaborate ceremony.

The drizzle had stopped and the sun was attempting to make an appearance. The reading of the verdict completed, the guards returned the prisoner to his coffin and seated him down on the rim. The chaplain, who had carefully chosen a relatively dry place to stand during the sentencing, now came forward and opened his prayer book. He read briefly something which no one could hear and shut his book. The prisoner gave a negative shake of his head, apparently his response to the question did he have any final words.

Still seated on his coffin, the condemned man had a blindfold tied over his eyes. The provost marshalled the firing squad into position, a scant ten paces from their target. The marshal held up his sword, and with a ready, aim, fire, brought his sword down in a slashing motion.

Lowe had expected the sharp crack of a fusillade, but the sound was more that of a skirmish, as the members of the firing squad fired at random rather than on command. The first few bullets seemed to miss the prisoner completely. Then one got him in the arm and he bent sideways. The next two or three found their mark and his body rocked to and fro, but he remained upright and seated. The next two shots Lowe heard appeared to be misses as the condemned man did not move.

Then a blast of three arrived almost simultaneously. The first caught the neck, then two blew off the top of the head. The man fell down next to his pine box. Sergeant Eaton whispered, the sport was to hit the man so that he fell back into his coffin. Nevertheless, the sergeant ventured that the officers would consider this a successful execution: he had seen others where the man had not died even after the second firing squad had been called in.

A surgeon stepped forward and verified the death. The troops were reassembled in columns and, following the band who this time played more cheerful tunes such as "Pop Goes the Weasel," were marched "eyes right" past the bloody gore.

That afternoon Lowe made another ascension. The weather had cleared a bit and he was happy to be back up in sky. Surveying the area through his spyglass, he found nothing out of the ordinary. There were no Confederate patrols anywhere, and their main army was now surely encamped comfortably in Richmond. He should have signaled to be hauled down, but he remained where he was, breathing the fresh air, glad to be free of the mud and filth, flies and mosquitoes, tobacco spit and cigar smoke, profanity, the smell of urine, and all the other things that seemed to be part of camp life. The officers, in general, seemed to be drunken fools, caring only for self-glory and advancement, if both could be obtained in safety at the rear of the line. And the poor soldiers, they were always tired, dirty, and hungry. Unlike the officers, they never seemed to have enough food and would steal anything edible when no one was watching. Lowe himself was tired, unable to sleep on account of the lice in his bed and the mosquitoes that hovered in his tent all night long. He missed his wife and daughters. He wondered when, if ever, this war would be over.

Looking down, the balloonist studied the parade ground where he had been forced to stand that morning as the deserter had been marched around and then executed. The place where the victim was interred had been graded completely level. Not a headstone, nor marker, nor even a hump of earth would be allowed to mark the spot of the wretched man's grave.

With smartly dressed bands blaring and battle flags waving, the Army of the Potomac departed its depot at White House Landing on May 17, 1862, and began its advance on Richmond. McClellan allowed the White House mansion to stand for two more months until he finished transferring his enormous accumulation of supplies to Harrison's Landing on the James River; then the vindictive general had the former home of George and Martha Washington put to the torch.

One of Lowe's men, who had been assigned to another unit and remained behind, later described the scene to the balloonist when they met up again at Harrison's Landing. The grand old structure had taken a whole day to die, the brightly blazing fire seen for miles by both sides. First the attic shook with flames that danced above the roof in the wind. Between pauses in the gusts, the rafters folded themselves into pleats, leaving the roof hanging limply like one of Lowe's balloons that had been punctured. After several hours of burning, the vaulted insides collapsed with the sound of an explosion. Reduced to embers, the next day only the chimneys on either end remained standing.

When the destruction of this historic landmark by Union troops became known, it aroused considerable public outcry in both the North and South. Numerous articles appeared in the newspapers condemning McClellan's decision, but too late; the devastation had already been done.

Despite still not having received their military commissions, Lowe and his aeronauts, bobbing along above the marchers' heads in the baskets of the three war balloons, were among the lead units in the Federal column heading for Richmond. This time, however, the balloon corps was not wandering on ahead all alone, but surrounded by a large body of protective troops.

After a three-day march, peppered with frequent driving rain, McClellan's army arrived at Gaines' Mill. They were now barely seven miles from Richmond, the Confederate capital and the supply and manufacturing center of the upper South. Lowe and General Stoneman stood on a height on the north side of the Chickahominy River, across from the village of Seven Pines, surveying the situation. Below them the normally shallow and sluggish river leapt white, swollen to a raging torrent, flooded by unusually heavy May rains. Every bridge not already destroyed by the retreating Confederate forces had been washed out by the rampaging water.

Lowe had chosen this hill for his balloon launching site. Stoneman would have his artillery on the next ridge. The general, who had initially complained that the Balloon Corps did nothing but draw enemy fire on his head, had come to appreciate the value of aerial reconnaissance.

Nearby was an imposing plantation identified on Stoneman's map as "Dr. Gaines' Farm." Wishing to see if the main house was occupied, the balloonist and three of his men rode toward the building across a large wheat field, its sun-bathed grain gently waving in the wind. As they emerged from the magnificent field, they were met by an angry farmer who questioned why they had trampled through his fine grain rather than come by way of the road.

Hoping to soothe the situation, Lowe introduced himself as Professor Thaddeus S. C. Lowe, a balloon observer and commander of the

Federal Balloon Corps. He asked who might he have the honor of addressing.

The man replied he was honored to meet Professor Lowe and introduced himself as Doctor Gaines, owner of the plantation. The two men shook hands, and Lowe apologized for ruining the wheat, but pointed out that General Stoneman would soon be arriving with his headquarters unit to set up his command post in this very field, which was the highest point in the surrounding area.

Lowe watched Doctor Gaines's face fall as he turned to see a troop of Federal soldiers on horses galloping through the same golden field. Lowe said he was sorry and revealed there would be more troopers coming after them. Feeling kindly toward Dr. Gaines, and wishing to spare his home the misfortune that had befallen the White House, Lowe ordered his men to guard the dwelling, while he went to fetch the rest of the balloon unit. They would pitch their camp in the grove of locust he had spotted next to the mansion. Stoneman's men would have to make do with the fields on either side.

That evening, as Lowe and his balloon unit sat down to their meager supper of army rations, servants appeared from the house carrying large trays of fresh garden vegetables, kale and black-eyed peas, a welcome gift from the doctor who appreciated the balloonist's concern for protecting his home and family.

Between May 21 and 25 the Army of the Potomac deployed along the north bank of the Chickahominy River, which sliced through the center of the peninsula, passing within four miles of Richmond at Mechanicsville. The engineers were busy at work attempting to repair the damaged bridges and building new temporary bridges using pontoons.

Just below Lowe's balloon camp, soldiers were working round the clock on a rough log bridge. A troop of Confederates on the opposite bank of the river were attempting to harass the operation with cannon and musket fire. The balloonist ascended in the *Intrepid*, and using the system of signal flags he had developed, began directing artillery fire from Stoneman's units on Gaines' Farm. Soon an accurate barrage of shells was falling on the Rebels who retreated into the woods along the banks. Knowing now that they were just under the nose of the "spy in the balloon," the Rebels gave up their attacks on this bridge, which when completed would play a critical role in a coming battle.

During the next few weeks General Stoneman made numerous ascensions with Lowe in the *Intrepid*, observing Confederate strong points blocking the Union advance. While Lowe and his other aeronauts were still uncommissioned, and rarely received their pay, their worth to General Stoneman was such that he remarked after one of his balloon observation flights, "that he had seen enough to be worth a million dollars to the government."

Perhaps bored now that the war seemed to have bogged down again, balloon flights became an extremely popular diversion with the officers camped along the Chickahominy. Anyone with any reason to go aloft looked up "Professor Lowe," as well as James Allen, who was operating another balloon camp nearby, and it was not just military personnel. The Balloon Corps had been considered extremely news-worthy since its controversial beginning. Now journalists and artists were showing up in increasing numbers, anxious to obtain a peek at the Confederate capital from the sky. This Lowe provided as he wrote: "From my balloon I was able to look into the windows of Richmond."

The British observer Captain Frederick F. E. Beaumont was a frequent passenger at this time. He kept copious notes on Lowe's activities, with the intention of establishing a balloon corps when he returned to Britain. He always called the balloonist "general" despite his civilian garb. When questioned about this, Beaumont ventured, "Lowe must be a brigadier at least." He was unaware of the real situation, that Lowe and his fellow aeronauts had no military commissions, and went mostly unpaid. Beaumont recorded in his notebook his observation that Lowe was "a clever man who was indefatigable in carrying out his work in the face of gravest danger." He mistakenly speculated that, considering the importance of his work, Lowe "must be one of the highest paid men in the Union Army."

In a paper dated November 14, 1862, Captain Beaumont gave this account of the Balloon Corps:

> It may be thought somewhat odd that such a thing as a balloon should accompany the advance of an army, but there appeared to be no difficulty in its doing so, and, of course, it was more likely to be of use there than farther to the rear. It was employed in making continual ascensions, and a daily report was sent by the principal aeronaut into McClellan, detailing the result of his observations; of course in the event of anything very unusual being noticed a special report was made. [Professor Lowe] by continued ascents, and by noting very exactly each time the position and features of the country below him, soon knew it, as it were by heart, and a glance is sufficient to assure him that no change has taken place in the occupation of the country.
>
> . . . From the balloon to Richmond, as the crow flies, was about eight miles . . . to the opposite bank of the Chickahominy, two.

At the altitude of 1,000 feet in clear weather an effective range of vision of ten miles could be got; thus the ground on the opposite side of Richmond could be seen; that is to say, houses, and the general occupation of the land became known. Richmond itself was distinctively seen, and the three camps of the Confederates could be distinguished surrounding the place.

An English reporter-friend of Captain Beaumont, who ascended with Lowe, wrote of encountering more excitement than he anticipated: "The Confederates fire on the balloon and the first shell passes a little to the left, exploding in a ploughed field. The next, to the right, bursts in mid-air. The third explosion is so close that the pieces of shell seem driven across my face, and my ears quiver with the sound."

By May 22 the number of people claiming to have a genuine need to make a balloon ascension had grown to a ridiculous number. Unable to cope with the many requests, Lowe prevailed on General McClellan to issue an order requiring any officer wishing to make a flight to first receive his authorization. No longer a darling of the media, McClellan was only too happy to issue a decree further banning news reporters from the balloons completely.

Shortly after McClellan's ban a young German observer turned up at the balloon camp. He hung around constantly asking technical questions of the men in halting English. Suspecting he might be another Confederate spy, although he was extremely well dressed and had excellent manners, Sergeant Eaton reported him to Lowe. The balloonist questioned the German, introducing himself to the man, who was all over himself with excitement at meeting the famous Professor Lowe. The German revealed that he was Count Ferdinand von Zeppelin, in the United States to study Lowe's methods of aerial observation so that he might set up a similar program with the army of his country.

The balloonist invited Count von Zeppelin into his tent for coffee. The two discovered they had many interests in common, not only science and inventions, but also the possibility of transatlantic flight by airships. Despite their language difficulty, the two became fast friends. The count very much wished to make an ascension. Lowe, however, having just prevailed upon McClellan to ban any civilian observers, was reluctant to ask for an exception so soon. Also, the Rebel gunners had been coming very close lately, prompting the Richmond newspapers to write that Lowe was "the most shot at man in the Union army." Instead, the chief aeronaut suggested that Count von Zeppelin travel to the main balloon camp at Poolesville in the Maryland mountains. There he would be able to make all the ascensions he wanted, out of harm's way. The count was reluctant to leave the front lines, but was happy to go to Camp Lowe when he learned that the aeronaut in charge there, John Steiner, spoke German better than he did English, and would be able to answer all his questions.

Unfortunately John Steiner would resign from the Balloon Corps in December 1862 over a pay dispute and would not be there when the count arrived. Zeppelin would not catch up to Steiner until August 17, 1863, in Saint Paul, Minnesota. There the disgruntled Union aeronaut, who had gone back to public ascensions in a rather battered balloon, would provide the count with his first balloon flight.

Zeppelin had been quick to realize the balloon's susceptibility to weather because of its shape. He discussed this with Steiner, who revealed his plan to construct a balloon with a very long, thin shape, with a rudder to provide directional control. Steiner's visionary idea would remain for him a dream, but for Zeppelin it was the beginning of what would become his contribution to aviation history.

Despite the many pressing things on his mind, Lowe became rather melancholy after Count von Zeppelin departed from the balloon camp. He could not recall having met anyone who shared his passion for travel by airship as much as the count had. Lowe had seen something prophetic in the German. In later years the balloonist would remark that he was disappointed that it had been John Steiner, and not him, who had given the count his first balloon ride. Lowe would also miss, by one year, the opportunity to read the newspaper accounts of the horrific damage bombs dropped from Zeppelin's airships did to Great Britain during the First World War.

Lowe's proximity to Richmond allowed the Federal balloons to be not just a tactical, but a psychological weapon as well. Whenever he was aloft, the balloonist was readily visible from the streets and houses of the city, a continuing reminder to the already worried citizens that the Army of the Potomac was bivouacked in their front yard. Lowe was now flying the *Constitution* and took great pains to ensure that the three tether lines were set so that the front of the balloon, festooned with red, white, and blue, and the name *Constitution* in large gold letters was always facing the Rebel capital.

Perhaps as a relief from the fear and gloom surrounding them, Richmond's population had begun to take a bizarre interest in Professor Lowe's flights. The city's newspapers, with one eye on circulation, kept the other eye on Lowe, endeavoring to keep their readership informed of his activities. On May 26 a Union spy slipped out of the capital with, among other information, copies of the local journals. McClellan, smiling at what he read, sent a copy of the paper to Lowe. The balloonist was rather pleased to learn the rumor he had heard—that he was rapidly becoming somewhat of a celebrity in the South—bore a ring of truth. The article in the paper, dated May 26, related: "The enemy are fast making their appearance on the banks of the Chickahominy. Yesterday they had a balloon in the air the whole day, it being witnessed by our citizens from the streets and house-steps. They evidently discovered something of importance to them, for about 4 P.M. a brisk cannonading was heard at Mechanicsville and the Yankees now occupy that place."

On the morning before, the 25th of May, Lowe and General Stoneman had gone aloft to seek to determine the Confederate strength at Mechanicsville, a sleepy hamlet of not more than a few houses scattered about a country crossroads, just four miles north of Richmond. The town was of strategic importance though as from there the Mechanicsville Turnpike ran down a gentle slope and crossed the Chickahominy at the Mechanicsville bridge.

Just west of the town Lowe could see the shining tracks of the Virginia Central Railroad, coming out of Richmond and disappearing into the haze in the north. The balloonist turned his spyglass to the south. On the opposite bank of the Chickahominy the slopes bristled with heavy cannon lurking behind dense earthen lunettes.

Stoneman was eager to drive out the Rebels and occupy Mechanicsville, thereby gaining control of one of Richmond's major supply lines. The town's importance notwithstanding, the two observers found few Confederate troops in the vicinity. Lowe, however, did detect some signs that caused him to warn Stoneman that some additional Rebel forces might be hiding in the nearby woods.

Lowe descended, and General Stoneman got out of the basket and hurried off to send the raiding party he had organized into action. The balloonist went aloft again, and from his thousand foot advantage was shortly directing a very accurate artillery barrage on the woods where fleeing Rebel forces had made themselves known. The skirmish was brief, and the Federals soon took Mechanicsville. Troopers on the ground were now so close to Richmond that they could catch a glimpse of its church spires through the branches of the trees.

Stoneman quickly moved his headquarters to Mechanicsville, and the head balloonist assigned his father, Clovis, and James Allen, there with the *Washington.* Neither of these two older men, however, were feeling especially fit, suffering from the effects of the damp weather. The *Constitution,* with the *Intrepid* as its backup, remained at Gaines' Farm, just across the river from the two Union corps commanded by General Heintzelman bivouacked near the village of Seven Pines.

18
McClellan Waits, a Kettle, Delirium

These were busy times for T. S. C. Lowe, as he had three war balloons in the Richmond area making frequent ascensions. He daily checked the activities at Mechanicsville to help out his father and James Allen, traveling back and forth by horseback the six miles between there and his main camp.

The English observer, Captain Beaumont, described the head balloonist's camp at Gaines's Farm in his journal. The balloon itself was "snugly ensconced in a hollow . . . surrounded by tents and cooking fires forming a small distinct encampment." While Beaumont's description makes the scene sound a bit idyllic, in truth the camp was a damp and mosquito-infested place, where the men had stripped all the usable lumber they could find from nearby barns and sheds to make floors for their "dog-tents" in a forlorn attempt to keep dry.

Although Lowe himself was quite fastidious and endeavored to keep his quarters clean, the same could not be said for his men. Sanitation at the balloon camp, as in most of the units in the war, was from bad to nonexistent. The troops paid scant attention to where they relieved themselves, a bush near a tent handier than a latrine fifty yards away. And some did not even bother with a bush. What had been Dr. Gaines's flower garden had been, despite Lowe's orders, completely defiled by the 150 men in his crew, creating a problem of even where to walk. When the wind blew from the south, the indelible stench of urine and feces was supplemented by the odor of garbage and the decaying offal of slaughtered animals that were disposed of nearby. All of this ensured a fertile breeding ground for the disease carrying flies and mosquitoes that swarmed everywhere. Mrs. Gaines had become so distressed by the whole matter she no longer held her Wednesday afternoon tea socials.

While the Army of the Potomac languished in camp, events had been occurring a hundred miles to the northwest, in the Shenandoah Valley, that would have a profound effect on McClellan's plans to capture Richmond. Jefferson Davis and the Confederate generals had become aware of Lincoln's fear of an attack on Washington and taken advantage of it. At the beginning of May, Stonewall Jackson had marched a large part of his army east across the Blue Ridge. Federal spies reported that they had been reassigned to the defense of Richmond. However, when the Rebel troopers arrived at Charlottesville they were secretly put on trains that returned them to Staunton.

From there Jackson led a force of nine thousand men over the mountains to the hamlet of McDowell, where they fought and defeated a Union force half again as large led by General Nathaniel Banks. This loss forced General John C. Fremont, who had been preparing to fulfill Lincoln's desire of liberating East Tennessee, to cancel his campaign and face Jackson.

Driving his infantry at a killing pace, Jackson was waging one of the war's most spectacular campaigns. His superior knowledge of the geography enabled him to quickly march west, knocking back Fremont's advance. Then he swept through the Shenandoah, deceiving Banks as to his whereabouts, breaking his supply line and forcing the Federals to retreat. Jackson's troops then mounted a ferocious attack on the fleeing columns, turning the withdrawal into a rout. Banks headed for the safety of the Potomac, some thirty-five miles away.

Stonewall Jackson's quick successes convinced President Lincoln and Secretary of War Stanton that a major invasion of Washington was underway. General McDowell, who had been marching his forces down the peninsula to join McClellan in the siege of Richmond, had his orders withdrawn. Two of McDowell's divisions were transferred from Fredericksburg to the Shenandoah to confront Jackson's forces, who appeared to march so quickly they were being called "foot cavalry." General Jackson calmly waited, resting his exhausted troops, then attacked the pursuing Federal columns, inflicting heavy casualties, before slipping down to Richmond. President Lincoln and his advisers, sitting in the War Department firing off telegrams to his commanders, had been thoroughly deceived. Jackson, by skillful use of only seventeen thousand men, had completely immobilized a Union force numbering more than fifty thousand.

On the Virginia Peninsula the abnormally wet weather had continued. By the end of May, McClellan found the Army of the Potomac bisected by the swollen Chickahominy. A large part of the army had been kept on the northeast side waiting to join up with McDowell's expected divisions. Several washed-over, makeshift bridges were all that connected the two elements.

Waiting apprehensively while McClellan prepared his siege, Jefferson Davis persuaded his recalcitrant commander, General Johnston, to mount a counteroffensive. Johnston chose to attack the Union's weaker left wing, on the south bank of the river. A torrential downpour on May 30 was to Johnston's advantage, as it washed out most of the temporary bridges connecting McClellan's army. This stroke of luck gave the reinforced Rebels an army of more than seventy-five thousand to send against the two isolated Union corps commanded by General Heintzelman. Johnston planned his attack for the next morning.

Lowe's observations of increased Confederate movements opposite Mechanicsville had convinced McClellan that Johnston planned to retake the town and then drive eastward to cut his supply line from the Pamunkey. However, on May 29, ascending in a slight rain, the balloonist noted unusually heavy Rebel activity on the other side of the river abeam his eagle's nest at Gaines' Farm.

Observing that the enemy units were going through considerable trouble to conceal themselves in the trees, the balloonist reported to McClellan, "I suspect the Confederates might be preparing for an attack on Heintzelman's separated units." For once McClellan did not procrastinate nor seek another opinion. Acting on Lowe's report, McClellan ordered what reserves he had available to assemble posthaste to move in support of the troops on the south bank.

The heavy rains of May 30 kept the Balloon Corps on the ground. Therefore, it was not until just before noon on May 31, when the last of the squalls had passed, that Lowe was able to go aloft at Mechanicsville. Looking north he strained to see any signs of the advance units of McDowell's anticipated forces, but saw nothing. Turning his spyglass south, the balloonist was shocked to find a column of troop and supply wagons departing Richmond to the southeast. It seemed as if a good portion of Johnston's army was heading in the direction of Seven Pines, the center of Heintzelman's forces. Nearer by Lowe discovered that the Rebel forces across the river from Mechanicsville had pulled out of their lines and were also heading south and east, as if to join up with the troops moving toward Seven Pines. He was sure now that the Confederates were planning a surprise attack on the weaker Federal force on the south side of the Chickahominy. The balloonist's telescope scanned the river; last night's torrential rains had wiped out most of the temporary bridges. Heintzelman was virtually isolated.

Not wanting to waste time, Lowe shouted through his megaphone to James Allen, ordering him to send a message at once to the main balloon camp instructing them to begin inflating the *Intrepid*. The balloonist sensed a major battle was coming and that he would need the power of the larger balloon to carry him and an observer with telegraph equipment to a thousand feet, high enough to be of any use.

Once on the ground, and finding the telegraph lines down, Lowe dispatched a messenger with a note relating his observations of the Rebel activities to his immediate superior Brigadier General Andrew A. Humphreys. Then, filled with a sense of purpose he had not heretofore experienced, Lowe leapt on his horse and galloped at full speed the six miles to Gaines' Farm.

Arriving at his balloon camp, Lowe was disappointed to see the *Intrepid* only partially inflated. Eager to make another observation of the Confederate movements, he immediately went aloft in the smaller *Constitution.* His suspicions were confirmed. During the time he had taken to ride from Mechanicsville, the two Rebel groups had converged on the New Bridge Road, in front of Seven Pines, and were taking up battle formations. The balloonist estimated that the Confederates had a full three divisions facing Keyes' and Heintzelman's two corps. Lowe gave the signal to be pulled down. Wasting no time once he was back on the ground, the balloonist wrote what he later would consider the "most important dispatch of his military career":

> Brigadier-General March
> Chief of Staff
>   There are large bodies of troops in the open field beyond the opposite heights on the New Bridge Road. White-covered wagons are rapidly moving towards the point of engagement with artillery in advance.
>
> T. S. C. Lowe
Chief Aeronaut

Having sent two warnings of Johnston's approach, Lowe now turned his efforts to the matter of inflating the *Intrepid.* He imagined his friend Heintzelman across the river, riding up and down in front of his men, shouting encouragement, and attempting to set the lines to his advantage. With the river flooded he had little chance of the reinforcements reaching him. Without knowledge of the enemy's movements and the concentrated artillery fire he could direct from his balloon, the Federal troops on the south bank were facing annihilation from the larger Rebel force. Consulting with his crew, Lowe learned they anticipated it would be another hour before the *Intrepid* would be fully inflated. Always the inventor, Lowe pondered a solution:

> I was put to my wits end as to how I could save an hour's time, which was the most important and precious hour of all my experience in the army. As I saw the two armies coming nearer and nearer together, there was no time to be lost. It flashed through my mind that if I could only get the gas that was in the smaller

balloon, *Constitution,* into the *Intrepid,* which was half filled, I would save an hour's time and to us that hour's time would be worth a million dollars a minute. But how was I to rig up the proper connection between the two balloons? To do this within the space of time necessary puzzled me until I glanced down and saw a 10-inch camp kettle which instantly gave me the key to the solution.

Lowe immediately ordered a camp tinsmith to cut the bottom out of this kettle so that it would serve as a funnel. In a few minutes a connection was made between the two balloons and the hydrogen from the *Constitution* was transferred to the *Intrepid.* Lowe and his telegraph operator Park Spring, who had rejoined him after Lathrop's death, climbed into the basket. The balloonist signaled his crew to release the mooring lines.

Then with the telegraph cable and instruments, I ascended to the height I desired and remained there almost constantly during the battle, keeping the wires hot with information.

Lowe would write many years later, "Of all the battles I have witnessed, that of Fair Oaks was the most closely contested and most severe."

From the beginning things went wrong for Confederate General Johnston. A misunderstood order caused James Longstreet to advance his division on the wrong road, where it became ensnared with troops of two other divisions, delaying the assault to mid-afternoon. When the attack finally did get underway, it was uncoordinated, moving one brigade at a time. The first Rebel thrust did manage to drive the Union forces back a mile through the crossroads at Seven Pines.

From his balloon Lowe could see that both sides were fully engaged now. Cannon smoke and the thick stands of trees made observation difficult, but the new Federal line seemed to be intact. The balloonist sent the message, "Heintzelman's units appear to be holding in face of superior enemy forces."

Directly below the *Intrepid,* Lowe could see two divisions of General Edwin V. Sumner's corps assembling in battle dress, awaiting orders to cross the flooded river. The log bridge Lowe had protected by his accurate direction of artillery fire was intact, but afloat. The only bridge available, it was prevented from being washed away by tree stumps and ropes attached to felled trees. With the water coursing rapidly over the walkway, it seemed impossible for the soldiers to cross. As the troops waited, the swirling water continued to rise.

Heeding Lowe's early warning of the Confederate advance, Mc-Clellan had ordered General Edwin V. Sumner's corps to cross the Chickahominy in support of Heintzelman and Keyes at any cost. The sixty-five-year-old commander, nicknamed "Bull," responded by personally leading his divisions across the raging river on the makeshift bridge, through water that poured over the men's ankles as they ran.

Rocking in the basket of his balloon, Lowe heard a loud shout from below, then watched as one brigade after another charged over the swaying bridge, the troopers' weight pushing the loose logs firmly into place. Once across, the men hurried on, the sound of the battle guiding them to their destination as they slipped and floundered in the muddy swamp. But they had gotten there in time. The Confederate forces were temporarily confused by the unexpected arrival of Sumner's men, allowing the Federals to escape a disastrous rout and take a stand at the railroad station at Fair Oaks.

As evening fell most of the fighting ceased. The Prince de Joinville and the French observers who had watched the engagement from McClellan's headquarters turned up at Lowe's balloon camp. They were very impressed by the part Lowe had played in the battle and congratulated him. They reported that McClellan's staff had been of the opinion that the attack on the south bank of the Chickahominy was just a feint to draw the Federal Army across the river, while the Confederates debouched on the north bank. But Lowe's report as to the number of Rebels advancing on Heintzelman's corps had put an end to their speculation. Although no one from McClellan's headquarters had suggested it, the Frenchmen felt Lowe's telegraph messages had saved the day.

Lowe had sent a report to McClellan expressing his fear of another Confederate attack the next day. The French observers told the balloonist that when they had left McClellan's headquarters the general was of the opinion the Rebels had returned to their fortifications at Richmond. Lowe disagreed.

Although not feeling well, and tired to the point of exhaustion, the balloonist decided to make one more ascension before retiring. The *Intrepid* climbed out more rapidly in the cool night air, and without the extra weight of his telegraph operator, Park Spring. Lowe studied the twinkling fire lights of the Confederate forces on the opposite shore. There were the smaller, duller, lights of the lanterns carried by the men moving through the trees diligently seeking out their wounded comrades. More numerous, however, were the brighter, static, blazings of campfires. The Rebels had left a sizable force in the field.

Ascending at dawn the next morning with his telegraph operator, Lowe's observations clearly indicated that the Confederate Army was still in position. Looking north, the balloonist espied additional forces moving down from Richmond. He scanned the barracks and earthworks near the city, finding them for the most part deserted. Lowe immediately began sending telegraph reports.

The second day's battle was waged sporadically throughout the day. It was mostly useless slaughter, with no side making any significant gains. Lowe remained aloft in the *Intrepid* at Gaines' Farm, while Allen was up in the *Washington* at Mechanicsville, both sending reports at fifteen-minute intervals. By now a line had been set up to the War Department in Washington, where President Lincoln listened to the battle almost "play by play." As the sun set, every forest lane and swampy field in Lowe's sight was strewn with the dead and dying. Bodies of Billy Yank and Johnny Reb lay peacefully next to each other.

Most of the forty-two thousand soldiers who had engaged in the bloody conflict at Fair Oaks/Seven Pines had fought in small clusters amid dense woods and knee-deep water in the flooded swampland. Wounded falling in the muddy water had to be propped against fences or trees to prevent them from drowning before stretcher bearers could arrive. Both sides conceded that the results of the battle were indecisive.

If any side could claim a small advantage, it would be the Federals, who inflicted six thousand casualties on their enemy while suffering only five thousand. The most significant casualty was the Confederate leader General Joseph E. Johnston, who took a bullet through the shoulder on the evening of May 31. Jefferson Davis replaced him with the demanding, but so far not very successful, Robert E. Lee. At the time this change pleased McClellan, who considered Lee to be "cautious and weak" and "likely to be timid and irresolute in action."

During the military operations of May 31 and June 1, 1862, Lowe and his Balloon Corps had successfully passed the test of the two most hectic days of their short existence. The head balloonist was convinced that the Balloon Corps service during the battle of Fair Oaks/Seven Pines had clearly demonstrated the value of military balloon observation. He felt that he had convincingly silenced any doubters. General Heintzelman did not hesitate to give his endorsement remarking, "From my own experience . . . I would consider your balloon indispensable to an army in the field and should I ever be trusted with such a command would consider my preparations incomplete without one of your balloons."

Major Adolphus W. Greely, chief signal officer of the U.S. Army, had an even higher opinion of the balloonist's services. Writing in an assessment of Civil War ballooning after the war he stated, "It may be safely claimed that the Union Army was saved from destruction at the Battle of Fair Oaks . . . by the frequent and accurate reports of Professor Lowe."

Not all of McClellan's commanders, however, were convinced of the value of the Balloon Corps to the regular army. General J. G. Barnard's remark reflected the thinking of many of the officers: "A balloon apparatus is decidedly desirable to have with an army; but at the same time it is one of the first encumbrances that if obliged to part with anything, I should leave behind."

Even Lowe's early supporter General Fitz-John Porter grumbled that the experience of Fair Oaks had demonstrated that professional aeronauts were "not of themselves successful observers because of their lack of military training." He recommended that the aeronauts should always be accompanied by an officer familiar with the terrain.

Nevertheless, at the moment Lowe sensed he was secure in his position with the Army of the Potomac. Although not feeling as fit as he would have liked, the balloonist continued to make ascensions during the month of June. McClellan was moving the bulk of his army to new lines south of the Chickahominy. While the army had escaped disaster at Fair Oaks, McClellan had lost the physical and psychological advantages he had held prior to the battle. The monumental Army of the Potomac had gotten as close as it was going to get to Richmond during this campaign. McClellan had decided to hunker down in his new positions and to prepare for a lengthy siege of the Confederate capital.

It was now early June. The incessant rains had given way to an unbearable heat wave. Lowe was aloft, enjoying the coolness and fresh air. However, he caught himself occasionally shivering uncontrollably. The balloonist dismissed his shakes as fatigue. He needed to get more rest. The mosquitoes, however, had become so numerous that they kept him awake at night. Training his spyglass on the other side of Richmond, all he could do was watch helplessly as a constant stream of Confederate reinforcements entered the city from the west. McClellan was waiting for replacements for the men lost at Fair Oaks, delaying his attack yet again.

Lowe signaled to be pulled down. In the bottom lands below him, another enemy was attacking the Union troops. The rank swamps and decaying woods were filled with disease-carrying insects. Two thousand soldiers had been invalided home. And many more men who were infected carried on, suffering repeatedly from fever and chills. As he stepped from his basket the balloonist looked for a familiar face that was not there. Lowe's own sergeant, the veteran Charles Eaton, had survived the Indian wars only to die of typhoid fever in Virginia.

Although McClellan may have considered Robert E. Lee cautious and weak, he was in fact facing a new and much more aggressive General Lee who would soon mold his forces into the legendary Army of Northern Virginia. Lee was aware that McClellan had now moved most of his troops south of the Chickahominy. He went about strengthening the defenses around Richmond, wielding a shovel himself, while at the same time devising a plan to attack the Union Army from an unexpected direction.

Curious about the strength of the force under General Fitz-John Porter left to contain the railhead on the north bank through which most of the Yankee's supplies were flowing, Lee sent his favorite cavalry officer, the colorful J. E. B. Stuart, on a reconnaissance ride around the Army of the Potomac.

On June 12, Stuart and 1,200 hand-picked men left Richmond and crossed the Chickahominy to the north. Then they swung east close to the huge supply base at White House Landing, brushing off any Union patrols they encountered. Rather than return the way he came the dashing Stuart made the bold gesture of riding completely around the Union Army, winning numerous skirmishes and capturing 170 prisoners and twice as many horses and mules on the way. When Stuart returned on June 16, his information confirmed Lee's suspicions about the weakness of McClellan's right flank. Lee decided to take an enormous risk. He would recall Stonewall Jackson's divisions from the Shenandoah Valley, where they were tying up Federal troops by feinting an attack on Washington. Then, leaving a weak defensive force in the trenches at Richmond, Lee and Jackson would pull a surprise attack on McClellan's exposed right flank.

Meanwhile the Union soldiers waited in their trenches. Rumors abounded. Troops lying on their backs on the ground could not help wondering what Lowe was observing and reporting to headquarters from his colorful balloon. A young regimental adjutant, Theodore Ayrault Dodge, who later became one of the nation's leading military historians, made the following entry in his journal on June 23, 1862:

> We turned out for inspection by Genl. Kearny this A.M., but it was postponed until tomorrow. A camp rumor (which you must know means nothing) says Prof. Lowe discovered this morning that the Rebels have evacuated Richmond, which was in flames. By the way this said Professor Lowe is a "big-wig"—rank of Colonel, pay ditto. Shoulder straps of bullion with balloon on

them in rich silver. Swell trains carrying inflators, 100 men at his disposal, hand and glove amity with Little Mac, fine cloth coats and little boots (so as not to weigh down the balloon, I suppose), handsome horses, wall tents, and commander in chief of Balloon Department of the Army of the Potomac! Fine high position whether up or down, is it not?

Col. Fardella doesn't believe in balloons, but in reconnaissances rather. He don't trust in the professor at all; but I think balloons are a great idea.

Despite Lowe's nearly constant observations, Lee need not have worried about leaving Richmond defended by only twenty-seven thousand men for as usual McClellan was convinced he was facing a far superior force. McClellan had been sending a steady stream of telegrams to Washington, explaining why he was not quite ready to launch his own offensive: the roads were too wet; his artillery was not all in place; the rest of McDowell's troops had not arrived. On June 25 he wired War Secretary Stanton that he was facing a rebel force of two hundred thousand, when in truth Lee had fewer than ninety thousand soldiers at any one time.

Training his spyglass to the north, Lowe, aloft in the *Washington* over Mechanicsville, spied large bodies of troops moving toward Ashland, only seventeen miles from Richmond. At that distance he could not tell if the forces were Union or Confederate. The balloonist balanced his spyglass against the load ring, refocusing the lens. The columns seemed to be shimmering and weaving before his eyes in a very odd way. Lowe considered it might be heat waves, then noticed he was shivering. He signaled to be hauled down; he would get a military observer and ascend again. On the ground he learned that a skirmish was going on at Fair Oaks. Rather than rush back there, Lowe chose to ascend again, hoping to determine what army was on the way.

Swaying in the gondola against a brisk wind that had come up, Lowe and his observer stared through their telescopes at the approaching dust cloud. Whoever it was clearly had a large body of troops and equipment with him, Lowe noted. The two men wished that it was General McDowell and his divisions coming down from Washington to aid in the attack on Richmond. But their hopes were soon dashed when, after a while, they were able to make out the flags of the lead units. It was the Confederate divisions of Stonewall Jackson, against whom McDowell was still blindly defending the capital. Lowe knew McClellan would not be pleased when he gave him this news.

On the evening of June 25, T. S. C. Lowe, wrapped in a woolen blanket as he felt unusually cold, sat eating with his men beside two blooming aloe trees. He had never seen such trees before and marveled at their attractiveness. Admiring their beauty, Lowe's mind slipped away temporarily from his constant fatigue and his other miseries. No campfires were allowed, so the group had thrown away their ration of fresh beef. As they always got it, warm with the blood still draining from it, it was not a tempting meal anyway. Even with cooking, the meat was often discarded as being inedible. Diarrhea was a common problem among the men, and the reserves of salt meat and adamantine crackers were easier on the stomach.

According to regulations, the soldiers were supposed to carry three days' rations in their haversacks at all times, but this was rarely the case. Most men never kept food on hand anymore than they kept money. Lowe observed that once in possession of something edible his men seemed to be overcome by an insatiable hunger, eating until everything was gone, whether they wanted it or not, trusting to the arrival of future supplies or to their comrades' generosity.

Although Lowe was shivering, the evening was warm and pleasant. A slight breeze was keeping away the bugs. The balloonist's group sat in a circle smoking and discussing those things soldiers usually talked about: the weather, the discomfort to their stomach, or their other ailments, and the folks they left back home. As if by some unwritten rule, no one ever mentioned past battles, nor fallen comrades. Unlike the officers, they had no whiskey to drown their thoughts. The balloonist noticed that, perhaps out of respect for his authority, there seemed to be much less cursing and swearing when he was present. Across the way the Rebel gunners were amusing themselves by sending a few light cannon volleys over the river and rippling through the trees. The incoming shells were mostly thirty-pounders, filled with sand instead of solid shot, startling, and annoying, but not especially deadly.

The strain showed on Lowe's face; he was feeling extremely tired. He had decided he would stay in Mechanicsville tonight rather than ride the six miles back to his main balloon camp. The balloonist's orders for tomorrow morning were to make an ascension and observe what McClellan stated "might be the start of an enemy reconnaissance-in-force," and then descend and make his report. After that Lowe was to have the *Washington* packed up and immediately sent back to Gaines' Farm. Along with it were to go the generators, wagons, tents, and all the other equipment, as well as the ground crew. He was not exactly sure why this was being done.

General Lee began his flanking action the next morning, June 26, the second day of what would become known as the Seven Days' battles. The weather was bright and clear. Lowe hung in his balloon, above Mechanicsville, catching glimpses of General A. P. Hill's Confederate forces massing behind the heights overlooking Meadow Bridge. The hilly landscape camouflaged the Rebels' activities and concealed their numbers. Below him only a token Union force remained. General Porter had withdrawn the main body of his men, planning to confront the Rebels at Beaver Dam Creek.

Flowing sluggishly through a small but sharp ravine two miles east of Mechanicsville, the creek, waist-deep in most places and bordered by swamps, formed a natural defensive position. Where Cold Harbor Road crossed the creek, a millrace and a grist mill had been constructed, ready-made fortifications for any force holding the east side of Beaver Dam Creek. The only approach from the west was across open fields and down the steep banks of the ravine. Unknown to McClellan, however, the Confederate strategy did not hinge on a direct frontal attack on Beaver Dam, but called for Jackson's forces to come around and hit Porter's exposed flank.

From his lofty perch, the balloonist could clearly see a large body of Confederate troops camped several miles further north. They did not appear, however, to be making any move to advance. The sun was now reaching its meridian. Lowe crouched in his balloon basket, sweat pouring off his brow. An unearthly silence hung over the area. In the stillness, even at a thousand feet, the balloonist could hear the song of the cicadas in the trees below.

On the hill overlooking Meadow Bridge, General A. P. Hill waited expectantly. He had roomed with his enemy, McClellan, at West Point, and even courted his wife Nellie before they were married. Only thirty-six years old, Hill was now the youngest major general in the Confederate Army. An impulsive figure, Hill had grown tired of waiting for Jackson's arrival. Not wanting to lose any more daylight, he signaled for the attack to begin.

At 3:00 a volley of cannon fire broke the silence. Lowe watched as Hill's men rashly charged across the Chickahominy on the Meadow Bridge. According to plan, the Union pickets offered little resistance as they fell back to their fortifications behind Beaver Dam Creek. Lowe reported the start of the attack, but did not give the signal to his crew to be brought down.

The balloonist watched as the Confederates advanced on Beaver Dam Creek. They must have known the Federals were there, but they came with a confidence brought on by J. E. B. Stuart's recent successes, which had been widely written up in all the Southern papers. To Lowe it seemed as if they thought they were already on their victory parade as they marched confidently down Cold Harbor Road and into the trap that had been set for them.

Union artillery opened up with an ear-splitting roar. A punishing rain of fire at once poured down on the columns, the fiery cannon balls and shot tearing great gaping holes in the Rebel brigades. Still the Confederates came on, colors flying bravely in the face of the flesh-rending hail of lead and iron. Another volley came howling in, a mad dog from hell, leaving dead and screaming wounded scattered all over the road and the sides of the ravine.

From under the trees below him the rolling clatter of musketry rose to the balloonist's ears. A cloud of smoke floated upward. The dazed survivors, some waving white handkerchiefs, were being picked off by Federal sharpshooters as they staggered to the rear. Lowe gave the sign to be brought down. As the balloon started its slow descent, he shouted angrily at his men to hurry. This was not war but butchery; he could not stand to watch the slaughter any longer.

With the screams and curses of the dying men ringing in his ears the balloonist leapt from his basket. Sweat poured from his forehead. His hands shook and his knees were weak. He ran for the privacy of a stand of trees. Lowe's motion put up a small fox from a bed of ferns. The bedraggled critter ran, skittering from one cover to another. The fox halted behind the safety of a rock, a scant six feet away and glared at the intruder. The balloonist imagined how the fox must be regarding this one-sided relationship. As the fox turned and ran Lowe bent over and threw up where he stood, again and again, heaving dry when there was nothing left inside him. Leaning against one of the pines, he mopped his brow. His head felt hot. Composing himself, Lowe returned to the men and gave the order to begin packing up the balloon camp.

The battle was over at sundown. The anguished cries of the wounded still rang in the heavy night air. It truly had been a slaughter, with nearly 1,500 Confederates killed or wounded, while the Union had suffered only 360 casualties. All day long, as the conflict raged, Jackson's three divisions had waited only a few miles to the north. But their commander, apparently weary from the strain of his rapid deployment from the Shenandoah Valley, or perhaps misunderstanding what his mission was, had made no effort to send his troops to Hill's aid. Many reasons were put forth for Stonewall Jackson's lethargy, but popular myth had it that the "Hero of the Valley" had simply lain down to take a nap and forgot to get up.

In his tent at Gaines' Farm, Lowe tossed about in a feverish half-sleep. A squadron of insects circled around his damp body. The demoniac sounds of battle echoed in his head. His small canvas world

was filled with the horrific screams of wounded men and the screeching of dying horses. The balloonist started from his troubled sleep. He
was aware of a tremendous amount of activity going on in the camp
outside. People could be heard shouting and hurrying about, but he
had no will to get up to determine what was going on, his head fell
back on the pillow.

Shortly before dawn on June 27, Lowe was shaken awake by his father. The balloonist had not slept more than three hours. Clovis told
his son that the balloon camp had been ordered to pack up and move
all three balloons and equipment across the river to the south bank,
between Powhite Swamp and the Lower Trestle Bridge. Lowe shook
his head, not believing what he had just heard. Why, he asked his father, were they retreating when the army won yesterday's battle?

Neither man knew that despite having achieved what he considered a "complete victory" at Mechanicsville, McClellan was not taking
the offensive. Fearing Jackson's forces attacking his right flank, which
was "up in the air," or unprotected, from the north, he had ordered
Porter's divisions to fall back four miles to a defensive position on the
high ground behind Boatswain's Swamp, near Gaines' Mill, to protect
the rail lines that were his main source of supplies. This was necessary because McClellan was moving his huge supply base at White
House Landing on the Pamunkey to Harrison's Landing on the James.
Eventually McClellan planned to have his entire army on the south
side of the peninsula. Fitz-John Porter's units would have to hold off
the Confederates while this retreat, which McClellan euphemistically
called a "change of base," was being accomplished.

Lowe stared up at his father, trying to make some sense of what he
had just been told; the man's face was blurred, swimming in front of
him. Clovis put his hand on his son's forehead and felt the heat of fever.
He went in search of a damp towel. When Clovis returned, his son was
already out of bed, preparing for his dawn ascension. The father protested, telling his son he was very sick and shouldn't go aloft. Lowe took
the towel, mopped his brow, and walked unsteadily out of the tent.

The head balloonist assembled his men and gave orders to immediately take the fully inflated *Intrepid* across the river. He would make
his ascension from the other side. His father and James Allen would
see to the movement of the other balloons and the rest of the camp
and equipment. As the unit was in its usual condition of being short
on supplies, Lowe instructed the men to leave nothing behind.

Over the previous weeks McClellan's engineers had managed to
install eleven bridges across the Chickahominy. And so, except for a
little banging and scraping on trees, and a man falling into the water,

the *Intrepid* was towed across the river without too much difficulty. However, with all the confusion and movement going on around them, it was not until 8:15 that Lowe and Park Springs finally managed to get the balloon attached to a telegraph wire and airborne.

Training his spyglass in the direction of his former headquarters, the balloonist could see the smoke of heavy cannon fire to the east in the vicinity of Gaines' Mill. He was still sweating, and his head spinning. Suddenly faint, Lowe gripped the side of the basket; the whole countryside was turning around in front of him, blurred. He shook his head in a futile attempt to stop the vertigo. Lowe could see nothing.

Slowly the balloonist dictated a message to be sent to McClellan's headquarters saying: "I am not well. Advise someone in good health take my place. I believe a major battle is coming and it is imperative the balloon be up constantly."

After a space of time that seemed to Lowe to be eternity, word came back that his father and James Allen were not available as they were still on the other side of the river trying to salvage the equipment. His ground crews having been appropriated for other duties, the aeronauts were struggling to get the fully inflated *Constitution* and *Washington* across with the help of only one other man, the assistant telegraph operator.

Nor were things going any better for the Confederates. Lee's attack again suffered from poor coordination between him and his division commanders. Once again Jackson was slow getting his forces into position and languid in attacking. And again A. P. Hill's units were fighting alone under the hot sun, moving across a deep ravine and through vine-entangled woods to attack well-entrenched Union troops, who poured a steady stream of fire on their ranks.

At 9:20, seeing the battle was fully in progress, and having heard no more from his father and Allen, Lowe sent word to headquarters: "Despite my illness, I am prepared to remain in the air as long as necessary. I request two orderlies to be sent to carry messages in the event the telegraph line is severed." Then he began his report: "North from here two and a half 2 1/2 miles from river, large bodies of troops in open field—too far right to be the enemy. Long line of skirmishers on hill to side of Gaines House. Field nearby on fire."

All of a sudden the balloonist's instinct caused him to turn away from the fighting and sweep his spyglass to the west. He shook his head and blinked his eyes. Now he was sure he was delirious. Rising over Richmond was a motley colored balloon, or at least he thought he saw another balloon. Park Spring was crouching on the floor of the basket, tapping on his telegraph key.

Pointing in the direction of the other airship, Lowe asked his telegraph man what he thought the strange thing was. Spring looked and
rubbed his eyes, then confirmed that Lowe was not seeing a mirage.
Whatever it was, the parti-colored object was indeed there; both men
could see it clearly. The newly arrived balloon was floating about
three hudred feet in the air. It seemed to be tethered in the south of
Richmond. The two men studied the globe through the spyglass. The
envelope was a patchwork of brightly colored fabric that shimmered
in the sun.

At the time, Lowe and Spring did not know the colorful Rebel balloon was captained by E. P. Alexander, the Confederate artillery chief.
Given the nickname the "Silk Dress Balloon," the multicolored craft
would have little effect on the outcome of the Seven Days Battles, but
would take its place in Southern folklore. Its fame would rest largely on
a story written years later by General James Longstreet, whose forces
were presently attacking Porter's troops at Gaines' Mill. In an article in
Century Magazine published in 1886, Longstreet would write:

> The Federals had been using balloons to examine our posi-
> tions, and we watched with envious eyes their beautiful observa-
> tions as they floated high up in the air, and well out of the range
> of our guns. We longed for the balloons that poverty denied us.
> A genius arose for the occasion and suggested that we send out
> and gather all the silk dresses in the Confederacy and make a
> balloon. It was done, and soon we had a great patchwork ship
> in many and varied hues. The balloon was ready to use in the
> Seven Days Campaign. We had no gas except in Richmond, and
> it was the custom to inflate the balloon there, tie it securely to an
> engine, and run it down the York River railroad to any point at
> which we desired to send it up.

Unaware of the Confederate balloon's intentions, the balloonist
watched the intruder for some time. Then, discerning the patchwork
balloon's poor construction and apparent lack of lifting power, Lowe
dismissed it as presenting him no more threat than the previous
Confederate balloon that had appeared several weeks before and was
never seen again. But the balloonist did consider that the next time
he was up he might take a musket along. He had no way of knowing it
would be another half-century before men realized they could murder each other in the skies as well as on the ground. The first "air kill"
would not be credited until October 5, 1914, when the French pilot
Frantz and his observer Quenault would shoot down a German plane
using rifle fire.

With one eye on the Confederate balloon, Lowe returned his attention to the battle going on below him. A chill shuddered through the
balloonist's body. His vision was blurring over again. Where were his
father and James Allen? He needed to come down.

Lowe had watched the *Constitution* being towed across the Chickahominy earlier. He could see the *Washington* presently wallowing on
the north bank waiting to cross as a steady column of troops moved in
the opposite direction.

The balloonist trained his spyglass on the opposite hills where the
Confederates could be seen advancing on Gaines' Mill. His mind still
concerned about his new sky partner, Lowe watched as below him
General Henry Slocum's troops crossed the river, heading in support
of Fitz-John Porter's besieged divisions. He wondered if the Rebel balloon had seen this movement and sent a warning of it.

At Gaines' Mill, the Confederate regiments could be seen swinging out in battle formation moving slowly across the open fields. A
cloud of smoke came from the woods on the opposite side. The gray
lines staggered and slowed, great gaps opening in the ranks. Some of
the men managed to keep going, sliding down the slippery slopes and
wallowing across the swampy ground. The balloonist could see staff
officers, astride their horses in the rear, admiring the troops' splendid
work. They were proud of their soldiers, who did not flinch under the
murderous fire, but went like heroes to their death.

The Union batteries on Gaines' Hill opened up, relentless volleys
following each other in quick succession along the entire line. A feverish Lowe was continuing to send information, but he had no way of
knowing if anyone was acting on it. Shells were falling on an enemy
force in the woods. The artillery seemed to have the range and the
direction as they fired rapidly and effectively.

At about 3:00 the Rebels made a bold push with their infantry. The
strongly pressed Federal brigades were moving back. They stopped to
face the Rebels and fired as they retreated, their colors in front, waving in full view of both lines. A shower of canister from their own cannon landed short, behind the retreating Union forces, cutting down
many of the men. The startled Federals turned to face a Confederate
brigade charging double-quick with fixed bayonets.

Fresh troops appeared from the rear and occupied the positions
just vacated by the dead. The Confederates too appeared to have an
unlimited supply of soldiers to add to the slaughter. The two armies
fought on, shells bursting, grapeshot flying through the air, minié
balls sailing with their peculiar deadly music. Running men stopped
in mid-stride and fell backward as bullets found their targets. A

feverish Lowe hung on to the wicker sides of his basket, watching as hour after hour the work of killing went relentlessly on. Long lines of wounded streamed to the rear, passing fresh troops on their way up. The wounded, covered in blood, screamed and cursed as they walked or crawled along, while the arriving men marched smartly singing patriotic songs.

Daylight was beginning to fade. No ground had been gained on either side, but the troops could not safely fall back until nightfall. The blood was up on both sides. Men had witnessed their comrades die. All the heedlessness of life and the abandonment of reason common to the heat of battle were in full play. Lowe could only wonder if either side would dare to call this slaughter a victory.

Darkness was falling. Unable to see anymore, Lowe signaled to be pulled down. His father was waiting for him on the ground with the news that James Allen was in the hospital with the fever. The two other balloons were secure, and camp had been set up. As the balloonist's foot left the basket and groped for the dark ground, the fever he had been fighting all day finally caught up with him. Overcome with delirium, Lowe fell, shaking and screaming, onto the cool earth.

19

The Hospital, Savage's Station, Going Home

The litter bearers carried Lowe into the lighted tent and placed him down among the wounded. The balloonist was speaking, but made little sense. Clovis' eyes adjusted to the dim light. He mopped his son's brow as Lowe moved in and out of consciousness. The lanterns hung around the walls flickered on red eyes and half-naked figures. Men who could walk paced fitfully up and down, their arms in slings. Those with more serious wounds, in the legs, body, or head, lay on their beds of corn-shucks, tossing in feverish sleep.

Aides bent over the injured washing their rent flesh from bowls of blood-stained water. In many wounds the ball or shot remained, surrounded by swollen and discolored skin from which foul-smelling fluids oozed. The most pitiful creatures were those who had been shot in the bowels. They crouched there clutching themselves, frightfully convulsed, shrieking and shouting. The volume of their noise was all they had to relieve their pain. A good number of the men were unconscious or sleeping, moving their fingers or lips as if trying to hold on to that last visage of life, not ready to be carried out and put on the growing pile of those who would move nothing ever again.

Clovis waited peevishly by his son for what seemed like a millennium. When no one came he decided to go in search of a doctor. The wounded men followed him with rolling eyes as he left the sickening smell of mortality and pushed through a flap into the cool night air.

The sentry at the door asked Clovis where he was going. He had not noticed the guard when they carried his son in. Clovis replied he was looking for a doctor for the balloonist. He was pointed to a smaller tent next door. This was also guarded by a sentry with a bayonet, whose orders were to keep out idlers, gossips, and journalists, but who seemed unconcerned when Clovis walked past him.

Clovis stepped inside to in a dimly-lit surgery. He was startled to discover what looked like amputation being performed. The surgeon, smoking a cigar, and with blood splattered on his bare arms and instruments, leaned over the unanesthetized victim, who was being held down by his horrified comrades. The men were trying their best to look away. Above the muffled screams of the patient, Clovis could hear the grating of the butcher saw on bone.

Overcome with nausea and feeling faint, Clovis ran from the tent into the open air. Groping around the back in the darkness, he tripped over something and stumbled. The living thing growled at him. His eyes adjusting to the darkness, Clovis saw it was a wild dog. The animal was eagerly grubbing through a pile of amputated parts: arms, legs, hands, and fingers. The dog growled again, unwilling to share his spoils with this intruder. Clovis stepped back, then let out a horrific scream. Startled, the mongrel ran off clutching the bloody mass of what had once been somebody's hand between his jaws. Clovis bent over double. In one sickening surge his stomach released its contents of undigested hardtack and beans.

Regaining his composure, Clovis returned to his son's side, but without a doctor. In a short time, however, a doctor appeared making rounds. Seeing a man not in uniform, the doctor dry-wiped his hands on a blood-stained coat, and took a piece of paper from his pocket. He asked what a civilian was doing there. Clovis explained that this was Professor Lowe, the man who went up in the balloon; he wasn't wounded, but had the fever. The doctor wrote something down in pencil on his paper, then walked away without saying anything. Clovis waited. When the doctor did not reappear, he decided to go in search of some quinine on his own.

A short time later the litter bearers returned and carried the balloonist back outside. They placed him down in the darkness, on a bed of corn-shucks, among the rows of heroes and cowards. Heroes were those whose wounds were beyond treatment and so were being left in their agony to die. Cowards were those suffering from things like diarrhea, dysentery, jaundice, and fever. Diarrhea sufferers were the most maligned. It was believed that only fear would make a man soil his underpants. The two bearers walked away laughing to themselves about the civilian they had just brought out who was ranting about flying across the Atlantic in a balloon and who claimed to have had breakfast with President Lincoln.

Having tracked down one of the few remaining sutlers who had not fled, Clovis returned to the hospital with a bottle of whiskey containing quinine he had bought at a wicked price. Not finding his son in the tent where he had left him, Clovis went to look among the long lines of miserable creatures lying out in the damp night. The light from his lantern picked out the torment on the men's faces as he moved down the long rows looking for Thaddeus. "Is that you doctor?" came the cry as he passed each man. The ground beneath him was soaked with blood dripping from the open wounds of the soldiers lying on the piles of corn-shucks. Flies and mosquitoes swarmed everywhere, feasting. He swatted at the insects with his hat, wishing he could help those poor abandoned creatures, but he was only one man, and an older man at that, and not feeling too well himself. Where was his son?

What was that? Over there, in the darkness at the edge of the group, Clovis thought he heard a voice talking about the wind and rivers in the sky. He found Thaddeus lying there with his eyes open to the night. Clovis put the bottle to his son's lips. He knew his son did not drink, but it was the only quinine he could find—if there really was any in the whiskey. Thaddeus was shaking violently. Then he noticed he was shaking slightly also. Clovis took a swig from the bottle. He had brought a woolen blanket, his only blanket. He was too tired to go back and try to find the balloon camp. Exhausted, the father lay down next to his son, wrapping his arms around the grown man who would always be his boy. Pulling the dirty blanket over the two of them, stroking his son's head, he curled up and tried to sleep.

Just before dawn Clovis was awakened by the cold chill. A thin fog covered the ground concealing the bodies of the men they had lain down with. He heard considerably less crying and moaning than last night. Some men were still sleeping silently. Others would not see the sun rise. There were gaps in the rows, men who had either wandered off in the night or been carried off dead. The sentries were gone. Clovis listened to his son's labored breathing; Thaddeus was still asleep. The father looked around, but saw no campfires. There was considerable activity, with many of the soldiers busy striking their tents. Clovis shivered in the damp gray air. He reached for the bottle of whiskey he had cached between his legs last night, but it was not there. Someone must have stolen it while he was sleeping.

Clovis got up and on stiff legs walked about the camp looking for the men from their balloon unit who had been appropriated for other jobs. The sun was beginning to penetrate through the branches of the trees. The camp looked lonely and deserted. There were few tents left standing; those that were belonged mainly to sutlers, who had abandoned their stores and left anyway they could. The general headquarters had long ago been vacated. Although he had not been told, it was clear camp was being broken. The date was June 28; McClellan's army was again in retreat. Clovis would need to find some men to help him save his son, as well as the balloons and generators.

The large hospital tent was empty, as the patients had all been turned out. Those who were fortunate had been placed on wagons and ambulances. The wounded and sick who could walk were started down the road and told to keep up with the regimental wagon train as best they could. A knot of men were standing around what had been a fire, as if the remembrance of it was giving them warmth. Clovis recognized some of the faces. They were soldiers from the balloon unit, and James Allen. Allen had been dismissed from the hospital as not being sick enough.

They returned and got Professor Lowe, who was now up and able to walk. A few of the men he had lain down with were also staggering about, but most of the bodies remained there in stiff, blood-hardened heaps. Learning that the Confederate army was not that far away, Clovis mustered his small group and went off to face the problem of saving the balloons. Finding no available conveyance, Lowe and Allen, leaning on each other for support, began walking down the road, hoping for an empty wagon to pass by and pick them up. But every wagon in the train was heavily laden and not inclined to make room for two civilians.

All around them bands of soldiers were engaged in looting what supplies had been left behind. The brigade commissary was being relieved of boxes of hard bread, barrels of flour and pork, and large quantities of miscellaneous items that had been thrown on a huge pile. Officers passed in and out of the abandoned sutler's tents, coming away with boxes of cigars, collars, clothing, tobacco, and sundry fancy items. Noncommissioned officers were then told to take whatever was left. Conscripts tried on officers' coats that had been selling for $18, throwing away ones that did not fit. Barrels of whiskey were broken open and poured over everything that remained. A match was put to the piles and the tents, and soon the entire camp was a blazing mass behind them.

A short distance down the road, the two floundering aeronauts were overtaken by the army's rear guard. The battalion's knapsacks were so loaded down with plunder that each man looked as if he was ready to start in the sutling business himself. Every sergeant had a box of cigars under his arm, and every man a cigar in his mouth. The column puffed away like a steam engine, the smoke serving to drive the insects from their faces. Pockets were crammed with enough bars of soap to keep the army in lather for a month. Newly acquired razor strops and pots of pomade could be seen hanging from the belts of soldiers too young to have need of shaving.

Lowe and Allen walked along, struggling to keep up with the

marching column, not wanting to be left behind. The balloonist wished for his wagons and his balloons to appear, but had no idea where they might be. It was clear that the army was in full retreat. Lowe, however, suspected that these men, now strutting with their swag, would not go far without having to turn and fight. He sensed that General Porter's corps was acting as a rear guard for the Army of the Potomac, falling back to select a position from which to take a delaying action in order to engage the enemy long enough to enable McClellan to get his overextended forces to Harrison's Landing.

As the Army of the Potomac pulled back toward the James River, Lee hoped to be able to hit it in its flank while it was on the move. His plan called for nine Confederate divisions to converge by six different roads against the retreating Federals. But once more poor coordination by his commanders, and again Jackson's slowness, coupled with stout Yankee resistance, would frustrate his efforts.

On June 29, at Savage's Station, only three miles from the Chickahominy, three Union divisions had encamped to protect a field hospital and large wagon train. Arriving at Savage's Station, Lowe and Allen found Clovis, who had managed to deflate the balloons and store them on a wagon. He also had a small group of men, some other wagons, and the generators. Clovis had stopped along with the rest of the wagon train he was traveling in.

Sensing that they should proceed to Harrison's Landing as soon as possible, Lowe, despite still feeling the harsh effects of his malaria, ordered his group to move on. Clovis argued they should remain at Savage's Station, encouraging his son to check into the large hospital that had been set up there. Although his men would protest, eager to share in the cigars and whiskey that were now being generously passed about, and some would disappear into other units, at Lowe's insistence the group started out. This would later prove to be a wise decision.

No sooner had the balloon unit departed Savage's Station than it began to rain heavily again. The men were fidgety and angry at having to leave the comfort of camp. As the damp air was full of sluggish mist, and Lowe's few guards had had a bit of whiskey before departing, every bush and fencepost became a Rebel picket at which they fired freely, if unsteadily. This kept Lowe in a fit of perpetual nervousness. He wanted to sleep, but dared not for fear that his skittish soldiers might mistakenly shoot at some actual Union pickets who would then return the fire. The group was made more anxious by the sounds of battle that could now be faintly heard behind them as his teams slogged slowly south.

Lee's plan was for Magruder to attack Savage's Station from the west, while Jackson came down on the right from the north. Magruder's men had begun the fight and were meeting stiff Union resistance. But Jackson was dawdling. On the general's orders, his men had spent most of the day rebuilding a bridge over the river at a point that his engineers had reported as being fordable even by infantry.

Expecting Johnson's forces to aid him, Magruder had only committed half of his division. Assuming, as usual, that they were being attacked by a superior force, the Federals would hold out until dark and then make a hasty retreat, leaving behind the hospital filled with 2,500 sick and wounded men from earlier fighting. It was the same hospital where Lowe had stopped before instinct told him to continue on.

The next day the Federal army would turn and fight again at Frayser's Farm near the village of Glendale. Lee had concocted an elaborate plan for a concentric assault on the retreating Yankees by seven of his divisions. Nevertheless, on this day only Longstreet and Hill managed to get their forces in action. In late afternoon they engaged in a fierce hand-to-hand battle against the main part of five Union divisions. Jackson again failed to do his part. Approaching from the north with twenty-five thousand men, Jackson sent a crew to rebuild White Oak Creek Bridge. Union sharpshooters drove the crew from its task. Confounded about what to do, Jackson delayed while Longstreet's and Hill's men bled and died two miles away. The Rebels gained little ground and lost 3,500 killed and wounded, twice as many as the Union Army.

When he received this report the next morning, Lee was furious. Once again his orders had not been carried out. However, he still had hopes of destroying "those people" as he referred to the Yankee army. He perceived the Union Army was becoming demoralized. Their route of retreat had become littered with a vast supply of equipment and arms. Confederate quartermasters and ordinance officers harvested a rich crop of captured matériel, including thirty thousand muskets, rifles, and pistols, and fifty cannon. In addition, Lee had captured over six thousand Union prisoners in the past six days.

A feverish and exhausted Lowe and his ragged balloon unit took refuge with the Federal Army at Malvern Hill. Here McClellan had turned around yet again and taken up a defensive stand. The position selected by the general was a naturally strong one. Three miles south of the town of Glendale, Malvern Hill was a mile wide and stood one hundred and fifty feet high. The slope was protected on both sides by fast-moving creeks that coursed through deep, tree-lined ravines.

Lee decided he would attack Malvern Hill frontally, and uphill, across woods, swamps, marshes, and creeks. Facing him were four Union divisions and a hundred guns, with four additional divisions and 150 guns in reserve.

Tuesday, July 1, 1862, showed early that the day would be hot and humid. Huge black crows strutted and pecked on the ground at the crest of Malvern Hill, where Colonel Henry J. Hunt had arrayed his cannon almost hub to hub for a mile. In the dense blue sky turkey vultures soared, anticipating the feast of torn human flesh that would soon be served up for them.

By noon all of the ninety thousand Federal troops were in position. As the heat rose from the damp ground in steamy waves, a silence gradually descended over the battleground. Even the crows were gone now. The men lay passive in the muggy air, the only sound being the noise of the flies circling around their faces. Gazing at the motionless trees at the edge of the field in front of them, they marked the time until, with a horrific yell, rows of gray clad forms would come busting out. These sweaty hours before the battle began passed with agonizing slowness, the hardest part of any fight being not the fear but the uncertainty; it strained men's nerves and made them live days in a moment.

But the soldiers, lying about smoking their pipes, or writing in their diaries, or picking lice from their beards, would have several more hours to wait before the killing began. As usual nothing was going right for General Robert E. Lee. The country through which the Confederates were advancing was not adequately mapped. Heavily wooded, with numerous streams, swamps, ravines, gullies, and narrow twisting country roads, the land gave the advantage to the hunted, not the hunters. An ignorance of the topography caused Lee's commanders to underestimate the importance of blocking roads and fords and destroying bridges. Required to offset these failures were solid tactics, close cooperation between divisional commanders, and sound staff work at army headquarters, none of which Lee's army yet had.

Malvern House had been appropriated by Porter for his headquarters. Lowe sat on the porch of the exquisite brick structure, wrapped in a blanket and shivering despite the heat. Sweat poured down his forehead. Although Lowe had all his balloons present, he had not been asked to send them aloft for observations. Porter knew that none of the aeronauts was fit, and the general felt he had a commanding enough view of the battlefield from his position at the top of the hill.

The battle was late getting started. Lee was having disagreements with his commanders about the plan for a frontal attack, while some of the lost units were still on the way. Longstreet had found two elevated positions north of Malvern Hill from which he thought the cannon might be able to soften up the Federal defenses and decided to have his guns set up there.

Lee ordered this artillery to commence firing at the knoll. However, on account of poor coordination by his staff, not all the cannoneers got the message. The result was that the weak fire did little but reveal the Rebel artillery's position. The Federals answered with an intense battery. As the shells landed the Confederate guns were blown into the air, coming down on any men and horses nearby. The wounded animals ran screeching to the rear. The Rebel units who had opened fire were soon torn to fragments. Thinking that the firing was the signal to attack, D. H. Hill's men charged forward, prematurely beginning the battle.

The Union soldiers heard a yell. They crouched, watching as gray clad figures sprang forward out of the woods advancing in cadenced steps up the slope toward the exploding fury of their blazing cannon. The Rebel line stopped and fired. An answering volley of cannon fire ripped a hole in their ranks. The second line came forward. Union musket fire flew out to meet the charging wave. Men screamed and went down, while others charged on. Ball and shot hissed hot in the dusty haze. The firing was horrendous, beyond anything that the war had seen so far .

The Confederate ranks, bayonets glistening in the smoke, surged bravely through the chaos, not stopping until they were almost to the muzzles of the Union cannon. But the Union line could not be breached. The charge became uneven, huge gaps in the ranks being ripped open by musket and cannon. The men had nowhere to go; many stood in confusion as their comrades fell alongside them. Then suddenly, without warning or command, the Rebel line broke. The soldiers ran in panic for shelter in a hollow beneath the ridge, crouching there only long enough to catch their breath before dwindling, exhausted, back into the trees.

Nothing had been accomplished by the battle. Confusion in the delivery of Lee's orders had caused the attack to be disjointed, with regiments advancing individually rather than together. This allowed the Federal artillery to decimate the charging troops. The few units that did manage to get close were soon brought down by withering musket fire.

This was the first time in history that artillery fire had caused more casualties than rifle fire. D. H. Hill, whose division was the most severely enfiladed, would remark caustically of Malvern Hill, "It was not war—it was murder." The 5,500 Confederates killed or wounded in the battle were more than twice the Union total.

A sad silence had fallen over Malvern Hill pierced only by the wretched sounds of the wounded and the dying. The setting sun revealed men in every attitude of anguish. Bodies lay scattered about dreadfully mutilated by the cannon. Some were cut in half. Many were headless. Fragments of torsos and limbs were strewn in such profusion that it would be impossible to match a part with its original owner. Most of the figures were lifeless, but enough of the men were alive and crawling about so that in the dim light the battlefield gave the appearance that the very earth was moving.

Lowe had watched the start of the battle from Malvern House with Porter and his staff. As the killing increased, the balloonist had ceased to look on and gone down and sat with his father and James Allen in the shade of one of the generator wagons. Although Porter had been responsible for the positioning of troops and artillery before the battle, he had little to do during the action with command or troop movement. Porter was, nevertheless, pleased with the result. He sent a message to McClellan describing his great victory, and suggesting, "We should hold this powerful position."

At 9:00 that evening Porter received his answer from McClellan, who was safely on board a Federal gunboat anchored in the James River suffering from a bout of dysentery: "The General Commanding desires you to move your command at once, the artillery reserve moving first to Harrison's Bar."

With darkness a brooding rain had fallen on Malvern Hill wrapping it in a ghostly mist. A feverish and weary T. S. C. Lowe and his greatly reduced crew prepared to join the Army of the Potomac on yet another march through the dark, and rain, and mud. Dispirited, haggard, and hungry, most of the troops were worn out more from marching than from fighting. The men knew a victory had been won, and would willingly have marched toward Richmond rather than away from it if the order had come.

Even the generals were of this belief. Although Porter merely wanted to maintain this position, the others, particularly General Philip Kearny of New Jersey, suggested an immediate advance on the Confederate capital. The pugnacious Kearny, who had lost an arm in the Mexican War, was so angered by McClellan's order to withdraw, he burst out, "I say to you all, such an order can only be prompted by cowardice or treason."

All through the grim night Lowe and his balloon unit struggled to make the eight muddy miles to Harrison's Landing and the protection of the Federal gunboats. The wagons crawled along, starting and stopping, guided by fires along the road hissing and sputtering in the rain. Lowe sat in a stupor, shivering under two blankets and a rain slicker, the water pouring off the brim of his wide hat.

The balloonist was suffering from the common vivax malaria, which had infected thousands of the men on the peninsula. While Lowe suffered from intense fever, sweats, chills, and general weakness, the attacks were chronic, usually occurring every other day. Often whole units suffered from this illness, soldiering on, no one wanting to report to the hospital for fear of the treatment they might receive.

Lowe's wagons kept to the roads with the other wagons, cavalry, and artillery. The route, no more than a dugway through the pines and overgrown, abandoned farms, was churned into a trough of liquid filth. What men remained with the balloon unit were constantly having to apply their shoulders to the wheel, or pull on the harness of a mule, to get the wagons moving. The foot soldiers found better going by keeping to the woods and fields sloshing along slowly in the muck. Men pulled each other along, struggling in the rain and darkness, drenched to the skin.

By dawn the rain had stopped. When daylight finally came, it revealed hundreds of stragglers sitting beside the road who, too exhausted to go on, had been left behind by their regiments. Many of the abandoned were wounded. Lowe espied one poor trooper, hardly a boy, who had been wrapped in a blanket and propped up against a tree by his comrades. His foot had been partly shot off, and he had been left there to die or be taken prisoner as fate might decree. The lad held a tin pannikin in his hand with which he collected fetid water from the ditch beside the road and poured it on his bloody foot. His empty haversack lay by his side, the few hard crackers that had been in it reduced to a soggy mess by the rain. Moved with compassion, the balloonist ordered his wagons to stop. Although his unit did not have rations to spare and did not know when their meager stores might be resupplied, Lowe jumped from the wagon offering food to the wretched boy.

The full road behind Lowe's group began to tie up. The following wagons were unable to pass on the narrow, slippery way. Almost immediately a convocation of teamsters assembled hurling oaths and outlandish swears at Lowe for having caused the stoppage. The balloonist climbed back on his wagon, while his own teamsters cursed at him with such a volley of horrid blasphemy as he had ever heard. All Lowe could do was sit there and listen. There was no disciplining these men as the teamsters were civilians as he was. They probably had only offered to drive for the Balloon Corps because they heard the erroneous rumor that Professor Lowe and the other aeronauts were some of the highest paid men in the army.

Lowe sat quietly as the wagons slogged along through the woods, pondering the fact that what he and his men had accomplished was probably of no great consequence. No single event that had occurred in this frightful, yet monotonous, campaign stood out in his mind with any importance. The balloonist mentioned this to James Allen, sitting next to him, who maintained a silence on the subject. He took off his black felt hat, like its owner crushed and somewhat the worse for wear, and drained the water from the brim. Then Lowe remembered the wounded boy sitting beside the road in the rain, his face a mask of seriousness and sadness. He would have liked to have taken him along, but, as the teamsters had argued, they could not stop for everyone. The wagons were already overloaded with the balloons and other equipment. And the horses and mules were tired; they needed rest more than the men.

Around ten o'clock the wagon train Lowe and his unit were traveling in finally emerged from the seemingly endless woods and joined the main part of the army at Harrison's Landing. The broad fields were covered with men: tired, worn-out, disgusted, and hungry, more dead than alive. Confusion reigned. Thousands of soldiers who had been separated from their units wandered about, asking every passerby for the name of their regiment. Ambulances, supply wagons, caissons, and artillery pieces clogged the roads. Tents were pitched everywhere. And transports and gunboats filled the river.

That afternoon heavy rainstorms began again, which was just as well as it caused Lee to withdraw his orders to J. E. B. Stuart to go in pursuit of Keyes's corps, which had been assigned the task of acting as the Federal rear guard.

July 4 was to be T. S. C. Lowe's last day on the peninsula. He was in his tent packing. The balloonist did not have many clothes, most being on his back, but he was stuffing his bags full of the reports and correspondence that were the record of the Balloon Corps activity so far. Admittedly, he was not very accurate at record keeping. Lowe would be the first to acknowledge that the stacks of papers were a mess. He hoped to get to them some day soon, perhaps while he was recuperating back at home in Philadelphia.

Bustling with excitement, an orderly arrived at Lowe's tent. He hustled the balloonist to a small knoll overlooking the river. His father and James Allen were already there. They pointed up the James toward Richmond. A balloon was approaching, being towed down the river by an armored ship. Lowe estimated the size of the balloon to be seventy-five thousand cubic feet. He judged by its patchwork surface that the Confederate balloon was the same one that had appeared over Richmond on June 27, while he was observing the battle at Gaines' Mill.

Lowe watched through his spyglass as the balloon tug rounded a bend. As the balloon was not very high and probably did not have an observer in the basket the Rebel boat unexpectedly came face to face with the Union gunboats U. S. S. *Monitor* and U. S. S. *Maratza*. Realizing it was completely out gunned, the armored ship, which Lowe could now see bore the name *Teaser,* attempted to immediately reverse its course.

At that point, however, the channel was very shallow. As it came about, the *Teaser* ran aground on a sandbar. Quickly surrounded by the two gunboats, the Rebel crew abandoned their ship, which was seized by the Federals along with the balloon. Aware that the chief aeronaut was still at Harrison's Landing, the Confederate balloon was brought down and presented to Lowe, apparently for him to analyze.

A pleasant zephyr cooled Lowe's face as he stood on the temporary pier waiting for the transport that was to take him back to Washington. He would be glad to be rid of the hoards of mosquitoes and swirling masses of evil-tempered flies, and of the fighting and killing. He was tired of seeing graves dug and of the malodorous smell given off by the bodies of dead horses as they burned.

The balloonist did not know if he would be back or the fate of the three war balloons he was leaving in the charge of his sixty-year-old father. What he did know was that he would bring the Confederate's parti-colored balloon with him when he embarked. On the way he planned to take out his scissors and cut the patchwork into its original pieces. What he would do with the pieces he was not sure.

Lowe left before the arrival of Abraham Lincoln who, on July 8, secretly came down from Washington to pay a visit to his battered army. The crushed and overburdened men would have to spend a day preparing for the honor, and doubtless would have been happier had they been given the day off. Salutes were fired, but there was not much of a parade. Only one small band could be mustered, as nearly all the band instruments had been destroyed or lost in the numerous moves, with most of the bandsmen having been reassigned to attending the wounded. The brigades were drawn up and a moonlight review was held, doubtless to conceal the ragged state of the men. As President Lincoln and General McClellan rode down the lines, the president towering by a head over his host, the soldiers cheered heartily—just as they had been trained to do.

20

To Home and Back, Called up, Fredericksburg

His joy of life newly awakened by the return river voyage from Harrison's Landing, and feeling somewhat strengthened physically, Lowe stopped briefly in Washington to give his report to the War Department. Secretary Stanton's tone conveyed to the balloonist that he was not especially pleased to see him. Lowe's complaints were the same as he had been hearing from most of his commanders lately: the government had failed to support him, his requests had been ignored, his orders were often contradictory. Stanton tersely informed Lowe he was restricted to reporting only on what actually transpired on the peninsula; he had no right to bring up other matters. Though infuriated by Stanton's magisterial air, the balloonist tried to remain calm reminding the secretary there were many accommodations he had made on the peninsula in the name of harmony and unanimity. Considering the many obstacles put in his way, he was impressed his men conducted themselves as well as they did. Thoroughly discouraged by the unexpected turn of this meeting, Lowe returned to Philadelphia with little hope for the future of the Balloon Corps.

Leontine was happy to see him and greeted him warmly, however not with the passion Lowe was anticipating. He noticed a tension between them, perhaps even an aversion, that had not been there before. As the balloonist stood at the door, shaking slightly from exertion and the aftereffects of his malaria, he sensed something stirring in his wife, a mixture of anger and fear combined with a glimpse of a new-found strength or perhaps aggression. He was not aware a rift had grown between them, caused by something that can cool even the warmest of relationships, the capital enterprise—money.

In Leontine's numerous letters to her husband she had frequently mentioned money, or more specifically her lack of it. In the past Leontine had always handled the financial matters. Lowe merely handed all his income over to her, which she managed very well. It had been that way since the beginning of their relationship. But now, to Lowe's great embarrassment, he had no money to give her. Although he was supposed to be receiving $10 per day in gold, the balloonist rarely received any compensation at all. And when Lowe did receive his salary, he usually had to use the money to pay for materials or services he had purchased for the Balloon Corps for which he had not yet been, or might never be, reimbursed. Thus it was with considerable abasement that he had consistently ignored his wife's requests. He occasionally was able to send her small amounts, but he knew that this was hardly enough. Always the impractical dreamer, the balloonist tended to ignore the question of how his wife was managing to get by.

As far back as March 1862 a desperate Leontine had sent her husband a telegram saying simply: "We are well. Nothing new. You must send money immediately." In a later wire the ever-patient Mrs. Lowe entreated: "Did not receive money. Need it badly. We are well."

In order to meet her financial obligations Leontine had been forced to take out another mortgage, at a usurious interest, on their town house. She also had released the cook, maid, and nanny. Her mother still lived with them, but was rather ill and of little help, needing considerable tending herself. When Leontine told her husband about the mortgage, he was furious. He suggested she should have sold some of her jewelry instead. Leontine reminded him that the last thing a refined lady did was sell her ornaments to pay her bills.

Leontine was also frightened of her husband's illness, which was another reason she kept her distance. As was typical of the disease, he would be fine one day and on the next be seized by fever, chills, and weakness. Little was known at the time about the cause of Lowe's malady, and Leontine suspected it might be contagious. She avoided him and did not let him have contact with their young daughters. He more often than not could be found sitting alone in a corner of the drawing room reading his newspaper.

A firm believer in the benefits of fresh air, Leontine encouraged her husband to take daily walks by the river. He took his daughters along, but she required him to wear gloves when he held their tiny hands. Lowe found these short walks difficult and consuming of his strength.

Breathing heavily and his shirt damp with sweat, Lowe sat down on a bench to rest. His daughters ran along the river bank in front of him. The spinning city landscape had taken on a red and pink hue. His feverish mind wandered. As the balloonist gazed at the flowing water it was not the Delaware he saw but the Potomac, York, Pamunkey, Chickahominy, or James. A violent spasm twitched his body. Once again he heard the boundless roar of cannon; saw the shattered bodies and the collapsing bridges; listened to the clumsy, gasping cries of drowning men; and the agonizing shriek of the wounded. Riderless horses wallowed in the mud along the banks snorting flames from their nostrils. Corpses, swollen to twice their size, ground out curses and blasphemies from their bloated mouths as they floated by on the spume. Summoned by he did not know what, the whole ghastly parade assembled around him, marching skyward, a relentless invasion of his senses. He shouted out something he had uttered before but did not understand and kept repeating again and again in a strange faltering descant.

Braver than their mother, his daughters, who Lowe would admit hardly knew their father, ran back at his cries. They stood there, not understanding, near him, yet maintaining the safe distance Leontine had prescribed. Lowe rubbed his eyes and shook his head, then assured the little girls he was alright. He dug in his pocket, took out the small bottle he regularly carried with him, and lifted it to his lips. While he frequently had such spells and attributed them to his illness, they could perhaps also have been caused by the various cures the balloonist was taking, which in addition to the quinine included calomel, tartar emetic, morphine, and laudanum.

Shortly after Lowe had returned from Harrison's Landing, President Lincoln and Secretary of War Stanton, who knew exactly what they wanted but not how to get it, replaced General McClellan with the bookish General Henry W. Halleck. On August 3, convinced that the Army of the Potomac would not advance, the new commander-in-chief ordered McClellan to withdraw his troops from the peninsula. The failure of McClellan's Peninsula Campaign was seen not only as a military failure, but also as the end of the idea of a "limited war for limited means." Henceforth, the North would not fight to preserve the old Union, but to destroy it, and build a new one out of the remains.

Anticipating the return of the battle-hardened veterans of the Peninsula Campaign, Lincoln sent General John Pope on an overland expedition to capture the Confederate capital. Headed to Richmond from the North, along the line of the Orange and Alexandria Railroad, General Pope's army was composed of those divisions that had been held in reserve for the defense of Washington.

Drawn into battle on the afternoon of August 29 with Jackson at Manassas Junction, Pope, full of bravado, wired Lincoln: "I am about to achieve a great victory." Lincoln was ecstatic. The next day, however, Lee and Longstreet joined up with Jackson, while none of McClellan's divisions had yet arrived. By evening on August 30, Pope's army was broken, driven back to the safety of Washington's fortifications in complete disarray. Pope had lost the day, his reputation, and with it fifteen thousand men.

Lowe put down his newspaper in disgust. He had just finished reading the account of Pope's failure, and could not believe the turn of events. At the beginning of that very summer he had been with the Army of the Potomac, with thousands of troops and more on the way, camped within four miles of Richmond. He had ascended daily in his balloon and looked down into the streets and houses of the Confederate capital. Now, thanks to their new commander General Robert E. Lee, the smaller Confederate forces had driven away the vast army that had been waiting in their front yard, and then whipped the army that was coming in relief.

In less than three months General Lee had successfully moved the war from the outskirts of Richmond to the doorstep of Washington, and now was preparing to cross the Potomac and invade the North. Lee was hoping that such a move would induce neutral Maryland into the Confederacy at last. An editorial in the same newspaper ventured that such a demonstration of strength by the South was sure to draw England and France into the war on the Rebel side.

Lowe rose from his chair; his blood was up. Whether the army wanted his Balloon Corps or not, they needed him before everything was lost. The balloonist's left leg shook slightly as he walked. He was still not well. Lowe had been told that his condition might never go away, but he had functioned when feeling worse. Leontine was in the kitchen preparing dinner. The two girls were there playing with cornhusk dolls she had made them. Standing away from her at the distance she required, Lowe announced he had decided to go back to the war. Leontine looked at her husband for a moment, then rushed forward and put her arms around him. It was the first time she had touched him since he had arrived. Seeing her, the two daughters ran and also put their arms around their father. Leontine burst into tears.

T. S. C. Lowe arrived back in Washington on September 5, 1862, the same day that Robert E. Lee took the Army of Northern Virginia across the Potomac and into western Maryland. In theory Lowe was still the chief aeronaut, although as yet he had not received a commission. The Balloon Corps had been relatively inactive during his absence, the only ascensions being those that Clovis had made in August for Commodore Wilkes, towed by a steamer on the James River.

Lowe's first objective would be to reopen a channel of communications to the military officialdom. By the time he had left the peninsula, the administration of the Balloon Corps had become considerably more complicated than when Lowe had worked directly with Hartman Bache and A. W. Whipple through the Bureau of Topographical Engineers. The balloonist had been supported by McClellan, who had put his staff officer, Colonel John N. Macomb, in charge of balloon operations. This had served well for Lowe, giving him a clear chain of command and freeing him from War Department bureaucracy. The head balloonist had been given permission to purchase matériel, and train and position his own aeronauts, as long as they accommodated the needs of McClellan's staff. However, Lowe's civilian status and his lack of familiarity with the procedures and rules of military accounting, plus his readiness to incur debts to ensure the quickest possible response to a problem, created serious difficulties within the chain of command. No one seemed to want to be responsible for Lowe's activities. He was shuffled from one officer to another, like a man infected with leprosy, until finally ending up under Brigadier Andrew A. Humphreys. Lowe and Humphreys took an immediate liking to each other. The two functioned well together all during the Peninsula Campaign, and the Balloon Corps had been able to perform efficiently within the framework of the Army of the Potomac.

Nevertheless, all this was lost during the time Lowe was back in Philadelphia. Returning to Washington, the balloonist learned that Humphreys had been promoted and was now commanding a division of his own. He would no longer be available to act as supervisor and mediator for the Balloon Corps.

Back now in his old room at the National Hotel, Lowe was uncertain what to do, not knowing who to turn to. He knew Lincoln would see him, but he did not want to bother the president as Lowe remembered the previous problems he had had when he went over too many heads. Looking over a list of the chain of command, the balloonist decided to begin his contact with the assistant adjutant general, A. V. Colburn.

Lowe mopped his forehead as he took his box of writing materials out of the drawer. He told himself it was a hot fall day, and there was no breeze in the room. As he put the pen to paper his hand began to quiver, the ink blotting on the page. The balloonist paused. Then his left leg began to twitch. He sat for a moment, wondering if these souvenirs of the Peninsula Campaign would be with him for the rest of his life. Slowly and painfully Lowe took out a clean sheet of paper and began again his letter to Colburn requesting travel orders that would permit him and his balloons to rejoin the army.

The assistant adjutant general received the letter and responded with reasonable promptness, but only to advise the balloonist to remain in Washington until word was received from McClellan, who would be contacted regarding his plans for the Balloon Corps.

General McClellan, who had been in Alexandria with his troops, but unable to make it in time for the second battle of Manassas, had been put in charge of reconstructing the shattered pieces of his and Pope's armies. In disgrace, General Pope had been relieved of his command and sent off to Minnesota to fight Indians. The refurbished Army of the Potomac, all ninety-five thousand men, was manning the Washington fortifications when Lee crossed into Maryland. Although no one knew where Lee's army was, or where he was going, McClellan had been ordered by President Lincoln to follow him.

For the next two weeks Lowe cooled his heels in Washington. His participation in the war had been reduced to sitting in the lobby of the National Hotel reading newspapers. He followed closely the results of the various battles, including the one just fought at Sharpsburg on Antietam Creek. Each new account gave him cause to wonder how the outcome might have differed had he and the Balloon Corps been able to be part of the action.

The war had not been going well for the Union during the past months, not only in Maryland, but also in the West. In both theaters the Federals held a strong advantage in numbers, but had failed to make use of it by mounting a vigorous and unceasing offensive. The desire to control territory, rather than compel the enemy to fight, was causing the Union to lose control of the situation. In Maryland, Kentucky, and Tennessee the North was fighting defensive campaigns. To foreign observers this made it seem as if the South was winning the war. Eager to be found on the victorious side, the British were on the verge of granting recognition to the Confederate States. The newspapers speculated that there would soon be a new country listed in the world's atlas of nations.

But at Sharpsburg, aided by pure chance, the tide had begun to turn in the Union favor. Preparing to move into Pennsylvania, Lee had split his army into three elements. But one of his officers had somehow lost his copy of the orders describing the troop deployments. These were found, wrapped around three cigars to keep them fresh, by two Union pickets, who could not believe it was not a joke. Sent to McClellan's headquarters, an officer there recognized the handwriting on the papers as that of one of Lee's assistants. Aware of Lee's plans, McClellan now had the advantage, as his army was closer to the Confederates' scattered divisions than they were to each other. If he moved quickly, McClellan could annihilate the Army of Northern Virginia.

But McClellan never moved fast. Lee ordered his troops to reassemble at Sharpsburg on Antietam Creek. Jackson, who had just captured the arsenal at Harpers Ferry, for once arrived on time for the battle that had been fought there on September 17.

The Union army attacked savagely all day long. Confederate units were forced to give ground, but the entire army never retreated. The next day, seeing Lee's battered forces still in position, McClellan chose not to renew his attack. That night Lee's worn-out army slipped back to Virginia. While tactically a draw, strategically Antietam had been a Northern victory of major importance. Lee's invasion had failed. The Union had regained the initiative. European governments drew back; it was not yet time to recognize the Confederate States of America.

The Battle of Sharpsburg/Antietam had another grim distinction; it had been the bloodiest fight so far. A combined total of nearly twenty-four thousand men had been lost. Never before in the history of war, or since, had so many men fallen in battle on a single day.

Finished with his newspaper, Lowe got up from his chair and began walking to his room. As the balloonist passed the front desk, a clerk handed him a telegram that had just arrived. It was an order from General Marcy, authorizing him to pack his wagons with balloons and equipment and proceed at once to Sharpsburg to join McClellan. Lowe was elated. The waiting was ended, but he knew he was already one day too late.

Even with General Marcy's orders it was not easy for Lowe to put together a new Balloon Corps. All his former crewmen had been dispersed; some to other units, others sick, wounded, or dead. The more fortunate had gone home. With manpower at a premium, Lowe had to fill his ranks from soldiers considered "least effective under arms," those men who were now assigned as stretcher-bearers, cooks' helpers, wagon loaders, and to various other manual chores. Many of these were men who had been trained as infantry, but fled in terror when the fighting started. Their commanders were more than willing to be rid of them by transferring them to the Balloon Corps. Lowe had no time to train this ragtag group, but would have to do it in the field. To drive his wagons the balloonist once again had to hire civilian teamsters. Lowe was sure they would disappear the first time their pay failed to arrive.

The war balloons themselves had experienced considerable abuse during their numerous moves on the peninsula and were badly in need of repair. The gas generator wagons would also require considerable work to get them operating again. The Balloon Corps' wagons and the teams were gone, having been appropriated by other regiments. For several days Lowe scoured Washington's arsenals and warehouses looking for what worn-out animals and dilapidated wagons were available to him.

As it was Lowe did well to arrive at Sharpsburg with his crew only one week after receiving his orders. He immediately met with Mc-

Clellan, who, besides the stress of his command, was showing the effects of a bout of dysentery he had suffered in Virginia. McClellan shook Lowe's hand warmly, glad to see his old friend. The general told Lowe he regretted not having the Balloon Corps available during the Battle of Antietam. He realized an observation balloon would have been invaluable to him during that engagement.

Forever the optimist, Lowe reassured McClellan it was only a matter of a few days before he would have his crews trained and the balloons fully operational again. The balloonist laid the blame for his delay on the difficulty of receiving orders, and then obtaining men and equipment. He attributed this to the fact that he had not yet received the commission he had asked for from the War Department, but was still a civilian employee. Lowe would write:

> From the first I had hoped to be allowed to command the Balloon Corps as a military branch and applied for a commission to command it. But all that 'the powers that be' would do was to grant me the privileges of that rank but not the authority, consequently I was subject to every young and inexperienced lieutenant and captain, who for the time being was put in charge of the Aeronautic Corps. These young fellows had no knowledge whatever of aeronautics and were often a serious hindrance to me than a help. But they were not all unintelligent, and all of the Generals under whom I served expressed a keen appreciation of my work, and this over-balanced the trouble I sometimes had with minor officers.

Lowe sat with McClellan late into the night in the general's tent, drinking coffee and discussing the Balloon Corps' problems. As McClellan fancied himself an effective organizer, he liked to delve into the difficulties facing those under his command. He also sensed that Lowe showed him a great deal of respect, which fewer people were doing those days. Lowe came away from the meeting feeling that the general was sympathetic to his situation. As the meeting ended, McClellan stated he would recommend the Balloon Corps be made a distinct branch of the Army with Lowe being granted a full commission.

The next day, eager to prove his worth, Lowe took up one of the battered balloons from his camp next to McClellan's headquarters at Sharpsburg. It was his first balloon ascension since the Peninsula Campaign. He had brushed his felt hat, cleaned his frock coat, polished his boots, and even trimmed his moustache. Always a dandy, Lowe was embarrassed at how he had let his appearance go while ill on the peninsula. If he was not an officer, at least he could look like one. His crew was a scruffy bunch; he would set them a good example.

As the balloon rose into the clear air Lowe felt happy to be back and be rededicated to his purpose. Or was he simply glad to be in the sky again? Gazing around him, the balloonist was pleased to see a whole new world. Gone was the dull flatness of the Virginia Peninsula, with its muddy swamps and vine-tangled forests. This was Maryland. Rich farms and orchards balanced on the gently rolling hills that disappeared into a backdrop of lush, blue-tinted mountains.

Lowe caught the sun glistening on the current of the foaming Antietam Creek as it twisted its way to the Potomac. Scanning the other side of the water through his spyglass, the balloonist studied the small groves, rock outcroppings, stone walls, and the dips and swells in the undulating farmland that had been the Rebel line. Focusing closer to home, he saw the Union camp below him: the wagons, caissons, cannon, tents, campfires, and marching men—McClellan's constantly drilling soldiers.

In the fields lay the detritus of war: the fresh dug graves, the overturned wagons, and the piles of dead horses rotting in the hot sun. The landscape had been changed, now and forever, the ground planted with canister and shot, the water running over a bed of abandoned weapons, and human and animal bones. In what had been rich cornfields few stalks remained standing. Poisoned with lead shot and human debris, it would be years before anyone would want to eat anything grown in that wasted soil.

Many of the haystacks that had stood in the fields were now only circles of charred black. The night after the battle the weather had turned cold. The hay had been set fire to by soldiers trying to keep away the chill, inadvertently roasting alive their wounded comrades who had taken shelter in the stacks during the day's combat. The men heard the screams too late and had no way of dousing the fires they had started. Lowe signaled to be hauled down. Nothing had changed in that battle-laden month he had been away. The curse of war had not been lifted from mankind.

For almost a month Lowe and the Allen brothers camped with McClellan's forces, making observation flights at Sharpsburg and from Bolivar Heights overlooking Harpers Ferry. However, they had little to report. General Lee and his ragged Confederate Army had escaped back to the safety of the Shenandoah Valley, nearly one-third of the men who so proudly forded the Potomac with him on September 5 having been wounded or killed.

McClellan remained in place at Sharpsville throughout October and early November while his army reorganized and reequipped itself. When he finally was ready to march south, McClellan sent Lowe and his Balloon Corps packing back to Washington, knowing that he would be moving through the Blue Ridge Mountains, where the balloons would be relatively useless in the rugged terrain. A disappointed Lowe protested mightily, but accepted McClellan's promise to send for him when his army got established further south.

Crossing the Potomac into Virginia, McClellan found himself in position to pick off, one at a time, the widely separated elements of Lee's army. Longstreet was at Culpepper Court House, and Jackson at Winchester. Lee, however, gambled that the cautious McClellan would hesitate to move against either unit. Once again Lee guessed correctly.

Thoroughly disillusioned with his commander-in-chief, President Lincoln removed McClellan from his post, replacing him with Major General Ambrose E. Burnside. This move was good news to Lowe's most constant aeronaut, James Allen, who looked forward to working with Burnside. Allen had originally marched off to war in Burnside's division; they were both from Rhode Island.

Although Allen was enthusiastic about the change, Lowe realized that in losing McClellan he had lost his strongest supporter. Moreover, when the Balloon Corps arrived back in Washington, James Allen suffered a severe attack of the fever he had contracted on the peninsula and decided to return to Rhode Island to recuperate. Lowe would have to open a channel of communication with the new commander-in-chief without the help of Allen.

On November 20, 1862, Lowe sent a letter to Major J. G. Parke, Burnside's chief-of-staff. The balloonist reiterated the Balloon Corps's contribution to previous campaigns and especially the importance of his personal contribution at the Battle of Fair Oaks. He outlined the corps's present condition and future needs. In conclusion Lowe stated, "My men and I stand ready to report for action as soon as we shall receive your orders."

Lowe's letter was well taken. Only four days later, the balloonist received a reply from Parke, ordering him and his men and balloons to report to the Federal army camped across the river from Fredericksburg as soon as possible. Parke also issued Lowe orders to the Quartermaster Department in Washington, and the Army of the Potomac, instructing them to "provide Professor Lowe with all the possible assistance he might need." Armed with his new authorization, the balloonist quickly replaced his more wornout wagons and teams and acquired a few more men and drivers, then started south.

The one thing Lowe hadn't changed was his attire. Once again the balloonist was going off to the war in his familiar black wide-brimmed felt hat and frock coat. Despite all he had accomplished at the various battles, and all the letters he had written, Lowe and his fellow aeronauts still had not been commissioned. They would continue to risk their lives as private contractors.

As the wagon wheels ground along on the rutted road, Lowe turned back to watch the smoke from the chimneys of Washington fading in the distance. A fresh wind blew up, causing the balloonist to tug his hat down more securely. He looked up again, wondering if this might be the last time he would see this scene. Would he be returning? Or would the coming months find the name Thaddeus Sobieski Constantine Lowe, balloonist, stricken from the government's register of those civilian employees still alive to receive their pay?

Six days after Lowe and his men set out, traveling in the cold on frozen roads, the Balloon Corps reached General Burnside's headquarters on the east bank of the Rappahannock River. Eager to get back in the air, Lowe was disappointed to learn that, as part of Burnside's strategy, the presence of the observation balloons was to be kept a secret until the army had crossed the river and the battle had begun.

Several weeks previous, Burnside had requested pontoon bridges be shipped for use in the river crossing. But their delivery had gone astray, supposedly because of his unclear orders as to where they were to be sent. After considerable delay the bridges had arrived; however, Burnside was still hesitating to attack. At the same time, Washington was full of gloom and discord. People were questioning why it was taking so long to accomplish what everyone was demanding—a decisive Union victory.

Winter had arrived. Days of freezing rain and intermittent snow showers followed one after another. While Federal troops continued to reconnoiter along the Rappahannock, the balloonist waited with General Burnside and his staff at his camp on Stafford Heights. This delay was fortunate for the Balloon Corps as it gave the Allen brothers time to return from Rhode Island. Since arriving the Allens had been as eager to go aloft as Lowe. The chief aeronaut kept stressing that his balloons could provide valuable information on the Confederate troop displacements. However, General Burnside, hinting at the need for complete surprise at their deployment, insisted they remain on the ground. Nevertheless, the Balloon Corps was itching for battle, as were the numerous batteries of Union artillery that lined the heights commanding both the river and the town of Fredericksburg.

One day, while passing time at Burnside's headquarters, Lowe made the acquaintance of a strange and eccentric little lady, who also felt she had better things to do than be run around by the military bureaucracy.

The two began talking and soon discovered a common bond in what they perceived to be their mistreatment by the War Department.

Hardly five feet tall, Mary Edwards Walker had graduated as the only woman in her class at Syracuse Medical College. Heeding Washington's call for physicians, Doctor Walker had applied to the War Department for a medical commission. Despite her credentials, the Surgeon General had rejected her application, reluctant to break with tradition by commissioning a woman, as all medical doctors were given the rank of officer. Despite her rebuff Walker volunteered as a nurse and was assigned to a makeshift hospital set up at the U. S. Patent Office building.

Becoming tired of this job, she resigned. Eventually she made her way to Burnside's headquarters, where her services as a doctor were readily accepted. However, she was serving without salary or commission. When Lowe met her she was resplendently clad in the uniform of a Union Army officer, with gold-striped trousers, the green sash of a surgeon, and a felt hat with encircling gold cord. The chief aeronaut, still attired in mufti, with only his homemade Balloon Corps buttons to distinguish him from a common sutler, asked the lady-doctor where she had obtained the authorization to wear a uniform since she, like he, had no commission. Dr. Walker only smiled, saying she had to go and check on the preparations being made at the hospital, as she was sure her services would soon be greatly needed.

Meanwhile, back in Washington, Lincoln's administration was sliding into serious trouble. The Emancipation Proclamation was receiving a lukewarm reception at best. Issued by President Lincoln on September 22, 1862, after much debate, the document promised the nation's three million slaves that if their masters were still in rebellion by the coming New Year's Day, they would all be set free.

Lincoln had avoided the urgings of the abolitionists for some time claiming, "My paramount object is to save the Union, and not either to save or destroy slavery." Had he issued the Emancipation Proclamation at the beginning of the war, Maryland, Missouri, and Kentucky probably would have straightaway joined the Confederacy. Now, with the war well in progress, there was no danger of this. On the other hand, if the slaves kept producing food for the Southern armies, there was a strong possibility the North could be defeated.

Lincoln's cabinet had approved the proclamation in July, at a time when the Union armies were suffering serious defeats, so they urged the president not to issue it. They feared it would appear to the slaves that the Union was appealing to them for aid rather than aiding them. Lincoln had agreed to the postponement, but promised that as soon as the Rebel army was driven out of Maryland he would issue the proclamation. The occasion came with the Union victory at Antietam.

Nevertheless, the fall elections had not gone well for Lincoln and the Republicans, the Democrats having sharply reduced their majority in Congress. Horatio Seymor, a Democrat not keen on the war, had been elected governor of New York. War weariness was also readily apparent in the West, with Lincoln having been warned that if the Mississippi River were not opened soon there would be a demand for a negotiated peace with the South. To win back popular support, President Lincoln was badly in need of military successes.

Burnside held the key. If he had crossed the Rappahannock when he first arrived opposite Fredericksburg, he might have given Lee, who did not have all his forces in position, a serious problem. But Burnside held back. Lee wisely decided not to engage in a battle for the city. Instead, he would contend the crossing of the river with a comparatively small body of troops, while his main forces manned an essentially invulnerable position on a line of low hills that paralleled the river two miles west of the city. The Confederates had both Jackson's and Longstreet's divisions in place in the hills, seventy-five thousand veteran soldiers ably led and in high spirits. They were dug in for a defensive battle at which they would be virtually unbeatable.

Burnside continued his wait for so long that Lee wondered if the Army of the Potomac might be planning to slip around Fredericksburg and attack somewhere else. In actuality, Burnside lacked the mental acumen to chance his plan and was merely struggling to discover some means of overcoming Lee's strategic advantage. Having only the most limited knowledge of the Rebel fortifications, information Lowe and his aeronauts could easily have supplied, and against the advice of his staff, Burnside decided to go ahead with his attack.

General Burnside's battle plan was rather simple. On the right, Sumner's troops would cross two of the pontoon bridges and move against the troops in the town. Franklin's men would cross three bridges downstream of Fredericksburg and attack Jackson's troops entrenched in the hills. In the center, Hooker's units would remain in reserve, moving his troops over a single bridge to support either flank.

In the cold early morning fog of December 11, 1862, Burnside's Corps of Engineers, working from rowboats, began to lay down their pontoon bridges. A freezing wind, mixed with snow, blew briskly down the river valley. The engineers rocked in their boats or waded in icy water as they struggled to lash the floating walkways in place. As the sun rose, burning the fog away, bullets from Confederate sharpshooters hidden in buildings on the opposite shore began zipping across the river like hornets. Without warning a helpless pontonier would topple from his boat into the river, turning the water crimson around him.

Seeing the heavy cost in men this project was taking, Burnside halted the work on the bridges and directed his artillery to fire on the town of Fredericksburg. The batteries went to work with enthusiasm, the frozen gunners eager to warm themselves off the hot barrels. The church clocks had just finished striking ten o'clock when round after round began slamming into the streets. Over 150 pieces opened up their iron muzzles and spat their howling shells down upon the un-suspecting community.

Cannon balls smashed through the thin walls of the houses, col-lapsing them. Roofs and chimneys came crashing down. Fires broke out randomly. People were running everywhere, attempting to escape the madness falling on them. Children fled their school only to return home to find their houses in flames, their parents dead inside. Chaos and panic flew in with each new volley. The Union cannoneers were enjoying the sport after weeks of idleness and boredom. But the hail of shoot had little effect on the Rebel skirmishers. When the firing ceased, and the dust and fog lifted, the snipers crawled from their shelters and continued their deadly work. Desperate for a plan, Burn-side put out a call for volunteers to stage a direct attack on the town.

Crouching down in the rocking boats against the wind and Rebel gunfire, three regiments were rowed to the other side. After con-siderable difficulty disembarking in the freezing water, and taking numerous casualties, the men assembled and with fixed bayonets charged the Rebel snipers holed up in the smoking ruins. The fight-ing was bitter. Hand-to-hand combat raged intensely from house to house. Losses were heavy, but the Rebels finally retreated and a Union bridgehead established.

Additional forces crossed the river and soon went about the busi-ness of ransacking the town. Union soldiers rampaged through the ru-ined houses, smashing whatever "rebel" possessions had survived the shelling, destroying furniture, pianos, glassware, books, and crockery. Seeming to take great delight in their efforts, the run-amok troopers demolished everything in sight. Finally exhausted by their vengeful work, the Federals left, taking away with them whatever small items of value they could carry. That night Burnside's men feasted on the meat, cakes, and whiskey they had looted. For many it would unfortu-nately prove to be their last meal.

Burnside was elated when, watching through a telescope from his headquarters at the Phillips House on Stafford Heights, he saw a Union flag raised above the smoke and rubble of Fredericksburg. Standing next to the general, Lowe ventured, as the town was now clear of snipers, that perhaps he should make an ascension and reconnoiter the Rebel fortifications. However, Burnside, full of his victory and more than ever convinced of the wisdom of his battle plan, told the balloonist to hold on; it was not yet time for the balloons to make their appearance.

All day long, on December 12, Federal troops poured across the newly completed pontoon bridges in blowing snow and freezing rain. Once on the opposite side, the units fanned out on a front along the river extending from the northern edge of Fredericksburg to Hamilton's Crossing a mile south.

The next morning Burnside finally issued his battle orders. The Union commanders were somewhat confounded by his plan, which was little more than a broad suggestion from Burnside that they move against the Rebel forces in their particular area, with the intention being to capture the entire range of hills directly behind the town. No particular objectives were specified, nor were any tactical movements indicated.

History records that Burnside's attack was ill-fated from the outset. Lee's artillery, posted along four miles of high ground overlooking Fredericksburg, totally commanded the half-mile of open fields that the attacking Union troops would have to cross. One of Longstreet's artillery officers was reported to have said, "A chicken could not live on that field when we open up on it." The Confederate regiments entrenched at the base of Marye's Heights directly behind the town were in an excellent defensive position. Longstreet's corps, dug in along a road behind a strong, four-foot high stone wall, was especially impregnable.

Lee was in no hurry, prepared to camp his army where it was until next spring. Burnside, however, could not afford to wait; President Lincoln needed a victory. Mulling the matter over, Burnside had come to the conclusion that "the enemy will be more surprised by a crossing immediately in our front." But General Lee was surprised only by the foolishness of this move. Lee had offered just enough resistance to the Union river crossing to give Jackson's corps time to move upstream and connect with Longstreet to extend the Confederate line an additional three miles.

21

The Stone Wall, Defeat, Blame, a Resignation

Just after dawn on the morning of December 13, Lowe and his balloon rose out of the lifting fog. Although the balloonist's position on Stafford Heights was relatively free of cloud, the river and valley were still shrouded in swirling vapor. Lowe hung there watching as the spires and shattered rooftops of Fredericksburg climbed out of the damp mist. The Confederate batteries on the opposite ridges could see him clearly now, and artillery fire was soon coming in his direction, with the shells landing a mile or so behind him. Lowe was tethered next to Burnside's headquarters at an altitude of less than five hundred feet so he needed neither signal flags nor telegraph, but merely shouted down his observations to Burnside's aides. His primary task was to report on the progress of the battle to Burnside, and to take up other officers as observers.

From his lofty perch the balloonist took in the array of General William B. Franklin's troops as they advanced across the plain toward Lee's hilltop fortifications. Heavy cannon fire showered down on them as they began their assault on Jackson's position on Prospect Hill. The Union batteries answered, opening up with Napoleons, Parrotts, Blakeleys, and siege guns.

At 8:30 A.M. Union General George G. Meade's men joined the battle by moving against Johnston's troops on the left. Lowe watched the Federals attacking through the mist, not in a mass, but in waves of blue, like the ocean breaking on the shore. Meade's division of Pennsylvanians charged bravely, line after line running uphill in the swirling fog. For a time it appeared that Meade's soldiers had found a seam in the Confederate defenses along a wooded ravine and might actually penetrate the fortifications to reach the top of the slope. This would enable Burnside to send Franklin's troops along the ridge against Lee's flank. But Franklin hesitated and the advantage was lost. By mid-afternoon double-timing Confederate reserves had counterattacked and driven the Federals back off the hill.

On the Union right the situation was even more grim. Four divisions had been thrown against the Confederates entrenched behind what came to be known as "that terrible stone wall" below Marye's Heights. The firing from behind the wall was so intense that it seemed as if "nothing could advance farther and live." Lines of Federal soldiers poured out of the town toward the heights. Following the ravines, through a marsh and a sunken drainage ditch, the charge arrived at the half-mile long stone fence at the base of the hill. Met by withering fire, the line of soldiers broke fifty yards short of the fence. The men turned and ran, trampling their own dead and dying as they fled. Behind the stone fence four ranks of Georgians and North Carolinians loaded and discharged their muskets with such rapidity it gave the effect of machine gun fire.

Lowe watched, powerless and impotent, as all afternoon brigade after brigade surged forward only to fall before the savage wall. This was masterful butchery, repeatable in its ease as long as Burnside gave the order to attack and his men obeyed.

Occasionally sweeping his telescope over the barren village, the only civilians the balloonist observed all day was the occasional person darting out into the enclosed space of a backyard to relieve themselves on the frozen ground, quickly returning to what was sometimes a half-burned-out shell of a house.

As the sun began to set behind Marye's Heights, Burnside, in a effort to alleviate the devastating fire falling on the men assaulting the stone wall, ordered Franklin to mount a fresh attack on the left. But Franklin's battered soldiers had had enough. Their commander ignored Burnside's order. The next morning Franklin would claim he hadn't received the order until it was too late to do anything.

At twilight Lowe's old friend, General A. A. Humphreys, attempted to save the day with a bayonet attack against the stone wall, his men charging bravely over the mangled and blackened bodies of comrades who had fallen earlier. Despite their heroic effort Humphreys' men too were driven back with great losses.

Darkness was falling. Below him, Lowe could make out the tiny figure of Dr. Mary Edwards Walker, wearing a bloomer-type adaptation of a male surgeon's gown, moving back and forth among the casualties, as she had done unstintingly all day.

Night came and he could see no more. Lowe gave the signal to be hauled down. As the balloonist slowly descended the wretched groaning of the wounded filled his ears. Those four hundred unobstructed yards in front of Marye's Heights had developed a fatal voice of its own. In the dark the lanterns of the litter bearers bobbed about the field as they searched for those they thought might be saved to fight another day. Lowe pondered how the soldiers could continue to show such bravery in the face of such stupidity by their commanders.

Upset by the disastrous outcome—after all he had not wanted to be put in command of the Army of the Potomac—Burnside blustered around his headquarters vowing to personally lead a victorious charge the next day. His staff officers, however, realizing the folly of more carnage, formed a united front and talked the general back to his senses.

Lowe lay in his tent shivering with the fever and fatigue he had ignored all day. Emotionally he was exhausted. The aeronauts had served as little more than commentators during the battle. The balloonist felt that he and the Balloon Corps could have contributed much more, perhaps even effecting a different outcome to the battle, had they been allowed to ascend earlier and reconnoiter the enemy's defenses. Lowe and the Allen brothers had been aloft all through the battle, their balloons positioned so close that the intelligence they reported was practically redundant. Burnside had stated that he "appreciated the information the aeronauts provided," although the general apparently made little use of it in his decisions. To the further annoyance of Lowe, Burnside had seemed to virtually ignore his efforts, while giving lavish praise to his old friend James Allen's contribution.

Lowe did take a number of officers aloft with him during the battle, with mixed results. General Daniel Butterfield was one of those who ascended, and two widely differing versions of the flight were recorded. Butterfield told his story some years later to Captain William A. Glassford, a U. S. Signal Corps officer who was writing a history of Civil War balloon operations. Butterfield related that although his flight had been very short, it had been enough to give him a comprehensive view of the field before leading his troops over the river into battle. However, he had not risen high enough to gain an extensive view of the Confederate forces behind the fence at Marye's Heights. The general commented that "my short ascent in the balloon had given me a view of the topography, ravines, streams, roads, etc., that was of great value in making dispositions and movements of troops."

Lowe's recollection of the brief flight varied significantly. After he left the service of the army in the spring of 1864, Lowe stated to one of his supporters in Philadelphia that General Butterfield had been a most outspoken critic of the Balloon Corps. The balloonist attributed this to the flight at Fredericksburg. Lowe remarked, "The general had been too frightened to look over the side and ordered me to take them down immediately. However, much to Butterfield's displeasure, I ignored his request and remained aloft while I completed my surveillance."

The balloonist was bitterly aware that the Balloon Corps had little effect on the outcome of the battle. Captain Glassford was the first to allude to the critical contribution the balloonist might have made, especially in view of Burnside's meager knowledge of Lee's troop deployments. "With the use of two or even three balloons at Fredericksburg," Glassford declared, "it seems strange that none of the reports available show that any of the aeronauts seemed to have observed the position of the famous stone wall from the protection of which was delivered a fire so deadly as scarcely to be matched in the history of warfare."

The balloonist defended himself by pointing out that Burnside had forbidden him and the Allen brothers from going aloft prior to December 13. When they did finally ascend, the area at the base of Marye's Heights was obscured by heavy fog that did not burn off until 10:00 A.M. Thus they had only two hours to espy the troops concentrated in that area. During this time they were also responsible for reporting on the other assaults that were going on.

When the first units went against the wall at noon, the Confederate strength along the shrunken road became apparent to everyone; or, perhaps it should be added, everyone but General Burnside. An animated Lowe reminded his detractors that he had been required to observe the battle from Burnside's headquarters, Stafford Heights, on the opposite side of the Rappahannock, a site which put him a considerable distance from the action. Even with his most powerful spyglass, it was difficult to see the details of what was going on.

Lowe was not haughty or vainglorious and readily concerned himself with the humblest workings of the Balloon Corps. In the past he had been forced to curry favor with his superiors to achieve his goals, so naturally rejoiced at any misfortunes of his critics. Thus the balloonist could not countenance being held responsible for a failure over which he was convinced he had no control.

Dissuaded by his staff from mounting another attack, Burnside delayed for two days deciding what his next move should be. Finally, on the cold and stormy night of December 15, the Army of the Potomac slipped back across the Rappahannock, its morale all but shattered. It had suffered nearly thirteen thousand casualties, almost the same number as at Antietam. Fighting from their well-protected positions, the Confederates had only lost five thousand men. Burnside's staff, however, attempted to conceal the true nature of the disaster by giving the Northern papers a smaller Union casualty figure to report. Dr. Mary Edwards Walker—who would later become the sole woman to receive the Medal of Honor only to have it taken from her years later—saw to the loading of the wounded aboard the transports that would take them back to Washington.

The terrible cost in human life, with nothing accomplished, created a crisis in morale not only in the army but on the home front. One Union soldier wrote: "My loyalty is growing weak . . . I am sick and tired of disaster and the fools that bring disaster upon us. . . . All think Virginia is not worth such a loss of life. . . . Why not confess we are worsted, and come to an agreement?" President Lincoln received most of the criticism for the debacle at Fredericksburg. "If there is a worse place than Hell," said the president, "I am in it."

For the next several weeks the two armies harried each other from opposite banks of the Rappahannock. Then Burnside decided to head upstream. His plan was to move beyond Lee's left flank and open up a new front. However, three days of steady, icy rain turned the dugways into bottomless mud. Conditions were so bad that one officer jokingly requested "fifty men, twenty-five feet high, to work in mud eighteen feet deep." This "Mud March" left Burnside's army completely bogged down.

For all practical purposes out of action for the winter, the battered Federals set up camp at Falmouth on the north side of the river. Lowe, the Allen brothers, and the rest of the balloon crew remained with the Army of the Potomac, but Burnside did not. The fiasco of the Mud March had been too much for President Lincoln, and he relieved yet another of his commanders. Major General Joseph Hooker, one of Burnside's subordinates who had intrigued to get the job, was put in charge of the Union's largest army.

Although the war was continuing in the West, with a desperate battle fought at Murfeesboro in Tennessee on December 31, the winter of 1862–1863 was a relatively inactive period for Lowe and the Balloon Corps. Bivouacked with General Hooker and the Army of the Potomac at Falmouth, freezing rain alternated with light snow to keep the aeronauts on the ground most of the time. When they did go up, supposedly to check on the Rebel troop movements, there was little to see. General Lee, camped in comfortable quarters across the river at Hamilton Crossing, was content to wait out the foul weather praying and Christianizing his men.

Despite the cold, Lowe still suffered with fever. This alternated with chills, which even the warmest campfires would not drive away. General Hooker and his staff slept in comfortable houses nearby, but the balloonist, who had still not received his commission, slept in a tent as did his father and the Allen brothers. Lowe became exhausted easily, so could not go aloft very often. The Allens and Clovis did make regular flights when the weather permitted, which helped to establish General Hooker's faith in balloon reconnaissance.

While he stayed on the ground most of the time, Lowe was not idle. Most of his day was taken up training new crew members and affecting repairs to the balloons and generators. In his free moments the balloonist drove away the thoughts of his wife and daughters, and a nice warm featherbed in Philadelphia, by experimenting with new signal techniques. Sitting at his desk with his drawing materials, Lowe continued to refine the system he had devised in early 1862 of using signal flags as a method of communicating in areas where it was not possible to use a telegraph. He had used this method somewhat at Gaines' Farm during the Peninsula Campaign and found it popular with the artillery officers as it did away with the delay caused by having to wait for a telegraph transmission. Working on his drawings, no matter what the purpose, had always been a relaxation for Lowe. The presence of a pen, ink, and paper in front of him greatly enhanced the balloonist's mental state. The activity of drawing allowed Lowe to compose and collect his thoughts, and take his mind off his cares.

During the two weeks he was forced to cool his heals at Burnside's headquarters waiting for the Battle of Fredericksburg to begin, Lowe had developed another system of signaling using small "caloric" balloons. The balloonist had discussed this method with Burnside and gotten approval to have a number of the small balloons constructed. Lowe's plan was that the balloons could be used to carry signal flags aloft during the day or lanterns at night.

Varying in diameter from six to twenty feet, the hot-air-filled caloric balloons could also be used to send messages from balloon camps and cavalry patrols back to main headquarters. The envelopes for daytime use sported distinctive markings as well as a variety of different colored signal flags. The nighttime aerostats carried red and green calcium flares. The balloonist anticipated the signal balloons would be able to be seen from as far away as forty miles.

To Lowe's surprise, the ordered sample balloons arrived considerably sooner than he had expected. He eagerly began his tests. Positioned in a frozen meadow, the balloonist and his father released the small balloons, which were intended to be blown to the Allen brothers standing at the field's other end. Much to Lowe's dismay the balloons frequently did not go anywhere near the spot they were supposed to land. More often than not the Allens had to run after them to keep the balloons from blowing away. These experiments were a source of great amusement to the soldiers who were watching and provided a pleasant change from their usual foul-weather pastimes of dice, cards, cribbage, and checkers. Many wagers were made on which color balloon might come down where. Given the uncertainty of the balloons' performance a fair sum of money was won and lost that winter over the chief aeronaut's mania.

Lowe was extremely disappointed with the results of his tests. He felt that he had been much more accurate in predicting the flight of the simple balloons he had used in his magic act. By March the balloonist had become convinced that the inferior materials the caloric balloons had been rapidly constructed of was his problem. Believing these trial balloons to be useless, he requested money to have a new group made. General George Stoneman, the army's cavalry commander, supported Lowe's proposal, convinced the signal balloons would be useful as a means of communication between isolated units. The petition, however, had to be reviewed by General Seth Williams, of Hooker's staff, who was of the opposite opinion and denied Lowe any funds.

Unable to get new balloons, or to make the caloric balloons he had function, Lowe and General Stoneman attempted to work out a system of communication using rockets fired from various positions along the Union line and observed by the aeronauts from the tethered war balloons. When this too proved to be unreliable, Lowe went back to his signal balloon scheme. Convinced of the system's usefulness, the balloonist continued to work on it even after his departure from the military service.

The bitter cold continued to grip Virginia. Lowe sat at his desk wrapped in as many blankets as he could requisition. Although he was technically in the "South," the winter seemed to him colder than those he remembered from his boyhood back in New Hampshire. A chill wind scudded in behind the orderly who entered Lowe's tent to hand him a letter. As he read the pages anger rose on the balloonist's face. Lowe was being asked—since the letter implied that he was presently doing nothing but lying about at Falmouth—to evaluate a list of improvements to the Balloon Corps operation that had been offered to various members of General Hooker's staff. Lowe was not an especially diffident person and so took offense at the request. As feverish as his mind was at the present, he took the list as a direct attack on his own operating procedures. He read the letter again. Furious, the balloonist began to pace up and down in his tent.

The suggestion that most annoyed Lowe was a proposal for a new method of balloon inflation concocted by a man named B. England. England, who was also from Philadelphia but unknown to Lowe, maintained that he could reduce the inflation time for a large balloon from fifteen hours to a half hour. Furthermore, England's proposal asserted his method would significantly lower the present cost of $400 per inflation and reduce the size of the wagon needed to sustain a balloon in the field.

Attempting to calm his anger, Lowe reread England's proposal a second time, and then a third. Then he went to his desk and moved aside the drawings for the caloric balloon signal system he had been working on. His hand shook. For a brief moment he stared at the page as the round balloon forms began to dance and swirl into the faces of his wife and daughters, smiling and laughing. "When are you coming home, Daddy?" one of the apparitions asked. "I don't know," he shouted angrily. Shaking his head, Lowe drove the image from his mind. Then he dipped his pen and began to draft his reply to England's proposal. A man who had on numerous occasions almost given up his life in the skies over the peninsula was not about to give way to some young upstart's unproven paraphernalia.

The balloonist's handwriting was not especially neat, an almost histrionic cursive, the ink instantly blotted so that the letters took on a transparent look. Nor did the tremors Lowe had developed after the Peninsula Campaign help his pen move across the clean page. He wrote slowly, weighing the cognitive essence of each word. To him B. England's claims were obviously false, but he would have to set this down in a clear and concise manner. Lowe was tired of writing letters, of always defending his program, always begging for funds, or asking when his commission would arrive. He was further annoyed that two of his former assistants, William Paullin and John Steiner, had attached personal statements endorsing England's plan.

Lowe maintained that England's claims were unsupportable. At present, he pointed out, only two and a half hours were required to inflate a war balloon, nowhere near the fifteen quoted by England, and currently the cost of the hydrogen needed to fill a balloon was only $60 not $400. Lowe also asserted that England had overestimated the size of the seven-wagon train required to support four balloons in the field. The chief aeronaut argued that England's balloon design was far too light and flimsy to be used on a battlefield. Nor did the balloonist see any improvement in England's "new system" of inflation over the methods currently in use by the Balloon Corps.

Finished with his rebuttal, Lowe folded the paper carefully and went next door to the Allens' tent. The brothers were there, drinking whiskey, smoking cigars, and eating chocolate. They invited the head balloonist to sit down and join them. Lowe accepted their invitation, but declined the whiskey, and did not smoke nor crave sweets. Instead he produced his document and went right to the heart of the matter, saying he had come there to request from the two gentlemen letters endorsing his system of aeronautics as currently in use by the Balloon Corps.

The brothers readily agreed and got out their writing box. In careful penmanship James Allen recounted his own early unsuccessful attempts to function as a military balloonist prior to the Battle of Bull Run. He admitted that his balloon and equipment had been inadequate for the requirements of the mission. Moreover, he stated that the government should be indebted to Lowe for his improvements in the construction of balloons and the invention of a portable gas generator. James concluded that without Professor Lowe's untiring perseverance and hard labor the U. S. Army would never have had the service of the Balloon Corps. In a much shorter letter, Ezra Allen cordially concurred with his brothers opinion.

Lowe stepped from the tent, letters in hand, into the newly revealed winter sun. The balloonist felt his energy returned, intensified by the blinding light. Earlier he had been so tired he could think only in terms of catastrophe; now Lowe concluded, his life was still worth living. He would march his letters to Hooker's staff and run the facts past their review—as usual sidestepping, dancing, and bobbing and weaving, as the case need be.

With the coming of spring 1863, the nation began to look for some activity from the long dormant Army of the Potomac. In the West the war had slowed down, with General Rosencrans inactive in Tennessee and General Ulysses S. Grant bogged down hopelessly in the steaming low country north of Vicksburg, Mississippi.

Over the winter General Hooker had done a fine job of rebuilding the Army of the Potomac, displaying talents as an executive and an organizer that no one suspected he had. Known only as a dashing, head-down fighter, and nothing more, he had set about seeing that the routine chores of military housekeeping were looked after. Having arranged for his men to be well fed, have decent camps to live in, and clean hospitals, Hooker set about restoring the pounded army's morale.

Despite all its material hardships, the South did have one great advantage over the North—its troops' spirit. The Confederate war aims were clear and definite. Even the lowest private could understand them in his mind, and more importantly with his heart. The South wanted its independence. Its soldiers were fighting off invaders who would take away their freedom. The ordinary Confederate trooper probably did not understand the intricacies of the "states' rights" question; he was simply fighting to protect his home, and that was enough.

By comparison, the Federal soldier seemed to be struggling for an abstraction. More often than not he had not chosen to be where he was. True, the call to make war for the his country had aroused deep feelings of patriotism. Nevertheless, as the hard months passed and he saw his comrades fall in battle or to disease, this rallying cry had lost its luster. The issues that were involved became hard to see through the smoke of battle. To defend one's country against a civil upheaval offered little to sustain the spirit when your muscles and bones were weary from marching and fighting.

That spring Lowe had faced a dilemma that had sapped his morale. No moral issue was involved, it was simply a game of power politics, played for revenge. Dismissing the claims of B. England was but a minor annoyance compared to the charges leveled at him by his old acquaintance, the Philadelphia lawyer turned aeronaut, Jacob C. Freno. Lowe had lost contact with Freno after he had dismissed him from the Balloon Corps in December 1862 for running a faro table in camp and for spreading "treasonous rumors." Now Freno had reappeared in the balloonist's life, with vindictiveness.

Freno had given a sworn statement to the provost marshal in Washington, D. C., charging Lowe with a list of serious offenses. First, Freno accused Lowe of keeping his father on the government payroll when the old man was at home sick in Philadelphia. Second, he claimed that the balloonist had stolen government property and included a list of stolen items that ranged from a saddle to an entire balloon. Finally Freno provided another list of alleged misappropriations by the chief aeronaut, including requisitioning government rations for himself and influential newsmen when he should have paid for these out of his own funds, and using army carriages to take his wife on pleasure trips around Washington.

It was obvious to Lowe that something else was brewing, or had already brewed; otherwise the provost's office would have dismissed these minor complaints. His usually reliable memory was straining to recall the details of these excruciatingly small incidents. The balloonist went to his papers and his scribbled notes. If Lowe was going to refute these charges, which were obviously false, he wanted to be as accurate as possible.

As Lowe recalled, the balloon he was supposed to have stolen was a small, experimental model, unwanted and unheralded, that he had taken to Philadelphia for repairs, and which had eventually ended up on a military trash-heap. He saw the charge concerning his father as another attempt to make a mountain out of a molehill. A devout member of the Balloon Corps, Clovis had been on duty for fifteen straight months without a leave, and should have been entitled to some sick pay. And his wife's only army carriage rides had been in October 1861, when she had come out to Fort Corcoran in Virginia to watch him attempt his first free flight reconnaissance. The next day she had another ride in an army carriage back into Washington, but only after she had, at great risk to herself, plucked her downed husband from behind enemy lines. For this heroic act she had received neither payment nor a medal.

Lowe sallied through his reply, confident that his superiors would accept his explanation over the charges of his accuser. Then, to launch his own torpedo, Lowe brought up the matter of Freno's having broken into the Washington balloon warehouse after he had been dismissed from the corps and vandalized the war balloon *Constitution*, which was undergoing repairs at the time. Lowe included statements from the Allen brothers, John Starkweather, and others supporting his charges. As a result the Washington district provost marshal's office issued a warrant for Freno, but he had disappeared.

The Freno incident, however, revealed to Lowe the fact that the War Department obviously maintained doubts about his ability with financial transactions and the disposition of government property under his control. That proper administration of the Balloon Corps's finances was a thing alien to Lowe's nature had been apparent to him for some time. The matter of a bill for lumber delivered to the aeronautical department by Messrs. E. Pickrell and Company many months ago, and as yet unpaid, was brought up as an example. Looking into the problem, the Quartermaster's Department had discovered that Lowe, ignoring all procedures, had merely signed the invoice "approved for payment" and sent it on to the secretary of war. There the invoice lay skulking away for months at the bottom of a pile of papers no one knew what to do with.

Lowe's method of inventory control was no more accurate than his accounting procedures. Although it was inconceivable, the chief aeronaut when questioned was unable to produce receipts for equipment, including whole balloons, that had been removed from service or transferred to other commands, believing that he might have lost the papers. The balloonist haughtily maintained that in the field he had been much more concerned with meeting the needs of the battlefield commanders than in keeping precise records for Washington bureaucrats. Lowe's attitude did little to gather him support among his interrogators from the War Department. His lack of receipts also made it difficult for the balloonist to clear himself of the charges leveled against him by Jacob C. Freno.

Months dragged by as the affair of the Balloon Corps' finances grew all out of proportion. Even Leontine was writing to him asking where the money was. Lowe had no idea. He certainly had not stolen it or he would have had some to send to his wife. The funds from the government always seemed slow in arriving, and when they finally did come they were already spent. For all his technical achievement, it was clear that Lowe's abilities in science were not matched by necessary administrative skill, leadership, and willingness to fairly consider the opinions of those who questioned his methods and theories. The same persistence and personal courage that had enabled him to overcome great obstacles at the creation of the Balloon Corps now seemed the source of a harmful, sometimes unjustifiable obstinacy.

Stories about Lowe's difficulties began to appear in the press, much to the delight of the Confederates who had considered Lowe's balloons as giving the Union a distinct advantage. The newspapers, which had wildly acclaimed the balloonist's achievements at an earlier time, now began to ridicule him. One paper sarcastically suggested that Lowe be given the title of "Brigadier General of the Skies," while another christened his ground headquarters "Camp Ohwhatawhopper."

On April 7, 1863, Lowe was dealt a fatal blow. General Hooker's assistant adjutant general, Seth Williams, issued Special Order Number 95, designating Captain Cyrus B. Comstock, who had made a number of ascensions with Lowe, as head of "the balloon establishment." Unlike Humphreys and the other officers in tactical command of the Balloon Corps who had been willing to issue orders while allowing Lowe freedom to exercise the actual control of the aeronauts and balloons, Captain Comstock intended to maintain absolute control of the entire operation.

A letter from Comstock, who had been the chief engineer for the Army of the Potomac, to Assistant Secretary of War P. H. Waterman, detailing his observations of the problems of the Balloon Corps, gave a hint that the War Department may have been behind Lowe's demotion. "On taking charge of the balloon establishment of this Army," Comstock remarked with apparent savor, "I found it as I thought, an unsuccessful experiment. Professor Lowe seemed to me to have been prompted more by his own interests than those of the government." Comstock surmised that the chief aeronaut "has been acting without the knowledge or authority of anyone connected with the Army of which he is an employee." Nor did the new head of the balloon establishment have much regard for the other aeronauts, concluding to Assistant Secretary Waterman that "any man of intelligence could learn to handle a balloon in a week's time."

Lowe quickly found himself at odds with Captain Comstock, who perhaps was jealous of the balloonist's fame and the princely salary he was said to be receiving, ten dollars a day in gold. This amount was equal to a colonel's pay, making it considerably more than Comstock was receiving. Comstock, therefore, introduced several changes. Lowe's pay was reduced to six dollars per day, the same amount the Allen brothers were receiving, and Clovis Lowe and John B. Dickinson were released. The Balloon Corps had now been reduced to three aeronauts, T. S. C. Lowe and the Allens.

Comstock demanded from Professor Lowe a complete accounting of all public property entrusted to the Balloon Corps. He also insisted on "strict protocol and adherence to channels of communication." When Lowe revealed that he had been assigning aeronauts directly through the secretary of war, Comstock wrote a formal complaint to the Chief Engineer of the Army.

"I have informed Lowe," Comstock's letter stated, "that such orders should come to me from the Adjutant General of this Army, and not from himself, that he is not in charge of the balloon establishment."

Comstock's actions infuriated Lowe, who wrote:

Now comes someone utterly ignorant of aeronautics who autocratically countermands every order I give and blocks every move I make simply because he is clothed in a little brief authority and thinks this is the way to show it. This instance of red tape might be expected in the regular army but aeronautics for military purpose is an entirely new thing and I frequently had been addressed by the Secretary of War.

Yet one more time Lowe appealed to his friends in high places, both civilian and in the military. This time, however, no one seemed inclined to take up the balloonist's cause.

Lowe was spending many sleepless nights endlessly going over in his head his problems with Captain Comstock. The balloonist was aware that the stress of dealing with the turbulent captain was having a debilitating effect on his already tenuous health.

Lowe wrote letters to his wife and discussed the matter with his father. On April 12, 1863, the balloonist made his decision. He presented a long letter of resignation to General Daniel Butterfield, Hooker's chief of staff. Lowe reiterated his service to the army. He especially called attention to the sacrifices he had made, in both time and money, in order that the United States might have a Balloon Corps. Lowe pointed out that he had originally been offered thirty dollars per day, but he himself had suggested the more reasonable sum of ten dollars per day. The balloonist letter went on:

> General, I feel aggrieved that my services should not have been appreciated. As it is, I cannot honorably serve for the sum named by Captain Comstock without first refunding to the Government the excess of that amount which I have been receiving since I have been in the service. This my very limited means will not allow, for it requires the full salary I have received to support myself in the field and my family at home; therefore, out of respect to myself and the duty I owe my family, it will be impossible for me to serve upon any other condition than those with which I entered service.

Lowe, however, was not yet completely ready to give up the Balloon Corps and hedged his resignation. The balloonist felt as if he was caught between two realities, his military service as he had lived it, and as Captain Comstock had concocted it for him. Still wishing to aid his country in view of the increased Confederate activity, and the probability of great battles yet to come, Lowe rashly volunteered to remain on duty without pay.

The balloonist's gesture, which he hoped he would not come to regret, had backed him into a corner. Lowe was sure his strong statement would return things to his old way of working.

Lowe sat at his desk, diligently going over his drawings for signal balloons and other new innovations, while eagerly awaiting the vindication he was sure General Hooker's reply would bring. But the balloonist was destined to be disappointed. To make things perfectly clear, Hooker returned Lowe's resignation with a stern rebuke for not having sent the document through "proper channels" after first having received Captain Comstock's approval.

After resubmitting his letter in the official manner, Lowe was shocked to learn that his resignation had not been accepted, but his offer to serve without pay had been. He was now in the dubious position of endeavoring to exercise his old authority—as an unpaid civilian.

In response to a request from the assistant secretary of war for a balloon and aeronaut to be detailed to Charleston, South Carolina, Lowe assigned James Allen. Discovering Allen in the midst of packing, Captain Comstock asked him where he was going and by whose orders. When the aeronaut revealed that he had been authorized by Lowe, Comstock flew into a rage. He immediately countermanded Lowe's order and issued one of his own. Then Comstock fired off a hostile letter to the former chief aeronaut, reprimanding him for not sending all orders through him. The new "head of the balloon establishment" was making it clear to Lowe that he now had little, or no, authority.

In spite of the humiliating treatment he was receiving, and the lambasting he was taking from the press who had gotten wind of his conflict with the military bureaucracy, Lowe remained with the Army of the Potomac at Hooker's headquarters at Falmouth. He loved balloons, and his balloons were there. And, although he was loath to admit it, he had grown to love the excitement of battle. The slaughter and waste repulsed him, yet he could not resist the satisfaction he got from being part of the great spectacle, and the knowledge that his small role might have significantly affected the outcome.

Lowe stood on Stafford Heights in the cool March air. Although he was ill and embattled, he was still young and cut a handsome figure. His eyes narrowed as he looked across the river. He could see the citizens of Fredericksburg going about the pitiful business of repairing their war-wasted homes as best they could. Like most mortals Lowe craved his place in history, even if it had to be carved out of other people's misery. He knew this and hated himself for it.

22

The Second Fredericksburg, Chancellorsville, the End for the Balloon Corps

Captain Comstock plunged himself into the operation of the "balloon establishment." Making daily ascensions with James Allen, the captain was rapidly becoming an experienced aeronaut. Although he belittled Lowe personally, Comstock was not foolish enough to ignore the balloonist's vast knowledge of aeronautics. He frequently asked Lowe technical questions concerning the manner in which the balloons had been operated in the past. Answering Comstock's questions gave Lowe a great deal of satisfaction, even though he was aware the captain would usually modify or change the procedure once he understood it.

On March 23 Captain Comstock made his first solo flight in the *Washington.* He remained aloft for an hour and a half. Against Lowe's advice, Comstock had the balloon towed three miles down the road while he was at the full height of the tether.

By the middle of April Comstock, Lowe, and James Allen were operating the *Washington* and the *Eagle* back and forth along the Rappahannock from Banks Ford on the Union right to White Oak Church in the rear, and to Fredericksburg itself. Meanwhile Ezra Allen was maintaining a separate operation at Hooker's headquarters at Phillips House on Stafford Heights. Lowe could sense that the great battle he was anticipating was not far off.

General Hooker began his movement on April 27, 1863. The spring winds had dried the dirt roads making them usable again. With jaunty optimism Hooker's army set off. He would not make Burnside's mistake of directly attacking the stout Confederate defenses at Fredericksburg. Hooker now clearly had the numerical advantage, and was deploying his forces with a strategic astuteness so far not shown by Union commanders. His plan was to cross both the Rappahannock and the Rapidan River twenty-five miles away, then swing back downstream and attack the Confederates' unprotected left and rear.

In the beginning Hooker's plan went well. He had more than seventy thousand men established around Chancellorsville, a crossroads a dozen miles behind Lee's left flank. Then he sent his cavalry to pounce down and cut the Richmond, Fredericksburg, and Potomac Railroad. Vastly outnumbered by the Union force approaching its flank, the Army of Northern Virginia appeared to have no option but to retreat. But once again Lee took a calculated risk and split his army into two units. Leaving only ten thousand infantry under Jubal Early to defend Fredericksburg, Lee marched north with the rest of his forces to meet the Union army, which was then struggling blindly through the scrub pines and dense vegetation of an area known as "the Wilderness."

Unlike Burnside, Hooker had his balloons in the air well before the actual fighting began. Lowe and the Allens were aloft regularly during the weeks before Chancellorsville, giving Hooker the information that Confederate troops had been moving out of Fredericksburg in the direction of his army. On May 1, Lowe, the aeronaut closest to the rebel camp, reported, "heavy columns of the enemy's Infantry and Artillery . . . moving up the river accompanied by many Army wagons."

The Federal balloons were readily seen by the Confederate troops marching to battle. An article in the *Richmond Examiner* of May 1 reported "a Yankee balloon aloft at great heights." Apparently some of the Confederate commanders just ignored Lowe's snooping and went about their business. To the contrary, Stonewall Jackson took elaborate measures to hide his movements from the aeronauts.

General Hooker took a special interest in the information issued by the balloon observers. Preparing for his campaign, Hooker requested numerous flights made at points he specified along the Rappahannock. Unfortunately he misinterpreted Lowe's early details of Rebel movements. Hooker believed that Lee was withdrawing his forces, which was the scenario he had written for him.

At midday, on May 1, the advance units of the two armies clashed a few miles east of Chancellorsville. The land there was clear, with no dense undergrowth. Because of the terrain, the Federal army, fighting in open country with superior numbers of men and artillery, clearly held the advantage. However, rather than pressing on with the attack, a somewhat bewildered Hooker ordered his units to fall back to rather hastily constructed fieldworks near Chancellorsville.

That night Lee and Jackson sat around a campfire conferring. Not knowing the strength of the Union entrenchment at Chancellorsville, Lee was reluctant to attack head on. The Federal left was anchored by the Rappahannock and he felt it could not be turned. Then J. E. B. Stuart arrived with reports from his scouts. Hooker's right flank was "in the air" only three miles west of Chancellorsville. This was the opportunity Lee needed, and Jackson would be the man to seize it for him. Despite being outnumbered nearly two to one, Lee decided to take the offensive.

The next morning, Jackson and thirty thousand men left on a daring twelve-mile march directly across the face of Hooker's main force. One of Jackson's officers had found a local resident willing to guide the troops through the wilderness of scrub oaks and thorny undergrowth along a track used to haul coal to an iron-smelting furnace. This most dangerous maneuver left Jackson's strung-out column vulnerable to attack.

Lee, however, was counting on Hooker to do nothing. Hooker had boasted to President Lincoln, "The question is not if I can take Richmond, but rather when I can take it." Nevertheless, now that Lee was showing some fight, Hooker seemed to have lost his nerve. Some of Hooker's staff speculated that his decision to go "on the wagon" three months earlier had been a mistake as he now seemed to be in the need of some "liquid courage."

Unfortunately Hooker had sent his cavalry south to throw a scare into Richmond, so they were not available to detect Jackson's march. Lowe, his fellow balloon observers, and an infantry unit had spotted Jackson's troop movements and reported it to Hooker, who apparently dismissed the significance. He was convinced that the thick woods were impenetrable and that the enemy activity was designed to cover a retreat.

Back at the balloon base, the aeronauts had been called down and were having their supper. Everyone was sure there would be no more activity that day. The same attitude prevailed among General Howard's men camped at Chancellorsville relaxing and cooking.

At 5:15 Jackson's seasoned veterans, their tattered uniforms made worse by the thorny undergrowth, burst from the woods with a wild yell. Deployed on a front two miles wide and three divisions deep, the charging Confederates hit the Union flank like a thunderstorm. A few of the Federal brigades recovered and fought desperately, slowing the Rebel advance. But most of the Union regiments, who had been facing south expecting an attack from that direction, were caught completely off guard and rioted to the rear. By nightfall Jackson had rolled the Union right flank back two miles. Hooker and Howard urgently improvised a new line of defense from four disparate corps in an attempt to stop the Confederate advance. In the end, however, it was the Southerners themselves, apparently just tired of killing, who came to a halt. The Union losses, which they would not be able to count for a few days, were tremendous.

On the Confederate side tragedy had struck one of their ablest commanders. Eager to keep the Yankees on the run, Stonewall Jackson and several of his staff had ridden ahead of their lines in the dark to reconnoiter for the next day's attack. Returning at a trot, the party had been fired on by their own pickets, who nervously mistook them for Union cavalry. Jackson was knocked from his horse by two bullets in his left arm. Rushed to a field hospital, Jackson had to have his arm amputated. The general put up a brave fight and seemed to be recovering, but took a turn for the worse when pneumonia set in. To the great sorrow of his men, Jackson would die eight days after he had been accidentally shot.

On May 3 Lowe rose from the balloon camp for his dawn observation. Lowe and the Allens were exhausted, having been aloft constantly since the beginning of the campaign. Not surprising to Lowe, when the shooting had actually started, although the aeronauts were some distance from the action and rounds rarely came their way, the intrepid Captain Comstock had found important things he needed to do that unfortunately kept him on the ground.

The word of the previous night's Confederate attack at Chancellorsville had come through, but as Lowe was almost nine miles away he could make out little of the carnage. Turning his spyglass closer to home, the balloonist watched as General Sedgwick's 6th Corps attempted to carry out Hooker's order to capture the heights behind Fredericksburg and then to push on Harry Lee's rear at Chancellorsville. Lowe did not have a telegraph operator with him, so had to descend and give his reports to one of Hooker's staff, who forwarded selected bits of information to President Lincoln, who was haunting the War Department's telegraph office. This was unlike the direct line Lowe had had to Lincoln at the first battle of Fredericksburg.

Although the balloonist was attempting to make his reports as clear and as accurate as possible, he heard that the president had complained about the fragmentary, and often contradictory, information he was receiving. This led Lowe to wonder if Captain Comstock or someone else on Hooker's staff might be editing his reports to put a better slant on the campaign.

Receiving intelligence that few Confederate troops remained in Fredericksburg, General Sedgwick mounted an attack against the Rebels entrenched behind the stone wall below Marye's Heights. This was the infamous stone wall where so many of Burnside's men had died in December. Lowe watched from above as Sedgwick's three divisions hurled themselves against the wall that lined a sunken road. In what appeared to be a repeat of the previous battle Jubal Early's undermanned division twice repulsed the Union charge. However, on the third try, with fixed bayonets, Sedgwick's blue wave carried the day, capturing the heights and sending the Rebels fleeing.

At the same time, back at Chancellorsville, Hooker was strangely inactive. He mounted no attack from the rear, but seemed to be waiting for Sedgwick's units to do all the fighting. He had even ordered one of his corps to fall back from an advantageous position on high ground at Hazel Grove, one mile west of Chancellorsville crossroads. This move permitted Lee and Stuart to rejoin their two armies, massing their artillery at Hazel Grove, one of the few places in the Wilderness where it could be employed efficiently.

The reunited Confederates mounted an all-out attack on Hooker's forces occupying the area around Chancellorsville. Despite the opportunity to strike Lee's flank, Hooker kept three corps out of action. To his subordinate officers he seemed confused. Then, in mid-morning, a cannonball hit Hooker's headquarters knocking him unconscious. The corps commanders immediately planned a counterattack. Before they could put their strategy in action Hooker recovered and resumed command. Much to the distress of his staff, Hooker ordered a withdrawal two miles northward to a previously prepared defensive line.

From his position aloft Lowe could see flames spewing from the Chancellorsville mansion. He could not discern, however, the figure of General Lee as he rode into the clearing in front of the burning building, waving his hat to the cheers of his exhausted, but exultant, troops. In the woods all around, smoke rose from the numerous brush fires that had broken out, ignited by exploding artillery shells. As if by mutual consent, the two armies had broken off the fighting to rescue the pitiful wounded who lay now threatened by fire.

Looking south, the balloonist could see that Sedgwick, having broken through the Rebel forces left to defend Fredericksburg, was rapidly marching north. His troops would soon pose a serious threat to Lee's rear. But General Lee must have received word of Sedgwick's movements, for a large force of Confederates had left the main body and were deploying near a country church halfway between Fredericksburg and Chancellorsville. Lowe sent this information to Hooker, who again seemed dismayed by the news and took no action.

As night was falling the balloonist made his final observation. He watched Sedgwick's column for some time, but it appeared that their advance had been halted near Salem Church. He could see numerous campfires flickering through the trees with groups of men sitting around them eating. Lowe got the distinct impression that both sides had retired from the business of killing for the day.

The light of next morning's dawn, May 4, found Lowe still stretched on his cot. On the table were the remains of the previous night's uneaten meal. The balloonist lay in a matted, damp pool of blankets, his face a mask of sorrow and resignation. "Professor Lowe!" He heard his name called but gave no response. The professor was suffering from one of his recurring malaria attacks, the severest in some time. Normally the cold stage came in the early morning, and arnica handled it nicely. But this time he had internal heat along with his external coldness, and he was sweating profusely. The balloonist reached for his belladonna. Lying there waiting for the medication to bring its relief, Lowe had no interest whatsoever in going aloft. He no longer cared if the army had a Balloon Corps or not. He was beginning to feel that he and his balloons served no real function, but were mere window dressing, showing off something the Union had that the Confederates did not.

Although he performed his observations very conscientiously and tried to give the best analysis he could based on his now considerable experience, he felt no one in the army was taking him seriously. They treated him like the civilian he was. And now that the word had gotten around that he was serving for no pay, he had lost what little credibility he previously had. If he reported that a large massing of Confederate troops appeared to be preparing for an attack, Lowe could be sure headquarters would see the movement as part of a retreat. The generals were highly paid professional soldiers, graduates of West Point; they did not like to be second-guessed. They were never wrong, or if they were did not admit it.

The medicine was taking effect. The balloonist rolled from his cot and tried to stand up. He was tired of watching thousands of men die because of pig-headed stubbornness. He was wrong to want a place in history built on the graves of so many brave men who had shed their lives in vain. When he had started his service, he had hoped to save lives by shortening the war. Now it seemed as if the generals on both sides saw no end in sight, and killing had become its only reason. If he made it through this battle he would go home.

Lowe was late making his first observation of the morning as he had ridden to the balloon camp at Banks Ford to be closer to the action. The balloonist reported that large numbers of Confederates were leaving their camps in front of Chancellorsville and moving toward Sedgwick's position. He estimated that there were fewer than thirty thousand Rebels facing Hooker, whom he knew to have upwards of seventy-five thousand men. Lowe, with the utmost discretion, sent a message to General Hooker suggesting that perhaps this might be an opportunity for an attack from the rear.

Possibly Hooker never received the balloonist's message, or he may have either disagreed with it or chosen to ignore it. At any rate, Hooker took no action. All Lowe could do was watch, as by late afternoon the reinforced Confederates mounted an attack on Sedgwick's forces. Sedgwick's men managed to repulse the somewhat disjointed attack and hold out until nightfall. Then, finally aware that Hooker was not coming to his aid, Sedgwick had his men snuck back across the Rappahannock under cover of darkness.

That same night Hooker held a meeting of his generals. The majority of the corps' commanders voted to mount a counterattack the next day. General Hooker, however, overrode this vote and ordered a withdrawal. The next evening, shielded by a driving rainstorm, the vast Army of the Potomac retreated to the safety of the east side of the river, avoiding the attack Lee had planned for the next day, May 6.

Although the Union army had escaped destruction once again, by any account the South had achieved a great victory. With little more than half the men of his enemy, General Lee had grasped the initiative and outmaneuvered the Federals, dividing and positioning his forces in such a way as to give them equal, and in some cases superior, numbers at the point of encounter.

Lee's victory at Chancellorsville, however, had not come without great cost. The Confederates had suffered thirteen thousand casualties, or approximately twenty-two percent of their forces. The Union had lost more men, at seventeen thousand, but this comprised only fifteen percent of their available manpower.

President Lincoln had remained at the War Department telegraph office almost constantly during the battle, distressed that the reports he was hearing were lacking in clarity and important details. According to a newspaperman who was present when the outcome of the battle became evident on May 6, "the president's face turned ashen." "My God! My God!" exclaimed Lincoln. "What will the country say?"

In effect the country had already spoken. The nation was not happy with the way the war was going. The patriotic jingoism of the previous year had been replaced by bitterness and sarcasm. Early in 1863, facing a severe manpower shortage, President Lincoln had been forced to sign into effect one of the most hated laws in American history, The National Enrollment Act. Aware of the strong feelings against the act, Congress had tried to sugarcoat the law by providing numerous legal ways to avoid military service. All this had done was to give rise to a vast network of brokers engaged in finding "substitutes" for the wealthy men who did not want to be called up. All that a poor man could do was resort to bounty jumping, false exemption papers, and desertion.

As the war dragged on, opposition to the Federal draft law increased. There was widespread dissent, with some draftees even fleeing to Canada. Two months later the discord would reach its violent peak in New York City. There, in bloody "draft riots," the city's poor white majority would turn on Conscription centers and their officers, and the free black minority. Using clubs, guns, and arson, roving mobs would vent the widely held sentiment, "Lincoln's war is a rich man's war and a poor man's fight." Resenting the Emancipation as one of President Lincoln's war aims, New York's largely Irish immigrant population would target blacks, with rioters setting the city's Colored Orphan Asylum on fire, and hanging a black man in Clarkson Street.

May 6, 1863, also marked the end of Lowe's service with the army. The balloonist left secure in the knowledge that his flights at Banks Ford and Fredericksburg had provided valuable military intelligence during the campaign. That this data had been used wisely was a matter of debate.

General Sedgwick, a strong supporter of Lowe, credited him with supplying information that enabled the successful attack on Marye's Heights. The general remarked, "The importance of careful balloon reconnaissance and accurate reports cannot be overestimated." Sedgwick believed an observation balloon, "flown by a skilled aeronaut accompanied by a trained military observer, could provide important intelligence that could not be procured by any other means." Once again the balloon operations during the Battle of Chancellorsville emphasized the lessons learned during the Peninsula Campaign, that balloon intelligence was valueless unless correctly analyzed and interpreted. As Hooker's staff had shown at Chancellorsville, field commanders could quite easily draw the wrong conclusions from rather explicit details.

Lowe called on Captain Comstock with the hope that his recent service during the Battle of Chancellorsville might have caused the officer to reconsider the issue of his salary. The balloonist was gruffly informed nothing had changed. He was not even offered the six dollars per day he had turned down. Learning this, Lowe asked to be relieved at the earliest possible moment. To this Comstock replied, "If you are going, you could probably be spared better now than at some later time." Lowe's desperate struggle to hold on to the Balloon Corps was over. He returned to his tent and began packing for the trip to Washington.

With Lowe's departure the Balloon Corps was left to the Allen brothers, who were now completely under the control of the military. Officers with no experience in aeronautics often ordered them to make flights against their better judgment in aging balloons that were deteriorating rapidly. The Allens wrote to Lowe, back in Washington, asking him to use any influence he still had with the secretary of war to obtain funds for the construction of new balloons. The brothers were firm in their desire to continue serving their country, but had little hope for the future unless Lowe returned to service. Nevertheless, when neither Lowe nor new balloons appeared, the Allens continued to carry on alone, and with their old balloons.

Lowe's resignation was widely covered in Northern newspapers. The *New York Herald Tribune* wrote that the chief aeronaut had departed "leaving the management of the corps to Mr. Allen . . . who is assisted by his brother. In their hands the silken spheres will continue to furnish a capital observatory from which to reconnoiter the movements of the enemy, and will prove, as they have heretofore, a great auxiliary in whatever operations the army may undertake."

Aloft during the first week in June, the Allens detected considerable movement in the Confederate lines. Heavy clouds of dust trailed the Army of Northern Virginia as it headed for Pennsylvania. Hooker did not know where Lee was going, but he thought it best to follow him. For reasons unknown, the Allen brothers were detached from the Army of the Potomac as it traveled north. This was unfortunate as they could have provided valuable information as Hooker shadowed Lee's forces as they moved up the Shenandoah Valley, the Union army wisely remaining between them and Washington, D.C.

The Allens were told they would be recalled for a great battle that was coming. But in fact the history of the Balloon Corps had come to an end, as they were not recalled for the Battle of Gettysburg. By August 1 the Balloon Corps had been completely dissolved and aerial reconnaissance had ceased to be part of the war effort.

After returning to Washington, an ailing and dispirited Lowe found his dreams for the Balloon Corps revived when Secretary of War Stanton asked him to prepare a complete report on his operations with the army. Lowe was sure that the lengthy report he was planning would vindicate him and hopefully have the Balloon Corps reinstalled under the War Department with him in complete command and with full military commissions for him and his aeronauts.

The balloonist sat on his bed at the National Hotel shuffling through the pile of dispatches, letters, telegrams, and reports he had just dumped from his luggage. True to his habits, this apparent mess contained the two-year history of the Balloon Corps. While Lowe was not good at filing and sorting, he carefully saved everything, important or not. He had a brilliant mind, but had only the most rudimentary grammar school education. Although he had assumed the title of "professor," Lowe was lacking in those skills such as organization and writing that he might have developed had he gone further in school.

Going through the papers with the balloonist in his room was W. J. Rhees, an associate of Joseph Henry at the Smithsonian. Rhees had been hired by Lowe to help him prepare the report for Secretary Stanton. In the trees outside their window a flock of wrens were cheerfully singing the song of spring. Hearing this, Rhees vowed that the report would be completed before the end of summer. With that, the two men began arranging the papers in front of them in a useful order.

Rhees was true to his word. In the projected time the document, executed in Lowe's cursive script and bound with red, white, and blue string, was delivered to Secretary of War Stanton. The finished report was quite comprehensive, including copies of of all the correspondence that had created and given direction to the Balloon Corps. Interspersed in the document's main text were Lowe's comments on the two years of activity. Written in anger and frustration, there was a sense of dignified sadness in Lowe's observations, a defensive tone that seemed to imply a feeling of self-doubt and failure:

> During the whole period of my employment I have directed all my mental and physical energies to secure the success of our forces. I have never shrunk from the discharge of my duty however hazardous, and holding no commission I have often been perplexed and put to inconvenience in doing the business of the Aeronautical Department which properly belonged to a commissioned officer. But for want of one acquainted with the business I was compelled to do it myself: I have also at all times been exposed to the danger of being treated as a spy had I fallen into the hands of the enemy.

Lowe's report was, of course, intended as an extended argument for the reinstitution of the Balloon Corps under his command. However, neither the war department nor the joint congressional Committee on the Conduct of the War, before whom the balloonist testified, took up his cause. When this plan failed, Lowe approached Colonel A. J. Meyer of the Signal Corps, offering to form a balloon organization under his command. When asked by Major General Quincey A. Gilmore if he would be presently available for service in Charleston, South Carolina, Lowe, in a monument of understatement, replied, "As the Aeronautics Corps is now situated, my absence, for a time at least, will not interfere with its operation."

Having failed with his own efforts to revive the Balloon Corps,

Lowe pressed his old friends to intervene for him. On August 29, 1863, Judge George Harding of Philadelphia sent a letter to Secretary of War Stanton on Lowe's behalf. In it the judge explained, quoting facts obviously garnered from Lowe, that the balloonist's "problems were the result of ill will harbored by General Butterfield, who had panicked under fire while up with Lowe at the Battle of Fredericksburg." But Stanton had heard this story before, and Butterfield had contradicted it himself. Harding then wrote to General George G. Meade requesting Lowe's reinstatement, also to no avail.

Lowe's wife and his daughters saw less and less of him as he continued to travel back and forth between Philadelphia and Washington. Although the balloonist was aware that he had few friends in the War Department, he continued to perform aeronautical ascensions in front of the Smithsonian hoping to convince the department to reinstall the Balloon Corps. All these demonstrations, however, proved worthless. As the war ground on, it was the rare officer or administrator who wanted to show any support for an experiment generally regarded as having been tried, and failed.

Lowe was also waging a futile battle to obtain $3,040.97 in back pay and other expenses he felt he was still owed from his service with the army. The balloonist had submitted an invoice for the $10 per day he had not been paid from April 8 to June 31, 1863. When Lowe had brashly suggested that he would remain on without pay, Captain Comstock had taken him at his word and used the opportunity to take the balloonist off the payroll. Lowe was now maintaining that he had only spoken in jest and wanted his money. He was also seeking $1,500 from the government for a balloon of his that he believed the government had agreed to purchase, miscellaneous travel expenses amounting to $1,558.47, and the $142.50 he had paid to W. J. Rhees for help in preparing his final report to Secretary of War Stanton.

Now the army laid its lethal paw on Lowe. He stood before Major General Edward Canby of the adjutant general's office, looking deceptively well, his face tanned, with deep lines set from long hours of standing in the sun in the basket of his observation balloon, but actually feeling quite ill. Although he had already been wounded by history, the balloonist was not inclined to grovel. General Canby rejected, without question, all but $280 of the reimbursement Lowe had requested in his letter. The general's reasons varied with each item. However, as he slowly enumerated each specifically, his acrimony and dislike for Lowe were manifestly evident. Lowe stood his ground with an almost debonair toughness. Canby concluded by rudely pointing out to Professor Lowe that the poor state of the Balloon Corps's files was his problem, not the army's, and they were not about to reimburse him for Rhees's help in putting the papers in order.

Lowe's leg began to tremble. He asked if he might have a chair, as when he was ushered into Canby's presence no chair had been offered. Rather, he had been forced to remain standing, flanked by two aides, one on either side, as if he were a prisoner. Lowe apprised the general of his condition and how he had contracted malaria while serving honorably with McClellan during the Peninsula Campaign. Canby, who as far as Lowe knew had not served anywhere but at his desk in Washington, was disinclined to show the professor any sympathy. However, seeing that the balloonist was shaking, he did order a chair brought.

Seated now, Lowe felt more at ease. His mind began to pine for the early days of the corps' beginning when he had taken breakfast with President Lincoln—who now, he was sure, had enough of his own problems. Immediately Lowe's inquisitor got back to his odious business. The army had not forgotten about Jacob Freno's charges. The balloonist was informed that the $280 in reimbursement he was being allowed would not be paid until he had explained a number of seeming inconsistencies. The transcript Canby handed Lowe read:

> Neither should the amount be paid until Mr. Lowe can satisfactorily account for a government saddle, which was concealed in a trunk by his father, and conveyed from Harper's Ferry to Philadelphia, October 3, 1862, two silk balloons for which he was responsible in 1862, and a lot of new Government tents, poles, and pins, which together with a new silk balloon belonging to the Government was conveyed by the Steamer Rotary from the Peninsula to Philadelphia on account of Mr. Lowe. Explanation should also be made by Mr. Lowe, in relation to forage said to have been drawn by him from the Government and sold to J. C. Jackson about 1st September 1862.

Lowe finished the transcript, then wiped the sweat from his forehead. He would have to do his best to disabuse General Canby of these charges. The malaria had given him numb intervals. As a result, there were times for which he had difficulty recalling anything at all. The balloonist's claims for travel expenses were all based on verbal orders, and hence not allowed. Lowe had no written evidence that the government had requisitioned the balloon he was seeking payment for, nor did he have proof that it had been ever used in the field, and that the envelope had either been disposed of or transferred to another command. And to Lowe the forage bills seemed like ones that he had already resolved in 1861.

In July 1864 a desperate Lowe turned to his old friend from the Smithsonian, Joseph Henry, for help in collecting money he believed the army still owed him. Henry put his assistant Rhees on the job. Between Lowe and Rhees the army was badgered enough to make a partial payment to the balloonist. Also the charges brought against Lowe for the missing balloons and equipment were eventually forgotten.

Despite numerous comments in the newspapers, no serious thought was given to the reestablishing of the Balloon Corps nor the hiring of other aeronauts. It would not be until 1893, thirty years after Lowe's last military observation flight, that the U. S. Army would add another balloon to its command.

The balloonist stood on the platform of the Washington railroad station, his scientist's mind admiring the smooth gliding approach of the train. He marveled at how the cars were able to come so close to the platform and yet never were in danger of touching it, something that worked right every time. The thought caused Lowe's haggard, aquiline face to melt into a half-smile beneath his full mustache. He wore the look of gracious fatigue in this dusty, dark coat and trousers and faded black felt hat. During his service with the army he had aged, his hair gone gray.

Someone spoke, addressing him as "Professor Lowe," but he did not acknowledge and walked away. Lowe heard nothing save the hissing of the train and the bustling of the people coming and going, some to the war and some returning from it. He, himself, was content to be leaving Washington and the war and the waste and senseless slaughter. Lowe knew now that no matter what role history would chose to assign him he clearly preferred peace to war.

He would go back to his experiments. Lowe's was an inventive mind, most content when he was dabbling at making improvements in mechanical devices. Although he was devoted to the idea of bettering mankind's lot, Lowe had no fascination with human nature and little interest in people in general. His scientist's mind had led him to the realization that during the short interval called a human life, which began and ended in darkness, everything in between, no matter how important it may have seemed at the time, was only one fleeting moment of light.

23

To the Mountains and Back, Aeronautic Amphitheatre, More Inventions

Although the war continued to rage, Lowe's main concern now was regaining his health. He spent several quiet weeks in Philadelphia hoping to recover from the effects of his malaria and from the stress of his still unfinished business with the government. Believing that a change of scene and some fresh mountain air might speed his recovery, Leontine suggested they travel to New Hampshire to visit his family.

The journey was long. The train, which ran only three times a week on a forgotten branch line, carried no more than a few passengers. Lowe, with his wife and first-born daughter Louise, sat in an archaic coach that must have been pressed into use to replace cars withdrawn from the line in order to service the war. The ancient cars, which exuded a strange and frightening sense of neglect, gave Lowe the feeling that he had gone back in time. Restless, he wandered from car to car, supposedly looking for one that was less drafty. Here and there a few people sat in the mostly empty cars, surrounded by their bundles. At a rural station deserted except for the station master who blew his whistle for the train to start, Lowe remarked to his wife as he looked out the window that it seemed odd that the railroad official was the only person he had seen wearing a uniform of any kind in over a hundred miles.

After the train, a short coach ride returned Lowe to Jefferson to step in the nostalgia of the familiar landmarks of his boyhood. Not much had changed in the little valley between the green hills, the whole panorama appearing as if it had just been unwrapped from being in storage while he was away. The sunshine, fresh air, and lazy simmering days, however, did make the battles the balloonist had seen appear as something that had never happened. But the war was evident even here. The small town was widely decorated with red, white, and blue bunting for his return. Patriotism and jingoism abounded. Recruiting rallies were regularly held, even though all the available young men had long ago either scattered to the hills or marched bravely off to the fight.

At first Lowe confined himself to walking in the woods and fields, avoiding the town. All of the local folks had read of his war adventures in the newspapers. While some considered him a hero, others wondered what he was doing back in Jefferson when the war was still going on. He also bypassed the town because it reminded him of the poverty and sameness that had driven him from the area at an early age. Everyone seemed stuck within themselves, within the day in which they were born, the life that had been dealt to them. Deceived by the silence of the mountains, time seemed to flow backwards, constantly retreating, only encountering the present when it was the past.

Lowe woke to the smell of fresh brewing coffee. He had not gone fishing in many years and was anticipating a pleasurable trip to the local reservoir with his brother Charles and his son Vyron. The catch was good, and the trio brought home numerous rainbow trout. Lowe cleaned the fish on the back stairs, tossing the heads to the many cats. Leontine prepared an excellent meal of the fillets using her special French recipe. Everyone appreciated her effort and complimented her lavishly, even though she apologized for not being able to find the seasonings she needed there in Jefferson. Lowe's brother laughed and reminded Leontine she was not in Paris. This chance remark made her sad. She remembered her dead father and France and the things she missed. Leontine worried that her husband was enjoying himself so much that he might decide to remain there in the mountains with his "bumpkin relatives." No, she was not in Paris, not even in Philadelphia.

Later in the week, when the fishing seemed to be especially good—legend had it that they caught four hundred trout—a banquet was prepared in the dinning room of the Waumbeck Inn to which all of the balloonist's relations were invited. When all the Lowe family, sons and daughters, uncles and cousins, and their offspring had gathered at the inn, it seemed as if most of Coos County was there. It appeared as if T. S. C. Lowe was trying to make up for all the meals of "salt horse and hardtack" he had endured while with the Balloon Corps.

After dinner the balloonist sat rocking in the setting sun on the wide veranda of the Waumbek Inn, looking down on the pine-crested valley of the Singrawac. As the chair swayed back and forth, his body trembled occasionally. Lowe suspected that this was from the aftereffects of his malaria, but he could not discount the recurring memories of the thousands of men he had seen killed or maimed that came fresh to his mind, or the knowing that in Virginia and Maryland and Mississippi and places in between, men were still shooting at each other and lying in the mud dying.

His father was there on the porch with him, leaning back in his chair, his abdomen protruding slightly through his waistcoat. Clovis had remained with the Balloon Corps for a short time after his son's departure, working with John Dickinson maintaining the balloons. But the martinet Captain Comstock was soon rid of both of them, claiming their hiring had been favoritism on Lowe's part. Shortly after his being cashiered, Clovis had returned to his home in Randolph.

One of the men sitting with them, puffing his cigar into the warm summer evening, chanced to ask Lowe, now that he was gone, if he saw any future for the Balloon Corps. All other conversation stopped as the gathering turned their ears to hear the balloonist's reply.

As the Civil War had become more savage, with extreme vindictiveness on both sides, newspapers in the North as well as the South had begun to press for a solution. Editorials remarked on the poor organization and decision making on both sides. Writers speculated that perhaps several of the bloodiest battles that had apparently accomplished nothing need not have been fought at all had the armies had better military intelligence. Many were asking what had happened to the aerial reconnaissance provided by the Balloon Corps, which had been so highly touted at the beginning of the war. One Southern paper even quoted General E. P. Alexander, the Confederate artillery chief, as saying: "I never understood why the enemy abandoned the use of military balloons early in 1863, after having used them extensively up to that time. Even if the observers never saw anything, they would have been worth all they cost for the annoyance and delays they caused us in trying to keep our movements out of their sight."

T. S. C. Lowe leaned back in his rocker. The man's question about the Balloon Corps was one to which he did not have an answer, or had received a clear answer in Washington, but had not accepted it. The balloonist remarked, "I have many letters from generals and other prominent officials wishing me a speedy recovery of my health—and a return to the army." As if he had been expecting to be challenged, the balloonist quickly produced a letter out of his pocket from General George Stoneman, the commander of the Cavalry Corps of the Army of the Potomac and began to read from it:

I beg to testify to you in writing, as I often have in words, my appreciation of the valuable services you have rendered the government during your connection with the Army of the Potomac, in the use of your "portable balloons" in various operations of that army. I have been up in them often and never made an ascent without coming down much better informed in regard to everything in my vicinity than I could possibly have been by other means.

Valuable as your balloons have been, I feel satisfied that you would have made them still more so had you been encouraged by having more facilities extended to you. I have ever regretted that our efforts, to have your system of signals by means of balloons introduced, were unsuccessful, as I feel satisfied that they can be made of great service both by day and night.

The men nodded their heads and grunted in respect of the general's letter, puffing their cigars hard to drive the evening insects from their faces. One of them quickly opined that the government should have made the Balloon Corps a permanent branch of the army, with "Colonel" Lowe in charge, looking to the balloonist for approval.

Clovis chimed in, even adding that the Allen boys had given up and returned to Providence, leaving six brand-new silk balloons, complete with generators, lying idle in the Columbian Armory. There was a murmur of incredulity at the stupidity of the government. And balloons weren't the only thing, Clovis prompted his son. He urged Thaddeus to tell the group about the calcium light he invented, which no one wanted.

The balloonist rocked back in his chair, describing how he had perfected an improved calcium light that the army could have used to carry on night operations, constructing bridges or breastworks. But the army would not even give it an official test. Nor had the government been interested in his system of varicolored phosphorescent signal balloons, Lowe went on, although he had shown them to be more brilliant than a rocket, and visible ten times as long.

The men were astounded by these revelations. "Doesn't the government want the very best for its soldiers?" someone asked. No one had any explanation other than the fact that it was all politics. An old veteran ventured it was the fault of the damn officers, who couldn't see beyond their noses, their main concern being their own promotions.

Lowe brushed the talk aside. He had heard enough of this firsthand; he wanted to tell them about his scientific side. He had not sat idle during those long nights in the field waiting for the killing to start, the balloonist offered. He explained how he had developed a magnifying lens by which aerial photographs could be enlarged from three inches square to as big as twenty feet. He anticipated that objects not clearly discernible to the naked eye might be distinguishable in an enlarged photograph. Lowe told the men that he had attempted to get Matthew Brady to cooperate with him on this experiment, but the army discouraged the photographer from participating. All his inventions would have to wait for a more enlightened generation, one less preoccupied with war, Lowe observed, sadly shaking his head.

Lowe gave as another example the successful balloon flights made by a Doctor Solomon Andrews of New Jersey in his powered airship *Aereon*. Andrews had attempted to interest the War Department in funding construction of his second airship for military purposes after Lowe had left the Balloon Corps, and had been rebuffed. Secretary of War Stanton had written him that he could not see any "practical utility" for the airship as the idea of using air power for military purposes was "too remote." Lacking funds to produce a new airship when his first one was destroyed in an accident, Andrews had purchased Lowe's *Union* and *Intrepid* from the army as war surplus, planning to salvage and revarnish the pongee silk and use it to construct a new *Aereon*. Lowe remarked that he, as Soloman Andrews did, foresaw the airship as a peacetime carrier of goods and passengers. Lowe noted, however, that neither of them had been very successful in attracting investors in their projects.

Speculating on the future of aeronautics, much to the delight of the small crowd that had now gathered on the veranda, Lowe predicted that the science would not advance until light, powerful engines were developed. He allowed as how he was extremely interested in this problem, but the manufacturing of engines required more money than he presently had available. Lowe's next prophetic observation sent the group reeling, especially coming from a balloonist. He declared, "The aircraft of the future will have nothing to do with balloons, but will be a kind of flying sled, that can ride the air just like a bird."

Lowe was talking freely and intimately now, the most he had said since returning to New Hampshire. The men and a few women who had gathered around him wanted more; this was not the stuff they got out of the daily newspaper. The balloonist told them: "My advanced methods of aerial observation have reached the attention of foreign generals, carried by the observers who had traveled with me during the Peninsula Campaign. My innovations are now in use with armies in both England and France."

It was getting late, the glowing sun slunk half hidden behind the mountains. Lowe was tired. His hand trembled slightly as he said good night, grasping the many arms extended to him.

For the present time he would dream just like any baker or farmer or tradesman fantasizes about ideas that might improve his lot. In the morning, at dawn, he would put on his wide-brim black felt hat and walk out the left-open back gate. The balloonist would spend the day, as he had the day before, wandering the labyrinthian woods and fields, his eyes on the ground, daydreaming. These were not the irrational, senseless nightmares of his feverish hours. Lowe was aware of his condition and he accepted it. He knew he was in the dangerous season, how difficult it was for him to achieve stability at all. He was determined to avoid destruction by his own mind. With time and care, he would regain his health and return to Philadelphia, where he hoped to transform some of his wildest ideas into realities.

The long summer days had no dusk. After his walk Lowe would stay up until darkness, laboriously covering page after page in his calligraphically precise hand, with drawings and notes for new inventions. Almost unnoticeably the stately mountains of his birth had had a healing effect on the balloonist. He was feeling much stronger after his period of rest and relaxation. A man of pride and restless energy, he was now eager to get back to his work in Philadelphia. His unfinished business had become stubbornly rooted in his mind.

Like most Northerners, Lowe was convinced that the tide had turned at the Battle of Gettysburg, that it was only a matter of time until the war would be over. His career as a military balloonist was ended, and he was ready to start a new phase of his life, although at the moment he was not sure what that might be. And, besides, notwithstanding the various amounts he was receiving here and there, Lowe was just about out of money.

Lowe had hoped to return to scientific work. His mind was full of new ideas for inventions. But their development required a great deal of ready cash. In an effort to improve his financial situation Lowe returned to that which he knew best, ballooning. Using much of the little savings they had left, the balloonist purchased the observation balloon *Washington* from the War Department as surplus. He planned to refurbish it and go back into the business of giving balloon rides.

The balloon was in such bad repair, and Lowe put in so much work on the project, that Leontine wondered if he would ever make any money from it, suspecting he may only have bought it as a souvenir. The *Washington* had been constructed by Lowe in the early fall of 1861. One of the first war balloons, it was sent to Port Royal, South Carolina, for use by John Starkweather. When Starkwater left, the balloon had been transferred back to Washington and then brought down to Lowe on the peninsula by his father Clovis. Thereafter it saw almost constant use during a number of campaigns.

In January 1863, after Lowe departed the Balloon Corps, the Allen brothers had made a test inflation of the *Washington*. Their report declared the balloon to be "in very bad order, finding the envelope full of numerous holes from 1/64 to 1/8 of an inch in size." James Allen attempted to patch the craft, but new holes continued to form in the worn fabric. The seams also were extremely rotten. Although the aeronaut informed the army that the grizzled balloon was unfit for use, Hooker's staff continued to order it aloft even in the worst conditions. An accident when high winds split a seam, almost costing Ezra Allen his life, finally caused the balloon to be taken out of service.

Lowe had worked day and night to get the *Washington* back in shape and was now offering the citizens of "The City of Brotherly Love" the opportunity to see their town from the air. A poster for flights in the *Washington* boasted: "15,000 persons have thus ascended in balloons directed by Professor Lowe, without the least inconvenience or danger." The balloonist made daily tethered passenger flights from a site at the intersection of Coates and Fifteenth streets and Ridge Avenue. On Wednesdays and Saturdays at 3:00, when the weather permitted, Lowe took his more adventurous passengers up for free flights.

Lowe and his family were now living north of Philadelphia in Norristown on a farm the balloonist had purchased when he returned from Washington, D.C. It was a small farm, bordering Pickering Creek, near the site where George Washington had wintered at Valley Forge. Lowe would do a little farming, hoping to retain his health, but mainly he planned for the barns and outbuildings to house the many projects he had in mind to work on. Leontine's days were spent caring for a growing family. Three more daughters would be born during the three years they lived on the farm.

While to many the balloonist may have appeared diffident or aloof, and sometimes just confused, Lowe was at heart the consummate showman. Sensing he had exhausted his small Philadelphia audience, Lowe decided to return to New York City to tap the larger market there. The balloonist purchased another surplus war balloon, the *United States.* This he rebuilt to his satisfaction. Then he went about setting up an elaborate enterprise that he called the "Aeronautic Amphitheatre," at the southern end of Central Park on the corner of 59th Street and Sixth Avenue.

In operation during 1865 to 1866, the Aeronautic Amphitheatre proved to be quite lucrative. An engraving made at that time depicted the interior of the amphitheatre as a rather large, dug-out, sloping space, with a covered walkway for spectators lining the top. On one of the inclines was a bleacher with five rows of benches, and open stairs for descending into the amphitheatre. Against another slant was a bandstand. On the other two slopes smartly dressed spectators, some of the ladies holding parasols, were seen standing or reclining.

Here, as in Philadelphia, Lowe offered tethered balloon ascensions and free flights. The balloonist, however, had added a number of sensational features in an attempt to attract the crowds. In the center of the arena was a large artificial pond on which mock naval engagements were staged using model ships that looked not unlike the *Monitor* and *Merrimac.* Surrounding the pond were massive shaped balloons on tethers. Chosen perhaps for their scale, these huge balloons had been designed and sewn into the shapes of an elephant, a whale, and a giant dancing man. At the center of the amphitheatre, directly in front of the bleachers, was the main attraction, the platform from which the famous Professor T. S. C. Lowe made his balloon ascensions.

Moreover, the balloonist had added to his aerial bag of tricks. Not content merely to rise up in the *United States* trailing the usual flags and red, white and blue bunting, Lowe had taken to dangling a trapeze artist below his balloon. Harry Leslie, a Manhattan gymnast and high-wire daredevil, performed acrobatic stunts on a swinging bar hung from the bottom of Lowe's basket.

When conditions warranted, Lowe also offered free flights. These were occasionally made between New York and the resorts at Atlantic City, with the arrival not always guaranteed. What passengers as could be found paid a steep price for the privilege of risking their lives getting to the New Jersey shore by balloon. While these cross-country balloon flights were a popular novelty, netting Lowe a substantial income because of the high price he asked, air travel had a long way to go before it would become a regular means of transportation.

In the shadow of all this hoopla, men were still fighting and dying. The war, always in the back of Lowe's mind as he felt somewhat guilty for having walked away from it, had begun to swing in favor of the North. On April 3, 1865, the Union Army commanded by General Ulysses S. Grant marched into a burning Richmond. Ablaze and rocked by explosions, the retreating Confederate Army had decided to destroy their war-weary capital rather than let it be conquered. The end came six days later in the bare parlor of a private residence in the town of Appomattox Court House, Virginia. Realizing that his worn-out army, undermanned and outgunned, was facing annihilation, General Lee wisely chose to surrender. The war was almost at an end.

Lowe had experienced a sense of relief, but no joy, when he heard the news of Lee's surrender. The hatred and bitterness that had torn the states apart was still there. It rose again on April 14 when the actor and rabid secessionist, John Wilkes Booth, shot President Lincoln while he was attending a play at Ford's Theatre in Washington. By the next morning the president lay dead.

Horrified by the news, Lowe put down his newspaper and walked to the window. Feeling faint, he opened the pane to let in some fresh air. At that early hour the rest of the family was blissfully sleeping. In the street the shadows of the trees absorbed the first sun of the morning. Lowe searched his mind. The name of the assassin was strangely familiar. Then he remembered a train ride on which he had shared a coach with a troupe of actors, a conversation with a rather troubled man. The immensity of the man's claims had frightened him. Hadn't the man said his name was Booth? Perhaps it was just a coincidence; it couldn't be the same man. No, he recalled the incident clearly now. When they had parted the man had shook his hand rather brusquely saying his name was Booth—John Wilkes Booth. Lowe remembered that name and that the man boasted that he was going to be famous someday.

Angered by Lincoln's death, the nation prepared to release its wrath on the already reeling South. While the balloonist's grief at the loss of a man he considered his friend was severe, he turned away from the cries for vengeance he knew Lincoln himself would have condemned. Lowe wondered if the gaping wound that now split the nation would ever heal completely.

Lowe had separated himself more and more from the the conflicts of the world, and escaped into his life of hard work and total dedication. All Lowe wanted to do now was go about his experiments, hoping that he might invent things that would improve people's lives through technology. He was, of course, not averse to any small fortune he might achieve from the marketing of his inventions. Of one thing the balloonist was sure though, he vowed to never again invent anything that could be used in any way to wage war.

Although Lowe rarely allowed himself any relaxation, his balloon ascensions at his Aeronautic Amphitheatre did offer him some lighter moments. The tall man with the dapper moustache, seen in Dr. John F. Boynton's wedding picture standing behind the doctor and his bride, looking as if he might be the minister, actually was Professor Lowe. The reason for his presence was that the couple's nuptial, on November 8, 1865, was the occasion of the famous "Balloon Wedding."

The Boyntons had hoped to be married above New York City in the basket of Lowe's balloon. Unfortunately they were unable to convince their minister, the Reverend H. W. Beecher, to go aloft to perform the ceremony. Instead they held their wedding at the Fifth Avenue Hotel, after which the couple and their attendants proceeded to Lowe's Aeronautic Amphitheatre for a honeymoon flight. Looking down at the Hudson River passing three thousand feet below, the couple did regain their composure long enough to exchange the informal vows they had prepared, before landing in a field near Mount Vernon, New York.

On the streets of Manhattan newsboys hawked papers featuring the novel event, and a fad for tying the knot in the sky had begun—among those couples who could afford to do so. One paper commented, "The sacred compact of Holy Matrimony was solemnized above the clouds, floating in mid-air, and in accordance with the laws of the Empire State." This balloon flight would be one of Lowe's last as he was showing less and less interest in aeronautics, his ever fertile mind rapidly shifting to new ideas.

Although Lowe abandoned ballooning completely in 1866, he still remained in contact with James and Ezra Allen, the only veterans of his Balloon Corps who had continued actively flying after the war. In that year, while he was experimenting with an artificial ice-making machine in the hope of preserving fruits and vegetables so that they could be shipped to various parts of the country, a tempting offer of a different nature came his way. As intriguing and lucrative as the offer was, he turned it down, passing it on to the Allen brothers.

Lowe had received a flattering letter from His Imperial Majesty, Pedro II of Brazil. The emperor had followed the American Civil War with interest, finding the activities of the Balloon Corps particularly engaging. Presently at war with Paraguay, Dom Pedro wished to establish an aeronautical unit for the Brazilian Army. He hoped the balloonist would come to Brazil to take command of this organization, and teach his system of aeronautics. The emperor was prepared to offer Lowe a commission in the Brazilian Army, $180 a month in gold, all expenses, a contract for the balloons and equipment, and a grant of land.

The balloonist savored the generosity of the offer, but did not think twice about passing it up. He had had enough of wars. The Allen brothers, younger than Lowe and still adventurous, were delighted to take the job, thus becoming the first two of what would be a long line of American aerial mercenaries.

The brothers wrote Lowe from Brazil saying that, unlike the United States Army, their ascensions were "well appreciated by all concerned." However, despite the efforts of the Allens, the war went on for four more years, finally ending in 1870 with the death of Paraguay's dictator, Francisco Solano Lopez, who had kept feeding his army to the slaughter despite tremendous losses. The war cost Paraguay fifty thousand square miles of her territory, and her prewar population of 1.2 million had been reduced to an estimated two hundred thousand women and twenty-eight thousand men.

Lowe received a letter of thanks, steeped in hyperbole, from Dom Pedro, "who gratefully acknowledged his indebtedness to the American aeronaut" and informed him "that by carrying out his methods, the war had been closed after a single battle." The emperor's letters brought home to Lowe how much a part of history he already was, even though he still dreamed of accomplishing much more.

Warm sunshine streamed in through the brick loft building's tall windows. Lowe puttered contentedly about his shop, which was a maze of tubes and pipes and bottles of compressed gas. A new life had begun for the balloonist. He had closed down his Aeronautical Amphitheatre after two lavishly money-making years and returned to Norristown, not to the farm, which had been sold, but to a large, and rather pretentious twenty-five-room house on tree-lined West Main Street. The spacious residence also had a carriage house and an elaborate side garden with tubbed palm trees, which could be wheeled into a greenhouse during the cold Pennsylvania winters. For his scientific projects the former balloonist had leased a sizable, well-lit building downtown, and had "Lowe Manufacturing Company" boldly lettered across the front.

Remembering the ice crystals drumming inside the envelope during his free flight from Cincinnati to South Carolina, Lowe began experimenting with the making of ice. His work with balloons had given Lowe a great deal of information about gases and the formation of ice at high altitudes. This knowledge led him to explore the possibility of developing a process of making artificial ice that would be more effective than the method then in use. In 1850 an ice-making machine had been patented by Dr. John Gerrie, which used compressed air, or carbon dioxide, cooling it with water, then expanding it in immersed coils until the water froze. As the bulky compressors were steam powered, Gerrie's system had proved unsatisfactory. Natural ice, sawed from frozen lakes in the winter, and stored in straw-lined warehouses until summer, was still the main method of refrigeration in use. This primitive system, of course, precluded the transfer of perishable foods by ship, which was precisely Lowe's objective.

Lowe obstinately put his mind to the problem. After considerable experimentation, he came up with a revolutionary improvement on the air-compression method. Lowe introduced the use of ammonia, the key element still employed in current refrigeration. The inventor proceeded from the fact that ammonia, in its pure state, was a gas at ordinary temperature and pressure, but when compressed and cooled it became a liquid. He knew that releasing pressure on the fluid would cause it to boil and return to gas, thereby absorbing a large amount of heat. Absorbing heat from water produced ice. The same process on air produced refrigeration. Lowe applied to the government for a patent on his "Ice Machine." He was successful, and on April 2, 1867, was granted U. S. Patent No. 63,405.

His ice-making machine worked so well that Lowe felt he was now ready to proceed with his plan to equip a steamship with refrigerated holds to transport fresh meat, vegetables, and fruit. To this end he persuaded a group of business men to put up the funds to purchase the steamship *William Tabor*, in which, after extensive modification, his refrigeration system was installed. This was the first-ever refrigerated ship. This innovation radically changed the transportation of perishable goods and was the beginning of a whole new era for world shipping. Lowe's refrigerated ship also laid the groundwork for the cold storage industry, which would come years later. Lowe was confident that this invention had fulfilled his goal of adding to the betterment of mankind through technology.

Lowe was ready to put the *William Tabor* to the test. After all, the second goal of his inventions was to provide the inventor with a significant monetary reward. With the compression system operating perfectly, the vessel was loaded with food products in New York and sent on a voyage to Galveston, Texas. Everything went well. Likewise, on the return trip, a cargo of Texas beef arrived without a single pound spoiled. The inventor was ebullient. That evening Lowe and his friends lavishly dined on freshly thawed steaks to celebrate the new enterprise, generously toasting the fortunes they were sure they would make.

The *William Tabor* was sent around Cape Horn to San Francisco with a full cargo of perishable goods. Again it arrived successfully, unloaded, and returned to New York with its holds full of California produce. The trip proved the merit of Lowe's system, but the voyage, in the era before the Panama Canal, took too long to be profitable. The group decided to concentrate on Gulf Coast products.

The glowing enterprise, however, would prove to be short-lived. Eager for profit, Lowe and his investors purchased another ship, the *Agnes,* and equipped her with refrigerated holds. However, as drying, salting, and canning were the most popular ways of preserving food at the time, the public was skeptical, and not easily convinced of the safety of food left untreated for a long period. After a brief trial run, the business proved to be a financial disaster. Lowe's investors were losing large sums of money, and one by one began to pull out to cut their losses. Undaunted, Lowe briefly carried on alone, but he too ended up with a personal loss of $87,000. Not one to take the blame, the inventor argued, perhaps rightly so, that this venture, like his balloon endeavors, was way ahead of its time. He rationalized that people were not yet ready for such a quantum leap of progress.

A different reason was put forward by his partners. Lowe, as a scientist, had concentrated on the technical matters to the exclusion of practical considerations. No study had been given as to the depth of the water at the Gulf Coast ports the company had chosen to operate from. The two steamships that were converted to refrigerated freighters had been oceangoing vessels with rather deep drafts, the idea being that they would have deep holds that could carry more cargo. As a consequence, the ships had difficulty operating in the rather shallow waters of the ports along the Gulf of Mexico, often having to stand off-shore for days waiting for the right tidal conditions to be able to land.

Undeterred by his floating fiasco, Lowe set out on a extensive cross-country tour to promote the merits of his ice machine. This undertaking was more successful. A skilled salesman, Lowe received numerous orders for his ice-making equipment. Ice-making companies, using Lowe's machines, were popping up in various cities throughout the country. While the seductive tinkling of the Good Humor Man's bell would not be heard for many years, the production of artificial ice, for commercial and home use, was beginning to find popular acceptance.

His early experiences as a balloonist also prompted Lowe's next invention. Coal gas, with which he had inflated his early balloons, was then in popular use both for heating and illumination. The gas was manufactured by heating coal in retorts to red hot, driving off all the volatile matter. Some of the matter condensed into tar and aqua ammonia; that which did not condense was the coal gas. The problem was the smoke and dirt associated with the gas and its low heat yield.

A much hotter flame could be obtained with water gas. This was produced by passing steam over red-hot coal or coke. However, the current method of producing water gas was inefficient and therefore costly. The difficulty was that the reaction that produced the gas absorbed so much heat that the coke soon cooled below the temperature necessary to support the reaction.

Lowe's children wondered what their father was up to when they saw him gathering all the spare flower pots from the greenhouse and loading them into his carriage to be transported to his workshop. When the children went there with their mother and found out what he was doing, they thought it was as they had feared—their father had finally gone mad. Lowe had stacked the pots inverted on a table and was building small fires under them. The inventor explained he was attempting to devise a system of packing coke in tall, fire-brick structures, and restoring the temperature by forcing air through the partly cooled substance. Lowe's experiments with the flower pots seemed to prove his theory, so he had a large model made, and his idea put to the test. His method worked so well and so increased the efficiency of production, that Lowe believed it would be commercially profitable to manufacture water gas.

In 1872 Lowe demonstrated his model coke oven to interested investors. A company was formed and capital raised to construct a water gas producing plant in Norristown. The plant was soon built and put in operation. In a strange turnabout, Lowe's plant was now providing water gas to his old balloon sponsor, the Philadelphia Gas Works. This Norristown plant was later incorporated into the United States Improvement Company, as Lowe formed several other companies to handle the spinoffs from his gas manufacturing process. One of these wares was an improved coke oven, which produced high-grade metallurgical coke, replacing the wasteful, old-fashioned "beehive" ovens. Closer to home, through his privately owned People's Fuel and Gaslight Company, Lowe had undertaken the task of laying gas mains down a number of Norristown Streets. This venture, however, would prove to be unpopular and unprofitable.

In a grand gesture designed to convince the public of the advantages of water gas, Lowe had the Windsor House, a five-story hotel, constructed at his own expense just outside the city of Philadelphia and illuminated entirely by water gas. Its opening was timed to attract some of the thousands of visitors that were expected to visit Philadelphia for the 1876 Centennial Exposition. While the Windsor House was an impressive structure and demonstrated Lowe's advanced applications of domestic gas, to his dismay it was not a successful hotel. Lowe had overestimated the public's desire to stay at a hotel outside of the crowed city. Although widely written about and much admired as a demonstration of the possibilities of gaslight, the Windsor House was yet another of the former balloonist's financial failures.

Never to be deterred, within two years Lowe had erected another factory and was soon doing a lucrative business turning out stoves, heaters, fireplaces, and other novel devices, all using water gas. In his laboratory at this plant Lowe produced one of his most outstanding inventions, the first incandescent gaslight. This was basically a Bunsen burner with a small coil of platinum wire. When the wire was brought to white heat, it gave off a fairly good light. Lowe's invention would later be improved upon by a German named Welsbach, who added a cylindrical mantle of carbonaceous cloth over the burner to produce a brighter light. Welsbach's name was given to the mantles, but it was Lowe who had shown him the way.

24
Time for a Change, California, New Mountains to Climb

Thaddeus Sobieski Constantine Lowe was well thought of in Norristown, where he could often be seen riding down West Main Street in his handsome double-brougham. He had given up the wide-brimmed felt that had been his trademark during his Balloon Corps days. Now he preferred a stylish opera hat and carried a cane. He still wore a long frock, but one made of the finest materials. However, it no longer covered a flat stomach, as Lowe had put on a bit of weight during the inactive period he had spent recovering from malaria. He rarely trembled these days, but, despite his tremendous energy, still tired easily. His hair and mustache had grayed considerably. One might say he no longer looked like the dashing balloonist he had been, but like the successful businessman he had become.

These were indeed prosperous years for Lowe. He had established thriving gas works in many eastern cities. His gas businesses had helped him recover from the losses he had taken on his other ventures. Things went so well that by 1879 Lowe had plants producing water gas for light and heat in thirty cities, and his process had been patented in France, Sweden, Great Britain, and other countries.

The Franklin Institute of Philadelphia twice honored Lowe for his accomplishments with water gas. A jury of distinguished scientists presented him with the institute's Elliot Cresson Gold Medal in 1885. And several years later he received the Institute's most coveted medal, the "Grand Medal of Honor for the Invention Held to Be the Most Useful to Mankind," for his water gas process. A model of the inventor's water gas apparatus was put on permanent display in the institute's galleries. His water gas system would remain in wide use until the early twentieth century, when it was gradually replaced by electricity.

Lowe was also honored abroad. In 1891 he received a medal in recognition of his inventions and achievements from the Paris Academy of Industry and Science. A contemporary periodical commented,

"[Lowe] had little more than reached middle life, and it is warrantable to suppose that his speculative and fertile mind will grasp and produce other valuable inventions."

Although he was increasingly becoming a public figure, Lowe's home life in Norristown was far from humdrum. He and Leontine now had ten children (seven daughters and three sons) living in their three-story gray brick house at 823 West Main Street. The house was surrounded by lavish gardens, with a greenhouse for the tropical plants, and a carriage house and stables. The compound also had its own private, Lowe-designed, water gas plant to supply light and heat.

The family lived well, with a staff of cooks, maids, and nannies to take care of the day-to-day details. Although Lowe had gained a bit of weight, he kept up his regimen of a healthy diet and exercise. He still had not taken up the popular habit of tobacco, neither smoking nor chewing. Lowe now, however, did take an oocasional glass of wine, and on winter holidays a hot toddy made with brandy.

The inventor loved holidays. His favorites were Christmas and the Fourth of July. An inveterate tinkerer, Lowe found the Yuletide season especially enchanting as it enabled him to spend his free time making unique toys for his children. One Christmas he delighted the family gathering with a bit of nostalgia, producing from his Santa's bag a small red, white, and blue balloon that rose to the ceiling, and then released tiny dolls that floated down on parachutes.

Lowe did his best to celebrate Independence Day. He spent large sums to have a huge display of fireworks, which could be seen from all over town, set off from his garden. He did the fireworks mainly to delight the children, his own as well as those of the neighborhood. While he watched, waving his flag and cheering each glowing burst with the others, his heart was not in it. He had seen too many rockets and heard too many bombs during the Peninsula Campaign and at places like Malvern Hill and Fredericksburg. The screams of terror, the bloody broken bodies, and the smell of burning flesh still lived in his mind. He recalled a saying attributed to the much maligned Robert E. Lee, before the war arguably America's greatest general, who through fate and a sense of honor had committed to the losing side: "It is well that war is so terrible, otherwise we should grow too fond of it."

In 1888, Lowe, having reached the age of fifty-six, was feeling a sense of weariness. Over twenty years of intense work on his inventions and businesses had begun to take a toll on his spirit. Although his water gas business and other enterprises had fully recouped the losses of his earlier unsuccessful ventures and provided him with a sizable fortune besides, he felt something was lacking in his life. Always a man of adventure, he was finding that the comfortable life he was leading in Norristown was leaving him bored. Lowe decided to confide his state of mind to his devoted wife. He told Leontine he thought it was time for him to make a change, both of pace and surroundings.

The sudden announcement had shocked Leontine. She thought at first that Thaddeus was referring to a change from her. She had little knowledge of what her husband did during those many times he had to be away. Although she never questioned him, and had been faithful herself, she sometimes wondered if he might have been deceiving her. After a pause, which she sensed was too long, Leontine guardedly asked her husband just what he meant.

Suddenly realizing what his wife was mistakenly thinking, Lowe took her in his arms and explained he was talking about giving up his water gas business and moving to a new place, to which Leontine replied that she doubted that he would ever be content away from the day-to-day pressures of his business activities.

Lowe revealed he no longer found his work interesting and considered Norristown too isolated. In the winter, when they were surrounded by snow, he felt as if they might as well be in Greenland.

Leontine jokingly suggested that if it was sunshine and adventure he craved, then they should move to California. To her surprise, her husband jumped at the idea. As usual when making important decisions, the family held a meeting. Unsure of what they would find in California, or "if the climate would be salubrious," it was decided that only the youngest children—Augustine, Blanche, Thaddeus, Jr., and Edna—would accompany their parents on the move to the West Coast. The two eldest daughters, already married, were living with their husbands. The other children still at home would remain at the house in Norristown in care of the nannies, and remain in school.

Once the decision was made, Lowe wasted no time in packing and arranging for the move. The thought of going to a new place excited him. He sensed the same stimulation he had felt on the peninsula when he regularly had to pack up his balloon camp and move it to a new location, not knowing what adventure, or terror, the change might bring.

In a short time the Lowes were settled near Los Angeles in the rich, colorful, residential community of Pasadena in a rented mansion on South Marengo Avenue. Almost immediately the newcomers received many invitations and became involved with the cream of Pasadena society. Finding his rented quarters not as opulent as those he was visiting, Lowe commissioned an architect to build him his own house at 905 South Orange Grove Avenue. For this he paid the then staggering sum of $65,000. The spectacular three-story, twenty-four-thousand-square-foot residence boasted a five-story circular tower with a mini-observatory and huge, lavishly decorated rooms for social gatherings. The gigantic basement was set up as a museum for Leontine's ever-growing collection of seashells and American Indian artifacts.

The construction excited the curious neighbors, and crowds gathered daily to watch the mansion grow. The building's progress was even reported in the newspapers. *The Pasadena Star* stated, "When completed [Lowe's] mansion will be the finest residence in the state." *The Los Angeles Herald* proclaimed, "Our people are learning more and more that this is Professor Lowe's way of doing things, generally better than anticipated."

On the first day they occupied the house, in the quietness of the morning hours, while the rest of the family was still asleep, the new owner ascended to his tower. As the heat of the dawn slowly rose around him, Lowe stood looking through his spyglass at the city of fine houses and expansive estates spread out below. He was higher above the ground than anyone else in town. All his energy, zeal, and stubborn determination had got him where he was, but he was not as high as he had been in his balloons. Lowe shuddered a little. Was it the fever, or just his memories? As the day lengthened, in the gaps between the houses Lowe could see people moving about, their comings and goings, everyone rushing somewhere. In his mind the town of Fredericksburg stretched out before him, its citizens dodging in and out of their crumbling houses to avoid the hell being rained on them by the Federal guns. He turned a circle to get his bearings and to drive the horror away. Looming to the north were the majestic peaks of the San Gabriel Mountains. These confronted Lowe with the more pleasant memories of his childhood, the mountains he had grown up beneath in New Hampshire.

Later that day, at a dinner party, Lowe asked about the possibility of climbing the San Gabriel's slopes, but was told the steep, rugged inclines made them inaccessible to all but seasoned mountain climbers and serious hikers. He questioned why such great beauty should be available to so few people. Lowe, always the dreamer, began to envision a railway winding its way up and around the rocky slopes, its cars filled with exhilarated people gasping at the natural beauty unfolding all around them.

Out of habit Lowe had become involved in some local enterprises, a bank and some real estate, but none of this stirred him as much as the thought of his mountain railway. His mind kept being drawn back to the idea. He saw the railway as an undertaking that could challenge his imagination, like the Balloon Corps, or his refrigerated ships. In his systematic way, Lowe began to research the project.

He was disappointed to learn that his was not an original concept; others had already explored the possibility of building a mountain railway and abandoned the idea. In fact Lowe found he was almost in a race of sorts with those proposing similar projects, all with the final destination being Mount Wilson.

Never one to shy away from a competition, this news only spurred Lowe on. As best as he could determine, the first mountain railway, using the cogwheel principle, was suggested by the naturalist Theodore P. Lukens. He had proposed to originate his line in Pasadena. Other men, likewise, had made similar propositions, but the obstacles were always the same—usually the routes planned were unrealistic and the funding was not forthcoming. The land boom of the 1800's had dwindled, and the economy became stagnant. Consequently money for such outlandish undertakings was hard to come by. A considerable number of railroad lines had been constructed during the period, but they were in the more populated areas of Pasadena and Altadena. The Altadena Railroad had opened in 1888. This allowed passengers to ride to the end of the line and enjoy a day out of the city, picnicking in the poppy fields of the highlands. Many travelers used this terminus as a starting point for hiking in the San Gabriel Mountains. Lowe quickly saw the possibilities and decided this was where his mountain railway would begin.

Four years earlier Clarence S. Martin, a California businessman, had hired an engineer to determine if a mountain railway was feasible. Martin and his engineer had hiked the steep slopes, surveying the terrain to determine what difficult construction problems would need to be solved. The two men had come to the conclusion that the only way a line could be built would be by using the cogwheel system. Their further research showed them that while construction might be possible, the cost would be prohibitive, and the venture was dropped.

Lowe discussed his idea with Perry M. Green, president of the First National Bank of Pasadena. Green put him in touch with David Joseph Macpherson, a widely known engineer who lived in the town. Although born in Canada, Macpherson had worked his way through Cornell University, while earning outstanding scores in mathematics, and finished a four-year engineering degree in three years. After that he had worked with the Santa Fe Railroad for several years before moving to Pasadena.

Green told Lowe that Macpherson was one of the staunchest believers in the possibility of a mountain railroad. In 1889 the engineer had begun walking the trails and making preliminary surveys in the mountains. Coupling his own findings with government topological maps, Macpherson had come to the conclusion that he had found a suitable route from Altadena to Mount Wilson. To prepare a convincing demonstration for potential investors, Macpherson decided to undertake a full-scale survey of the proposed right-of-way. An enthusiastic Perry M. Green was the first to sign on as a subscriber to the survey, and others soon followed.

The funding arranged, an official survey team, headed by Macpherson, started into the mountains on February 4, 1890. After ten days of rough walking, rock climbing, and camping out overnight, they had staked out what they believed to be a workable route. However, securing investors for the actual construction proved to be considerably more difficult than finding sponsors for the survey. For several months Macpherson traveled Southern California meeting with potential backers, only to be consistently rebuffed. Green's story held Lowe's interest. It seemed to him that Macpherson's project was at an exciting stage of development. Lowe confided to the banker that this was good enough for him and asked Green to arrange an introduction to the engineer.

The first meeting between Lowe and Macpherson occurred at Lowe's imposing residence on Orange Grove Avenue. Full of enormous rooms, vaulting doorways, and ornamental decorations, the Lowes' new mansion made his Norristown house seem modest by comparison. The engineer was especially impressed by the front of the ornate structure, which featured a five-story, circular, observation tower. Macpherson could not help believing that he had finally met the man who had the wherewithal to make the mountain railway a possibility.

Lowe was taken with Macpherson almost immediately. After a cordial dinner, during which the two went over the many details of Macpherson's plan, they agreed to combine their resources to achieve what most people said could not be done. Macpherson would supply the engineering know-how, while Lowe would provide the capital and such technical help as he was capable of. Macpherson would immediately assemble a team to complete a more in-depth survey and calculate an estimate of the cost.

From the start the partners began to encounter serious obstacles as negotiations got underway to secure lands for the right-of-way to Mount Wilson. The owners of the properties at the summit, who had argued among themselves for years over boundaries and access rights, were the main snag to Lowe's plan. Confident in the belief that the mountain railway had to terminate on their real estate, the owners set preposterously high prices and sat back to wait for Lowe to come to their terms. As it was, their wait was in vain. More serious obstacles to the ascent to Mount Wilson were presented by the terrain. The engineer and his crew had made testings that indicated that the rock that made up the wall of a canyon, which needed to be crossed, was too weak to sustain a railroad trestle. Also it was discovered that the area was susceptible to major landslides in rainy weather, which would make it difficult to maintain any roadbed that might be laid.

Professor Lowe grew impatient as the project began to lose momentum. To a man used to doing things, the frustration of waiting was unbearable. But Lowe was not willing to give up. He came to Macpherson with an alternate plan, as the engineer would later write:

> The professor became restless at the delay and one day asked me if we could not find a point close at hand to which we could run a cable and which would make a good hotel site. After making investigations I reported back to him that starting from a point where the survey to Mount Wilson crossed the Rubio Canyon a cable could be run to the top of the point now called Echo Mountain. Then, with his characteristic vim, he came down with his fist on the table and said "Confound it, I can do that much myself."

With that, Macpherson's plan to build the railroad to the summit of Mount Wilson was abandoned. In January 1890 the partners assembled a party of surveyors to look for another route. Led by Lowe and Macpherson, the group struggled on for over six hours, crawling their way along ledges fit only for mountain goats. Lowe was overwhelmed by the natural beauty, the grandeur of the many gorges and canyons, the cascading waterfalls, the tall pines and spreading oaks, and the abundance of deer, birds, and other wildlife. Taking in the panorama from the shoulder of a lofty peak where one could see as far as the ocean, Lowe announced this was the place where he was going to build his hotel. He would call it Alpine Tavern.

When the party arrived back in Pasadena, they discussed their findings and came to the conclusion that they had discovered a workable route. The one problem was that Macpherson agreed with the earlier assessment made by Clarence Martin's engineer that only a steam-powered cogwheel railway would be able to make the climb. But Lowe was not convinced. His eyes wrinkled, filled with despair at the notion. He felt that there must be some way to avoid the smoke and ashes that would be produced by a steam-operated system.

Exhausted from climbing the mountain and still trembling a little from his malaria, Lowe retreated into his study. For several days he could be heard skulking back and forth in intense concentration. Then he emerged, his face flushed with fervid energy, and revealed his idea for a cable incline supplemented by an electric trolley line. The inventor showed the plan to Macpherson, who agreed that it did provide a unique solution to the problem. Lowe's next task would be to find the funds for this grandiose scheme.

With the help of P. M. Green, Lowe organized what was at first called the Pasadena Mountain Railway. To demonstrate his confidence in the new operation, Lowe invested most of his own fortune. The citizens of Pasadena picked up the remaining $600,000 in bonds. On June 3, 1891, the railway was incorporated with T. S. C. Lowe as its president and general manager; P. M. Green, vice-president; Edward Groenendyke, secretary; and T. W. Brotherton, treasurer. D. J. Macpherson headed the advisory board, as well as being Chief engineer and construction supervisor. Less than six months later, on a crisp day in December 1891, Professor Lowe, always the showman, doffed his hat, rolled up his sleeves, and formally drove the first spike.

The mountain railway was begun at Mountain Junction in Altadena, formerly the Terminal Railroad depot, bordered by Lake Avenue on the east, Mendocino Street on the north, El Molino Avenue on the west, and Calaveras Street on the south. The new railway began with a single track, narrow gauge line for electric cars. Track laying proceeded rapidly on this line, which ran from Mountain Junction, along Lake Avenue, to the entrance of Rubio Canyon. This fairly level section was soon completed, and on April 12, 1892, construction was begun on the cable incline.

That September, Lowe accompanied a group of Pasadena businessmen on a horseback trip into the San Gabriels. As the party rested on a crest, Lowe took in the lush green of the undulating mountains. The shadows of the clouds gave a depth to the iridescent ocean beyond. Numerous butterflies fluttered in semiobscurity in the grass beneath the horses' hooves. Gazing indulgently at this pastoral setting, Macpherson asked if anyone knew the name of this particular peak they were on.

As no one in the party, which included men who had lived nearby all their lives, including H. H. Markham, a future California governor, allowed that the place had any name, Macpherson quickly suggested the peak be called Mount Lowe, to honor all the work Professor Lowe was doing to bring a railroad to the mountains.

The group needed no prodding, but readily agreed. A committee was thereupon set up, with Macpherson at the head, to go about the matter of naming that particular peak Mount Lowe. Eager for news about Lowe's mountain project, the proposal to name a peak after the railway's sponsor, and famous Civil War balloonist, T. S. C. Lowe, was widely reported in the newspapers. The article attracted the attention of Andrew McNally of the Rand McNally mapmaking firm. McNally followed the progress of the proposal closely. When the name became official, McNally saw to it that Mount Lowe, properly located, appeared on all their new maps of the area.

Everything about Lowe's railway was newsworthy. The papers delighted in reporting how a former grocer's son, who had run away from home barefooted, was changing the shape of a mountain. The progress of the construction was closely followed with stories full of facts and some fiction. By spring the first section, from the terminal at Altadena to Rubio Canyon, was completed. Incredibly, a portion of the roadway had been carved through solid granite, vast quantities of dynamite being the only solution. The difficult feat had been accomplished by the primitive method of dangling workmen from the cliffs by ropes who, working by hand, had hacked and blasted at the hard rock.

Lowe and Macpherson next turned their attention to that stretch of the railway that would come to be called the Great Cable Incline. Rival engineers ridiculed Macpherson's plan to go directly up the steep rise, asserting that any railway from Rubio Canyon to the summit would have to go by way of a winding shelf cut into the side of the mountain at great expense. Lowe, however, refused to accept the popular opinion and ordered the roadbed graded up the steepest slope. The incline initially rose sixty-two percent at the bottom, leveling to forty-two percent near midpoint. The rise was so perpendicular that the water and cement used to construct the walls and buttresses had to be hauled up by burros. And when the way became too difficult for the animals, the workmen had to shoulder the materials themselves. The process was arduously slow. Lowe wrote in his notes about this frustrating period of the construction:

> The first year was a continual outlay for surveys and bridle roads necessary to reach the work to be accomplished and to furnish supplies; the difficult grading and roadbed building along the perilous canyons and mountain sides; the building of the numerous bridges and the heavy work of spanning the canyon at the foot of the Incline with heavy timbered structures; the opening up of Rubio Canyon to popularize the resort at the opening of the road; the slow tedious work was of conveying

the supplies by pack animals; the hauling in by horse of heavy construction material and machinery to the foot of the Incline; the construction of the Incline after grading . . . all of these were new and difficult problems, a constant challenge, necessitating Herculean strength to overcome.

The two most difficult problems confronting the engineering skills of Macpherson and the wit of Lowe in the design of the cable incline were a massive gorge and a steep ridge that intersected the right-of-way only a short distance from the base of the mountain. Crews worked a total of eight months cutting through the formidable ridge, depositing enormous slabs of rock and other debris, mostly by hand, into a nearby ravine so that the site of the Rubio Canyon loading platform located directly below them would not become filled. After carving through "Granite Gorge," as that precarious piece of landscape had come to be known, Macpherson still had to come up with a plan for bridging the wide abyss behind it. His solution was a magnificent trestle.

Spanning a straight line distance of two hundred feet, on a sixty-two percent grade, this extraordinary bridge ascended 114 feet from beginning to end. When Lowe first saw the completed bridge, he was so taken by the innovative structure he was moved to proclaim, "I take the liberty of naming this splendid triumph of engineering the 'Macpherson Trestle' in honor of its designer." Macpherson, who had been standing next to Lowe, thanked the professor for his gesture. Known to the residents of Pasadena as a man "never given to self-aggrandizement who shunned publicity for himself," Macpherson, nevertheless, admitted to being modestly pleased.

Macpherson's original plans for the incline indicated two separate tracks, with the two cars passing each other in the middle. It was soon apparent the width the roadbed for four tracks would require very large retaining walls. These proved too costly to construct, so another solution had to be found.

Lowe's scheme to defeat the incline involved the use of two counter-balanced cable cars, each using its own outer rail but a common center track. Halfway up the three-thousand-foot slope would be a turnout, where the right-of-way widened, and the single center rail split into two separate rails to allow the cars to pass one another each on its own track. Lowe's system worked perfectly, both in theory and practice.

After the usual difficulties attached to having to do all the work manually, the roadbed was completed and the track laid. On December 28, 1892, a temporary three-thousand-pound construction cable was installed on the incline to speed up the construction. The heavy cable was drawn into position by horses harnessed to an iron windlass at the top of Echo Mountain. When it was installed, the cable was used to haul flat cars, loaded with construction materials on a slow journey to the summit of Echo Mountain, where two hotels were under construction. Later on specially constructed cars, completely open so as not to obstruct the view, were attached to the endless cable that tugged them up and lowered them down the grade. The two main incline cars, named Rubio and Echo, were described in an article in the February 3, 1894, issue of *Scientific American*: "Two cars of peculiar construction are provided with transverse seats arranged in three compartments, rising above each other like steps."

This stepped appearance caused some passengers to refer to them somewhat humorously as "opera box cars." While others, taking a key from their bright white paint schemes, called the cars "white chariots."

A cautious Lowe insisted on many safety devices in his cable system, which he had designed by Andrew Smith Hallidie, the man famous for the San Francisco cable cars. An additional cable beneath each of Lowe's cars, measuring one and one-half inches in diameter, could stop the cars within two feet in the event the main cable should fail. The incline's system was over-designed to place only five percent of the maximum load on the main cable when both cars were fully loaded. Despite the fears of some nervous riders, the line never had a serious accident in its forty-four-year history.

The machinery used to run the railway also showed Lowe's creative genius. Electricity to power the cable cars was generated by water wheels and dynamos beneath Rubio Pavilion operated by piped water descending from Echo Mountain reservoir. Gas-fired steam engines, located at Altadena Junction and Echo Mountain, provided supplemental power in the event of a dry spell. From the Echo Mountain powerhouse, current was provided to the geared motor that turned the "grip-sheave." This huge wheel, fitted with seventy-two steel jaws, forty-five of which were in constant contact, gripped the endless cable and pulled the cars up and down the hill.

While construction of the mountain railway presented a lofty challenge to Macpherson's engineering skills, the work was creating an even greater strain on Lowe's financial situation. As the line progressed, Lowe escorted numerous groups of potential investors to the top of Echo Mountain to view the construction. In spite of his dwindling funds, Lowe had not lost his flair. Lowe would announce after each phase's completion that the event was a reason for a celebration. And the celebrations were by no means modest.

On February 13, 1893, when the track from Rubio Pavilion loading platform to Mount Echo had been laid, Professor and Mrs. Lowe hosted a grand ball in their twenty-four-thousand-square-foot mansion, to which hundreds of Pasadena's social elite were invited. The guests at this elaborate celebration toasted not only Lowe's impressive progress on the mountain railway, but also the couple's thirty-eighth wedding anniversary.

The press was always welcomed at these events, which assured rosy reports in the local newspapers. The journals also kept Southern California readers apprised of the progress of the railway. With growing excitement, the public anticipated the line's completion. On May 14, 1893, the day the first electric-powered car made the run from Mountain Junction to Rubio Canyon, in an attempt to satisfy the public's curiosity, complex descriptions of the lines' workings filled the newspapers. The *Los Angeles Herald* carried the notation, "Rapid advancement is being made on the Pasadena Mountain Railway, and it will be only a few weeks before this most unique, and in many ways most remarkable, railroad will be in actual operation."

Finally, on June 12, 1893, with investors and the press watching apprehensively, Lowe proclaimed the Great Cable Incline ready for testing. Then, with the flick of a switch by Lowe, the drive motors came ominously to life. An article in the *Pasadena Daily Evening Star* described what happened next: "The cable began to move, smoothly, noiselessly and accurately, as if it had been gliding along its accustomed channel for months and years. This is a historic event."

A cheer went up from the assembled observers. With his customary bravado, Lowe announced he was planning a gala opening celebration the likes of which never had been seen in Southern California before. Behind the scenes his crews were already at work on the final clean-up operations, and the rest of the small details that had to be accomplished to prepare the facilities for the vast crowds that were expected.

For the rest of the week the *Los Angeles Herald* ran the following advertisement in its Pasadena items section:

> Hotel Rubio, higher than the Catskill Mountains, New York, is now open for the accommodation of guests, and is conducted on the European Plan, rooms from $1.00 to $2.00 per day according to size and location. The finest mountain air, water, and scenery that can be found on the globe.

At the moment, however, construction was still underway at the Rubio Hotel and Pavilion. Located at the terminus of the first section of the line, at an altitude of 2,200 feet, where the electrified railway ended, the Rubio Hotel was the first of Lowe's mountain resorts. Set in a glen, the hotel had a sweeping panoramic view, with more than a mile of planked walkways radiating from the broad verandas of the pavilion. With its huge ballroom and banquet hall and gardens lighted by two thousand Chinese lanterns, Rubio Hotel and Pavilion was a fantasy land that would attract huge crowds from its very beginning.

The first official passengers on Lowe's new railroad were a large, invited group of investors and friends. The party of 140 people required several cars to arrive at the Rubio Canyon Incline Station on the morning of June 29. The group stared in amazement at the three thousand-foot Cable Incline, which appeared to go straight up the side of Echo Mountain. Lowe personally escorted his guests on a tour. The inventor had to admit, however, that the cable cars were undergoing a little maintenance, so they would not be able to take a ride that day. Many were disappointed, but some were secretly relieved at not having to make the steep ascent.

Finding his fortune considerably diminished by the expense of creating his vast "empire in the sky," Lowe had resorted to selling tickets and operating his railway well in advance of his scheduled "opening day" of July 4. As early as June 30, curious travelers were allowed to take preview rides on the railway and see for themselves the wondrous sights Lowe had promised for their entertainment. Passengers riding in the open cars had the feeling that they were floating in the air as the trolley hugged the edges of yawning precipices or sailed across one of the eleven trestle bridges. As Lowe had anticipated, the early visitors could not help but be impressed and went home singing the praises of the new mountain railway, most hailing it as the greatest thing they had ever experienced.

At that time of the year the sun began its climb early over the peaks of the San Gabriel Mountains. In the long shadows below, most of Pasadena was still asleep. Hundreds of men and women, however, had risen before dawn and were busy at work at Mountain Junction, Rubio Canyon, and Echo Mountain. The date was July 4, 1893, Independence Day. There would be picnics, parades, and fireworks, and the official opening celebration for Lowe's Mountain Railway. Trolley drivers and crews, hotel and kitchen staff, and an army of newly hired employees, cleaned, polished, and cooked, and otherwise prepared for the festive crowds that would arrive with the heat of the day.

The Terminal Railway had scheduled six round trips to carry passengers from Los Angeles to Altadena. They could have scheduled six more as each train departed filled to capacity, with disappointed people left waiting on the platform. Local horse-drawn trolleys were on hand to pick up the excess and drive them to Mountain Junction. Persons fortunate to have their own teams could bypass the most congested section of the line by driving over the ranch at the mouth of the section.

Appearing more like a parade float than a trolley, the first car, covered with flowers and palm fronds and festooned in patriotic red, white, and blue bunting, departed Mountain Junction. Next came a breathtaking two-mile ride in the open cars, which seemed to hang on to the canyon right-of-way. Nor was the arrival at Rubio Hotel and Pavilion a disappointment, as there Professor Lowe had carefully planned every detail so that his guests' slightest whims were catered to.

After a walk around the grounds, many travelers sought relief from the heat of the day in the cool interior of the Rubio Pavilion, with its dark woodwork and tables covered with crisp white linen. Complimentary cake and ice cream was dished out to all. On the airy, shaded porches, a band provided rousing music for the bustling crowds. Outside the Pavilion, entertainment could be found in the picturesque interior of the canyon. There, more than a thousand steps linked wooden walkways that crossed mountain streams, roaring waterfalls, and other natural wonders such as Mirror Lake and Suspended Boulder. There was no shortage of private spots for a romantic afternoon picnic.

Looking around wide-eyed, visitors began to anticipate the coming magic of the evening, as they noticed every conceivable corner of the canyon had been hung with an electric Japanese lantern. People marveled at being in the "wilderness," yet having all the amenities of Los Angeles available to them at the same time. All this had been provided for them by Professor T. S. C. Lowe for the mere price of a trolley ticket.

And there was the professor, in the middle of it all enjoying himself immensely, his tall figure, white hair, and full moustache standing out above the throng. One of the many reporters who seemed to follow Lowe everywhere those days asked if he was pleased with the crowds. Lowe replied he was extremely pleased, and dodged any further questions by encouraging the young fellow to take a ride on the cable incline.

The professor checked his gold watch. It was almost noon. He made his way to the white car waiting at the base of the incline and began shaking hands with members of the Pasadena City Band, who were to make the first trip of the day. Lowe gave them a salute and they were off. The area suddenly became quiet, people staring as the odd-looking car began its smooth, seemingly effortless journey up the sheer face of the mountain while the band played "Nearer My God to Thee."

Cars ran up and down the incline all day taking visitors to the summit of Mount Echo, the future site of the elaborate Echo Mountain House. There they could hike the trails or visit the already built, but much smaller and quaint, Chalet. The porch of the Chalet offered a quiet place to relax while sipping lemonade and admiring the spectacular view of Los Angeles and the ocean beyond.

As the sun set over the Pacific the Japanese lanterns were turned on, illuminating the Pavilion, and dotting the canyon with their warm glow. The patrons who had stayed on watched in awe as a spectacular display of fireworks was set off from Echo Mountain and nearby peaks. The former balloonist did not see the fireworks. Feeling fatigued from the excitement of the day and perhaps a bit of his recurring malaria, Lowe had gone home. He was not that fond of fireworks anyway, having seen enough explosions and aerial bursts in his Civil War service.

Writing in the *Los Angeles Times,* a reporter estimated the crowd in Rubio Canyon for the opening to be between two and six thousand, remarking that, "the financial success of the undertaking is assured." These were doubtless welcome words for Lowe, who had staked what was left of his fortune on the success of this venture. Although huge crowds had gathered at Rubio Canyon to see the marvel, only four hundred passengers paid the five dollars each to brave the trip from the terminal at Altadena to the top of Echo Mountain and return.

Despite his professed love for natural beauty, Professor Lowe proved he was not averse to tampering with nature if it got in his way. Carrying on with his project, Lowe had the summit of Echo Mountain hacked off and made level. There the inventor erected the promised three-story hotel named Echo Mountain House. Relaxing on its wide porches while taking in the fresh air, guests could enjoy the sweeping panorama, including a high cascade that Lowe named Leontine Falls in honor of his wife.

Lowe's renown as the founder of what was now being called Mount Lowe Railway was spreading rapidly throughout the United States and abroad. The press widely hailed Lowe's cable incline as the greatest mountain railway in the world. Distinguished visitors came from all over to see the railway for themselves. Count Pomendensky, the Russian Imperial Superintendent of Roads, declared it to be "the most outstanding feat of mountain engineering I have ever seen."

Not content with the notice that he was getting in the regular papers, Lowe started his own publication, the *Mount Lowe Echo.* The publication's offices were in the Echo Mountain House. The editor, George Wharton James, a well-known writer and historian, kept the weekly paper full of news and events at the Lowe resorts. James suggested that as Lowe was a unique figure in the Civil War, the readers might be interested in some first-hand accounts of his exploits. But Lowe declined, saying someday he would write it all down and get it published. Like the military commission he so much desired, but never received, this also was not to happen. It was not until the last year of his life that Lowe found the time to write his story down; his papers, however, were not published until 2004.

Having completed the incline railway and two resort hotels, Lowe was now ready for the third stage of his mountain project. His next plan was to build an electric trolley road along a shelf of solid granite and through a dense forest of tall pines, thereby extending his line four miles to Mount Lowe Springs. The new track, which had 127 curves, was graded so gradually that passengers had no sense of ascending. At the railway's mountain terminal, almost a mile above sea level, the inventor erected yet another resort hotel.

The new resort, called Ye Alpine Tavern, was a large structure done in the style of a Swiss chalet. The hotel had twenty bedrooms and a dining room that seated two hundred persons. Heat was provided by a hot water system designed by Professor Lowe himself. Lowe and Leontine greeted the crowds like royalty at Ye Alpine Tavern's formal inaugural on December 14, 1895. The opening was a lavish affair with distinguished guests coming from all over the country. As Lowe anticipated, the tavern, located at the end of the line, soon became the most popular feature of what was now being called Lowe's "White City of the Clouds."

Recalling the countless hours he had spent as a young boy lying on a haystack in a farm field in New Hampshire studying the stars, Lowe decided to build an observatory in his mountain kingdom. He took the plan to his investors, who could not see how a profit would be made from such an enterprise. Undaunted, the inventor decided to go ahead with the project at his own expense.

Seeking the best assistance, Lowe invited Dr. Charles W. Eliot, president of Harvard University, to come to California to advise him in determining a suitable location for the observatory. Lowe and Eliot walked the mountain together, rejecting several sites before settling on a slope of Echo Mountain. The observatory was soon constructed, in a short time, but at great cost.

Next, Lowe invited Dr. Lewis Swift, who was known as the "indefatigable comet-seeker," to come west to oversee the installation of the telescope. The seventy-two-year-old astronomer was so impressed with Lowe and his operation that he stayed on to become the director of the new Lowe Observatory. Attracted by the fame of Dr. Swift and the discoveries he had made, numerous visitors, both serious astronomers and the general public, came to the Lowe Observatory from all over the world.

Unfortunately the previous year, 1893, the year the mountain railway opened, had seen a great depression in America. People had less money to spend on things like pleasure trips to the mountains. Lowe, heavily in debt from the construction of his railway and the added expense of his observatory, was hit hard. He was forced to give up his other dreams for the mountain: extending the line beyond Ye Alpine Tavern, and establishing an institute of science where young inventors could work undisturbed in the seclusion of the mountain. He appealed to donors for aid with these undertakings. He could not, however, raise the necessary funds so had to abandon these projects.

Despite the popularity of the mountain railway and the vast number of people still patronizing his hotels and taverns, Lowe's entire enterprise was losing money. His debts were mounting alarmingly. The problem he had with the Balloon Corps had resurfaced. The inventor, like the balloonist, never watched his accounts carefully. A bit of a free spirit, when Lowe had money he spent it. Fortunately for a time he had been earning more than even he could run through. Now Lowe was forced to admit that his financial situation had become untenable.

By 1898, Lowe's debts exceeded his assets by over $200,000. He attempted to find additional refinancing, but to no avail. Pressed by his creditors, the inventor had no recourse but to declare bankruptcy. His properties were sold at auction for a mere $175,000, considerably less than they had originally cost. The mountain railroad was bought by the Pacific Electric Railway, the operator of Los Angeles' trolley lines. They would continue to operate it for the next forty years.

As with his other failed enterprises Lowe was undaunted by the demise of what he considered his "greatest achievement." As usual he was philosophic, feeling he was the victim of circumstances beyond his control: "I sold the road because I was ten years ahead of my times and the time was not ripe. Therefore I lost with no regrets, for I realize that many millionaires would sacrifice their lives to attain a monument for themselves such as Mount Lowe will be to my name when I have passed away."

As Lowe predicted, the mountain with his name on it would be his only lasting monument as, one by one, nature removed the objects he had imposed on it. Most of the buildings were gone long before his own passing. In 1900 a blaze swept Echo Mountain House, burning it to the ground. A strong windstorm, which started a fire, leveled most of the remaining structures on Echo Mountain in 1905. The observatory would stand until 1928, fifteen years after Lowe's death, when it would be collapsed by another severe storm. Nor would the inventor witness the fire that gutted his beloved Ye Alpine Tavern in 1936. Two years later, a cloudburst would devastate most of the mountain railway. Changing times had made the operation of the railway unprofitable, so the badly washed-out tracks were never restored. For years all that remained of Lowe's spectacular "White City of the Clouds" were the twisted tracks, collapsed bridges, and a few piles of charred lumber.

25

More Projects, Planet Airship, Leontine Dies, Remembered

The collapse of his financial empire had taken its toll on T. S. C. Lowe. Now well past middle age, the toil of his years was beginning to show. The inventor's white hair was balding rapidly, and he had taken to wearing a black silk skullcap to disguise this fact. He still sported a bushy moustache and small goatee, but they too were pure white. His dark eyes sparkled nonetheless, although now through genteel pince-nez. He could yet be considered handsome, but in a dignified rather than dashing manner.

The loss of his mountain empire had been a deep personal tragedy, but even more so had been the sale of his beloved Pasadena mansion at 905 South Orange Grove Avenue. Located next door to the estate of millionaire brewer Adolphus Busch, the Lowes' grand and spacious residence had been a elegant showplace, serving as both a home and an art museum.

Over the years Leontine had become a patron of archaeology and the arts. She traveled the world, enthusiastically collecting paintings and antiques. Her collection of the work of Arizona Indians, in whose culture she took an especial interest, was one of the most outstanding in the West. Leontine exerted a strong cultural influence on her husband, and they often had friends over who showed similar interests. The Lowes had been frequent entertainers, giving extravagant parties and balls that were often the highlight of the local social season.

Now this life was all gone and Lowe was faced, yet again, with the problem of resurrecting his monetary situation. Even as he surveyed the wreckage of his fortune, the source of a new and prosperous future was taking shape in his mind. The inventor had never completely lost interest in the technology that had been the basis of his successful years in Norristown. He decided to turn back to the production of gas and coke as a means of restoring his finances.

Researching the matter with his usual thoroughness, Lowe discovered that Southern California industries were desperately in need of additional stocks of coke. However, the region contained no coal to make it from. Lowe hit on the idea of using California's abundant heavy crude petroleum as a substitute. Retiring to his laboratory, Lowe experimented until he came up with a method for "cracking" the crude oil to produce gas and coke. The "cracking" process subjected the crude oil to an extremely high heat, which caused it to vaporize, thus separating its lighter components from its heavier residues. Lowe became a pioneer in this technique, still widely used by the petroleum industry today.

For his next act, Lowe trotted out the water gas process that had been the source of his original fortune. He had continued to experiment with water gas during his early years in Pasadena, and even while working on the mountain railway. Learning that gas customers in the los Angeles area were paying as much as $1.50 per thousand cubic feet, Lowe decided that he would produce and sell it for $1.00 per thousand. He was successful at attracting some prominent investors and secured a franchise.

Using the investors' funds, Lowe erected a plant that covered six acres and laid pipes into selected residential districts. The inventor's offer of cheap gas was an immediate success, with many customers subscribing to his service. Alas, Lowe once again proved that his skill as a scientist far surpassed that of a businessman. He soon was selling gas for less than it was costing him to make. His corporation quickly went out of business, absorbed by the Los Angeles Gas Company.

Once again, despite his setback, Lowe was not deterred. He was convinced that not only would he regain his fortune through gas production, but also that he would become a major player in the industry in the Western states. To this end he set up, with his son Thaddeus Junior who heretofore had been working in the theatre, a vast network of gas-serving systems under the imposing corporate title of the New Lowe Gas System for the United States, Canada, and Mexico. In San Francisco, Lowe put another of his sons, Leon Percival, in charge of a coke-and-gas company that he organized under the name of the California Gas and Electric Company. True to form his gas companies proved to be losing ventures, and were all taken over by other firms.

Out of the gas business, Lowe returned his interest to artificial ice making. He became the director of two local icehouses, the Citizen's Ice Company and the Pasadena Packing Company. He was beginning to run out of energy, but gave his all to the ice business. However, unlike his success of the past, these endeavors failed to replenish his fortune. Lowe was reduced to selling real estate.

There was yet remaining one more of T. S. C. Lowe's interests he had not revisited—aeronautics. Inspired by stories of the Wright Brothers and other flyers such as Glenn Curtiss in the United States and of Louis Bleriot in France and his old friend Count Ferdinand von Zeppelin in Germany, Lowe announced he would design a better flying machine.

Lowe began working on plans for an airship with the traditional globular gas bag. The inventor considered the horizontal gas bag of Count Zeppelin's airship clumsy and impractical and believed that its heavy, internal, framework presented too much surface to the wind. He felt the dirigible's lifting power was small compared to its bulk. Although Lowe acknowledged that the long, slender craft was handsome to look at, he believed that the vertical balloon was by its very design inherently more stable. Furthermore, it required no framework to remain rigid and could therefore carry more weight, and was never in danger of tilting.

With renewed enthusiasm for flying, Lowe set about drawing up the elaborate design for a huge airship. Having regained some of his old hubris, the inventor plunged into this new project, sure that he was about to revolutionize aerial transportation. He planned for his airship to be equipped with the newly available light, reliable, and high-powered gasoline engines. Lowe anticipated these engines would enable his new balloon to circle the globe in thirty days. With one eye on the future and the other on public relations, Lowe gave his new venture the hyperbolic name Planet Airship.

In his typical fashion the Lowe Airship Construction Corporation was set up by Lowe to market stock in the enterprise. The investors of Southern California, however, showed little interest in the offering.

The Aerial Publishing Company of Los Angeles issued a booklet in March 1910 describing the Planet Airship in detail. While the paper did a great deal to spur Lowe's efforts on, it did little to encourage investors. Discouraged, Lowe abandoned the Planet Airship project and began work on a completely different aerostat. This he described as a balloon to which a car resembling a large boat would be attached. The airship, which was to be equipped with a 150-horsepower motor, and contain a galley and sleeping quarters, appeared very much like the designs he conceived for his balloon *Great Western,* in which he proposed to make the first transatlantic flight.

Still experimenting at the age of seventy-nine, Lowe arrived at what he believed to be an even further advance to his method of coke making. Now considered a bit gaga by those who knew him in California, Lowe was no longer able to find financial support in the West.

So, in the winter of 1911 Lowe traveled back to the East. As Leontine was not well, and his children busy with their own lives, the old man went alone.

Arriving in midwinter, Lowe called on two old friends, John D. Rockefeller and John Wanamaker, hoping to convince them to invest in his coke-making scheme. They both received him politely, but made it clear that they were not interested in this or any other of his inventions.

Discouraged and worn out from his traveling, Lowe went to Norristown to visit one of his daughters, Mrs. Augustine Brownback. While they spent some pleasant days together, Lowe was discouraged to see how the town had changed. It was not as elegant and stylish as when he had lived there. Norristown had not brought back fond memories of the past, but rather had depressed him with images of what might have been.

The weather was cold with flurries and snow covering the ground when Augustine took him to the Norristown train station to begin his journey home. Lowe reassured his daughter she should not worry about him; he would soon be back in the warmth of California. Crossing the railroad tracks in a driving snow, the old man suddenly slipped on a patch of ice and fell down. Augustine helped him up, suggesting perhaps he should delay his departure and see a doctor. But Lowe, who was no friend of doctors since his Civil War experiences, declined. Although the pain was excruciating, he got up, saying it was nothing. With the whistle of the locomotive screaming in the background, Lowe brushed the snow off his clothes and got on the train. Throughout the long ride home the landscape out the window seemed to pale, and his body to become more brittle. He hobbled through several train changes and had almost passed out, so he overnighted in Chicago, a city stinking of pigs he had hoped to avoid. By the time he reached the breathless and windswept prairie, the shaking of the train car was unbearable. Consuming all of what laudanum he had brought for his malaria induced a dull and lazy state that got him over the mountains, which seemed yellow and distant. Unknown to Lowe, the fall at the station had fractured his hip.

Back in California, his problem diagnosed but impossible to treat, Lowe's hip allowed him to only get around with great difficulty. To further complicate matters, although her mind and spirit remained keen, Leontine's health was failing rapidly. Lowe, the devoted spouse of fifty years, now spent most of his time caring for his beloved companion. On May 16, 1912, the mother of ten passed away with her husband at her bedside.

After his wife's death, alone and financially distressed, Lowe moved in with his daughter, Mrs. Edna Lowe Wright, in Pasadena. Time passed for him uncounted, the days making unfamiliar notations in their passage. The inventor tried bravely to fill the void in his life that Leontine's death had created. Sometimes he imagined he saw his wife and spoke to her, waiting for a reply. But more often he could not remember what he had been saying. Leontine's appearances became strange to him, and he became strange to himself. He felt empty, but it was not a logical emptiness. It was as if with his wife's death something had gone out of him that he would soon follow into the next world.

Lowe forced himself to return his attention to the plans for his Planet Airship. However, without the encouragement of the woman whom he had praised as "the most constructive influence in my life" he lacked the spirit for even the simplest tasks. He spoke little about his grief, and his daughter could only speculate at the depths to which his spirit had plunged.

Lowe's health began to decline, and it became apparent to his daughter that he would not live much longer. On the cold California morning of January 16, 1913, Professor Thaddeus Sobieski Constantine Lowe, self-taught scientist, balloonist, inventor, and entrepreneur, passed from this earth.

Ironically, Lowe, who had made and lost numerous fortunes in his lifetime, died so heavily in debt that his creditors would not be satisfied. Even his modest funeral expenses could not be met. His few remaining possessions were auctioned off—some medals, a pocket watch, two gold-headed canes, and a souvenir sword and pistol. The amount raised was nowhere near enough to satisfy Lowe's obligations, so his son Leon Percival paid for the funeral out of his own pocket.

Even in death the balloonist was not granted that reward he had most wanted from his country. Because he never received his commission, not having been granted military status during his time as Chief Aeronaut for the Union Army, even though he had served honorably in the Civil War, T. S. C. Lowe was denied burial in Arlington National Cemetery.

T. S. C. Lowe eventually would be honored by his government, but not until sometime after his death. In 1930, seventeen years after he passed away, in fulfillment of his often expressed wishes, the balloonist's Civil War records, mementos, and photographs were presented by his daughters to the Smithsonian Institution.

On September 10, 1957, on the occasion of the 125th anniversary of Lowe's birth, an airfield was dedicated to his memory. The Lowe

Army Airfield has continued in operation to this day at Fort Rucker in Alabama. While there never were any balloons at the airfield, for years student aviators there have learned to fly helicopters. Although helicopter pilots perform many roles in support of ground troops, one of their key duties has always been aerial reconnaissance, the activity pioneered by T. S. C. Lowe during the Civil War.

And in Richmond, Virginia, the city the balloonist observed so closely during the Peninsula Campaign, on Memorial Day 1962, a monument to the birth of military aviation in America was unveiled as part of a Civil War centennial celebration. Carved into the granite were the names of all the Civil War aeronauts. Prominent among them was that of Professor Thaddeus S. C. Lowe.

Sources

Books

Aymar, Brandt, ed. *Men in the Air.* New York: Crown Publishers, 1990.

Block, Eugene B. *Above the Civil War: The Story of Thaddeus Lowe.* Berkeley, Calif.: Howell-North Books, 1966.

Burden, Maria Schell. *Professor T. S. C. Lowe and His Mountain Railway.* Los Angeles, Calif.: Borden Publishing Co., 1993.

Cagle, Malcolm W., and C. G. Halpine. *A Pilot's Meteorology.* New York: Van Nostrand Reinhold Co., 1970.

Catton, Bruce. *The Civil War.* New York: The Fairfax Press, 1980.

Crouch, Tom D. *The Eagle Aloft: Two Centuries of Ballooning in America.* Washington, D.C.: Smithsonian Institution Press, 1983.

Dodge, Theodore Ayrault. *On Campaign With the Army of the Potomac.* Edited by Stephen W. Sears. New York: Cooper Square Press, 2001.

Duke, Neville, and Edward Lanchbery, eds. *The Saga of Flight: An Anthology.* New York: The John Day Company, 1961.

Freehling, William W. *The South vs. the South: How Anti-Confederate Southerners Shaped the Course of the Civil War.* New York: Oxford University Press, 2001.

Herrin, Lamar. *The Unwritten Chronicles of Robert E. Lee.* New York: Saint Martin's Press, 1989.

Hoehling, Mary. *Thaddeus Lowe: America's One-Man Air Corps.* Chicago: Kingston House, 1958.

Kessler, Lauren. *The Happy Bottom Riding Club: The Life and Times of Pancho Barnes.* New York: Random House, 2000.

Kirkland, Frazar. *Anecdotes and Incidents of the War of the Rebellion.* Hartford, Conn.: Hartford Publishing Co., 1866.

McPherson, James M. *The Battle Cry of Freedom: The Civil War Era.* New York: Oxford University Press, 1988.

Mondey, David, general ed. *The International Encyclopedia of Aviation.* New York: Crown Publishers, 1977.

Pratt, Fletcher, ed. *Civil War in Pictures.* Garden City, N.Y.: Garden City Books, 1955.

Seims, Charles. *Mount Lowe, the Railway in the Clouds.* San Marino, Calif.: Golden West Books, 1976.

Shamberger, Page, and Joe Christy, eds. *Command the Horizon.* New York: A. S. Barnes and Co., 1968.

Taylor, John W. R., and Kenneth Munson, eds. *History of Aviation.* New York: Crown Publishers, 1977.

Magazine Articles

Cullen, Joseph P. "The Battle of Mechanicsville." *Civil War Times Illustrated,* 5, no. 6 (October 1966).

———. "The McClellan-Lincoln Controversy." *Civil War Times Illustrated,* 5, no. 7 (November 1966).

Evans, Thomas H. "There is no use trying to dodge shot." *Civil War Times Illustrated,* 6, no. 5 (August 1967).

———. "At Malvern Hill—A First Person Account." *Civil War Times Illustrated,* 6, no. 8 (December 1967).

Fearson, Jim. "Chain Bridge—A History of the Bridge and its Surrounding Territory, 1608–1991." *Arlington Historical Magazine,* 9, no. 3 (October 1991).

Grimsley, Mark, ed., and Bernatello Glod, trans. "The Journal of the Compte de Paris." *Civil War Times Illustrated,* 24, no. 3 (May 1985).

Hassler, William W. "Professor Lowe—A Personality Profile." *Civil War Times Illustrated,* 6, no. 5 (1967).

Hoffsommer, Robert, ed. "The Rise and Survival of Private Mensard." *Civil War Times Illustrated,* 24, no. 9 (January 1986).

Jones, Gordon W. "Sanitation in the Civil War." *Civil War Times Illustrated,* 5, no. 7 (November 1966).

Lowe, Thaddeus S. C. "The Army Takes to the Air." Edited by Charles Cooney. *Civil War Times Illustrated,* 24, no. 5 (September 1985).

McCaffrey, James. "A Short History of the Civil War Sutler." *Civil War Times Illustrated,* 24, no. 4 (June 1985).

Margreiter, John L., Jr. "Anesthesia in the Civil War." *Civil War Times Illustrated,* 6, no. 2 (May 1967).

Robinson, June. "The United States Balloon Corps in Action in Northern Virginia During the Civil War." *Arlington Historical Magazine* (October 1986).

Rudolph, Jack. "Taking Up Arms." *Civil War Times Illustrated,* 23, no. 2 (April 1984).

Thomas, Martha. "Amazing Mary—Army Surgeon Dr. Mary Walker." *Civil War Times Illustrated,* 23, no. 1 (March 1984).

Wert, Jeffrey D. "Mutiny in the Army." *Civil War Times Illustrated*, 24, no. 2 (April 1985).

Westwood, Howard, and eds. "A Portfolio: The Port Royal Experiment." *Civil War Times Illustrated*, 25, no. 3 (May 1986).

Additional Materials:

Ainsworth, Brigadier General Fred C., and Joseph W. Kirkley, eds. *The War of the Rebellion: A Compilation of the Official Records of the Union and Confederate Armies.* Published under the direction of the Honorable Elihu Root, Secretary of War. Series 3, vol. 3. Washington D.C.: U. S. Government Printing Office, 1899.

Compton's Pictured Encyclopedia. Chicago: F. E. Compton & Co., 1922.

Funk & Wagnalls New Encyclopedia. New York: Funk & Wagnalls, Inc., 1979.

Lowe, Thaddeus S. C. *Memoirs of Thaddeus S. C. Lowe, Chief of the Aeronautic Corps of the Army of the United States During the Civil War: My Balloons in Peace and War.* Edited by Michael Jaeger and Carol Lauritzen. Lewiston, N.Y.: Edwin Mellen Press, 2004.

———. *Practical Aerial Navigation in Peace and War.* Unpublished paper, Library of Congress, AIAA Files, Box 82.

Medicology. New York: University Medical Society, 1912.

World Book Encyclopedia. Chicago: Field Enterprises, 1977.